RUDYARD KIPLING

RUDYARD KIPLING

BY

LORD BIRKENHEAD

WEIDENFELD AND NICOLSON
LONDON

CONTENTS

ILLUSTRATIONS

ACKNOWLEDGEMENTS

The quotations from papers in the Royal Archives printed in Appendix B were included in the text by gracious permission of His late Majesty King George VI, for which the author was deeply grateful.

The author acknowledged a great debt of gratitude to Kipling's sister, Mrs A. M. Fleming, who was immensely helpful while he was doing the research for this book. She not only had long talks with him but also answered a great number of questions, in writing, from her home in Edinburgh. Other close relations to whom he was most grateful for personal reminiscences included Kipling's first cousins, Mrs Margaret Mackail (née Burne-Jones) and Stanley Baldwin, by then Earl Baldwin of Bewdley, and Kipling's brother-in-law Dr Theo Dunham, who with two charming daughters entertained him in his old brownstone house in New York and generously put at the author's disposal the letters of the Balestier family, which had been in his wife's possession.

He was very grateful to Ethel, Lady Dilke, daughter of Mrs W. K. Clifford, and to Lady (Sybil) Colefax, who as a child had known Lockwood Kipling in India and remembered Henry James, Kipling and Wolcott Balestier in London, and to Sir Louis Dane and Sir Henry McMahon for information about Kipling in Lahore. He was also fortunate enough to be able to talk to General Dunsterville, the original 'Stalky', and to Major G. C. Beresford ('M'Turk').

Among friends made by Kipling during the South African War, Sir Roderick Jones was outstandingly helpful, writing a long account of Kipling for the author, and he and his wife (Enid Bagnold) introduced him in Rottingdean to people who had known the Kiplings when they were living in the village. Another friend from this period, Mr H. A. Gwynne, later editor of the *Morning Post*, also gave him great assistance and wrote special notes as well as answering many questions verbally. Mr Nelson Doubleday, son of Kipling's American publisher, had a long talk with the author in his house on Long Island and was kind enough to allow him full access to his papers.

Other old friends of Kipling whose help the author would have wished to acknowledge with gratitude include Mrs Táufflieb; the Hon. Mrs Leigh; Mr A. B. Ramsay, Master of Magdalene College, Cambridge; Sir Herbert Baker; Sophie, Lady Hall, widow of Sir John Hall, who commanded the Irish Guards at Warley while John Kipling was there; Countess Roberts and Lady Lewin; Lord Dunsany and Sir Sydney Cockerell, who both lent him letters from Kipling; and Enid, Lady Bathurst, proprietor of the *Morning Post*, to whom Kipling wrote frequently about politics and the policy of the paper and who was kind enough to put these letters at the disposal of the author; also Lord Dawson of Penn, at one time Kipling's physician; and Sir Alfred Webb-Johnson, Kipling's surgeon and close friend during the last years of his life; Mrs Angela Thirkell; Lady de Chair; Miss Blaikie, for many years Elsie Kipling's governess; Field-Marshal Sir Archibald Montgomery-Massingberd; Viscountess Milner; Sir Leonard Woolley; Major C. S. Jarvis; Mrs W. M. Cazalet; General A. S. Little, head prefect at Westward Ho! when Kipling made a return visit; Major-General Sir Fabian Ware; Mr Edwin Haward; Sir Desmond MacCarthy; General Sir Ian Hamilton; Sir Henry Badeley; Sir Percy Bates; Mrs Belloc-Lowndes; the Rt Hon. L. S. Amery; Mr Chalmers Roberts, for fifteen years Doubleday's representative in London; Lady Rodd; Mr Gerald Stanley; Sir Shane Leslie, nephew of Moreton Frewen; and Madame Cattani, proprietress of the hotel where Kipling stayed in Switzerland, who kindly sent the author letters written to her by the family; also neighbours of the Kiplings in the country – the first Viscount Hailsham, Mrs Christopher Hussey, Mr Roland Gwynne and Earl Stanhope, all of whom were most helpful.

The author would have wished to express his warm thanks for all the kindness that was shown him in Brattleboro. Unfortunately during the preparation of his manuscript for publication, after his death, a fire at his home destroyed a number of notebooks, some of which contained information about his stay in Brattleboro, and it is therefore impossible for his debt to be fully acknowledged. Mr Howard Rice and Mr Cabot Holbrook kindly allowed him access to their private papers and he was most grateful to Mrs Holbrook for arranging for him to meet and talk to people who had known the Kiplings in Vermont.

The author was particularly grateful to Mr Douglas Rees, whose co-operation in listing and analysing the Kipling papers when the

author was working on them in his London house was literally invaluable, and his remarkable memory has been equally helpful to those involved in the publication of this book; also to Mr Murray Brooks, who in 1946 was of great assistance in supplying many points of detail. Over thirty years later, now over ninety years of age, he has again given most generous help. The author would also have wished to thank Mrs June Robertson-Rodger, who typed the first draft of this book.

He acknowledged with gratitude the help given to him by the Kipling Society and the librarians and staff of the Houghton Library, Harvard, the Library of Congress, Washington D.C., the New York Public Library, Columbia University Library, The Pierpont Morgan Library, New York, the New College Library, Oxford and – as always – the London Library.

Permission given by the National Trust, Macmillan & Co. of London and Doubleday of New York with A. P. Watt and Son, to quote from published and unpublished Kipling material is gratefully acknowledged.

S. B.

The publishers are most grateful to the following for kind permission to reproduce illustrations: Elspeth, Countess Baldwin of Bewdley 1, 2, 3, 5, 9, 10, 26 and 34; Roger Lancelyn Green 4, 8; R. E. Harbord (and John Freeman, Photographers) 6; Haileybury College Governing Council (and R. Lancelyn Green) 7; Mansell Collection 11; Royal Commonwealth Society (and John Freeman, Photographers) 12; Kipling Society 13 and 24; Houghton Library, Harvard University (Henry James Archive) 14; Dr Theo Dunham (who gave the picture to the author) 15; Sir Rupert Hart-Davis (and Mansell Collection) 16; F. Cabot Holbrook and Howard C. Rice, Jr 17, 18, 19, 20 and 21; Library of Congress 22; British Library (and National Trust) 23; Royal Commonwealth Society and the Kipling Society 25; Radio Times Hulton Picture Library 27, 28, 30, 31, 32 and 33; Press Association 29.

INTRODUCTION

TOWARDS the end of the Second World War my father was looking forward eagerly to leaving the army and returning to literary work. He had already written biographies of his own father and of Strafford, both of which had been well received. A chance meeting with Captain Bambridge, who was married to Kipling's only surviving child, led him to undertake a life of Kipling.

It was a splendid opportunity. Kipling had been a reserved and secretive man of whose private life little was known beyond the glimpses he had revealed in his writing. But his life was well documented and there were still survivors to be interviewed who had known him very well at every stage of his life: as a child, at school, in India, back in England, in America and in South Africa. The timing seemed perfect in every way. Kipling's literary reputation had plunged into the trough that so often follows an author's death and my father, who had always admired his work, felt that it was due for a reappraisal.

There were, however, signs that the author might have to write under the close supervision of Kipling's family. The biography had already been attempted and abandoned twice; first by Hector Bolitho, who found Mrs Kipling's supervision too exacting, then by Captain Taprell Dorling RN (Taffrail). After Mrs Kipling's death, Eric Linklater considered the project but could not come to terms with Mrs Bambridge.

This daunting history might have put any biographer on his guard and made him determined to obtain a contract that protected his interests. The contract which my father and Mrs Bambridge signed did the reverse, being equally unfavourable to the author in its provisions for copyright and finance. Among its clauses were the following:

(3) ... The Author will (if requested by Mrs Bambridge to do so) visit at his own expense the United States of America to inspect the Brattleboro property. . . .

(4) The Author will also if he considers it desirable and Mrs Bambridge consents visit (a) India ... and/or (b) South Africa..... The amount of the Author's personal expense of any such visit shall be borne as to Two Thirds by Mrs Bambridge and One Third by the Author.

(5) The Author will visit at an early stage Earl Baldwin and Mrs Fleming and such other persons as Mrs Bambridge may indicate....

(7) The Copyright in the work shall be the property of Mrs Bambridge and the Author shall when called upon execute any document which may be necessary in order to vest the copyright in her.

(8) The Author shall submit his work to Mrs Bambridge in convenient sections as he proceeds and shall omit from the completed work such passages or documents (if any) as Mrs Bambridge may desire....

(9) The arrangements for the publication and exploitation of the work in any material form whatever shall be subject to the approval of Mrs Bambridge who shall have the entire control of the work when completed and all arrangements for publication, exploitation and sale in any form and on any terms shall be effected by Messrs. A. P. Watt & Son of Norfolk Street, Strand, upon and subject to her instructions.

(10) As consideration for his services the Author shall receive and be paid one Third of all sums received by Mrs Bambridge from the publication, exploitation and sale in any form of the said work less all commissions and other payments or expenses....

(9) [sic] In the event of the death of the Author or on his being unable for any cause to complete the work within the agreed time the manuscript so far as it exists and all material relating thereto shall be delivered to Mrs Bambridge who shall be entitled to arrange for the work to be carried out by such person and on such terms as she shall in her absolute discretion think fit when remuneration shall be provided for out of the one third of the net receipts which would have been payable to the Author as aforesaid....

It will be seen that through this contract Mrs Bambridge retained complete control of the book. She could remove any passages from it which she disliked (Clause 8) or ban it completely through her retention of the copyright. She could dictate who my father was to see and to some extent where he was to go. She was to receive two thirds of the book's proceeds and was to contribute to its costs only if my father visited India or South Africa, and she had the right to withhold her consent from these visits. The American trip, written into the contract, was to be undertaken at his own expense.

Although this contract clearly gave him no protection, my father looked for his security elsewhere. His relations with the Bambridges were excellent and Captain Bambridge promised him that when the time came for publication he would see that everything was all right. This assurance and his own eagerness to write the book made him sign the contract and, as soon as the war was over, begin work on it.

The Bambridges continued to be most cordial and co-operative, sending their Kipling Papers from Wimpole Hall to his house in London where he could study them at his convenience. He made the trip to America and conducted a great number of interviews both there and in England. Many of those he saw were extremely old but still crystal clear in their memories of Kipling. Mrs Fleming, Kipling's sister, and Lord Baldwin and Mrs Mackail, his first cousins, spoke to him about Kipling's childhood; General Dunsterville and George Beresford, the originals of 'Stalky' and 'M'Turk', told him of their days together at Westward Ho! Sir Louis Dane remembered him as a cub reporter in Lahore and Sir Henry McMahon also contributed stories of his life in India; Dr Dunham, husband of Kipling's sister-in-law, and the son of his publisher F. N. Doubleday were among the many who had known him in America; his part in the Boer War was told by Sir Roderick Jones and H. A. Gwynne, founder, with Kipling and others, of *The Friend*, the British Army newspaper, and later editor of the *Morning Post*. All these and many less prominent died between the time my father interviewed them and the commissioning of another biography.

Captain Bambridge himself died while the book was being written but Mrs Bambridge continued to correspond with my father on the friendliest of terms. When he finished his work in 1948 and sent the first draft to Wimpole Hall for her approval, he saw no reason to be apprehensive. Her response was all the more shattering: an immediate and complete ban on its publication.

He wrote to her asking whether there were any particular passages or interpretations which she found objectionable and whether they could meet and talk about it. After some delay he received an uncompromising reply.

'. . . It is very unpleasant for me to have to tell you,' Mrs Bambridge wrote, 'that I consider it so bad as a book that any attempt at palliative measures such as you describe, re-writing here, and altering there is not feasible.' Other general criticisms followed, then the unkindest cut of all: 'The distasteful task of conveying my opinion to you is accentuated by my own personal feeling of disappointment. *So* much time has been wasted.'

She could not be swayed from her decision; Sir Desmond Mac-Carthy, who had read the book and admired it, tried to see her but was refused an audience.

Mrs Bambridge did, however, have one eminent supporter. After suppressing the book, she showed the manuscript to T. S. Eliot, who said it was too slight for a definitive biography of Kipling; so far as we know, she did not explain to him that it was a first draft.

A different view of the book was provided by Sir Roderick Jones, who had known Kipling since the time of the Boer War. 'The new material alone,' he wrote to my father, 'which you have assembled is enough to electrify the average Kipling reader... You have made me realize how little I knew of the real Kipling. I think that would be the effect on most of his friends.' Others who read the book at this stage and were mystified by Mrs Bambridge's decision included John Betjeman and Robert Blake.

Mrs Bambridge lost no further time. By 20 November she was discussing compensation and on 3 December she offered £3500, an offer which was eventually accepted. My father's feelings can well be imagined. Three years of what he felt had been his best work had been rejected out of hand and denied publication for no ascertainable reason except that Mrs Bambridge disliked it. The shock and bitterness engendered by Mrs Bambridge's action, together with the obvious reluctance with which she made her offer of compensation, explain his next move. He pressed her for more compensation and received another £1500 on condition that he made an undertaking never to publish or cause to be published any biography of Kipling.

Whatever the provocation, this temptation should have been resisted. He was much younger than Mrs Bambridge, who had no heir, and in the normal course of events he could have expected to publish after her death. He was not greatly interested in money and the sum involved was not important to him, but in return for this un-needed £1500 he gravely compromised the book's chances of appearing during his lifetime. It is doubtful if he really understood what he had done. His correspondence is full of hopes that the book could come out after Mrs Bambridge's death.

In 1951 Mrs Bambridge found another biographer, C. E. Carrington, whose authorized life of Kipling appeared in 1955. Other biographies have been published since, but only Carrington and my father had access to the Wimpole Hall Archives.

My father's Kipling biography remained in first-draft form until the 1960s when, encouraged by rumours of a thawing in Mrs Bambridge's attitude, and having acquired more background material from visits to India and South Africa, he made an extensive revision of the book and brought it up to date. An old friend of the Kipling family was engaged to read the new draft for passages that might seem offensive to her, but Mrs Bambridge refused to read it.

My father died in 1975 and Mrs Bambridge in 1976. It then became possible to publish the book, and it will appear just over thirty years after the original draft was first suppressed.

I have often been asked why Mrs Bambridge banned the book, and my answer that I didn't know was seldom believed. My interrogators were clearly convinced that some shameful secret must have been exposed to provoke such a violent reaction. Even if this had been true Mrs Bambridge, under the terms of their Agreement, could have erased it from the text and published the approved part of the book. Her own explanations have been vague and inconsistent. Her first letter contained three general criticisms: that Kipling's love and knowledge of the English countryside was barely mentioned; that there was too much emphasis on his political life; that his literary work was underrated and inadequately assessed. While not agreeing with all these criticisms my father was prepared to compromise with her on them, only to receive a second letter saying that the book was so bad that it could not be saved by any changes. She later told Carrington that it was full of amateur psychoanalysis, and that my father being allied to 'The Bright Young Things' – a truly ludicrous description – could not understand Kipling's age. Later still she claimed that he hated Kipling and his works. Her final word was she had banned the book, but she could not remember why.

It is possible that my father made a mistake in submitting a raw and unedited first draft to someone who, although the daughter of a great writer, had probably never read a book in such a form. Whatever the explanation there is no doubt that something in the book shocked her deeply; nothing else can explain the change from her friendliness in early 1948 to her implacable hostility in September.

ROBIN BIRKENHEAD

CHAPTER I
A PEACEFUL CHILDHOOD

WHEN Rudyard Kipling in old age looked back upon his early childhood, certain scenes and visions came clearly to him out of the past. His first impressions were of walks in the early morning to the Bombay fruit market; of 'day-break, light and colour and golden and purple fruits at the level of my shoulder' in the strident Indian dawn; of his father walking up and down the veranda brushing his beard, and the trumpeted flowers, dappled by the sunshine through the creepers; of the syce Dunoo, who tended his pony with the ring saddle; of Meeta, his Hindu bearer, who made toys out of oranges and sometimes took him into the Hindu temples where he gazed in awe at the dim friendly gods, or for walks by the sea in the evening in the shade of the Mahim palm-grove woods. 'When the wind blew, the great nuts would tumble. ... I have always felt the menacing darkness of tropical eventides, as I have loved the voices of night-winds through palm or banana leaves, and the song of the tree-frogs.'

He remembered watching the Arab dhows stretching away over the iridescent waters on their long voyages and the Parsees wading out in gaudy clothes to worship the sunset. Close to the Kiplings' little house on the Bombay Esplanade was the grim place to which the Parsees made their last earthly journey, the Towers of Silence where the vultures squatted on the turrets, agitating their great wings in anticipation as the dead were carried in, afterwards hopping away gorged into coma. He was to remember that lost kingdom of India vividly in the bitter years to come, and in exile would tell his sister Trix stories of her red and green push-carriage, and the brougham smelling of old leather, horses and ammonia, where they sat opposite their mother in her bright dresses and drove to the bandstand or along Black Bay, and of the stuffed leopard's head on the nursery wall, which the *ayah* had told him was a talisman against sleeplessness and the night-terrors of childhood.

Across a green open space near the Kipling house was a place of mystery, bare rooms smelling of paint and oils, where there were un-fashioned lumps of clay with which Rudyard played, a place presided over by Mr 'Terry Sahib', to whom his small sister was devoted. This was the *atelier* of his father's School of Art.

John Lockwood Kipling, always known as Lockwood, was one of the pioneers of art education under governmental auspices in India. Eldest son of the Reverend Joseph Kipling of the Wesleyan ministry and Frances Lockwood, he was born at Pickering, Yorkshire, in 1837 and sent to the Connexional School at Woodhouse Grove. At the age of twenty-two he was apprenticed to the Burslem potteries in Stafford-shire as a modeller and designer of terracotta. One of the managers of the pottery, recognizing great potential ability, encouraged him to learn French, and he soon left the potteries and worked for a time in an artist's studio, until he received an appointment on the staff of the executive art department of the South Kensington Museum.[1] His father died at Skipton in the West Riding in 1862, but his mother sur-vived there until 1886, 'the Skipton grandmother' so often spoken of in Rudyard's childhood, and the grandparent of whom he had the clearest recollection.

In 1865, Lockwood married Alice Macdonald, daughter of a well-known Wesleyan preacher, George Browne Macdonald. Frederick Macdonald, her brother, had met Lockwood in Burslem, where the latter had made an immediate impression in a narrow religious com-munity, bringing into it the breath of something new and mysterious, the atmosphere of an artist's life, the hint of a different world and an enlargement of their small horizon. Interested in everything, sympathetic and critical, and with a wide general knowledge, Lock-wood Kipling brought to Macdonald's life an intellectual quicken-ing which no one else could arouse, and when Macdonald's sister Alice came to visit him in Burslem, he introduced her to his new friend.

Mentally [said Macdonald], they had much in common, though with certain obvious differences of temperament. She was keen, quick and versatile beyond anyone I have known, saw things at a glance, and des-patched them in a word. His mind moved more slowly, and was patient and meditative. It was a case of the masculine and feminine mind each in high typical development, and the result, as so often in such cases, was a kinship of thought and feeling that soon ripened into something more.[2]

They became engaged after a day spent together at Rudyard Lake, a piece of ornamental water lying between the villages of Rudyard and Burslem, and from this place Kipling's strange Christian name was derived.

One of George Macdonald's ministries had been in Birmingham in the 1850s, and it was here that his eldest son Henry began his friendship with Edward Burne-Jones. When Burne-Jones moved to London, where he shared a studio with William Morris, Henry, his younger brother Frederick, and his sister Georgiana were frequent visitors to Burne-Jones's house, and Georgiana married the painter in 1860. Four years later they moved to 'The Grange', North End Road, which was one day to become a place of refuge for Rudyard in his hour of agony.

It was from this house that Georgiana made the arrangements for her sister's wedding. Lockwood and Alice were married at St Mary Abbot's Church on 18 March 1865,[3] a raw and sombre day, but the eminent writers who attended the reception, including Swinburne and the Rossettis, caught not a glimpse of the bride and bridegroom, who had already made their momentous decision to sail for India on a ship that weighed anchor the same day. Earlier in 1865 Lockwood Kipling had been appointed Professor of Architectural Sculpture in the School of Art at Bombay, a school which he created and launched with the same vigour with which he later made famous the Mayo School of Art in Lahore. Lockwood and Alice landed in India in May, and on 30 December the same year Joseph Rudyard Kipling was born in Bombay. His mother spent six days of agony in a dangerous and protracted confinement, 'as long as it took for the creation of the world', as she said afterwards. In a cheerful letter to her mother she 'hoped the baby would dine with them on Christmas day', but on Christmas eve her real labour began. It is possible that Rudyard's eyes were affected by that ordeal, for his sister and both parents had exceptionally strong sight.

Sometimes, later, there would be malicious whispers from men stung by Rudyard Kipling's sudden and astonishing success that he had black blood, that he was 'four annas in the rupee'. Such insinuations, fostered perhaps by his sallow, swarthy complexion and his Indian boyhood, cannot survive the slightest examination of either side of his parentage.

'We used to be small Nidderdale Yeomen', he said, 'and I believe that in a humble way few stocks carry back cleaner Yorkshire blood for a long time. I think we are West Riding for a matter of two hundred years, a thing of which I am not a little proud.'

On his father's side the accusations become even more ridiculous when we examine his family history, which stretches back into the dim records of the West Riding, and the Norman Survey itself.[4] We find that Kiplin (with no final 'g') in the parish of Catterick was the home of the Baltimore family who founded Baltimore in the USA in 1633, and near it was Richmond, where Kipling's ancestors lived, and where most of the Kiplings lived afterwards.

We find indications that Kipling's forebears originated in 1519 the 'Kiplin Cotes', the oldest, longest, and most testing horse race in England. Rudyard Kipling's great-great-grandfather came from Bedale or Richmond, and in 1800 the Wesleyan Methodists at Lythe, a little north of Whitby, were presided over by the author's great-grandfather, John Kipling, who married Ann Hansell. Their eldest son, Joseph, the grandfather of Rudyard, was born at Lythe. Joseph, a preacher of fire and local renown, was dark-complexioned with piercing black eyes, and Frances Lockwood, the daughter of a Skelton-in-Cleveland architect, is said also to have been dark-eyed and brunette, although as has since been noticed 'her offspring alternated between "Spanish" brunettes and apple blossom blondes'.[5]

The Macdonald strain was equally free from any dark admixture of blood. It can be traced to one of the most savage periods of Scottish history, and sprang from the Highland clansmen dispersed after the rebellion of 1745 and the slaughter on Culloden Moor, men whose world had suddenly fallen to pieces and who left Scotland for ever to strike new roots over the seas. Some ventured to the British colonies across the wastes of the Atlantic. Others sought refuge in the North of Ireland. Among these were the Macdonalds, and James Macdonald, quickened by the eloquence of Wesley, joined the Methodist Society in 1785. For eleven years he laboured in that bleak countryside – hard days of austerity and self-instruction in Latin, Greek and Hebrew, in French, Italian and Spanish – days of journeying on foot and horseback through his wide circuit, spreading the Word in distant hovels among rough herdsmen who lived on hills covered in bog-cotton.[6] Appointed to an English circuit, he died in 1833, to be succeeded by his son, George Browne Macdonald, who also entered the ministry.

There is a continuity of devotion in this family in which three generations of Wesleyan preachers pursued their calling in unbroken succession for 144 years, as a tablet in Wesley's Chapel in the City Road, London, proclaims:

In grateful and loving memory of
THREE GIFTED METHODIST PREACHERS
FATHER, SON, and SON'S SON
Whose ministry in unbroken succession covered 144 years

	BIRTH	MINISTRY
1761	James Macdonald	1784–1833
1805	George Brown MACDONALD	1825–1868
1842	FREDERICK WILLIAM MACDONALD	
	(President of Conference 1899)	1862–1928

George Macdonald, after a tragic first marriage, married Hannah Jones and had a family of eleven children, with five daughters of unusual beauty. Four of these daughters married, with what appeared to be varying degrees of worldly success: Georgiana to the rising Pre-Raphaelite, Burne-Jones; Louisa at Bewdley to a rich iron-master, Alfred Baldwin, destined to sire a Prime Minister, Stanley Baldwin, and become Chairman of the Great Western Railway – parties in strange contrast, it must have seemed, to the penniless curator of an obscure School of Art in India. On the day of Louisa's wedding her sister Agnes married a friend of Burne-Jones, the artist Edward Poynter. The fifth sister, Edith, was the maiden aunt with whom Rudyard corresponded to the end of his life, and the only one to survive him.

Lockwood and Alice settled easily into the new life in Bombay. They had little behind them beyond their own characters and accomplishments but with these they were liberally endowed – Alice *petite* and attractive, with blue eyes and fair hair, a sharp tongue and a mind so swift that the onrush of thought frequently outstripped the power of expression; Lockwood, with his immense appetite for knowledge, his sympathetic understanding of Indians and his technical mastery of his craft, which perfectly fitted him for the task of reviving and nourishing the languishing craftsmanship of India and turning its practitioners away from the slavish aping of modern Western forms. Beginning with sculpture, he acquired professional knowledge of all branches of Indian art and a remarkable manual dexterity, but was never confined narrowly to his own profession, being a man of wide reading, and gifted with an enviable prose style.

In this teeming Indian city, which seemed half-drowned in the sea and lay flat against the dark promontory of the Malabar Hills, with its festering rabbit-warrens of streets and appalling contrasts of wealth and squalor, Rudyard Kipling's infancy was passed.

Lockwood came to feel an affection mingled with exasperation for the Indians working in his studio.

We have as you know [he told Edith Macdonald] open sea on one side of the narrow neck of land on which we live, and the ship-crowded harbour on the other. Things are so funnily like and unlike what they should be. A Hindoo makes a shot at the right thing and he hits or misses by chance so that no one thing is quite right. No masonry is square, no railings are straight, no roads are level, no dishes taste quite like what they should, but a strange and curious imperfection and falling short attends everything, so that one lives in a dream where things are just coming about but never *quite* happen. I don't suppose if I were to talk for a week I could make you quite realize how far the brains of a native take him and where the inevitable clog of his indolence and that'll-do-ish-ness stop him short. But it's very odd and strange. Ruddy is a great lark but he won't be a baby much longer. He gets into imminent peril with the chairs and things daily. It's the quaintest thing in the world to see him eating his supper intently watched by three dogs to which he administers occasional blundering blows with a little whip and much shouting.[7]

There are photographs of Rudyard as a baby. The first sent to the grandparents, a *carte de visite*, showed him asleep in the lap of a dark-skinned Madras *ayah*, an upright, dignified woman, with a bare head and thick black hair coiled on her neck. One of Rudyard's uncles on being shown the photograph said: 'Dear me, how dark Alice has become.'[8]

The child was already difficult to control, but his mother soon developed a method of distracting his attention from unpleasant necessities. A bout of whooping cough was met by a nightly emetic. Alice would read an interesting book while waiting for the medicine to work, and Rudyard would say: 'When I hold up my hand and say "now", stop reading.'

Rudyard's birth had nearly killed Alice, and when she was again pregnant in 1868 the doctors sent her to England in February, so that her second child might be born under better conditions. The steamer was infested with spoilt children, amongst whom Rudyard soon became one of the most dominating and odious, and it was with relief that Alice brought him safely to shore. They went to the quiet, beautiful village of Bewdley, where her parents lived in an old-fashioned three-storeyed house on the River Severn. Rudyard, used to an Indian bungalow, found the staircases irresistible. He clattered round the house from kitchen to attic, peering into every room, regarding with particular interest the large bedroom belonging to his grandparents, and complaining to his mother: 'They have taken the best room in the house for themselves.'

He slept in the same bed as his aunt, Edith Macdonald, whom he kicked steadily through the night when he was not waking her up demanding drinks of water. His grandfather George Macdonald, exhausted by years of preaching and travelling, old and ailing, resented this disturbing interruption of the quiet routine of his house, and whenever possible sent his grandson out of doors. The child would walk down the village street muttering, 'Ruddy is coming, Ruddy is coming,' and if a village showed signs of interest, 'An angry Ruddy is coming.'[9] Edith used to say that Ruddy's noise had hastened and embittered his grandfather's last days, and Uncle Fred Macdonald, who had children of his own, wrote to his brother in America:

Alice and her two children have been staying with us before they go back to India. The little girl is already a beauty, and we should like to steal her, but Ruddy aged three is a power and a problem with strange gifts of upsetting any household. He adores his father luckily, and I hope John will be very firm with him for dear Alice is as wax in his small fists.

Alice had had a second dangerous confinement in June, for her new-born daughter weighed eleven pounds and was apparently stillborn, with a broken arm and black eye, and remained so for an alarming time till the doctor whipped her alive with a towel wrung out in iced water. The child, named after her mother, was born at the Burne-Joneses' house, 'The Grange'. Years later Trix said: 'Aunt Georgie Burne-Jones was so impressed by my size and whiteness, as I lay like a Blake drawing, abandoned on the floor, that she picked me up and asked the doctor if nothing could be done. He said briefly, "Slap her", · which she did very gently with her little hands till he could attend to me.' When her breathing became regular she was rolled in a blanket and placed on a chair in Burne-Jones's studio, and exposed to the further hazard of nearly being sat upon by a fat picture dealer awaiting an appointment. Rudyard had by now temporarily discarded his Hindi, the vernacular idiom that he had thought and dreamed in, and adopted a broad Worcestershire accent.

'She is like a little Rubens girl,' said Alice, bathing the child.

'Yes', Ruddy agreed with his new voice, 'hur is very like Reuben.'

Reuben was the coachman, and at that time Ruddy's intimate and ideal. Lockwood, to Alice's surprise and amusement, was shy of the baby, and when she was five months old and they were on their way back to India, he seemed not to know how to talk to her. He said she was a 'tricksy baby'. From then on she became 'Trixie' or 'Trix' to all the family.

Rudyard's *ayah*, a Roman Catholic from Goa, took charge of the new baby. On their walks with Trixie in her perambulator, she would pray at a wayside cross, the little boy standing beside her. The children spoke to the *ayah* and to the Indian bearer in their own language and had to be reminded when they were sent into the dining-room, correctly dressed, to speak English to their parents.

On 15 April 1871 the children – Rudyard now five and a half and Trix rising three – left Bombay for England with their parents; their mother had lost a baby the year before. This departure was the beginning of the most miserable period of Rudyard's life, and of a sudden desertion by his parents, the causes of which are still obscure. The Kiplings, answering an advertisement, had decided to take their children to England and board them out with two strangers at Southsea. Their name was Holloway and they took in children whose parents were in India. The Kiplings had no acquaintance with the Holloways, who apparently had not been personally recommended to them. Relatives on both sides of the family had offered the children homes. Grandma Kipling lived in Skipton, and had a daughter, Ruth, living with her and another nearby. 'Aunt Ruth', said Trix long after, 'was a sweet young woman with a soft voice, fine eyes in a plain, dark face, and the lovely expression some old nuns have, but she had it from early youth. A married daughter lived near with a large family, chiefly of flaxen haired girls with apple-blossom cheeks.'

Nearer home there had been a plan that Ruddy should be divided between the Burne-Jones family and his godfather and uncle, Fred Macdonald, spending all his holidays with Trix for the five years Alice Kipling was to be away. But Mrs Kipling, who was a few months older than Lockwood and in any matter relating to the children dominated him completely, had said that the brother and sister must not be parted, and Lockwood had agreed.

It is a matter of pure speculation to suggest that Mrs Kipling might have been influenced by a faint jealousy – that she might have preferred to give her children to strangers rather than to risk the danger of their growing too intimate with other relatives during the long absence. It is possible, too, although this is also conjecture, that

Lockwood and Alice were restrained by pride from appealing to the generosity of relatives, thus emphasizing the social gulf that already existed between them, and that this pride demanded that they should pay their own way without being beholden to others.

Harsh and unnatural as this arrangement seems to be, we should remember that it was a common practice for the English in India to board out their children in England, to be catered for by special establishments. The staff on which Lockwood Kipling worked at the time was poorly paid by the Government, and the Kiplings could ill afford to take the children to the Hills in the hot season, while the oppressive heat in Bombay and the many Eastern scourges, as yet unmastered by science, made it a place of extreme peril for European children. Rudyard was, his parents thought, badly spoilt when he left India, and the more so for his precocity and cleverness.

Yet we cannot overlook the fact that it was in the parents' power to place the children with relations who knew and loved them, that they jumped at the excuse that the aunts could only take one child each, and insisted on the children being together;[10] that, perhaps to avoid lacerating their own emotions, they failed to prepare the children in any way for this grim separation, which was, said Trix, 'like a double death, or rather, like an avalanche that had swept away everything happy and familiar'.[11]

So on 15 April 1871 the days of light and darkness, heat and shade in India were over, and there was a time on a ship, the old P & O paddle-wheel *Ripon*, seething through the night. 'There was a train across a desert (the Suez Canal was not yet opened) and a halt in it, and a small girl wrapped in a shawl on the seat opposite me, whose face stands out still. There was next a dark land, and a darker room full of cold, in one wall of which a white woman made naked fire, and I cried aloud with dread, for I had never before seen a grate.'*[12]

---

* His two journeys home from India as a child seem to have become mingled in Kipling's memory.

CHAPTER II

THE HOUSE OF DESOLATION

THEN there came another house, which was to be Rudyard's home for more than five years, a house afterwards seldom referred to, and then only with horror as the 'House of Desolation', or 'Forlorn Lodge'. There was a miserable parting in a misty dawn – a cab waiting – a father and mother overwhelmed by grief who told Rudyard that he must learn quickly to read and write, so that they might send him letters and books, and then a hasty departure. The children were bewildered by this unexplained desertion:

A simple reiterated explanation of the necessity of leaving us in England would easily have been understood by a six-year-old boy of my brother's intelligence, and he would have made it clear to me. As it was, we felt that we had been deserted, 'almost as much as on the doorstep', and what was the reason? They had seen [added Trix] the horrible little house before they left us there, they knew how far it was from the sea and the Common, with a garden the size of a pocket handkerchief, too small even for battledore and shuttlecock. They had seen Harry's* crafty eyes, they had heard Aunty's false voice; they must have known that she was of the seaside landlady type, and yet they let her be my only teacher and companion till I was ten years old.

The cab drove away and the children entered 'Lorne Lodge', the house in which they were to learn the meaning of captivity. Mrs Holloway, a woman probably over-abused, was to be known to Ruddy and Trix as 'Aunty Rosa'. Her husband, 'Uncle Harry', was a retired naval captain, once a midshipman at Navarino, with a dry black scar on his leg, relic of an accident with a harpoon line while whale-fishing, a scar at which Rudyard used to gaze with horror and fascination. The house stood in the suburbs of Southsea. Nearby in Portsmouth Harbour 'the timber for a Navy that was only experimenting with iron-clads such as the *Inflexible*, lay in great booms in the Harbour. The little training-brigs kept their walks opposite Southsea Castle, and

* The Holloways' son.

... outside these things lay the desolation of Hayling Island, Lumps Fort, and the isolated hamlet of Milton.'

Rudyard was soon to know all these places in his walks with the scarred sea-captain who, apart from Trix, was his only friend in the 'House of Desolation' – the mud banks with their screaming sea-birds, the great harbours with the ships riding at anchor, their slimy jetties and seaweedy smell, the dockyards with the hammers ringing, the marine-store shops with tar and ropes, and the brass-countered offices where the captain went every three months with a slip of blue paper to claim his wound pension.

That desolate scene lingered in his mind long afterwards: 'The sea had not changed. Its waters were low on the mud-banks, and the Marazion bell-buoy clanked and swung in the tide-way, on the white beach-sand dried stumps of sea-poppy shivered and chattered together.'

When Rudyard and Trix looked at their new home, they saw a small house in a short street of small houses. The road petered out into the waste land where Trix was sometimes allowed to play, and every detail was indelibly printed upon this child's extraordinary memory.

The house was covered in shabby stucco and had a front garden about the shape and size of a prayer-carpet, where nothing grew except a bank of St John's wort which sloped down to the playroom window in the basement. At the back was ugly brick-work, and a mean little scullery and coal-shed, but there was a small grass plot, three speckled Portugal laurels, one laurustinus, a small laburnum, and a few scent-less flowers.

'Lorne Lodge' was entered through a hall as narrow as a passage, which crooked an elbow at the front door and took a sharp turn before it disclosed the dining-room door at the right, the drawing-room opposite, and the steep narrow staircase. In the dining-room where 'Aunty's' meagre rations were consumed was a highly polished table and a perennial odour of cabbage, in spite of the ventilation of the little greenhouse leading out of it, which contained the only beautiful things in the house, pink oleanders among dull ferns, stunted mauve primulas, and leggy white geraniums.

The drawing-room smelt of plaster and damp, what Ruddy soon called 'a buried-alive smell'. No fires were allowed to pollute the glittering steel fireplace, and it was in this room that Trix's icy fingers struck false notes on the little cottage piano in the grim practices before breakfast in the depth of winter.

The kitchen was down a short flight of slippery matted stairs; so was the little dungeon of a playroom, a dark place never warmed or aired, for the ground was a trifle above the window. It was a mush-roomy-smelling little hole, with wall cupboards where even a doll's china dinner-set grew mildew after two or three days, with a rusty grate but no fire, a room that produced broken chilblains from December to February, and where Ruddy stood his solitary confine-ments.

The bedroom above the drawing-room, which Trix shared with 'Aunty', had a little dressing-room holding a hip-bath as there was no bathroom in the house. There was a brass bed with a stiff white honeycomb quilt and a nightdress case with GOOD NIGHT braided on it in red, to match the SOILED LINEN bag that hung behind the door, and the BRUSH AND COMB bag on the toilet table. A large framed text of scarlet poppies, wheat-ears and blue cornflowers commanded one to CONSIDER THE LILIES. The wallpaper was a dull grey, patterned with small purple roses, as was that in the spare room opposite, where there was also a glazed chintz ottoman, cool and agreeable to slide off in warm weather.

In this house it was upon Rudyard that the main brunt of the harsh evangelical discipline fell. Mrs Holloway had long wanted a daughter, and she soon made a pet of Trix, who escaped most of the torture.

It was [said Kipling sixty-five years later, his memory still sharp with a sense of outrage] an establishment run with the full vigour of the Evangelical as revealed to the Woman. I had never heard of Hell, so I was introduced to it in all its terrors – I and whatever luckless little slavey might be in the house, whom severe rationing had led to steal food. Once I saw the Woman beat such a girl, who picked up the kitchen poker and threatened retaliation. Myself I was regularly beaten. The Woman had an only son of twelve or thirteen as religious as she. I was a real joy to him, for when his mother had finished with me for the day he (we slept in the same room) took me on and roasted the other side.[1]

It was soon evident that the regime would be a severe one for the lonely little couple, whose united ages did not amount to ten years. Separation from each other and solitary confinement for twenty-four hours with 'Aunty' as jailer were imposed for spilling a drop of gravy at dinner, forgetting to put a slate away, or 'crying like silly babies' when she read them letters from Bombay. 'Discipline' was one of her favourite words, and it was applied with no sparing hand to

Rudyard, whose life now resolved itself into a series of humiliating fiascos.

If you cross-examine a child of seven or eight on his day's doings (specially when he wants to go to sleep) he will contradict himself very satisfactorily. If each contradiction be set down as a lie and retailed at breakfast, life is not easy. I have known a certain amount of bullying, but this was calculated torture – religious as well as scientific. Yet it made me give attention to the lies I soon found it necessary to tell: and this, I presume, is the foundation of literary effort.[2]

The Holloways' son Harry – 'the Devil-Boy', as Rudyard thought of him – was the children's most painful cause of suffering, deeply religious, mentally and physically cruel, and adored by his mother. Rudyard was condemned to share an attic with him, sleeping in a hard iron bed against the wall, where the roof sloped down on the left of the floor, and the early parts of his nights were rendered hideous by Harry, who fortunately liked his sleep and could not maintain the persecution long before falling into snores.

By day he tried to trap the two children with spurious sympathy and, if successful, reported their complaints to his mother. Trix soon learned, when Harry approached her with 'Has the old cat been making you cry, Trixie?', to answer, 'If you speak of your mother in that way I shall tell her.'

Luckily for Ruddy, Harry was always at school until tea-time, but they soon realized that a friendly attitude on his part was a sign of trouble. He was the worst part of their exile, more feared even than 'Aunty', particularly after his father's death. 'Uncle Harry', dimly aware of what was happening, thrashed Harry one day when he saw Trix's arms marked with black bruises from pinching. He thrashed him again when Harry was detected trying the 'wrenching torture' on the children which, as the boy modestly said, he was 'rather good at', but his father's death in 1874 removed the last check upon him, and Jane, the harassed little maid-of-all-work, would hide Trix when 'Aunty' was out and Harry in a cruel mood.

After 'Uncle's' death, Rudyard knew that he would be beaten or sent to bed supperless if he offended Harry or committed some trivial offence. Trix did her best to protect him, and Jane helped her, even sharing her frugal supper with Trix when she staged a hunger strike. Jane, while she stayed, was their ally, and Trix loved the driven little slavey, except when she used to damp-plait her long hair into many tails and iron them on the kitchen table with a hot iron. Trix, however,

was not altogether cowed, and when Harry got older and used pomatum on his hair – which even the adoring mother said made him look
like a butcher's boy – would avenge cruelties to Rudyard by putting
flour on Harry's pillow.

The children never ceased to speculate miserably as to why they
had been deserted. Mrs Holloway told them it was because they had
been naughty, and she had taken them out of pity, but her husband
told them kindly that it was only 'Aunty's' joke, and that India was
too hot for children. They did not believe him, for they had been to
the Hills for the hot weather in Ruddy's fourth and fifth years. Harry
told them with unction that they were workhouse brats, who had been
taken in out of charity, and that none of their toys belonged to them.
'He began to break my doll in proof of this, and was most surprised
to receive a full-sized cuff on each side of his head, before Uncle, who
was a man of few words, said, "You can go and tell your mother what
you got that for and then go to bed. Dry bread, remember." We were
both very sorry when Uncle died.'[3]

The last time Trix saw Uncle Harry, whom she called 'Daddy', he
was lying in bed, looking very strange on a starched pillow. His nurse
sat her down on the bed, with her white socks and blue shoes straight
out in front of her, and said: 'Sing your pretty hymn to poor Uncle.'
She began to sing 'The King of Love my Shepherd is', beating time
on his cold and unresponsive hand, but to her surprise and chagrin,
when she came to 'In Death's dark Vale I fear no ill', 'Uncle's' face
suddenly puckered and he began to cry. Nurse led her away, and she
never saw her friend again.[4]

After many years it was Trix's belief that 'Aunty' did her best to
weaken the affection between brother and sister by a long process of
sapping and mining. She took the line that Trix was always in the
right and Ruddy in the wrong, but Ruddy said that she was a jealous
woman and of such low caste that she did not matter. He ignored
her efforts to sow dissension. She was a *Kuch-Nay*, a Nothing-at-all,
and the contemptuous name became a secret and a bond between
them, as did the use of other Hindi words, for Trix could understand
them a little and Ruddy spoke the language fluently.

They made no attempt to communicate their unhappiness to their
parents, and although both wrote regularly to Bombay their letters
were often dictated by Mrs Holloway and always strictly censored.
They did not realize that an unstamped letter would have been delivered in Bombay, imagining that it would be returned and recoil
upon their own heads.

This harsh novitiate affected their maturity in a strangely similar way. To Rudyard it 'drained me of any capacity for real, personal hate for the rest of my days. So close must any life-filling passion lie to its opposite.' To Trix:

Perhaps hate is a disease, like measles, that it is well to recover from early, and up to the age of eleven I hated Harry so wholeheartedly that I have only disliked a few people, in a mild tepid way, ever since. I am ashamed to say that only last year, when I found a scrap of his detested writing on the fly leaf of an old book, I tore it out, and burned it at once, and dark eyes set near together, and black hair plastered with pomatum still make me shudder with dislike.[5]

The constant process of accusation, detection, homily and punishment should have produced an introvert, but Rudyard showed no particular signs, during this period, of living in a world apart, or having any special powers or life of his own until his mother came home in 1877. He was too busy struggling to adjust himself to these crazy and inexplicable conditions, and to keep his head above water.[6] Even at night, when he might have let his thoughts ride, he was constrained by Harry's nearness in the next bed in that low-ceilinged attic.

Rudyard had not been able to read when he was five years old, and he could not read for pleasure until he was seven, very late for those days. It is possible that if he had learned earlier his short sight might have been detected. Mrs Holloway taught the children to read together. The lessons took place in the dining-room, on the over-polished dinner table, for she could not face the damp of the basement playroom. Rudyard wore a man-o-war's blouse with a lanyard and whistle, short blue knickers, striped socks and strap shoes. There were 'pothooks and hangers' for him and 'strokes' for Trix, and *French Without Tears*, and their pencils squeaked on the slates. Trix learned to read before Ruddy, but he soon passed her in lessons, explaining her superiority in reading: 'You're so little, you see, you're not old enough to take in the hard things about reading, and that's why you can do it quicker than me, because you've got less brain to see where it's difficult.'[7]

There were not many books in the 'House of Desolation', but Rudyard fell upon what he could find, a bound copy of *Aunt Judy's Magazine* in which appeared Mrs Ewing's *Six to Sixteen*, *The Old Shikarri* with its steel engravings of charging boar and tigers, and a severely moral tale called *The Hope of the Katzikopfs*, containing verses that began 'Farewell Rewards and Fairies'. There was also a thick blue book that described nine white wolves coming over the wold, and another, fat and brown, was full of lovely tales in strange metres: 'a girl was turned into a water-rat, an urchin cured an old man of gout with a cool cabbage leaf, and somehow "forty wicked goblins" were mixed up in the plot, and a "Darling" tried to sweep stars off the skies with a broom.'[8]

Once he was taken to Oxford, and introduced to a venerable old man who, he was told, was the Provost of Oriel, and once to an old gentleman in a house in the country near Havant:

Here everything was wonderful and unlike my world, and he had an old lady sister who was kind and I played in hot, sweet-smelling meadows and ate all sorts of things. After such a visit I was at once put through the third degree by the Woman and her son ... but it was beyond my comprehension. My sole concern had been a friendly pony in the paddock ... and once again the pleasure that I was seen to have taken was balanced by punishments and humiliation – above all humiliation. ... The son after three or four years went into a Bank and was generally too tired on his return to torture me, unless things had gone wrong with him. I learned to know what was coming from his step into the house.[9]

Trix was denied even these modest escapes, making only one note-worthy excursion from 'Lorne Lodge' in seven years, when she was taken to Brighton. Her sole relief was to be taken to tea with 'kind Miss Tayler' who was much older than 'Aunty' and who 'lived in a long damp green drawing-room, that smelt earthy, and looked out upon a long damp green garden'. The walls were hung with Landseer pictures in Berlin woolwork.

'Miss Tayler was very small and very bent and wore a heavy brown wig, tied to her head with a wide black ribbon, and I liked her to the verge of love, till, out of the kindness of her heart, she gave me my first lesson in Death. It was Christmas Eve, and she told me she had something very pretty to show me, "a sweet little kitten"; then she brought out a large penwiper with a tiny stuffed dead kitten on it. I cried so much that I was taken home in disgrace, but my nerves were shattered and I still think I deserved credit for not being what Aunty called "vulgarly sick" till we were in the road.'[10]

It is strange that not one of the 'beloved aunts', according to Trix, once visited the children at Southsea, and that in all those bleak years they never sent Trix a card or a Christmas gift. Although she carried throughout her life the impression that she had suffered complete abandonment by all her relations, Trix's formidable memory was here at fault, for her grandmother's diary for 1872 shows clearly that on

several occasions that year she paid visits to 'Lorne Lodge' especially
to take the children for an afternoon outing:

Aug. 29. Came to Southsea with Agnes [her nurse] and Ambrose. Called at
   Mrs Holloway's to see Ruddy and Alice. Found them well and happy.
   After much searching found rooms at 7 South Parade....
Sept. 2. Ruddy and Alice called after tea.
Sept. 6. Ruddy and Alice spent the day with us.
Sept. 10. Drove to Mrs Holloway in the afternoon and took the children
   for a drive.
Sept. 13. Went to the beach with Mrs Holloway and the children who dined
   and spent the day with us.
Sept. 15. Left Southsea with my daughters and came to The Grange.[11]

For one month each year Ruddy spent his Christmas holidays with
'Aunt Georgie' Burne-Jones at 'The Grange', North End Road, a
month which alone saved him from despair. But even during this bliss-
ful month of emancipation he never confided his misery in Aunt
Georgie, and appeared happy and well. So, occupied with her own
children and, as she afterwards told her nephew Stanley Baldwin, to
her deep subsequent regret, she never went to 'Lorne Lodge' to see
for herself. At first Rudyard was escorted to 'The Grange'. Later he
was allowed to go alone, and arriving at the house 'would reach up
to the open-work iron bell-pull on the wonderful gate that led me into
all felicity. When I had a house of my own, and The Grange was
emptied of meaning, I begged for, and was given that bell-pull for
my entrance, in the hope that other children might also feel happy
when they rang it.'

Well might he have been happy when he entered this place, so different from the little stuccoed prison at Southsea. It was the house
in which Richardson had written *Clarissa Harlowe*, *Pamela*, and
Grandison. There was a garden of three-quarters of an acre, a fine old
sloping mulberry tree on the lawn, peaches, plums and apricots ripening against the wall in their seasons, and enough apple trees to justify
calling part of it an orchard. When the Burne-Joneses had first taken
possession in November they had found late-blooming monthly roses
and a hedge of lavender. There were still great elms growing in the
roadway of North End, and wild roses to be picked in a turning out
of it. In those tranquil days, before the havoc wrought by the arrival
of the District Railway, the space at the open end of the garden led
into fields; there was a walnut and an elm tree, through the branches
of which you could see the moon riding high on summer nights. The
walnut-tree field was used for carpet beating, and Burne-Jones told

an apprehensive Italian model that the noise was that of Englishmen beating their wives.[12]

Edward Burne-Jones's daughter, Margaret, vividly remembered Rudyard's arrivals at 'The Grange' for his summer and Christmas holidays. He was about six when he first came. He arrived from 'Lorne Lodge' in a reefer-coat with brass buttons, and a bursting carpet-bag, a stout cheerful little boy, fond of play and climbing trees. He showed no signs of ill-treatment and made no complaints about his Southsea life. So little concerned indeed was the loving Aunt Georgie that she noted casually that the children 'had with them their young cousin Rudyard Kipling, now beginning the Anglo-Indian child's experience of separation from his home'.[13] He was already precocious.

It seemed to his cousin Margaret that his imagination was abnormally active. Stories were teeming in his head, and he recited them to her with eager fluency. She thought that a depth of emotion, rare at such an early age, was already perceptible behind this creative instinct. The younger aunt would come up to the bedroom to say good night to the children, and Margaret remembered an evening when he had tried to keep her there, and how the aunt had said that she wished she could cut herself in half so as to be half upstairs and half down. When she had gone Rudyard's face suddenly assumed an expression of horror Margaret never forgot, and he gasped: 'I have just seen her cut in half.' He was filled with terror, as at a vision, and Margaret realized that he had visualized his aunt cut in two with extraordinary intensity, and with horrible glimpses of lacerated internal organs.[14] He became easily frightened of the dark during those holidays and frightened of what might be under the bed. The more robust Margaret had to rake underneath it with a walking stick to satisfy him there was nothing there.[15]

Inside the house there were pungent smells of paint and turpentine which took him back to the *atelier* in Bombay, smells that were wafted from the first-floor studio where his uncle worked, painting the eyes in the portraits first, and leaving the rest in charcoal. There was a rocking-horse in the nursery and a table that, tilted up on two chairs, made a toboggan-slide, a magic lantern in the hall and Aunt Georgie to read *The Arabian Nights* to them in the evenings, while Rudyard lay on the sofa sucking toffee and calling his cousins 'Daughter of my uncle' or 'O True Believer' – a form of facetiousness that unhappily persisted into maturer years. At bedtime they hastened along the passages, where unfinished cartoons lay against the walls, to the top landing, 'where we could hang over the stairs and listen to the loveliest sound in the world – deep-voiced men laughing together over dinner'.

William Morris, 'Uncle Topsy', was frequently in and out of the house, discussing picture-frames or stained glass, but taking little notice of anything outside the orbit of his own interest. Yet he had a sort of genius for the unexpected, and Margaret and Rudyard, eating pork-dripping on brown bread in the nursery, were surprised when Uncle Topsy came in and said that he would tell them a story. They sat under the table which they used for a toboggan-slide, while Morris climbed heavily on to the rocking-horse. Then, rocking slowly backwards and forwards to the groanings and crepitations of the horse, he told them a story about a man who was condemned to dream bad dreams. One of them was that of a cow's tail waving at him from a heap of dried fish. Morris then descended from the rocking-horse and departed as suddenly as he had come.

Burne-Jones spent all day in his studio. Breakfast was at 8, and after breakfast he went to the studio at about 8.45, and painted till dark.[16] There was an intimate and happy relationship between Rudyard Kipling and his uncle. Kipling never afterwards forgot what he considered his profound debt to this man. Their pleasure in each other was continued in their correspondence when Rudyard was a young man in India, and they tried to score off each other by faking old drawings, manuscripts or curios, and exchanged letters packed with schoolboy banter that sometimes make uneasy reading today.

In those Arcadian days at 'The Grange' the sharp divergence on politics, which was afterwards to sap his admiration for these Pre-Raphaelite relatives, could find no place in the mind of a child. It was in the years ahead that he was to write with retrospective bitterness, describing the 'intellectual' society in which he lived as a boy:

purveyors of luxuries [as he called them], but utterly dependent on the fabric around them being kept safe. They fought tooth and nail, and in the general revolt, as I think, the Fabian Society was spawned. Of war, or its necessity, they knew as little as they did of any life which did not directly touch their own emotions and prettinesses. But as you can imagine, to a youngster it was intensely interesting – for a while.... Burne-Jones was in all ways the biggest. He had the most glorious sense of humour; Morris had none; it annoyed him as flies annoy cattle. But to have the two together discussing the working side of their art – fabrication of colours, design of glass windows, the inlay of little bits, and how the lines cut each other, as they loafed in the studio between whiles, was a thing to be grateful for, even though one did not comprehend it.[17]

There was only one other escape from Southsea for Rudyard. The Baldwins had taken a house in 1875 which he was sometimes allowed to visit. It was in Albert Terrace, afterwards Albert Gate, where Charles Reade had once lived, a rickety place with doubtful sanitation and a beautiful view over the Park. Here the children would sit on the walls and watch the carriages bowling down the street. Rudyard's memories of this house were of smoky oil lamps, the smell of which lingered in his nostrils all his life.[18]

On a certain day at the end of the month, a day which he tried hard to put out of his mind, the respite was over, and he would return to the 'House of Desolation' and cry himself to sleep for the next two or three nights, until he became absorbed again in the grinding routine. On the whole he endured it with stoicism. He never plotted revenge on 'Aunty' or Harry. He could never love the one and he hated the other, but he accepted them with the unquestioning resignation of childhood. Only once did he break down completely. His eyesight even at this age was rapidly failing, and his work at the little day-school in Southsea, where he had been sent at the age of eight, began to suffer.

On one of his holidays at 'The Grange' he had suddenly begun to lash with his stick at an apple tree in the garden. When asked why he had done this he announced: 'I thought it was Grandmama, and I had to beat it to see.' Margaret Burne-Jones thought the episode so strange that she told her mother, and Rudyard was taken to an oculist. This was the first time that his bad eyesight was noticed, and the doctor diagnosed his attack on the apple tree as an optical delusion. He was to suffer from them in later life when overworked, and to describe one with terrifying effect in *At the End of the Passage*.

There came a moment in March 1877 when he was shut away from Trix for two days on the grounds that he was a 'moral leper'. On a Monday morning with a bitter wind blowing, Trix, who had not seen Ruddy since Friday, was told to practise the piano and not to move from the stool for forty-five minutes. The piano was in the drawing-room, the only room downstairs that looked to the front, and she asked to see her brother, but was scolded and told he was going to school and 'perhaps', added Harry, 'you'll never seen him again, and a good job too'.

She waited till she heard the attic door unlocked, then she fastened that of the drawing-room and drew the lace curtains well over the window. She heard 'Aunty' storming at Ruddy in the little hall, and drowned the noise by playing strident scales. Then, looking out of

the window, she saw him going down the little garden, walking like
an old man. A placard covered the whole of his back – it was strong
cardboard – neatly printed by Harry:

KIPLING
THE
LIAR

Trix locked the drawing-room door behind her and, taking the key,
ran after him. She caught him up on the piece of waste ground beyond
the second house to the right, and tried to tear the placard. It was
so thick that she could not even bend it and it was sewn to his blue
overcoat with strong twine. She had to take Ruddy's knife, and cut
and unpick each stitch – while he said weakly:

'Don't, don't, dear. Leave it alone – it's no good – she'll only beat
you too.'

Trix continued to hack at the placard and at last wrenched it off
and danced on it in rage. Ruddy crept on to school, broken down
at last, and Trix ran back, her long hair whipping her face, to meet
a 'scarlet-faced virago' brandishing the cane she had never used on
the child. Trix screamed at her: 'You are a wicked woman. I'll never
speak to you again. How dare you sew that wicked placard on poor
Ruddy?'

There was an ugly scene, but Trix met 'Aunty's' threats by saying
that she would tell everybody how cruel she was to the children, and
how they hated her. 'Aunty' blustered: 'You don't know anyone to
tell.'

'Yes, there's the doctor – and you can't stop me telling the vicar.
I'll stand up in Sunday School – and I'll tell the postman, and the
policeman on the corner of Palmerston Road.'

'She threatened me with the cane, and I said: "That's right; thrash
me as if I was Ruddy – you know how I bruise and when I'm black
I'll go to the police and show them, and have you punished." I am
ashamed to say that I reduced her to tears – but I was fighting for
Ruddy as well as myself – it was the end of my childhood. He was
too broken by fasting and beating to have any kick left in him.'[19]

In March 1877[20] Mrs Kipling left Lahore for England, and descended, apparently without warning the children, upon the house in
Southsea. Trix, who during all these years had known intimately few
women other than Mrs Holloway, Jane and Miss Tayler, was not prepared for a person so different from these as her mother proved to
be. In her mind was a vision, long nourished, of another friendlier

but related 'Aunty', and her first impression when she saw her mother, of whom she retained not the slightest recollection, was of the gentleness of her voice, the softness of the face pressed against hers, and the startling blueness of the eyes that surveyed her, held at arms' length. Alice wrote that night to Lockwood that the children had welcomed her very sweetly and seemed delighted to see her, but she had been a little disappointed by the way they had both hung round Mrs Holloway in the evening.

'She did not know,' said Trix, 'that well-trained animals watch their tamer's eye, and the familiar danger signals of "Aunty's" rising temper had set us both fawning upon her.'

Rudyard said he would have known his mother anywhere by the way she jumped out of the cab and ran to meet them, but when she went into his bedroom to kiss him good night he flung up an arm to ward off the blow he had learned to expect. So came to an end the squalid episode of the 'House of Desolation'.

That Kipling remembered vividly and bitterly his privations in this place to the end of his days is beyond doubt. He and his sister never afterwards talked of Southsea days: 'They hurt too much';[21] and forty-three years later, when he was in Southsea to inspect the submarines, his wife noted in her diary: 'Rud takes me to see Lorne Lodge near St Bartholomew's Church and near Outram Road, where he was so misused and forlorn and desperately unhappy as a child, and talks of it all with horror.'[22]

In India, as a young man, he was to deliver that bitter castigation *Baa Baa Black Sheep* against the Holloway family. But it would be unjust to ignore the fact that Rudyard probably gave Mrs Holloway frequent cause for irritation, and that many of his punishments may well have been richly deserved. He was clumsy, ill-mannered and undisciplined, and it had been said that he had hastened the decline of his grandfather at Bewdley. He was also noisy, argumentative and abnormally slow to learn to read and write, so that it was perhaps not surprising that 'Aunty Rosa' thought it her duty to correct these boorish tendencies, and that she did so with a heavy hand.

Baa Baa Black Sheep was written eleven years after Kipling left 'Lorne Lodge'. He was living at the time with Professor and Mrs Hill, and it is probable that he deepened the shadows to enlist Mrs Hill's sympathy. She claimed afterwards that she had helped him to write it, and it was one of the few stories that he did not send to his family, either in manuscript or in proof. It was a grievous blow to the Lockwood Kiplings when they read these savage outpourings in cold print, and, unwilling to recognize their own contribution to this suffering, they tried to make Trix say that it was all exaggerated and untrue, but even to comfort them she could not pretend that they had ever been happy.

Yet it is essential not to overestimate the effect of this ordeal on Rudyard Kipling's emotional life. An impression, persuasive but misleading, was conveyed in Edmund Wilson's brilliant book *The Wound and the Bow*, of a character warped *in limine*, and for ever afterwards shot through with hatreds and neuroses, of a man twisted by childhood suffering into an almost pathological introvert. Strange and jealously guarded as Kipling's later character became, it is a grotesque travesty of truth to regard it as so tender a seedling, delicate and vulnerable as a tuberose. Rather did he possess such formidable powers of recuperation that he emerged from 'Lorne Lodge' unscathed by anything much worse than evil and enduring memories. He had then, as afterwards, an endless reserve of vitality, resilience and bumptiousness on which to draw. He went to Southsea so spoilt and wayward that even his sister, who shared his suffering to a lesser degree, admitted: 'Personally I think that the bitter experiences and injustices of life in "Lorne Lodge" were the making of much that was best in Rudyard's character; they supplied the discipline that was lacking.' He likewise weathered the kickings and beatings. He remained to the end of his life a firm believer in corporal punishment. 'I have often been beaten,' he said, 'and I richly deserved it.'[23]

We shall see him soon among the rude buffetings and Spartan severity of Westward Ho!, the barbarities of which so shocked Edmund Wilson, but it will not be a crushed, shrinking little figure that will emerge. It will be 'Gigger', with all his arrogance, precocity and resource, who has already shaken off the cares of Southsea as a dog shakes the water off his back. And again we shall see him appearing as resilient and bumptious as ever in India, insulting angry seniors in clubs, and writing at nineteen with the smug worldly wisdom of a greybeard. For the young Kipling's character was too effervescent to be affected for long even by the most depressing adversity, and the buoyancy remained to the end of his life, when he would suddenly emerge in tearing spirits from long bouts of agonizing physical pain and spiritual apprehension.[24] Yet something from Southsea days was to cling to him throughout life. We shall see it in the morbid reticence in which he was to shroud every secret corner of his mind from external scrutiny – in a constant, almost animal wariness and timidity, and an undying instinct for self-protection.

It was with joy that Kipling left 'Lorne Lodge' with his mother on the day of liberation. There were many memories in his head, and they were to remain there for ever: that miserable parting in the misty dawn almost six years ago; the 'buried-alive smell' of the drawing-room and the mildewy reek of the playroom below stairs; the ominous footfall of Harry returning from his bank, his black hair glistening with pomatum; Jane with her work-worn hands crying after a rebuke; the dreadful day of the placard seen swimming through a mist of tears; 'Aunty's' busy fingers sewing; solitary confinement in the dungeon; the primulas in the greenhouse and the smell of seaweed on slippery steps in his nostrils while 'Uncle Harry' told him of the Battle of Navarino.

CHAPTER III

EPPING INTERLUDE

M RS Kipling decided that the children needed a complete change from the discipline of Southsea. She also felt that this was the moment when she must study them, and come to know them. She decided to let them run wild for six months, so that Rudyard could rest brain and eyes. She had taken them to the home of a family called Pinder for a visit after she had rescued them from 'Lorne Lodge'. Pinder was Lockwood Kipling's chief in the Staffordshire potteries, and the daughter of the house described the arrival and sad state of the shy, half-blind, gauche little boy. 'He was an oyster,' she said, 'he would tell us nothing of what he had endured.'[1]

They went now to a little farmhouse on the edge of Epping Forest. The place in those days was wild and the forest deserted. The farmer and his elderly wife were kind to the children, who had the freedom of the farmyard from the beginning. They were initiated into the lore of the country, of which they were completely ignorant, learned to recognize the right middlings from half a dozen sacks all alike, to make a fattening swill for the young pigs, and how to keep apples on shelves in a fragrant-smelling apple-house. The farmer, Mr Dally, on their first morning told them they could do what they liked on the farm, provided they did not leave gates open, throw stones at the animals or break down the orchard trees. Mr Dally told their mother that he only owned half a bull, that Red Roger was twenty miles off, and that all his cows had good natures.

Next evening they were riding home in the dusk on the broad backs of Duke and Captain, and were soon helping to milk the cows and drive the pigs from the fields to their sty. They collected acorns in the outlying fields and in Epping Forest for the farm horses, Black Beauty and Cleopatra. They made friends with 'Jarge', the farm-boy, who was about Harry's age, but who never teased them, answering their questions in a 'serious satisfactory way', letting them ride in the red and blue farm-wagon when he went to the mill for middlings –

'a windmill out of a fairy story' where Ruddy made friends with the miller, and was made free of 'lovely rumbling floury places'.

'Jarge' showed them how to cut drinking straws before the milk pails went to the dairy. Ruddy did not like drinking the warm milk; there was too much 'taste of cow' about it. When they were tired of sliding down straw slopes and cajoling the half-wild barn cats on rainy afternoons, they would lie in the hay till tea-time, and he would tell Trix stories, improvising from such themes as an old log in the duck pond, or a ruined cottage half-seen in the Forest.

Scarlet fever broke out at Wilden, and their cousin Stanley Baldwin came to the farm for a long six weeks' visit. He brought a cricket bat and tried to teach them the game, but the country had got into their blood and they would have none of it. Ruddy had just been put into powerful magnifying glasses. No books or lessons were allowed, and his kitten, Sprats, sat on his shoulder, hooking the new glasses off from time to time with an inquiring paw. Mrs Kipling wanted the children to forget Mrs Holloway and her influence as soon as possible, and placed few restrictions on them, jibbing only when Rudyard began returning to meals 'red-booted' from assisting at the slaughter of pigs – a foul occupation indeed for a small boy – or reeking after the exploration of attractive muck-heaps.

This assisting at pig-killing, always, in the days before humane killers, a disgusting and haunting spectacle, sounds perhaps even worse than it was, and Mr Hilton Brown has drawn attention to it as indicating a brutal strain in Kipling's nature. Stanley Baldwin was with him at each pig-killing, and Trix observed loyally that 'his habitual pose as a stalwart countryman, afraid of nothing' spurred Rudyard on into an unnatural display of bravado. They took part in hoop races downhill, Rudyard's heavy iron hoop called 'Eclipse', Trix's 'Kisber', and Baldwin's 'Blair Atholl'. They assaulted a wasps' nest on an islet in a muddy pond, and twice a week rode donkeys under the care of a gypsy called Saville, who led them deep into the green glades of Epping Forest, where they collected mosses and ferns and learned how to set snares for pheasants and rabbits.[2]

Their celebration of All Hallows E'en was extended as far as Guy Fawkes' day. They gathered hedge-clippings and fir-cones for a bonfire; 'Jarge' contributed stacks of faggots, and Mr Dally let them pick his largest mangel-wurzels to make turnip lanterns. They made five of these flickering lamps and fastened them on the big iron gate, while the passing cyclists shouted with kindly simulated terror. They fired rockets on Guy Fawkes' night and danced round a blazing bonfire,

afterwards roasting potatoes in the embers, potatoes which tasted delicious and smoky in spite of large raw centres as hard as peach stones.

With the winter this exciting holiday came to an end. It had done
much to remove the bitter taste of Southsea from Rudyard's mouth.
The breath of the country had passed over him like a cleansing wind;
the memory had for the moment faded of blows and discipline and
loneliness, and smells of cabbage at silent meal-times. He felt sure,
when he left the farm, that he would never be happy again far from
the cool glades of Epping, the cows and Black Beauty, swarthy Saville
and his troop of donkeys, the dairy and the hay-scented barn.

But there was another happy period in front of him. He came from
Goldring's Farm to a small lodging house at No. 227 Brompton Road
prepared to hate his life in London, but within a week found the new
scene as fascinating as the old. The house was rented by an ex-butler
and his wife, and it was here that the night first got into Rudyard's
head. He got up and wandered about the silent house, and then into
the little walled garden to see the dawn break: 'I did not know then,'
he said, 'that such night-wakings would be laid upon me through my
life, or that my fortunate hour would be on the turn of sunrise, with
a sou'west breeze afoot.'

His favourite room in the house was the sitting-room looking
directly upon the street, with no railings or area. On the ceiling was
stuck a new, unused penny stamp, the object of which greatly puzzled
him. In foul weather, when passing hansoms splashed the window
panes, he would sit looking out on to the street, absorbed in watching
the people. He made up intriguing little packets and dropped them
on the pavement, studying with interest the reactions of the passers-
by. It diverted him to watch a well-dressed person, after a furtive
glance around, eagerly tearing open the parcel and then throwing it
away in disgust at the sight of a piece of wood or a lump of coal.
His best packet was put in a real jeweller's box, sealed, and addressed
to a hypothetical J. Pettleworth Esq., 5 Myrtle Street, Peckham Rye,
and was picked up by an old gentleman in a top hat and found to
contain a walnut shell.

At the back of the house was a tempting expanse of roofs and leads.
The long narrow bedroom, papered with a pattern of shaded ivy
leaves, looked out upon a small bakery, and he could tell by a fragrant
aroma when they were making beefsteak pies. On the roofs, forbidden
to the children by their mother, the cats screamed, courted and fought,
'large splendid tabby chieftains, like young pumas, with magnificent
pelts and square sullen heads'.

The children bought evil-smelling meat in the Brompton Road to feed the cats, whose numbers quickly grew, and to solace the blind man's dog on the corner. At these cat-fishing parties on the leads they fished without hooks, dangling the meat on long strings to the screaming, leaping animals below. Kipling was accused later in life of callousness and indifference to animals, but Trix said with conviction: 'If it were possible to find, in a Zoo or out of it, any animal that Rudyard hated, I would undertake to kill it with my bare hands and eat it raw. He, like his father before him, loved all living things, and neither of them ever owned a gun.'*

In the London of those days there were many cheap and fascinating toys: scenes and characters to be coloured as marionettes for a toy theatre, wooden Dutch dolls with painted smiles, pistols firing real 'caps' and wooden pill-boxes full of Pharaoh's Serpents. On these and other toys in the windows of the glittering Lowther Arcade they spent their pocket money – a doll's silver tea-urn swinging on a stand, a Giant Book of Transfers, and a prize-pig in white sugar with red ears and eyes for a penny. There was a window called Larberg's in the Brompton Road which appealed to them more than any other, and they stood by the plate glass looking at the gleaming cutlery inside, knives and scissors, some of them gold-chased, and saw a medley better than any toy-shop – for everything was real.

Mrs Kipling bought Ruddy and Trix tickets for the old South Kensington Museum across the road, then housed in a row of dingy sheds. They spent so much time in the wet weather exploring the Museum that the policeman would help Trix to spell out her middle name, Macdonald, as she signed on student days, and he would hold back her long untidy hair from blotting the page or falling into the inkpot, and salute them solemnly when they arrived with grown-ups.

From the big Buddha with the little door in his back, to the towering dull-gilt ancient coaches and carven chariots in long, dark corridors ... we roved at will and divided the treasures child-fashion. There were instruments of music inlaid with lapis, beryl and ivories; glorious gold-fretted spinets and clavichords; the bowels of the great Glastonbury clock; mechanical models; steel- and silver-butted pistols, daggers and arquebusses ... a collection of precious stones and rings. ... These experiences were a soaking in colour and design with, above all, the proper Museum smell; and it stayed with me.[3]

---

* This statement is misleading, for Kipling shot both in India and England with enjoyment, whether he owned a gun or not.

CHAPTER IV

WESTWARD HO!

It was now time for Rudyard Kipling to go to school, where he was to spend the years 1878 to 1882, and he made yet another change of lodgings, again a happy one. His mother, on returning to India, entrusted Trix and Rudyard to the care of 'three dear ladies', Mrs Winnard and Misses Mary and Georgina Craik, who lived at the end of Kensington High Street by Addison Road.* With them he spent all his holidays from school, except those of 1881, in a pleasant atmosphere of books and kindness.

'One of the ladies,'† he said, 'wrote novels on her knee, by the fireside, sitting just outside the edge of conversation', beneath two clay pipes tied with black ribbon, which had once been smoked by Carlyle. 'All the people one was taken to see either wrote or painted pictures, or, as in the case of Mr and Miss de Morgan, ornamented tiles, and there was choice in the walls of bookshelves of anything one liked from *Firmilian* to *The Moonstone* and *The Woman in White* and, somehow, all Wellington's Indian Despatches, which fascinated me.'

Kipling represents the ladies as usually listening and himself talking, but he in turn must have listened to Miss Georgina, who was garrulous as well as kindly, taking five minutes to finish her preliminary talk about the weather. The ladies' *milieu* was that of Coniston, and they spoke often to Rudyard about how their friends were invited by Ruskin to Brantwood.[1]

In January 1878 Rudyard arrived at the United Services College, Westward Ho!, for which he was soon to find that the draconian regime of Mrs Holloway had been no bad preparation. The various accounts of Kipling's schooldays are clouded by irritating differences on points of detail. One of these was written by L. C. Dunsterville, the original of 'Stalky' in Kipling's later book *Stalky and Co.*; another was the

* Trix returned to 'Lorne Lodge' for part of the time when Rudyard was at Westward Ho!
† This was Miss Georgina Craik.

work of George Beresford, called 'M'Turk' in that book, and a third version was that of Kipling's autobiography, *Something of Myself*. To these may be added such moments of historical truth as occur in *Stalky and Co.*, but these, as we shall see, are few.

The tone of Beresford's book, written like that of Dunsterville many years later, is one of patronizing and embittered disparagement of his brilliant contemporary Kipling, who had so far outstripped him in the race of life. 'Beresford,' said Dunsterville at the age of eighty, 'was quite the type of stage Irishman who is agin anybody and everybody, and he kept this up till the day of his death. He was then a swank photographer in Yeoman's Row, but filled with hatred and contempt for his fellow men.'[2] And to Kipling, Beresford had a tongue 'dipped in some Irish-blue acid'. Dunsterville's recollections of the United Services College are more mellow and tolerant than those of Beresford; Kipling's, in *Something of Myself*, reticent and cautious, anxious to give nothing intimate away, as in the rest of this tantalizing, unsatisfactory book.

Beresford describes the founding of Westward Ho! in 1874 with icy disdain for its humble origins and boorish character. 'It was started by some Army and Navy Service people,' he said, 'who through the niggardliness of fortune, had to look on both sides of a shilling', and he proceeds with gusto to sneer at its buildings, its staff, its morals, its lack of tradition, its sanitation, and its bad cooking.

But to Dunsterville: 'Beresford had the right idea, but put it in a nasty way. The school was only started in the seventies, a sporting effort of a lot of old retired Navy and Army officers to found a school on public-school lines, in which they might be able to give their sons a decent education at a price they could afford. They obviously could not afford high salaries and must have had some difficulty in securing their staff. The masters I remember were on the whole a decent lot, but not men of real ability.'[3]

The founding of the United Services College was an effort to eliminate 'Crammers', who at that time were charging the heavy fee of £250 to £300 per annum to coach a boy for the Cadet Colleges.[4] The system and spirit of the new school were largely derived from Haileybury whence Cormell Price, headmaster of the USC, had come. Most of the boys were the sons of officers and themselves destined for the Army, and there was a strong Anglo-Indian *ambiance* about the place. But although the object of the school was to enable boys to pass the Army Examination there was a refreshing absence of militarism in its curriculum, which can be attributed to the libertarian tendencies of the

headmaster, while the fact that the trappings of the Army, Cadet
Corps, bands and drill-hall were also absent was inevitable in a school
conducted on such slender resources.

The normal religious pressures were equally wanting in this unconventional school, and the atmosphere was almost entirely secular. Unlike most headmasters of the day, Cormell Price was not in Orders.
There was no chapel; prayers were held in a grim all-purpose hall,
and the school remained immune from outside influence. Thus,
although religion was one of the most absorbing issues of the day,
and young men in their thousands were succumbing to Evangelical
and Anglo-Catholic persuasion, Rudyard Kipling passed through his
schooldays completely untouched by either of these strong and cleansing winds.

Dunsterville had arrived at the College three years before Kipling
and had found there an atmosphere of appalling and unchecked brutality common to many Victorian public schools. The bullying had
already greatly declined by Kipling's first term. Dunsterville, a boy
of exceptional strength and resource, never forgot his early period in
this forcing-house: 'Like a hunted animal I had to keep all my senses
perpetually on the alert to escape from the toils of the hunter; good
training, but likely to injure permanently a not very robust temperament.'[5]

Boys were held out of windows five storeys high by their heels. They
were hanged from the top-floor staircase blindfolded, with slack on
the rope to give a violent jerk under the arms when they fell into space,
a torture which at least once resulted in broken limbs. Their ears were
held up against the thin wooden panel of a form-room door, and a
violent blow was struck by a hammer opposite the earhole on the other
side of the panel, producing the sensation of a bomb exploding in the
head, followed by a violent headache and sickening humming of the
tympanum. They were taught to swim by being allowed to subside
to the bottom of the bath on the end of a fishing rod, while the unheeding sergeant-instructor gossiped with a crony, or, in the absence of
the sergeant, by being thrown into the deep end by other boys. The
wise new boy guarded his Christian name jealously, or, if it was
bizarre, altered it. Kipling arrived in this daunting atmosphere fresh
from the green lanes and kindly farmer of Epping and the gentle ladies
of Kensington High Street.

'Into the small boys' house at Westward Ho!,' said Beresford, 'in
the grey chill January days of 1878 there fluttered a cheery, capering,
podgy little fellow, as precocious as ever he could be. Or, rather, a

broad smile appeared with a small boy behind it, carrying it about, and pointing it in all directions.'[6]

The modelling of Kipling's head was peculiar. His skull appeared of moderate size in relation to his rather large face; his forehead retreated sharply from a heavy brow-line, in fact, so sharp was the set-back from the massive eyebrow ridges that he appeared almost 'cave-boy'. His lower jaw was massive, protruding and strong, and the chin had a deep central cleft that at once attracted attention. Owing to its width, his face appeared somewhat Mongolian; his complexion was dark and the curve in the shoulder region and a small head close to the shoulders earned him the nickname of 'The Beetle', but this was current only among a few. His spectacles consisted of pebble lenses framed in blue steel, and without them the eyes were 'strange, vibrating and blind, seeing only clearly a few inches, but of a brilliant blue'.

Across his upper lip lay the downy menace of a moustache, which was thick by his sixteenth birthday, and accompanied by rudimentary whiskers.[7] When in 1881, at the age of sixteen, he spent his holidays with his father's friends, the Pinders, Miss Pinder observed that he was abnormally mature. He shaved daily, and his chest, legs and arms were covered with black hair. He also smoked continually, and Mrs Pinder felt that she must remonstrate:

'Don't you think, Rudyard,' asked, 'you are much too young at sixteen to smoke so much?'

'I know my birth certificate gives my age as sixteen, but you know as well as I do that I am twenty-six in everything else.'[8]

He was the only boy in the school wearing glasses, and the name 'Gigger' was given to him by a local card known as 'Rabbits Eggs', described by Dunsterville as a rather dull-witted peasant frequently under the influence of drink. 'Who's old Giglamps?' he had inquired, looking at Kipling, and the name was adopted and shortened to 'Gigger'.

Kipling described his first term as 'horrible'. The numbers in the school had been made up by the headmaster by drafts from Haileybury and a number of 'hard cases', problem boys from other schools who were not wanted elsewhere. 'Even by the standards of those days,' he said, 'it was primitive in its appointments, and our food would now raise a mutiny in Dartmoor.'

One of the physical charms of the school was its position at the little seaside resort in Bideford Bay called Westward Ho! after Kingsley's novel. The school buildings were a row of twelve bleak lodging-houses by the shore near the curve of the Bay, bought by the proprietors of the school and linked by a covered passage running the length of the buildings. At one end was a barrack-like hall used for assemblies, daily prayers, and exercise in wet weather. The row of houses looked out across the sea, turbulent and white-horsed in winter, to Hartland Point and Baggy Point which enclosed the Bay, and the broad estuary of the Torridge. On the left a rocky shore led to Clovelly with its sheer cliffs and woody coombs above: to the right lay the flat, dreary expanse of the Northam Burroughs, a waste of scrub and sandhills protected from the sea by the Pebble Ridge where the heavy Atlantic swell crashed eternally on the shingle.

Whatever the deficiencies of the school, there can be no doubt that Cormell Price was the ideal headmaster for Rudyard. 'Uncle Crom', one of the 'deputy uncles' at 'The Grange', was the main reason for the Kiplings' choice of Westward Ho! A school-friend and intimate of Burne-Jones, who called him 'Crommie', he had been master of the 'modern side' at Haileybury, a school modelled in the image of Arnold's Rugby, and was for twenty years headmaster of the United Services College. He was one of a group of friends from the King Edward School, Birmingham, in the days 'when the whole town reeked of oil and smoke, and sweat and drunkenness'. These now forgotten men, Richard Watson Dixon, the historian, Edward Hatch, the theologian, William Fulford and Macdonald, used to meet Burne-Jones and Cormell Price at the latter's house in Upper Sun Street, Birmingham. Later they went to Oxford, where Burne-Jones visited them, and there were parties in William Morris's rooms in St Giles and walks to Summertown. Cormell Price had taken a hand with Burne-Jones in painting the Pre-Raphaelite frescoes at the Oxford Union, but soon abandoned the artistic life. Before settling down as a schoolmaster he had studied medicine, and visited Russia after the Crimean War as tutor to a boy in a Russian family.

Cormell Price does not escape Beresford's lash. He is depicted as an intellectual snob, precariously hanging on to the fringe of the Pre-Raphaelite group, and capitalizing his artistic connection for all it was worth in the grim struggle of academic life. Beresford adds offensively that Price wore a beard in order to conceal a weak chin, a statement rejected with contempt by Dunsterville. It is true that Beresford refers to Price's good qualities, but the effect of five pages of favourable biography is quickly effaced by a sneer on the sixth.

Clearly, the Headmaster of *Stalky and Co.* was a fiction of Kipling's mind, that 'nursing mother of Jingos, a trainer, a guide, and an inspirer of Imperial fuglemen, and stimulator of prancing frontier officers, who was cheered wildly by the school for flogging them *en masse*'. This absurd description bears no relation to the gentle, cultivated Price of real life, and it is a picture which, as Beresford sourly observes, 'requires some accounting for when one discovers that during a summer holiday in the days of the Russo-Turkish war, Price organized, hand in hand with Burne-Jones, a "Workman's Neutrality Demonstration" in denunciation of our Imperial Beaconsfield, in the blameless district of Islington'.[9] Whatever Beresford's view of his headmaster, Kipling's was one of enduring gratitude and affection.

There are many differences in the various accounts of Kipling at Westward Ho! Kipling in *Stalky and Co.* writes about fags, and Beresford objects that the institution of fagging did not exist at the United Services College, a view afterwards borne out by Kipling in his autobiography. But in Dunsterville's recollection: 'Certainly the system of fags existed in the College. I was a fag myself, and later our study shared a fag. I was seven years at the College, as in the opening years there was no junior school. R.K. and Beresford were each only about four years. By the time they joined they would have been past the fag age.'[10] This is a curious contradiction, and it is possible that by the time of Kipling's arrival the compulsory system had been relaxed into a voluntary one, run on a sort of commission basis where small boys 'obliged' for a consideration.[11]

There are further discrepancies in the various accounts of the masters in the different books written about the school. The first boys at Westward Ho! were called 'a job lot' by Dunsterville, and this description was, no doubt, equally applicable to the masters. To find men of adequate scholarship and standing to take up posts at a new and obscure public school, clearly to be dogged by poverty throughout its existence, was a formidable task for the headmaster. Indeed it was a tribute to him that he succeeded in assembling a staff of any kind in the circumstances, and although it was uneven in quality, several outstanding men emerged from it.

Rudyard's first year at the school, which was spent almost entirely in the company of Beresford, was poisoned by the chaplain, an odious cleric of sadistic tendencies called J. C. Campbell. This Dickensian figure, like so many of his kind, combined emotional sentimentality with a keen enjoyment in the infliction of corporal punishment. In his relations with this man Rudyard gave early indication that his character was one that never forgot an injury, and that his memory was long and tenacious. The chaplain, who departed in Rudyard's second year, preached a leaving sermon of such rich pathos that some of his more gullible pupils were moved to forget the past, and even to suggest a valedictory gift to the outgoing master. They were silenced by Rudyard's growl that: 'Two years bullying is not paid for with half an hour's blubbering in a pulpit.'

Rudyard found himself on easier terms with Campbell's successor, Willes, who can be identified as 'Gillett' in *Stalky and Co.*, and who prepared him for confirmation without any noticeable quickening of his spiritual impulse. He arrived at a *modus vivendi* with his housemaster M. H. Pugh, an innocuous dullard whom he afterwards ridiculed as 'Prout' in *Stalky and Co.*, and formed a happier relationship with H. A. Evans ('Hartopp'), who was fond of staging theatricals, and encouraged Rudyard and his friends in their wanderings over the Devonshire countryside.

But the most dominating influence on Kipling, after Cormell Price, was William Crofts, who appears in *Stalky and Co.* as 'King', and who instructed him in Latin and English literature. Here was a man towering above his puny colleagues, and there developed between master and boy a strong intellectual antagonism. A man of formidable personality, he recognized in Kipling a dawning genius smothered in ignorance and conceit. He set himself to trample on pretension and vulgarity in Kipling's compositions with a brutality spared less gifted pupils. Rudyard was intelligent enough to recognize the incomparable benefit he was receiving from these savage maulings and, while frequently wincing under the lash of Crofts's tongue and suppressing his own rage, coolly rifled the treasury of the master's experience: 'Tennyson and *Aurora Leigh* came in the way of nature to me in the holidays, and C[rofts] in form once literally threw [Browning's] *Men and Women* at my head. Here I found "The Bishop orders his Tomb", "Love among the Ruins" and "Fra Lippo Lippi", a not too remote – I dare to think – ancestor of mine.'[12]

Any opinions expressed in *Stalky and Co.* are open to question, particularly in connection with the masters, and Kipling's caricature of Crofts in the book bears no relation to his true opinion of that master which, as can be seen in *Something of Myself*, was a blend of admiration and fear:

My main interest as I grew older was my English and Classics Master, a rowing-man of splendid physique, and a scholar who lived in secret hope of translating Theocritus worthily.... I wish I could have presented him as he blazed forth once on the great Cleopatra Ode – the 27th of the Third Book. I had detonated him by a very vile construe of the first few lines. Having slain me, he charged over my corpse and delivered an interpretation of the rest of the Ode unequalled for power and insight.

This was clearly no ordinary man, whose brilliance remained fresh in Kipling's mind after fifty years, and the favourable judgement is repeated in *Regulus*. In another story, *The Propagation of Knowledge*, Kipling refers to a 'happy and therefore not too likeable King', and indeed it is probable that Kipling did not like 'King', who certainly did not like him. But he respected his personality and admired his scholarship.

In Dunsterville's words: 'Crofts was a fine man in every way both mentally and physically. R.K. pays a right tribute to him in *Something of Myself*. Why he wrote that quite wrong description of him in *Stalky and Co.*, I could never make out. He had my admiration, but admiration has nothing to do with liking, and I disliked him as heartily as he disliked all boys.'[13]

Beresford's opinions of the masters do not really confuse the issue; he was writing from the bitterness of a disappointing and desultory career, and from the consciousness of personal failure, and his picture of the staff at Westward Ho! should be regarded with reserve. He sneered at Cormell Price and turned Pugh – whom Kipling and Dunsterville regarded at the time as a well-meaning ass – into a half-witted oaf. Kipling's tolerant contempt of Pugh, however, was turned into violent hatred by the revelation made to him by Dunsterville in India in 1886 that Pugh suspected him of homosexual behaviour at Westward Ho! He expressed his indignation in a letter to Crofts:

...Dunsterville pointed out a little fact to me which has made me rabidly furious against M.H.P. You will not recollect that he once changed my dormitory – just before I left – and insisted upon the change with an unreasoning violence that astonished me. Thereafter followed a row, I think. I objected to be transferred because my little room was a snug one, had no prefect, and allowed me to spread my boxes and kit. About this time M.H.P., who must be a very Stead in his morals and virtuous knowledge of impurity and bestiality, transferred me to my old room, clearing out the other two boys who occupied it. It never struck me that the step was anything beyond an averagely lunatic one on the part of M.H.P. – I was not innocent in some respects, as the fish girls of Appledore could have testified had they chosen – but I certainly didn't suspect anything. Dunsterville told me on Wednesday, in the plain ungarnished tongue of youth the why and the wherefore of my removal according to M.H.P., and by the light of later knowledge I see very clearly what that moral but absolutely tactless Malthusian must have suspected. It's childish and ludicrous, I know, but at the present moment I am conscious of a deep and personal hatred against the man which I would give a good deal to satisfy. I knew he thought me a liar but I did not know that he suspected me of being anything much worse. However, I have my consolation. He shall be put into my novel – that novel which is always growing and is never finished; and to finish the revenge I'll marry him to a woman who shall give him something else to think about! But 'tis an unsavoury subject and a *most* unsavoury man. Let us drop him off the pen point and burn incense to cleanse the room.[14]

At the end of Kipling's painful first term he was told that his parents could not come to England for the Easter holidays. He spent them, not unhappily, at Westward Ho! An extraordinary change in atmosphere comes over a school when the term is over, and most of the boys have left. A sudden peace descends upon the place. The deserted form-rooms are silent; the playing fields empty; rules are relaxed, and masters friendly and tolerant. So Kipling found it:

When we survivors were left in the echoing form-rooms after the others had driven cheering to the station, life suddenly became a new thing. The big remote seniors turned into tolerant elder brothers, and let us small fry rove far out of bounds; shared their delicacies with us at tea; we had no special work to do and enjoyed ourselves hugely. On the return of the school 'all smiles stopped together'.[15]

For compensation Rudyard was given a holiday when his father returned from India, and they went together to the Paris Exposition of 1878 where Lockwood was in charge of Indian exhibits. Rudyard was allowed to wander alone through the city and the exhibition grounds, and his adoration for France began from that moment.

Our happy expedition crossed the Channel in a steamer, I think, made of two steamers attached to each other side by side, (was it the old Calais-Douvres designed to prevent seasickness, which even the Gods themselves cannot do) and, late at night, we came to a boarding house full of English people at the back of the Parc Monceau. In the morning, when I had waked to the divine smell of roasting coffee and the bell-like call of the *marchand d'habits*, my father said in effect: 'I shall be busy every day for some time. Here is –' I think it was two francs. 'There are lots of restaurants all called Duval, where you can eat.' Then he was swallowed by black-coated officials and workmen in blouses.[16]

The originals of 'Beetle', 'M'Turk' and 'Stalky' soon came together at Westward Ho!, and the alliance was formed before the end of the first year. Here we should emphasize again that *Stalky and Co.* is fiction. There were no such boys, and no such Napoleonic manœuvres and strategy.

'The three characters, however,' said Dunsterville, 'correspond more or less to the characters of Kipling, Beresford and myself. We were rather like that, but not quite so clever. The events described are actual events in most cases, but very much written up. Some of the events really concerned others, and not us three. Looking back on my own life of over eighty years, I think that events have shown me as possessing the same sort of traits of character depicted in Stalky.'[17]

Elsewhere he wrote, with the need of castigating Beresford in mind: 'We were only just a lot of potty little schoolboys with playful ingenuity perhaps rather unusually highly developed.'

The mysterious 'Turkey', with his tongue 'dipped in Irish-blue acid' and his unknown home life, would arrive a day or two late by the Irish packet, aloof and saturnine, but 'Stalky' was the unquestioned executive leader of the three. Even the sour Beresford is startled into praise – a unique schoolboy, he admitted, who really had a mind and aspirations like those of the boy in *Stalky and Co.* – although, as if ashamed of this involuntary lapse into warmth, he hastens to add that the real-life character was a watered-down version of the glittering Olympian of the book, the fabrication of Gigger's brain.

These three boys visualized their life simply as a series of pitched battles against the masters and the sergeant, varied in Kipling's case by incessant reading, and writing of verse on cream-laid vellum. They were refreshingly indifferent to the accepted standards of the normal public school. They cribbed frequently in their work, and sneered at the idolatry of games. They were not interested in bullying. They despised rules, discipline, the herd instinct, and the public-school spirit. They smoked pipes and cigars and read Ruskin, Carlyle and Whitman in their hut in the middle of the densest patch of furze bushes, or in a tiny room they hired from one of the cottagers.

The secret entrance to these places was in bounds, and the hut out of bounds, but there was no danger of capture on entering or leaving. The furze thicket was on a steep slope, and the tunnel of approach between bristling gorse bushes only just wide enough to admit a boy. In the winter they used the little room they had hired from 'Rabbits Eggs', a pigsty which they cleaned, and where they enjoyed the same secret delight of occupancy as in the hut, of security and escape. There they cooked stolen blackbirds, potatoes, turnips, hens' eggs and apples over a spirit lamp.

There were clearly some good points in this unconventional school. Proficiency at games did not carry the same wildly distorted significance as at most public schools. Bounds were wide, and freedom given to wander over the Devonshire countryside. In spite of the violent adventures of 'Stalky and Co.', the trio actually did little. They were not boys of action. They did not throw stones at bottles on the beach, or join in a favourite recreation of Victorian boys, the tormenting of cats.

Kipling was at this time strangely blind to his surroundings for one who was to become a creative artist. He knew little of the natural history of flowers or the movement of the seasons, and regarded the country as a place in which to dream or to think about the books he had read. When Beresford and Dunsterville went into the country with Kipling they went at peace with all nature, and the rabbits, rats and chattering jackdaws had nothing to fear from them. But as at the pig-killing at Epping, Rudyard succumbed on occasions to the more revolting deviations of youth, and Beresford tells us in macabre detail:

There was only one biological thing I saw Gigger do, and that was really worth the while of a gigantic intellect. He produced on a plate in our big study a find worthy of Milton or Coleridge. It was nothing less than a frog which was being chewed to death, devoured alive by hefty maggots, all inside him and coming out here and there through holes. It was a work of mercy of high ethical value. The skilful surgeon that he turned into was armed with a delicate pair of tweezers, and began with dexterous art to remove the maggots one by one, making them cease from their hideous task. He kept on dislodging them and placed them aside on another plate, presumably for some kind of execution. This is so poignant a picture that memory refuses to register anything further than the spectacle of the amateur Surgeon toiling philanthropically with his tweezers, and the patient pitiful frog, the tearful *bonne-bouche* of innumerable maggots, and also on the plate the pile of wriggling animalculae destined to a crushing doom under a broad boot-sole. And what of the frog?... one merely puts forward the surmise that some boot-sole, the disease being incurable, made for this reptile a surcease to torture and to life.

It is probable that Kipling is too modest in the part he assigned to himself in the trio. The ductile character he depicted is not corroborated by either Dunsterville or Beresford, the latter of whom makes him a power in the school in virtue of his erudition and precocity. And in Dunsterville's opinion:

'Beresford is quite right. Kipling's wide knowledge and natural wisdom were great assets to the Three in their various plots. R.K. refrained from stressing this point owing to a natural modesty. You can't say "I was mentally far and away above all the boys and all the masters." I think that was a fact. Crofts recognized it, and that was what led him to hold R.K. up to scorn and derision on every possible occasion. It was again a case of admiration coupled with dislike.'[18]

The first year was hard, but Kipling was well conditioned and not particularly unhappy. At this time he wrote to his aunt, Edith Macdonald:

There was a body found on the beach last week. Several ships have gone to pieces on Morte Rock and they say there are nearly thirty-five men missing. That means a good deal to some bodies in Bideford and Appledore. Bideford Quay was covered with little knots of men talking over the news and the way the widows 'took it'. An old fellow in a jersey was terribly upset, I never saw anything so strange in my life. He was as grey in the face as the river and shaking like a leaf. I have got something swollen in my neck; they say it's a gland and I'm regularly blistered with iodine in consequence. It makes your neck look like a crocodile skin, and utterly ruins your temper.[19]

His bad eyesight made it difficult for Kipling to play games. From this Beresford automatically deduced that he had the intellectual's contempt for games and for those who played them, to which Kipling afterwards gave savage expression in the lines about the 'flannelled fools at the wickets, and the muddied oafs at the goals' that so perplexed many of his less discriminating admirers. It was rather regret at his physical incapacity and a loathing for compulsion that made him occasionally bitter about athletics. The astringent lines in 'The Islanders' sprang from his despair at the lethargy and frivolity of his countrymen in the face of national disaster, rather than from an instinctive contempt for athletics.

Dunsterville and Beresford agreed that Kipling's eyesight prevented him playing games at all. Kipling said with rather pathetic pride: 'I played footer (Rugby Union), but here again my sight hampered me. I was not even in the Second Fifteen.'[20] It is probable that he was excused compulsory games, taking part only when he wished. His role was more often that of a spectator pacing the touch line on those bleak winter days of north winds, staring with unseeing eyes at the scrum churning up the field, at the slimy ball slung from hand to hand, and the steam of the players ascending into the air as the daylight waned. He stood there, hunched in an overcoat, with a few shivering fellow sufferers, while the thud of the toe on the ball was answered by the moan of wind and winter sea and the crashing of the surf on the Pebble Ridge, until he was free to escape from the field while others ran to the mouldy-smelling locker-room and removed the caked mud from knee-cap and face under the tap.

In summer these grim duties were relaxed. Cricket was played in the sunshine on the living Devonshire grass, when he could loaf with

a book in the drone of high summer, with the smell of the mounds
of new-cut grass, the soporific noise of the mower, and a whiff of lin-
seed oil from the pavilion, interrupted only by an occasional and always
brief innings, punctuated by hilarity and cries of 'Giggs'. He and
'Stalky', clad in knickerbockers and jersey, took part in the paper-
chases that sometimes varied cricket in the summer, and, leaving the
field at the first opportunity, they would wait in a gorse bush while
the steaming procession panted on its ordained path. After a pleasant
solitary ramble they would rejoin the main body just before home. He
showed even less enthusiasm for the gymnasium, where his bad sight
would not have hampered him.

> The athletic inhibition [wrote Beresford] was almost as strong in the pre-
> sence of dumb-bells and Indian clubs as it was in the neighbourhood of the
> careering cricket ball. Gigger displayed an almost total abstinence from
> superfluous bodily exercises. Nor, in spite of the passion for describing the
> conversations and functions of crankshafts and tappet-valves, and the
> absorbing interest in the mechanics of how things worked, did he at West-
> ward Ho! take any interest in craftsmanship or show any aptitude with his
> hands. He would look in and smile, but decline to assist in efforts to plane
> a board. People no doubt figure him as one of those boys who had a pet
> lathe and made models, and carried machine-parts and spares in their pockets
> ... and imagine that he looked eagerly forward to his *British Mechanic* and
> *World of Science* each week or month. This would be an incorrect deduction;
> for it was not until after years that Gigger found an interest in machines
> and machinery. From what deep well in his being he pumped up all this affec-
> tion for pistons and connecting rods one knows not; how compound marine
> engines and railway bogies came to claim him for their own is a dark mystery.

But after these supercilious remarks, Beresford added with perception: 'But it must be that all was fish that came into his net, and if
these semi-animate monsters were to be material for the art of expression and depiction, then they must be made friends with and somehow
coaxed to take their place on the stage of letters.'[21]
    Kipling spent his happiest moments at Westward Ho! on the sea-
shore and the sands. The beach lay beneath the line of the Pebble
Ridge, smooth and unbroken by quicksands. Sometimes you would
find on it a stranded whale stinking to leeward, or the wreck of
an old schooner with blackened spars. He was taught to swim in the
long salt-water baths beside the shore, the Nassau, or Cory's Baths.
He learned in the accepted manner of the day, a belt of webbing under
his armpits, with 'Foxy', the gym-instructor, holding one end of the
supporting pole, and as Beresford sneeringly observed, 'our sweet

singer in his belt at the danger or fish end'. The brutalities of Dunsterville's initiation had now ceased, and there was little ducking at
the baths. Although Kipling was never a good swimmer he loved the
sea and was happier in it than in any other outdoor activity. He loved
the stinging impact of the cold sea water on a burning sweaty body,
passing, as Scott Fitzgerald described it, 'from the heat to the cold
with the *gourmandise* of a tingling curry eaten with chilled white wine'.

He loved the excitement of bathing in the open sea beyond the
Pebble Ridge where the Atlantic white horses plunged into Bideford
Bay. You went at once into deep water, into the great green combers
that beat upon the ridge. You went to meet them so that they burst
upon your head, when for an instant you glanced down arched per-
spectives of beryl before all broke in fizzy electric diamonds. Up on
the crest, and you saw Hartland Point, Baggy Point and Lundy Island,
that floating amethyst with its ever-changing colour and depth of tone,
and then a swoop down into the sunless trough to a sense of dark
solitude. Kipling loved the exhilaration of being the sport of the great
rollers, carried on the crest of their green ridges while the gulls
screamed above, as he declaimed to the rhythm of his side stroke:

> Who shall seek – who shall bring
> Who restore us the day
> When the dove dipped her wing
> And the oars won their way
> Where the labouring Sympleglades whiten
> The Straits of Propontis with spray?

By about 1880 the three boys had come together in Study No. 5,
which is described in *Stalky and Co.* They had been removed from
their first study, of which 'Stalky' was not a member, by a master,
and Kipling had found a new room on the same landing which had
been the padre's bedroom.

This little hole had a large piece bitten out of it, making it L-shaped
with a recess. It had one table, three kitchen chairs and some coconut
matting. They decorated it, stencilling Greek honeysuckle on dado
and chimney-piece, thus depriving the room of the usual grim signature of the athlete – those photographs of burly youths with bare
knees and a football, foils, boxing gloves and first eleven caps. They
made expeditions to an antique shop in Bideford, walking there
between the wild-rose and convolvulus-spangled hedges of the Devonshire lanes. The pieces in the shop were mostly mended or spoilt, and
they acquired them cheaply – a beaker of Famille Verte, antique

Worcester, Derby, Rockingham, Plymouth, Lowestoft and Wedg-
wood. All these treasures appeared in the study, further emphasizing
the distance between 'Stalky and Co.' and their less aesthetic fellows.

Cormell Price was satisfied by 1880 that Kipling would be a writer,
and prepared to help him. His freedom from compulsory games was
a priceless asset. His first published juvenilia had appeared in *The
Scribbler*, a home magazine organized by the younger members of the
Burne-Jones and William Morris families in 1878. Kipling, then thirteen, made several contributions, including poems, signed 'Nick-
son'.[22]

Now, with brilliant educational flair, Cormell Price took a decisive
step. In 1881 he appointed Kipling to the editorship of the school
paper, *The United Services College Chronicle*, and

gave Beetle the run of his brown-bound, tobacco-scented library; prohibiting
nothing, recommending nothing. There Beetle found a fat arm-chair, a silver
ink-stand and unlimited pens and paper. There were scores and scores of
ancient dramatists; there was Hakluyt and his voyages; French translations
of Muscovite authors called Pushkin and Lermontoff; little tales of a heady
and bewildering nature, interspersed with unusual songs ... There was
Borrow's *Lavengro*; and an odd theme, purporting to be a translation of
something called a 'Rubaiyat', which the Head said was a poem not yet come
to its own; there were hundreds of volumes of verse.... Then the Head, drift-
ing in under pretence of playing censor to the paper, would read here a verse
and here another of these poets, opening up avenues. And, slow-breathing,
with half-shut eyes above his cigar, would he speak of great men living, and
journals, long dead, founded in their riotous youth; of years when all the
planets were little new-lit stars trying to find their places in the uncaring void,
and he, the Head, knew them as young men know one another.[23]

Price even grounded Rudyard in Russian, and insisted on précis writing, that severe craftsman's discipline of the compression of dry-as-
dust material, omitting no essential fact.

The whole was sweetened with reminiscences of the men of Crom's youth,
and throughout the low soft drawl and the smoke of his perpetual Vevey
he shed light on the handling of words. Many of us loved the Head for what
he had done for us, but I owed him more than all of them put together, and
I think I loved him even more than they did.[24]

Kipling was afterwards to pay his debts by looking after Price's son
with that kindness and generosity to youth which was one of his finest
qualities.

Kipling was writing hard after his second year, and the 'dear ladies' of Kensington High Street were his audience, a more sympathetic one perhaps than the disturbing 'Stalky' and the saturnine 'M'Turk', and it was to them that the first fruits were uncovered, prose on foolscap, verse on cream-laid notepaper. He wrote offensive limericks about his friends and compiled an 'Inferno' in an American-cloth bound notebook with appropriate tortures for the masters. He read *Hiawatha*, *Atalanta in Calydon*, and the poems of Elizabeth Barrett Browning and wrote an essay on 'a day in the holidays' so vile that one of the masters publicly informed him that he would die 'a scurrilous journalist'.

But Kipling already had a wide background of reading, which had first solaced his days in the 'House of Desolation' and was continued at Westward Ho! This reading had never been properly directed and had followed no preconceived course, but was, for his age, of remarkably wide range. Besides Tennyson, Browning and Swinburne, he had read the robust novels of Smollett and Fielding, and had been an early captive of Thackeray, Dickens, Bunyan and Defoe. In this impressionable phase of his development the influence of Poe is almost as frequently discernible in his early verse as that of Browning.

But there were many other shrines at which to bow – Longfellow, whom he rated far higher than did most critics of the day, Whitman's *Leaves of Grass*, the poems of Emerson and the earthy genius of Mark Twain. Some understanding of their greed for knowledge can be gained by the fact that the three boys read and discussed at length such forbidding works as Carlyle's *Sartor Resartus* and Ruskin's *Fors Clavigera* in the privacy of their hut in the furze bushes. And Rudyard was so ardent a disciple of Bret Harte that when his own book of verse *Departmental Ditties* was published a few years later in India, it was with the work of that poet that his own verse was most frequently compared.

His importance in the school increased with his appointment as editor of the *Chronicle*, which he conducted for his last two years at Westward Ho! His first contribution to the magazine was the unfinished and uncollected tale *Ibbetson Dun*. He acted in Sheridan's *The Rivals*, and it was observed in the *Chronicle* that Kipling's 'Sir Anthony' was a capital performance, somewhat marred by an unfortunate catarrh and a voice too slender.[25]

Like all schoolboys, Kipling and his friends enjoyed discussing women. Physically as well as mentally developed to an unusual degree, swarthy and hirsute, he was already more a man than a boy. At sixteen he was, as he had told Mrs Pinder, in all other respects a man of

twenty-six. The reference to the fish girls of Appledore in the letter
to Crofts, together with another letter of a similar nature to Dunsterville, suggests that Kipling had gone a good deal further than most
schoolboys in his experiments with women. But such experiences must
have been perilous and rare. The boys' opportunities in this direction
were mainly confined to digging up pretexts for ringing the bell of
the headmaster's front door, which would be opened by a beautiful
girl with a perfect figure emphasized by tight lacing. Employed by
Price, and being, they thought, *chic* as a Parisienne, she was given
the hybrid name of 'La Pricienne'. Kipling, when women were discussed, took refuge in a knowing secret smile, allowing the impression
to develop that he had had a wide experience which it would be ungentlemanly to explore. His opinions on this absorbing topic were
eagerly sought and widely circulated.

But apart from the fish girls of Appledore, he could only speak from
a single experience. Rudyard first met Florence Garrard when he was
fourteen, and she two years older. Florence, who was attending an
art school, had gone to 'Lorne Lodge' as a paying guest after Rudyard's departure for Westward Ho! and while Trix was still an inmate
of that sad dwelling. He had visited Southsea in the holidays to take
his sister out, and at once fallen in love with Florence, who was
later to appear as 'Maisie' in *The Light that Failed*. Her influence upon
him was still strong when he left for India, and it is probable that
he remained in love with her in a vague and irritating way until he
was twenty-four, his mind distracted by a thousand new excitements,
and his emotions never painfully engaged.

Her background had certain romantic drawbacks, and she would
complain to him that she came from a hopeless family, that both her
father and mother had had delirium tremens, and that her sister
suffered from curvature of the spine, incipient sex mania and a hungry
gushing manner. There was also, she told Rudyard, a rowdy handsome brother Jack, who was fond of pinching young girls and asking
them to sit on his knee. Kipling's affection for her lasted from 1879
till 1891, revived, when he returned from India and was living in rooms
at Villiers Street, Strand, by a chance encounter in a London fog,
described in *The Light that Failed*, when the old passion gripped him
again at once and the same cold indifference ruled her. It may be noted
that he gave the name Florence to the blind woman in *They* and to
the beautiful drug addict of *In the Same Boat*. Trix's vivid memory
brings this shadowy figure into clearer focus:

'Flo was very slender with a long plait of brown hair, as thick as your arm, and the same thickness all the way down, swinging below her knees. Her head was too small for her body, her hair too heavy for her head, hair like Rapunzel; her eyes too big for her face, such eyes, of the true grey with no hint of blue or hazel, and the thickest straightest black lashes I have ever seen. An ivory pallor that never flushed or changed but always looked healthy. The mouth in repose was a straight line, and the small features as delicate as a cameo. She gave most of her dress allowance to her sister, who always looked like a rag-bag, and fluttered out of doors like a worrycrow, or bird-scarer, while she wore old Holland dresses or the simplest blue serge.'[26]

A tall well-mannered goat called Becquot followed Flo like a dog, and endeared itself to Rudyard by butting 'Aunt Rosa'. Kipling was reticent as always about this unsatisfactory early affair, and we know little of the details of his long pursuit, or how deeply his feelings were engaged. He who was so reserved that he shrank from the description of the passion of others in his written work – who excused himself on the grounds that he disapproved of 'wenching in public' – was unlikely to leave signposts for posterity to his own emotional life. We can only say that although the memory of this dreary *allumeuse* haunted him for ten years, Kipling, throughout his life, shrank from emotional intimacy with women, and we shall see no other passionate liaison formed amid all the golden opportunities of India. His mother liked to believe that this unrewarded devotion kept him free from lesser loves. Flo never married, and when she died in 1902 Rudyard told Trix of her death:

'Do you remember Flo?'

'Of course, I shall never forget her.'

'Well, she died three months ago: neglected lungs I think, she never took the least care of herself'; and that was the end of 'Maisie'.[27]

In 1881, a year before Kipling left Westward Ho!, his parents collected the poems which he had enclosed in his letters home and had them printed in India in a volume called *Schoolboy Lyrics*. It must have seemed to many a dangerous experiment by fond and foolish parents. Edward Shanks cites this incident as an example of Lockwood Kipling's prescience and recognition of his son's stability, and of the extraordinary discretion of the boy in keeping all knowledge of the publication from his friends at Westward Ho! as described by Beresford.[28] This tribute is doubly mistaken. It was Mrs Kipling, and not Lockwood, who wanted her son's verses preserved in a permanent form, those juvenilia secretly entered in his Russian-leather, gilt-edged, cream-laid MS books. Lockwood was against it. The boy was clever and precocious, but it would be a disaster if he got a swelled head. As for Kipling's reticence at Westward Ho!, he knew nothing of the matter at all until he arrived in Lahore and saw one of the little books, when he flew into a rage and sulked for two days.[29]

It is necessary to make some reference to this early work, although none of the verses have been reprinted in the standard collections of Kipling's poetry. The poems are derivative, and the influence of the authors he had read can be clearly traced in them. That of Browning is evident in the first, 'An Echo':

> Let the fruit ripen one by one
>   On the sunny wall;
> Who is it suffers. What harm is done?
>   None at all.
>
> An Eve in the garden am I;
>   Behold this one
>   In the Sun
> Falls with a touch, and I let it be,
>   My first one.
>
> One fresh from the bough; I break it,
>   The red juice flies
>   Into my eyes.
> Shall I swallow, leave, or take it,
>   Or despise?
>
> Sweet to my taste was that second
>   And I hold it meet
>   That I did eat.
> But ah me! Are the bruised ones reckoned
>   At my feet?

A typical poem, on the average level for a groping adolescent, it is followed by a 'Schoolboy Lyric':

> Our heads were rough and our hands were black
>   With the ink-stain's midnight hue,
> We scouted all, both great and small –
>   We were a dusky crew;
> And each boy's hand was against us raised,
>   'Gainst me and the other Two.

> We chased the hare from her secret lair,
>   We roamed the woodlands through;
> In parks and grounds far out of bounds
>   Wandered our dusky crew;
> And the keepers swore to see us pass –
>   Me and the other Two.

Immature lines, perhaps, but they are contemporary evidence that Kipling did, during his schooldays, think of himself and his friends as the adventurous outlaws whom he afterwards depicted in *Stalky and Co.*

The third poem of interest, 'Ave Imperatrix', inspired by the attempt of a lunatic to assassinate Queen Victoria, conveys for the first time a strong impression of the later Kipling, but it is strange that he should have written it at this moment, his mind still untouched by any yearning for Imperial greatness.

> Such greeting as should come from those
>   Whose fathers faced the Sepoy hordes,
> Or served you in the Russian snows,
>   And, dying, left their sons their swords.
>
> And some of us have fought for you
>   Already in the Afghan pass –
> Or where the scarce-seen smoke-puffs flew
>   From Boer marksmen in the grass.
>
> Once more we greet you, though unseen
>   Our greeting be, and coming slow,
> Trust us if need arise, O Queen,
>   We shall not tarry with the blow.

There is another instance, far more remarkable, of Kipling's extraordinary maturity. In March 1882 Trix wrote to Rudyard:

> 226 Warwick Gardens,
> March 18, 1882.

I showed your new poem – 'A Discovery' – to Mrs Winnard and Miss Georgie, and thereby hangs a tale funnier than any of Oscar's. I thought it was simple to the verge of childishness – obvious is the word I mean – but the dear ladies summoned me to a conference! Mrs Winnard said – 'The verses are musical but –'

'It's a sonnet', I said foolishly – 'Yes dear, we know that, but what does it mean? Do you know?' I said I thought I did – it was fairly clear – and looked

at Miss Georgie – She said in in her gentle voice that they understood that
a beloved cage-bird had flown away and been found dead, but the emotion
expressed was disproportionate – exaggerated.

'But it is not a bird – it's a kind of allegory – it means dead love – Cupid
you know.'

'Did your brother explain that to you?'

'No, he only said it was a new poem, and he wanted to know if you liked
it ...'

Then Mrs Winnard said in her 'more in sorrow than in anger' voice –
'Really Trixie I hoped we had eradicated your unfortunate tendency to think
yourself wiser than your elders, but I fear we have only repressed it. Do you
seriously think a little girl of your age can understand somewhat abstruse
verse better than two educated and mature ladies?'

'Oh no – of course not. Only I know Ruddy so well, and the way he thinks
and writes, that I feel I can understand him better than anyone.'

'Well I can hardly agree with you. But Georgie shall write to him at once.'

Miss Georgie did so, and Trix's opinion was vindicated, and the
note that Kipling scribbled on the sonnet more than a year later shows
how he felt about the misinterpretation of this remarkable poem by
a boy of sixteen, with a background of the 'House of Desolation' and
a minor public school:

DISCOVERY

We found him in the woodlands, she and I.
Dead was our teacher of the silver tongue,
    Dead, whom we thought so strong he could not die,
Dead with no sorrow loosed, with bow unstrung.
    And round the great grey blade that all men dread
There crept the waxen white convolvulus,
    And the keen edge that once fell hard on us,
Was blunt and notched, and rusted yellow red,
    And he our master, the unconquered one,
Lay in the nettles of the forest place
    With dreadful open eyes, and changeless face
Turned upward staring at the noonday sun.
Then we two bent above our old dead King:
    And set the dry baked earth above the thing.

Westward Ho!

This was later endorsed by Kipling: 'Mrs Winnard said that the King
was a dead Canary, for which mistake (a genuine one) I find it hard
to forgive her.'

By July 1882 Kipling was in his last term at Westward Ho! He was now committed to writing. For a while, a year earlier, he had played with the idea of becoming a doctor, but after a little time given to the Latin, which he studied in Caesar's *Commentaries*, he abandoned it, although still haunting the precincts of St Mary's Hospital at Paddington, where he picked up much half-knowledge of medicine.

Then came a day when Cormell Price told him that a fortnight after the end of the summer holidays of '82 he was to go to India to work on a newspaper at Lahore 'for one hundred silver rupees a month'. This was an underestimate, for he was to receive 150 rupees per month.

Some time before, Lockwood Kipling had written to a friend saying that he intended to bring Rudyard out to India and find him work on a newspaper. He could not afford to send his son to Oxford, and he felt that the boy wanted the sort of occupation that would test his energy and ability. He believed that Rudyard would appreciate this decision. But Rudyard had at this moment no conception of what a priceless opportunity was about to be disclosed to him. Nor did he realize that in the teeming sub-continent he would discover something new and strange, a sudden and rich commotion in the blood, and an inspiration he could not have found anywhere else in the world. He was far from happy at the news. 'Stalky' and 'M'Turk' were also going to India, but Dunsterville was going as a soldier, and Beresford as a civil engineer. India would offer them both wide opportunities; but Rudyard already saw himself as a writer, and believed that his proper place was London, and not as a cub reporter in Lahore.

He spent the last few hot August days before sailing with Aunt Georgie in the cottage that the Burne-Joneses had bought in the enchanting little fishing village of Rottingdean, the village from which he was to be driven many years later by the persecution of tourists. 'There I looked across the village green and the horse-pond at a house called "The Elms" behind a flint wall, and at a church opposite; and – had I known it – at "the bodies of those to be in the House of Death and of Birth".'[30]

The figure of Kipling at seventeen now begins to emerge. He had had a cruel experience in childhood and his unhappiness was accentuated by a failure to understand why it had happened. He never forgot it, and 'spoke about it all with horror' to his wife years afterwards. But its immediate effect upon him, although powerful, was evanescent, and the recovery astonishingly quick, as the evidence of all who knew him at the time conclusively proves. He went to a minor public school at which he had a rough and hard time, but he had a constant refuge

in writing and reading in the 'tobacco-scented library' of Cormell
Price. He was precocious and physically mature, and was saved by
his eyesight from long periods of compulsory games.

His interests were entirely literary, and what time was left from them
he spent in the swaying fortunes of the constant battles against the
masters. He was no prig; smoked heavily at sixteen, cribbed in examinations, possibly had sexual relations with local girls, and often
used coarse language. He was not then or afterwards greatly moved
by the beauties of nature, seeing in them, as in everything else that
attracted his penetrating eye, a subject for writing.

His interest in craftsmanship had not yet awakened; he was not
a boy of action, and he took no interest in militarism or imperialism.
With no experience yet of the Army, he was not fired by subaltern-
worship, or the endearing 'cards' of the ranks, and the Bobby Wickes,
Brushwood boys, Infants, Cherubs and Mulvaneys all lay in the
future. 'It always amused us,' wrote an early friend, 'that he should
have become so fervidly the prophet of Action and the laureate of
the Deed; for as a boy – and I never knew him after – he was a book-
worm, entirely absorbed in the life of books, unathletic, unsociable,
and sad to say – decidedly fat.'[31]

'He did not enthuse,' said Beresford, 'to any vision of national or
racial greatness. War was no subject in those days for him to celebrate.
His development in the direction in which he did expand was utterly
unforeseen by all. In those days it was the individual that interested
him, his struggles and triumphs, his failure, his fate, his doom.'[32]

Kipling's mind had already taken this turn when he wrote *Stalky
and Co.*, and it was the mind of young 'Kuppelleen Sahib', with his
civilian's passion for the Army already strong within him, who then
wrote of his schooldays, the facts distorted in retrospect, depicting
the horde of bronzed Old Boys thronging down to the 'Coll.' for Old
Boys' match, addressing the mild libertarian Price as 'Head Sahib',
and reciting with clipped modesty stories of camp and bivouac to a
gaping audience of future soldiers of the Empire in the Dormitory.
The Kipling who was now setting out for India cared as yet for none
of these things; for the moment it was all words, 'gaudy words'.

CHAPTER V
THE YOUNG JOURNALIST

ON 18 October 1882, sixteen years and nine months old and looking twenty-two, wearing side-whiskers which were at once prudently removed at the earnest entreaty of his mother, Rudyard Kipling found himself again at Bombay. He seemed aware of a smell he knew at once, a smell evocative of memories and full of a strange excitement, a mixture of spice and woodsmoke, of jasmine, dust, and cow-dung smoke, the smell of Bombay; and the past came back, and he began to speak in the vernacular sentences whose meaning he did not understand, as other Indian-born boys have done before.

Then after four days by rail he came to Lahore, where

my English years fell away, nor ever, I think, came back in full strength. That was a joyous home-coming. For consider! – I had returned to a father and mother of whom I had seen but little since my sixth year. I might have found my mother 'the sort of woman I don't care for', as in one terrible case that I know; and my father intolerable. But the mother proved more delightful than all my imaginings or memories. My father was not only a mine of knowledge and help, but a humorous, tolerant and expert fellow craftsman. . . . I do not remember the smallest friction in any detail of our lives.[1]

The Museum – 'the Wonder House', as the Indians called it – stood near the Mall, a broad avenue leading from the European quarter to the ancient native city of Lahore girt by a wall, where the mystery of the Indian night first took possession of Rudyard Kipling. The excitement of this walled Mohammedan city after dark got into his blood – a place thrilling and sinister, like some illustration by Edmund Dulac from the *Arabian Nights*, where the packed inhabitants from every part of Asia had their mysterious being under the shadow of the Mosque of Wazir Khan, and the moonlight fell upon the enchanted Shalimar Gardens.

Beyond the wall was the Mian Mir military cantonment, where there was permanently stationed a British infantry battalion and a

battery of artillery. Outside the city were the bungalows in cool
gardens, schools, shops and offices, and the Punjab Club, of which
Rudyard was soon an honorary, and frequently irritating, member.
Nearby, behind a row of acacia trees, housed in two wooden sheds
was the printing office of the *Civil and Military Gazette* where, in
November, he was to begin his labours under the grandiloquent title
of Assistant Editor.

This provincial newspaper, on which Kipling was broken in like
an obstreperous colt, was founded by James Walker and by a leading
member of the Lahore Bar, William Rattigan. The *Civil and Military*
had thrived because it was underpinned by the printing house which
held the contract for the provincial administration. It was widely, if
unfairly, supposed, as Rudyard was soon to discover to his cost, that
as a consequence the editorial policy showed a servile deference to
that of the Punjab Government. Rattigan and Walker had also
acquired an interest in a larger and more important newspaper, the
Pioneer, which had been founded by George Allen for the down-
country at Allahabad, and which soon won a reputation for fearless
reporting, for remarkable sources of information, and for covering
the news on a national rather than a parochial basis.

Kipling's employment on the *Civil and Military Gazette* had been
arranged by Lockwood Kipling. Both Walker and Allen were old
friends of Lockwood, but Rudyard's appointment was probably
arranged in Lahore with Rattigan, one of the principal shareholders
and a director of the company, as the Chairman, Allen, was then in
England. It was felt that as Rudyard was disqualified for any of the
public services by his defective eyesight, and appeared to have a bent
for writing, he should enter journalism.

He lived in a cool white house with high, white-walled rooms and
wide verandas, and after a year a corner in the hall was partitioned
off for him to write in, on the door of which he inscribed in elaborate
letters with a breezy and unfortunate humour which was now developing: 'Respect the apartments of the great.' His parents had chosen
a brick-built bungalow in a compound of its own, apart from its
neighbours, because the Kiplings believed that diseases were carried
by insects, and that bushes round a house provided them with a fertile
breeding ground. Their friends called the bungalow 'Bikanir House'
because its dusty compound reminded them of the Great Indian
Desert.

Rudyard slept in a plain bedroom with white walls, matting on the
floor, book-shelves and polo sticks, and a polo ball on the mantelpiece,

in a narrow austere bed just large enough to accommodate himself and the adored Vixen, a white fox-terrier, who always slept with her head on the pillow. His equipment was in strange contrast to Westward Ho! He had his own servant, his own horse, a bay pony called Joe, his cart and groom, his own office hours, and his own office box.

He rode after tea, sending his horse home from Montgomery Hall. This was a *rendez-vous* where the small English community of Lahore met three times a week to gossip and read the papers, to play tennis and dance before dinner. He would drive home in the family coach, a big barouche and pair. Until he was in his twenty-fourth year he no more thought of dressing himself than shutting an inner door and, what to some may appear a decadent habit, he was shaved by his Indian bearer, the son of his father's servant, while he was asleep. In this house the Kiplings enjoyed a singularly happy family life, and while Rudyard's labours in the office, particularly in the hot weather, were prodigious, he found a sure refuge at home from the gruelling routine and strain of his work.

This work was so severe that it became at times a physical endurance test which no one without Kipling's bounce and recuperative powers could have survived. This untrained boy of seventeen represented half the editorial staff of the single Punjab daily, and as he grimly remarked, 'a daily paper comes out daily, even though fifty per cent of the staff have fever'. His chief, Stephen Wheeler, whom Kipling at first loathed but afterwards came to respect, although he always thought him a dull dog, broke him in without mercy. He never worked less than ten hours, and sometimes sixteen, a day, and as the *Civil and Military Gazette* went to press at midnight he did not see the midday sun except on Sunday.

Yet such was his vitality and absorbed interest in this new, fascinating world that he usually returned from his office in high spirits, unless Wheeler, who was known in the Kipling family as the 'Amber Toad', had been particularly disagreeable. On these occasions Rudyard was pale and angry, but never remained long in this mood. These passing moments of depression were due to the fact that he was working under a man who had little appreciation of his talent and who kept him employed on work for the most part dull and uncongenial.

It was his duty to prepare for press the telegrams of the day; to provide all the extracts and paragraphs; to make headed articles of official reports; write editorial notes; and be responsible for sports, outstation and local intelligence. He also read all the proofs except the editorial matter. And in addition there was the eternal sub-editing, the weary cutting of amateur contributions ranging, he tells us, from discourses on abstruse questions of Revenue and Assessment by a great civilian with foul handwriting, to literary articles about Milton. 'Here Crom Price's training in précis work helped me to get swiftly at what meat there might be in the disorderly messes.' It is melancholy to look through the back files of the *Civil and Military Gazette* and to see how at first Kipling's inventive wit only flashed out in introductory lines to summaries of Government reports and the side headings of scissors-and-paste paragraphs. Charged with these menial duties his exuberance was astonishing. He had bad moments, which he conquered with splendid courage, as in 1883 when his father went on leave to the Hills:

I assure you [he wrote to his aunt, Edith Macdonald] that for one weary week my fear in the day time was that I was going to die, and at night my only fear was that I was going to live till morning. I wasn't seedy, but I was washed out and boiled down to the lowest safe working point. The Pater had gone to Dalhousie for a week and as soon as I was alone in the big dark house my eyes began their old tricks again and I was so utterly unstrung (you'd be as bad if you sweated twenty-four hours a day for three weeks on end), I could only avoid the shadows by working every minute that I see, and I can say, with my hand on my heart – I mean my head – that I cured myself by doing sixteen hours grind a day at the office, at original matter and much précis writing – videlicet condensing a Bill which has been introduced into the legislative council, from ten columns to two and writing the grimmest sort of stuff and nonsense about its possible scope, or probable inefficiency. It cured the blue devils but it about used me up.

These black periods came in the hot weather when all who could had escaped to the hill breezes, when the newspaper office became a baking inferno. He well remembered those nights of torment, and how vividly he was to describe them:

It was pitchy black night, as stifling as a June night can be, and the loo, the red-hot wind from the westward, was booming among the tinder-dry trees and pretending that the rain was on its heels. Now and again a spot of almost boiling water would fall on the dust with the flop of a frog, but all our weary world knew that was only pretence. It was a shade cooler in the press-room than the office, so I sat there, while the type ticked and clicked, and the night jars hooted at the windows, and the all-but-naked compositors wiped the sweat from their foreheads, and called for water. The thing that was keeping us back, whatever it was, would not come off, though the loo dropped, and the last type was set, and the whole round earth stood still in the choking heat with its finger on its lips, to wait the event, and as the machines spun their fly-wheels two or three times to see that all was in order before I said the word that would set them off, I could have shrieked aloud.

An Indian press room was indeed a strange sight on a hot weather night, lit by a flickering hurricane lamp. Half-naked men turned the big presses in the uncertain light, lolling against the black walls, awaiting their call, and from the far end came the death-watch tick-tick of the type being set up by the compositors. The native foreman would nod at his desk while Kipling sat down at a dirty table to wait for the last telegrams and take the last proofs. There was a mixed smell of printers' ink, baled paper, deodar wood and sweating coolie, and the muskrats scuttered about the wainscot.

His routine was varied, as soon as Wheeler could trust him, by the reporting of local race meetings and the opening of bridges, when he spent the night with the engineers. He reported village festivals and communal riots under the shadow of the Mosque of Wazir Khan, where the waiting troops lay patiently in timber-yards and alleys until the time came to intervene, and the 'growling, flaring, creed-drunk city would be brought to hand without effusion of blood'. He reported the visit of the Viceroy to the neighbouring princes, murder and divorce trials, and, a task that made him shudder, an inquiry into the percentage of lepers supplying beef and mutton to the European community of Lahore. He reported reviews of armies expected to move against Russia at any moment, and receptions of an Afghan chieftain. He was soon to be shot at in the Khyber Pass.

All these details of this new, fascinating world he sent home in letters to his Aunt Edith. In June 1883 he wrote:

I was counting on a holiday to-day but the Sind Punjab and Delhi railway needs must derail a train and slay thirteen coolies and there was no reporter handy *of course* when the preliminary inquiry opened. It's not the least use being above any sort of work in this land so I had to ride over to the court, and report as best I might. The heat was terrific, the court crowded with natives; and I don't expect you to believe me when I tell you that the thermometer marked 128 on the wall behind me.

I was there for four hours, took down four columns of matter – cross-examinations, and technical details for the most part, recopied it from short-hand to long, and am waiting now for the proofs to turn up in time for to-night's paper. A two mile ride in the sun has skinned my nose, and the iron of my giglamps has burned a blue horseshoe over the bridge of it, but there are times when life is really worth living and those half a dozen hours of high pressure work come in as a tonic to the regular office routine. My chief has complimented me unreservedly – a rare thing for him as he believes in 'sitting on' the young idea when possible.

And Kipling added in facetious verse:

Dear Aunty, your parboiled nephew reclines with his feet on a chair,
Watching the punkah swing through the red-hot fly-full air;
For, when work is nearly at an end and the telephone ceases to ring
Then the soul of the poet awakes and the Stunt begins to sing,

Sings as Sterne's Starling wailed, watching the blazing sun
'I can't get out' – at least till after the sunset gun;
For the heavens are red-hot iron and the earth is burning brass,
And the river glares in the sun like a torrent of molten glass,

And the quivering heat haze rises, the pitiless sunlight glows
Till my cart reins blister my fingers as my spectacles blister my nose.
Heat, like a baker's oven that sweats one down to the bone,
Never such heat, and such health, has your parboiled nephew known.[2]

The first impression which Kipling made on the English community of Lahore was not always favourable. The education he had received at Westward Ho! did not seem to include good manners. He was untidy, rather uncouth in society, and had, at first, what a distinguished Anglo-Indian civilian described as a 'caddishly dirty tongue'. The official added that no one minded a robust expletive, but that Kipling's constant dirty language became boring, while his inability to play games added to his unpopularity in a community much given to polo, gymkhanas, archery and other Anglo-Saxon activities. He was also inclined to be bumptious, aggressive and casual.

Sir Henry MacMahon recalled a military exercise in the middle of which he found himself in Lahore, and retired to the Club. Here he soon reached the bar, which was the centre of social life in all Indian clubs. There, among a group of men, was a small figure with a heavy moustache in civilian clothes. Someone said: 'Kipling, I want you to meet MacMahon.' Kipling replied: 'Why should *I* want to meet MacMahon?' and turned away. This was said with such gratuitous insolence that MacMahon said angrily: 'Well, whether you like it or not you *have* met me, so come outside, and I will give you the biggest thrashing you ever had in your life.' This, he said, he fully intended to do, but a stand-up fight was averted by the other members.[3]

Kipling, from the moment of his arrival in India, was entranced by the native quarter of Lahore, and in his heart he probably despised many of the beefy conventional men who surrounded him, the army officers with their polo and gymkhanas and provincial flirtations, and the Government officials who were inclined to look down upon him as a mere journalist, and to shake their heads over his explorations in the back alleys and dim-lit temples of the bazaar. But his new life now held him completely in thrall:

I'm in love with the Country [he wrote to a friend] and would sooner write about her than anything else. Wherefore let us depart our several ways in amity. You to Fleet Street (where I shall come when I die if I'm good), and I to my own place, where I find heat and smells and oils and spices, and puffs of temple incense, and sweat and darkness, and dirt and lust and cruelty, and above all, things wonderful and fascinating innumerable.[4]

As his travels over India deepened his knowledge of her, he became obsessed by the harsh spell of the country of which he was later to write:

What do you think of a big, red, dead city built of red sand-stone with raw green aloes growing between the stones, lying out neglected on honey-coloured sands? There are forty dead Kings there ... each in a gorgeous tomb finer than all the others. You look at the palaces and streets and shops and tanks, and think that men must live there, till you find a grey squirrel rubbing its nose all alone in the market place, and a jewelled peacock struts out of a carved doorway and spreads its tail against a marble screen as fine pierced as point-lace.... I have been there and seen. Then evening comes, and the lights change till it's just as though you stood in the heart of a king-opal.

He relished the new strange scenes with sensual delight: 'The bamboos and the custard-apples, the poinsettias, and the mango-trees in the garden stood still while the warm water lashed through them and the frogs began to sing among the aloe hedges.'

There was much adverse comment in the English community over the young Kipling's immersion in the bazaar and in other aspects of native life, and many gloomy forecasts were made of the manifold dangers lurking therein for so young a man. For a time even the adoring Lockwood Kipling was seriously disturbed, but his anxiety was unnecessary. This boy of seventeen was patiently amassing a profound knowledge of Indian life and character. 'He acquired in the bazaar,' said one who well remembered Rudyard in India, 'an immense knowledge of Indian ways, language, and trade customs. He was extraordinarily accurate in his Indian details. What he could not get from personal exploration, he was able to get from his father.'[5]

Now again, as in childhood in the boarding house in the Brompton Road, the night got into his head in the mysterious city of Lahore. It was in the hot weather, when the midnight edition had gone to press, that he wandered in vain about the empty house in search of sleep, with swimming eyeballs, carrying his bed from room to room in quest of air; or lay naked on the roof in the stifling heat with the waterman pitching skinfuls of water on his body which brought on fever but prevented heat-stroke. When sleeplessness became insupportable he would wander until the flush of dawn round the liquor shops and opium dens and native dances, and down the side alleys where there were puppet shows, often challenged by the police, but secure in his father's name and the immunity of the journalist. 'One would come home just as the light broke, in some night-hawk of a hired carriage which stank of hookah fumes, jasmine flowers and sandalwood; and if the driver were moved to talk, he told one a good deal.'

Thus it was in no academic manner that he wrote of the sights and smells that sent his pulses hurrying with strange emotions on those breathless nights when the cicadas kept up their din with insensate zest, and the punkah whined in the dead air; when he passed through deserted Mohammedan burial grounds, where the skulls had worked to the surface, down long ranks of the native dead, and sometimes saw a sleeping leper rigid and silver in the moonlight. At moments he caught the twang of a stringed instrument behind a lattice and heard the guttering of a hookah on a flat roof, while the kites snored like old men on the domes and minarets before the Muezzins called the Faithful to prayer. It was on such nights that Kipling took his midnight prowls, and he loved it all, the stink, the oven-heat, the lust, the cruelty.

The pitiless moon shows it all, shows too the plains outside the city, and here and there a hand's breadth of the Revee without the walls; shows lastly a splash of glittering silver on a house-top almost directly below the Mosque Minar. Some poor soul has risen to pour a jar of water over his fevered body; and the tinkle of the water strikes faintly on the ear ... a small cloud passes over the face of the moon, and the city and its inhabitants – clear drawn in black and white before – fade into masses of black and deeper black. Still the unrestful noise continues, the sigh of a great city overwhelmed with heat, and of a people seeking in vain for rest. It is only the lower class women who sleep on the housetops. What must the torment be in the latticed zenanas where a few lamps are still twinkling? There are footfalls in the court below. It is the Muezzin – faithful minister, but he ought to have been here an hour ago to tell the Faithful that prayer is better than sleep – the sleep that will not come to the city.

All work and recreation in Kipling's day in India took place against the constant background of death; sudden death from cholera, typhoid, and other horrible oriental diseases against which the medicine of the day was pathetically impotent. Kipling attended ghostly dinners at which subalterns in charge of the infantry detachment at Fort Lahore 'amid marble-inlaid empty apartments of dead queens' casually added thirty grains of quinine to their sherry. 'The dead of all times were about us,' he said, '– in the vast forgotten Moslem cemeteries round the Station, where one's horse's hoof of a morning might break through to the corpse below; skulls and bones tumbled out of our mud garden walls, and were turned up among the flowers by the Rains; and at every point were tombs of the dead.'

Rudyard was left alone in the bungalow for months on end in the last part of the year 1883, when his father was absent on the business of the Museum and his mother in England. But a great stimulus was given to his life when Alice returned in the New Year bringing his sister Trix with her, now fifteen years old and full of astonishing cleverness and precocity.

In January 1884 Kipling wrote to his Aunt Edith to tell her that he had made his first public speech:

Yesterday the Punjab Club gave a big dinner to our retiring honorary Secretary, who is going to be married. There were about forty at table and I had to reply for the Press of India – it was my maiden speech so that fact must be my excuse for quoting it as the reporter showed it to me. As a matter of fact it wasn't anything half so polished as I was in the middle of a 'hoss-trade' with a friend when my name was called. Wheeler had sloped silently and left me to pull through as I could. This is what I am said to have said:

'Gentlemen' (I know that's all right) 'this is a flattering and, I confess, a most embarrassing honour. So far as a youngster of my position and inexperience can claim to represent the Press of India believe me I thank you most heartily for the toast you have just drunk.

'You know the proverbs about the "strength of the chain being its weakest link", and that "little boys should be seen and not heard". May I ask you to "take in the chain" and forgive the baldness of my maiden speech? It may sound a startlingly original [sic] sentence but I am "unaccustomed to public speaking"!'

This little bit of nonsense took very fairly and they all made a big row and beat upon the table with their fists. So I'm through my baptism of fire in the public oratory line.[6]

In February of the same year the first attempt to bribe him was

made and he described the episode to his aunt in a letter which throbs
with the excitement and zest of this strange new life:

Verily India is a strange land, and its people are still stranger. Yesterday
morning I got an invitation to come to an old Afghan's house somewhere
in the city. You must know that we have more than one of the Afghan Sirdars
who fought against us in the war, as prisoner in Lahore. They are under
no sort of surveillance but they have to stay here and keep quiet. When I
got the note – couched in flowery English and flowerier Persian I rode off
into the city wondering what on earth the old sinner could want with me....

In the end I was shown his house and I rode into the square courtyard
with the Sirdar's mounted follower at my heels. Then we went up stairs –
such *filthy* stairs – to Kizil Bash's room, a dirty place stuffed full of embroideries, gold cloth, old armour and inlaid tables. The old boy was sitting at
one end of the room, rose to meet me and made me sit down after enquiring
how I did. We conversed in Urdu to the following extraordinary effect:

KB: Your honour's health and prosperity, are they well assured?

I: By your favour, Khan, they are so.

KB: I have heard of the fame of your honour, so far North as Peshawar
– that you have the ear of the Lat-Sahib (our Lieutenant Governor) and
that he fears your *Khubber-Ke-Kargus* (newspaper) more than God or
the Sheitans. Therefore, (this with the air of a King) I have sent for you
Sahib.

Here I began to feel rather uneasy and answered:

'The Khan honours me too greatly. Who am I that I should know the
heart of the Lat-Sahib or that the Lat-Sahib should fear me? It is true, (here
I couldn't help advertising the *C.M.G.*) that my *Khubber-Ke-Kargus* is heard
from Karachi and Sind to Benares, and from Peshawar to Delhi – but it is
a little thing, O Khan. How should I help you?' Then the old boy began
in a low tone about the iniquity of his being a prisoner in Lahore....

'My wives and my women are at Cabul, but I am here. Write in your *Khubber-Ke-Kargus* Sahib that I will do anything they ask me, write that it is
cruel and unjust to keep me here. Write', and so he went on for about twenty
minutes like a madman, and finally wound up by throwing me a bundle of
currency notes and asked me to count them. I did so and found them Rs.
16,000 – that is to say about £1300. These I was told would be the price of
merely recommending him to be released, a thing I might have done in ten
lines on the front page any day, if I had only known about his case. Of course
it wasn't possible to do anything after an insult like that, but I daren't give
him a piece of my mind in his own house for fear of accidents – fatal ones
maybe, so I threw back the notes and told him, that the years had impaired
his eyesight and I wasn't a Bunnochi or a Baluchi (two races the most cove-
tous on earth) but an English Sahib.

Then he pulled up and thought for a few moments. Finally he blurted out
that we English were 'fools' and didn't know the value of money but that

'all Sahibs knew how to value women and horses'. Whereupon he sent a small boy into an inner chamber and, to my intense amusement, there came out a Kashmiri girl that Moore might have raved over. She was very handsome and beautifully dressed, but I didn't quite see how she was to be introduced into an English household like ours.

I rather lost my temper and abused the Khan pretty fiercely for this last piece of impudence and told him to go to a half-caste native newspaper walla for what he wanted (all the same I'm afraid I kissed the damsel when the Khan's broad back was turned). At the end of my harangue I felt that I couldn't make a dignified exit as I had intended, 'cos the door was shut and bolted. Then I pulled up and told the old gentleman to open the door. It was a funny scene to think over afterwards because, all the time I was talking to the Khan, he was shrugging his shoulders and waving his hands in protest, and I could hear the devil's own noise in the courtyard – sounds of horses and men.

Never having been in a position like this I naturally began to sweat big drops, and cursed the Khan female relatives in a manner which made the Kashmiri titter. It seemed that the man only wanted to get his horses out to show me and when that was done he went down to the yard. I followed – and saw about seven of the most beautiful beasts it has ever been my lot to look on. There were two bay Arabs, one Kathiawar mare, and four perfect little Hagar country breds. Then I'm afraid my resolution began to waver, 'specially when he said I might pick any three I liked – they were such beauties and had such perfect manners.

However, I explained very gravely that I wasn't going to help him a bit, and he ought to have known better than to 'blacken an Englishman's face' in the way he had done and if I had my own way I'd keep him in Lahore till he died. When I come to think of the way I slanged him I'm rather astonished he didn't stick one then and there. No one would have been any the wiser and there would have been one unbeliever the less.

However he kept his temper very fairly and told me to come upstairs again and have a smoke and some coffee. If I refused I knew he would think I was afraid of poison, and if I accepted I was afraid I should get some *dhatura* with the coffee.

However I accepted the offer and we went upstairs again and here began the cleverest part of the old man's policy. I saw when I came in that he meant no bodily harm, for the money was out on the table, from my couch in the window I could see the horses being marched to and fro in the yard and the Kashmiri was superintending the coffee and getting my pipe ready. The Khan took his seat out of sight of me and left me there to sip and smoke, and watch, if I chose the money, the horses or the girl.

This went on for nearly half an hour, and I was so thoroughly indignant with the old beast that I resolved to inflict myself upon him for a time till I sobered down. When I had smoked out one pipe, drunk my coffee and talked oriental platonics with the Kashmiri I rose up to go and my host didn't attempt to hinder me. He had lost about three cups of coffee, one smoke, and a couple of hours of his time (but that didn't count) and had heard some plain truths about his ancestry. Of course I couldn't do anything for him, – tho his case is a hard one I admit but I can mention the subject to Wheeler, and he can, if he likes, take notice of it, so that I shan't be concerned in the affair. When I mounted my old Waler (he did look such a scarecrow) I found that beneath the gullet plate of the saddle had been pushed a little bag of uncut sapphires and big greasy emeralds.

This was his last try I presume, and it might have seriously injured my brute's back if I hadn't removed it. I took it out and sent it through one of the windows of the upper storey where it will be a good find for somebody. Then I rode out of the city and came to our peaceful civil station just as the people were pouring out of Church – it seems so queer an adventure that I went and set it down and am sending you the story thereof. I haven't told anyone here of the bribery business because, if I did, some unscrupulous beggar might tell the Khan that *he* would help him and so lay hold of the money, the lady or worse still the horses. Besides I may be able to help the old boy respectably and without any considerations.

Wasn't it a rummy adventure for a Sunday morning?

CHAPTER VI

MILITARY INCLINATION

IT was at this period, if we are to believe Kipling's memories as an old man, that he conceived his lifelong devotion to the Army, and his intense veneration of the man of action to the detriment of the thinker and intellectual. This interest does not seem to have been strong at the beginning of Kipling's years in India, but, once aroused, it stayed with him for life. He wrote, in old age, of the regiments he visited in youth in a curiously proprietary manner, almost as though he were a soldier himself, or at least felt a strong tinge of envy for the military caste.

He had grown to know the soldiers of those days in visits to Fort Lahore and the Mian Mir Cantonments. Long afterwards he wrote almost in the manner of a regular Lieutenant Colonel reminiscing fondly about the past:

My first and best beloved Battalion was the 2nd Fifth Fusiliers, with whom I dined in awed silence a few weeks after I came out. When they left I took up with their successors, the 30th East Lancashire, another North-Country regiment, and, last, with the 31st East Surrey – a London-recruited confederacy of skilful dog-stealers, some of them my good and loyal friends....

I am, by the way, one of the few civilians who have turned out a Quarter-Guard of Her Majesty's troops. It was on a chill winter morn, about 2 a.m. at the Fort, and though I suppose I had been given the countersign on my departure from the Mess, I forgot it ere I reached the main Guard, and when challenged announced myself as 'Visiting Rounds'. When the men had clattered out I asked the Sergeant if he had ever seen a finer collection of scoundrels. That cost me beer by the gallon, but it was worth it.[1]

It is clear that Kipling derived a vicarious delight from the atmosphere of a military ante-room, from the orderlies, the regimental trophies, and the army 'shop', and that he deeply venerated the ritual of the Mess, 'which', as he wrote, 'no one but an officer can understand' – silver on the table, and the big men in Mess kit heaving themselves to their feet to drink the loyal toast. He was to describe it all in tender detail in a brilliant story, *The Man Who Was*. And we are told by his American friend Mrs Hill, whom we are soon to meet, that 'his great sorrow was that he could not enter the Army, owing to his poor eyesight, and it was particularly hard for him to associate constantly with those who were preparing for the service'.

How different is this picture from the Kipling of Westward Ho!, and we can only assume that in these early Indian days this strong preference for the man of action began suddenly to ripen, and his distrust of politicians, later almost obsessive, first struck roots. Small of stature, and physically disqualified as he was for active service, there is sometimes an element of pathos in this avid military enthusiasm, but his splendid sympathy with the common soldiers should always be remembered, and the improvements that he brought about in their miserable lives.

'I came to realize,' he said, 'the bare horrors of the private's life, and the unnecessary torments he endured on account of the Christian doctrine which lays down that "the wages of sin is death".' He was outraged by the fact that it was considered impious that the disease-riddled prostitutes in the bazaar should be medically inspected, or that the soldiers should be given elementary instruction in prophylactic precaution, a moral delicacy that cost the Army in India nine thousand men a year lying stricken in the Lock Hospitals, to which Kipling paid lugubrious visits on behalf of his paper. These depressing tours of inspection, he said, 'made me desire, as earnestly as I do today, that I might have six hundred priests – Bishops of the Establishment for choice – to handle for six months precisely as the soldiers of my youth were handled'.

He left posterity a magnificent, and in fact the only record of the old Volunteer Army,

the sweltering barracks ... the red-coats, the pipe-clayed belts and the pill-box hats, the beer, the fights, the floggings, hangings and crucifixions, the bugle calls, the smell of oats and horse piss, the bellowing sergeants with foot-long moustaches, the bloody skirmishes, invariably mishandled, the crowded troop-ships, the cholera-stricken camps, the 'native' concubines, the ultimate death in the work-house. It is a crude vulgar picture, in which a patriotic music-hall turn seems to have got mixed up with one of Zola's gorier passages, but from it future generations will be able to gather some idea of what a long term volunteer army was like.[2]

Kipling's Army contacts also served journalistic purposes, and an old soldier of those days recalled:

My old Battalion, the 2/5 Fusiliers, were stationed in 1885 in Mian Mir, near Lahore. I was colour sergeant, acting Sgt. Major, when one evening in May I was asked by the orderly officer 2 Lt. Hill to introduce a friend of his, who was with him, to typical scenes of barrack room life and to afford him the opportunity of coming into contact with the men. Mr Kipling, then a man of 19, just out from school in England, explained that he had been commissioned to turn out a series of articles descriptive of army life gathered in from personal contacts and experience.

I knew that the only place to suit his purposes was the regimental canteen and there I conducted him. By chance I found a suitable knot of men in the shape of 8 or 10 'boozing chums' who belonged to the musketry fatigue party, headed by Cpl. MacNamara. I did my best to give them an idea of what Mr Kipling wanted, warning them not to give themselves away by mis-statements and so on, and I left them.[3]

Kipling repeated his visits during that hot-weather season. Years later, in 1921, he wrote to Fraser, the author of the above reminiscence, in the familiar fellow-soldier tone:

I've always looked on the 5th as my own regiment. I remember our meeting in the Sgts. mess. In 1885 on St George's Day of that year I had some trouble in getting a very bosky private (with roses in his helmet), who had tried to hold up my ticca gharri, past some of your Sergeants who seemed to have some sort of idea that he was not quite sober.

Kipling had other contacts with the Army. We have it on the authority of General McMunn that there lived at Solon near Simla in the eighties QMS Bancroft of the Bengal Horse Artillery, of the old army of John Company, and that from this garrulous old relic, whose reminiscences were privately printed at the time of the 1897 Jubilee, Kipling was to get much of his 'Mulvaney', and the whole story of 'Snarleyow', a troophorse in G. Troop, 2nd Bde, in which Bancroft was a gunner.

It is worth noting that Kipling had left the *Soldiers Three* stories far behind him by the Jubilee, so Bancroft's book could not have been much use to him, but Bancroft retired to live in Lahore, where Kipling probably met and listened to him, and it is true that extracts from Bancroft's book show a typical 'Mulvaney' accent and dialect. It is impossible to say whether Kipling drew his three soldiers, 'Mulvaney', 'Ortheris' and 'Learoyd', from living men. But with the continuous transfer of troops from one station to another, it would have been difficult, if not impossible, for Kipling to have had a sustained friend-ship with any three particular men.

Kipling's personal military record in India is in melancholy contrast to his own avid enthusiasm and the scenes of carnage that he was to describe with extraordinary pictorial intensity in *The Drums of the Fore and Aft*. The martial virtues, so loudly extolled, withered in his own person. He was, for a time, a private in 'B' Company of the 1st Punjab Volunteers, but no one ever saw him in the ranks. Having exhausted every device for getting him on parade, the Company Commander called upon Volunteer Kipling to make good the capitation grant which he had failed to earn. 'The amount claimed,' said the superior officer, 'was promptly remitted under cover of a letter frankly admitting the justice of the penalty and expressing regret for neglect of duty.'[4]

In April 1884 Kipling was able to write home that he had won his spurs as a descriptive special correspondent, and a message of congratulation came from the proprietors of his newspaper. He had been sent in March to the native state of Patiala to write as much as he could of the visit there of the Viceroy, Lord Ripon, and he found stirring copy in the fantastic jewels, the champagne, the treachery and intrigue, the swaying elephants and the fours-in-hand. Only two years separated this boy of nineteen from the bleak discomfort of Westward Ho! – from the bare corridors and locker-rooms smelling of carbolic soap. Now he found placed at his disposal an elephant, a four-in-hand, and as many horses as he could use daily, and lived like a prince, with sentries, guards of honour, and every consideration except the salute, from which he was debarred by his non-official position.

At the end of the visit he was presented with fruit and nuts, and a bribe of 1000 rupees at the bottom of the fruits in a conventional attempt to enlist his help in augmenting the number of guns in the Maharajah's Salute. Kipling stalked off in his shirtsleeves in the blazing sunshine to the Durbar and violently abused the Council of Regency, the Prime Minister and the Finance Minister for treating him like a servant, and not a friend. The *Civil and Military Gazette* was greatly feared in the state of Patiala, where the Maharajah was a minor, and after suitable apologies the greasy notes were returned to the Finance Minister. Other reporters present were less scrupulous and two of them cleared 2500 rupees apiece; – 'but', said Kipling contemptuously, 'they were half-castes, and, as I tenderly explained to one of them, it's like getting money from your father.'[5] He achieved a scoop on this visit, and described it with relish in a passage which suggests that when on professional business he was none too scrupulous about the rights of property:

I managed to cut down these gentry and get my letters into the papers before any other journal could get ahead of us, by a starlight ride of sixteen miles to the nearest railway station, and sixteen miles back. I left Patiala station at 9.20 one night (on a borrowed horse belonging to a native lancer), caught the half past ten train to Lahore and got my letter in. Then my horse shut up and I had to hunt about the platform of the station till I found a trooper of the irregular horse asleep with his beast picketed in the sand. I didn't wake the man but took his horse and tied my tired one to the lance and fled back to Patiala – covering the thirty-two miles in a trifle less than two and a half hours, getting my letter into the paper next day – to the disgust of the other men. [6]

He found India in the cold weather delightful, healthy and invigorating, but always in his mind was the thought of the hot weather lying ahead like some terrible enemy, when life became a struggle for survival, and the implacable sun an object of loathing. Late in April Kipling wrote to his Aunt Edith in a state of gloom at the prospect of the hot weather:

Wheeler and I have made a compact to work the paper at the lowest possible pressure throughout the hot weather, which is 'best for him and best for me'. Nearly everyone who can get leave has gone away and this little go of fever is a not too delicate hint to Mrs Kipling to take her daughter to Dalhousie as soon as may be.

I'm only anxious to get them well away for the next four months, as we shan't have a particularly healthy hot weather – measles and typhoid and small pox among the natives in April are pretty certain to grow unpleasant in July and August. As you are seven thousand miles away I don't mind telling you that there has been a case of sporadic cholera already, and, as this is the third year since we had the last epidemic, we are anticipating a festive season later on.

It is very funny to watch the progress of any disease. It begins like an engagement with dropping shots, falling no one knows where and gradually settling down into a steady roll – a death roll if you please.

In a few weeks he had taken up his bachelor existence with his father – 'a collarless, cuffless, bootless paradise of tobacco, unpunctuality, and sloth, when they both wandered aimlessly about the house in any garment that came handiest', and Lockwood propped up the *Illustrated London News* against his glass at dinner to eke out waning conversation.

In September 1884 Kipling had another of his black periods. Throughout the year cholera had been rife in the old city of Lahore, and had spread to the English settlement where there were eleven cases

out of the seventy members of the white community. So accustomed
did he become to this constant proximity to death, that he was able
to write casually to his aunt:

Our great consolation through it all is to hear the Mother at Dalhousie
talking of velvet and plush and wood-fires far away in the Hills. Thank good-
ness she and the child are out of it, which is well, for the Abominable has
come into the Station and it seems as though she would stay with us for
a month or two or three. I saw her, the other day, knock a man down. He
died in a trifle under two hours, and his friends told me that it was the 'Will
of God'. I was never so angry with anyone in my life before as I was with
those dusky mourners. Just think, a human life (not that it is of any importance in this densely crowded land), thrown away before one's very eyes
through rotten melons and bad arrack![7]

There were no professional nurses, and when the dreadful sickness
came, said Kipling, 'the men sat up with the men, and the women
with the women'. His father went on leave, and he was left alone in
the house. The Station was almost empty, and in spite of hectic efforts
to keep going he became very depressed. Then a night came when
he had a terrifying experience, about which he wrote to his aunt with
typical frivolity:

I haven't been quite well and look on creation as through a glass darkly.
Last night I was shot out of my little bed with spassims [sic] in my tummy
and all sorts of aches forbye. Threshing round in a pitch dark empty house
and calling for servants who won't hear, and hunting for medicines one can't
find, isn't the pleasantest thing in the world.
When I had dug up my man he lit a lamp and took a look at me and
straightway bolted out of the house. This made made me fancy that I must
have a touch of the 'sickness that destroyeth in the noonday', as distinguished
from the other articles and I poured myself out a pretty stiff dose of chloro-
dyne and sat down to await the march of events and pray for the morning.
I had hardly rolled onto the floor, however, before my man turned up for
the second time with a naked oil lamp, a little bottle and a queer looking
weapon in his hand. The fellow had brought me opium and a pipe all complete and then and there insisted upon my smoking as much as I could. Well,
I wasn't in a condition to argue, so he rolled the pills and I set to. Presently
I felt the cramps in my legs dying out and my tummy more settled, and a
minute or two later, it seemed to me that I fell through the floor.
When I woke up I found my man waiting at the bed side with a glass of
warm milk and a stupendous grin. I must have looked queer, for Macdonald,
my help from Allahabad, declares that I came into the office with every sign
of advanced intoxication. This however has worn off and left me almost well
– an evening ride will put me straight, I trust. My man is awfully pleased

with himself and walks round me as though I was a rare and curious animal, occasionally putting his hand on my shoulder. He vows and declares that I was going to have a touch of the sickness that is loose in our city now. Whether he is right or wrong ... he certainly cut short a spell of the acutest pain I have ever experienced in my life and no woman could have tended me more carefully than he through those terrible hours between eleven and two.[8]

Sometimes the nights were cooler, and it was on such a night that he went to a moonlight picnic in the Shalimar rose-gardens, 'one of the loveliest places under heaven', to which they rode in couples. In the moonlight the Shalimar Gardens had a cold and unearthly beauty, with great sheets of still water and inlaid marble colonnades, and round them thick trees; there were acres of night-blooming flowers that filled the Gardens with scent and over all the aroma of Marshal Niel roses. He was reminded of Tennyson's description of the garden of the Princess Ida by moonlight. 'We just sat round and talked and then the women began to sing *naturally and without pressing* and the voices came across the water like the voices of spirits.'[9]

August 1884 had seen the publication of a little book called *Echoes*, the fruit of the Kiplings' habit of playing pencil and paper games in the evening. These consisted largely of writing parodies, for which Rudyard had an extraordinary aptitude, and it was from these scribblings that *Echoes* was assembled. It made a modest but favourable impression when published by the *Civil and Military*, and was the joint work of Rudyard and Trix. He sent a copy of this little book to Aunt Edith with the inscription:

> Though the *Englishman* deride it,
> Though the captious *Statesman* chide it,
> Your dear judgment shall decide it
>   Yours alone.
> For the good that in each line is,
> From the title page to Finis
>   Is your own.
>   R.K.

On the copy given to his mother he wrote only 'To the Mater from Ruddy, August 22nd 1884'. *Echoes* was to acquire a high scarcity value: a correspondent informed the author that having bought a copy from the penny tray in a bookshop, he forgot it for seventeen years, selling it in 1929 for £328. Aided by a building society, he bought a house with the proceeds and called it 'Echoes'.

When Rudyard's parents were in the Hills and he was alone in the house he watched himself closely to avoid running to seed in details of living. Sometimes he would break the monotony by digging out a few listless fellow-sufferers for a dinner-party; and then, 'the pitiful, scorched marigold blooms would appear on the table and to an accompaniment of glass, silver, and napery, the ritual would be worked through, and the butler's honour satisfied for a while'.

These exacting stretches of duty were broken by his Simla leaves. He would leave the oven of Lahore in exhausting dusty stages by rail and road, and come to his destination in the cool of the evening, to a bedroom with a log fire, and thirty days of leisure ahead. He devoted every spare moment in Simla to the study of his fellow-men as the raw material for his books. Their secret vices, their abortive love affairs, their sycophancy to superiors – he registered them all with a merciless and photographic eye. Although he carried on stilted flirtations, his intense preoccupation with his craft filled his mind to the exclusion of almost all other thoughts. He persuaded himself that the pallid ghost of 'Maisie', standing reproachful at his shoulder, alone kept him from major entanglements. 'I flirted with the bottled up energy of a year on my lips,' he wrote. 'Don't be horrified for there were about half a dozen of 'em and I took back the lacerated fragments of my heart as I distributed my PPC cards and returned the whole intact, to Flo Garrard's keeping as per usual.'

His most intimate correspondence leaves no doubt of the extent of this self-delusion, nor of the influence which he believed this girl still exercised on him. It is a love affair about which we cannot read without impatience and disbelief, and his letters deploring her coldness are spurious and cloying. He referred to her as 'My Lady', but at the same time thought that anyone in his condition was stupid beyond words. He even, in a spiteful moment, called her 'this – Tillie Venner'.*

If he had consulted his inclinations he would have written to her every day and all day:

I don't wait for her letters. I get one, and go on till I get the next, my nose to the grindstone for fear of thinking. When a horrible Sunday comes and I am thrown back upon myself, I know how long I have waited and then I get all the arrears of suspense in one gloomy lump. I have written and told her that, save and except her letters, I have nothing, – absolutely nothing, and that is a fact.... I can't imagine a man deliberately keeping sacred letters. If it all dies, they would hurt more than any woe. If it lived he would have the reality and the memory. That is, if he could repeat the

---

* A spoilt empty-headed girl in *Plain Tales from the Hills.*

letters off by heart, as I can. You will see from this my Lady does not favour me with any lengthy outpourings. She doesn't gush, and I try in my letters to her to keep myself within that decent insular reserve that is the hereditary mask of the Englishman.[10]

All these letters present a picture of a man brooding miserably in the lonely evenings over this frigid and indifferent girl, and it is probable that Kipling saw himself as the central figure in a macabre drama of frustrated love. But it was writing and India with her savage allure which now held the true key to his seduction. His preoccupation with the unresponsive 'Maisie' has a quality that is both literary and synthetic, the sentences flowing on with a significant lack of truly experienced grief: 'There is this strange quality in Love, that it has in common with Death – the curious and unquenchable remorse for carelessness in the past, for pique and misunderstandings that ravaged the golden time.' It was soon to recede, grow dim, and disappear, washed away on a stream of more compelling interests. Perhaps we may discover in this youthful involvement the seeds of his character in maturity, for among the emotions that were later to agitate him so fiercely a capacity for the passionate love of women never seems to have found a place.

He rode and danced with married women, observing them narrowly, and often using them for a copy, a circumstance which they understandably resented. He sent them verses, sometimes indifferently using the same lines twice. 'Better alter the colour of the eyes,' said Trix cynically, and she recalled his casual attitude to girls by a revealing but brutal little story:

'Once I remember he was attracted by the face of a girl seen in church. A chaplain's daughter – small, dark and slender with fine eyes. He used to go to church to look at her – I was eighteen then. I found her pretty and commonplace – though of course I did not tell him so – I introduced him to her at one of the afternoon dances. The next dance began; I looked for Rud and the dark-eyed maiden; they seemed to be sitting out. Came the third dance – and she was sitting out alone. No sign of Rud – and he did not drive home with us. After dinner I questioned him.

'"My useless sister, why didn't you tell me? Dragons and great deeps were not in it."

"What do you mean?"

'"She has the breath of the tomb – emanations from the Pit. She has a lovely smile I know, but when she leant and whispered something to me I could have fainted. Never again!"'

' "Poor girl, she probably only needs to see a dentist."
' "Worse than that, – corruption!" '[11]

Kipling's real passion was writing, and it was not only from the indiscretions of women that he derived inspiration. The story of the 'Gadsbys', he tells us, derived from the drunken babblings of a friend at a ball, which, in the morning, he begged Kipling to forget. This besotted creature, Captain Beames of the 19th Bengal Lancers, had little idea, when he poured out his infatuation for a young girl to Kipling late at night, that every humiliating word and gesture was being professionally noted, and that the progress of his affair would be immediately relayed to Rudyard's friend, Mrs Hill. 'He is coming in tomorrow afternoon,' said Rudyard casually. 'I shall stay in because I want him for a story – he'll work in beautifully, though some of the things he says are very hard to bear without wincing. But he has given me the material I want, and if I can catch him after his engagement his carcass will give me more flesh for the dissecting.'[12]

In Lahore the centre of Kipling's life was the Punjab Club, then at Nedou's Hotel. In the dingy dining-room he ate monotonous ill-cooked fare in the company of fellow-members whose tempers grimly deteriorated as the heat increased, and whose every mannerism became maddeningly familiar. Here Kipling's aggressiveness got him into trouble again, and there was still living in 1910 in Lahore an elderly lawyer who would relate with relish how disgusted he and a fellow-barrister had been by Kipling's flamboyant behaviour at a luncheon-party. Having monopolized the conversation throughout the meal, Kipling had, at the end, held forth egotistically about his desire for a new experience: the angry lawyers took him outside and provided him with it in the form of kicking him downstairs.

On another occasion some contemptuous remarks of Kipling's about the Indian Civil Service brought Michael O'Dwyer,* then a young official, to his feet in a rage and the two glowering young men were separated with difficulty by friends. These were isolated incidents, and on the whole Kipling was a popular member of the Club and of its less raffish and grander sister in Allahabad, although he had to face some unpleasant episodes. In 1883 the Liberal Government, 'acting', said Kipling sarcastically afterwards, 'on Liberal principles', decided to introduce a measure which came to be known as the Ilbert Bill, to enable native judges, in this case overwhelmingly Hindu, to exercise jurisdiction over European British subjects. The

---

* Later Lieut. Governor of the Punjab.

community was outraged by this proposal and fought it tooth and claw, even going so far as to boycott the levées of the Viceroy. Kipling's paper had begun with an attitude sharply critical of the Bill and it was with astonishment that he read the leader as usual one night when the paper was put to bed. 'It was the sort of false balanced semi-judicial stuff that some English journals wrote about the Indian White Paper from 1932 to 34,' he said long afterwards. He asked Wheeler what this *volte-face* meant, and was sharply told to mind his own business.

When Kipling that night entered the long dreary dining-room of the Club with its communal table, the room hissed like a nest of cobras.

'Who are they hissing?' asked Kipling, startled.

'You', was the reply. 'Your damn rag has ratted over the Bill.'

The Adjutant of the Volunteers spoke up quickly in a decent attempt to save Kipling: 'Stop that! The boy's only doing what he's paid to do.' Someone else said: 'You damned young ass! Don't you know that your paper has the Government printing contract?'

Of this recollection of Kipling's, Mr Haward, editor of the *Pioneer* in 1926–8, observed to the author:

'In Kipling's autobiography allowance must be made, of course, for the passage of time, which does not tend to help accuracy, but I cannot help thinking that he was very unfair to the owners of the *Civil and Military Gazette* in his suggestion that the policy of the paper was switched on the Ilbert Bill because of the Government contract. Din Mahomet, who was the news foreman in my time, was the son of Ruk-Um-Ud Din who was the press contractor of Kipling's time, and I never found that the Government contract, which we endeavoured to shake off without success when I was manager, had any influence over editorial policy; in fact the editor would have been indignant if we on the managerial side had ever attempted to use the lever. Close examination of the date is also against Kipling. He came to the staff of the *Civil and Military Gazette* in 1885 and the tumult over the Ilbert Bill had subsided, for Lord Ripon left India in 1884.'[13]

This statement is incorrect, for Kipling was working on the *Civil and Military* from the end of 1882, and so had every opportunity for observing the episode, whether he remembered it correctly or not.

After this humiliating experience, Kipling began to take an interest in certain persons who had seen good in the Bill, and had 'somehow been shifted out of the heat of Lahore to billets in Simla', and in the many devices and pressures that a Government can exert on its employees in such a country as India:

So, when the great and epoch-making India Bill turned up fifty years later, I felt as one re-treading the tortuous by-ways of his youth. One recognized the very phrases and assurances of the old days still doing good work...the very slightly altered formulas in which those who were parting with their convictions excused themselves. Thus: 'I may act as a brake, you know. At any rate I'm keeping a more extreme man out of the game.' 'There's no sense running counter to the inevitable' – and all the other Devil-provided camouflage for the sinner-who-faces-both-ways.[14]

Kipling relied heavily on the Club in those breathless evenings, heavy with the smell of the newly-watered Mall. The flowers in the Club gardens were dead and black on their stalks, the little lotus-pond was a circle of caked mud, and the tamarisk trees were white with the dust of days. In this hot weather the survivors sat in the Club snapping venomously at each other, construing the mildest pleasantries as studied insults. A member suddenly fell to the floor under the first impact of cholera. The remorseless thermometer turned the minds of some to darker things than quarrels. There was a night when someone brought in a half-dead viper to dinner in a pickle bottle. One of the most dejected of the company kept fiddling about with the angry little reptile on the tablecloth until he was warned to stop:

A few weeks after some of us realized it would have been better had he accomplished what had been in his foreboding mind that night.... The Complaint Book bristled with accusations and inventions. All of which came to nothing when the first Rains fell, and after a three days' siege of creeping and crawling things whose bodies stopped our billiards and almost put out the lamps they sizzled in, life picked up in the blessed cool.[15]

Much as he depended upon the Club, it sometimes made deep inroads on his nerves:

I have returned to the old wearying, Godless futile life at the club – same men, same talk, same billiards – all *connu* and triply *connu*, and, except for what I carry in my heart, I could swear that I had never been away. However, it will pass in time, and I look forward as I have never looked forward to anything in my life for its ending, and the relief...but as it all fits in with my plans it must be got through, and now that I have the Gift I don't care.

In spite of Lockwood's charm and learning, and the sharp intelligence of Alice, the Kipling family had not yet succeeded in making the longed-for entry into viceregal society in Simla. Lockwood's position as the curator of a museum was considered a lowly one by the army officers and Government officials who competed for the Viceroy's invitations, and his pay was meagre. It had not yet been discovered what a social asset this brilliant family could be, but their position was to be entirely changed by the arrival of the new Viceroy, Lord Dufferin, at the end of 1884.

In the meantime Rudyard had various escapes from the grinding routine at Lahore. In March 1885 he reported for the *Civil and Military* the reception at Rawalpindi of that staunch friend of the British, the Amir Abdurrahman. The ceremony, conceived with oriental splendour, was swamped by the torrential rain of the hills. He followed the Amir's progress to Fort Jamrood at the mouth of the Khyber Pass, and it was here, venturing a little too far into that dangerous territory, that he came under fire from a suspicious tribesman. In May he was on the move again on an adventurous expedition on the craggy road that winds from the Himalayas into Tibet.

He spent the hot weather of 1885 in Simla, his second season in the summer capital, and July found him special correspondent for his paper, his salary now raised to £420 a year. For that sum he was supplying editorial notes, reviews, articles, and social Simla letters. To his Aunt Edith he sent, in facetious vein, the first of a lifelong series of complaints about the pirating of his work:

By the way a tenth rate journal called *The Times*, I think, calmly bagged an article of mine upon the geology of a little-known part of Central Asia without a word of acknowledgement. Next time you meet Mr Buckle tell him with my compliments that I object to special information being utilized in this way.

He refers for the first time to his novel *Mother Maturin*, which was never published:

Further I have really embarked to the tune of 237 foolscap pages on my novel *Mother Maturin* – Like Topsy 'it growed' while I wrote, and I find myself now committed to a two volume business at least. It's not one bit nice or proper, but it carries a grim sort of moral with it, and it tries to deal with the unutterable horrors of low-class Eurasian and native life as they exist outside reports. Mother says it's nasty, but powerful, and I *know* it to be in large measure true.[16]

'In vain,' said General McMunn, 'have several of us looked and hoped for it, for it promised to be the story of stories. I have however ascertained that *Mother Maturin* kept a questionable house of entertainment for sailors of the South China Seas at Saigon.' Another version was that she was an old Irishwoman who kept an opium den in Lahore, but sent her daughter to be educated in England. The return of this daughter, and her marriage to a civilian in Lahore, was the explanation of why Government secrets often leaked to the bazaar.

The last reference to this unpublished work is on 3 July 1900, when Kipling's wife Caroline was to enter in her diary that the manuscript of *Mother Maturin* had been sent to Kipling by his literary agents, A. P. Watt. Later, parts of this book were used in *Kim*.

Rudyard Kipling found Simla an almost inaccessible town, clinging to the mountains like a swallow's nest amid peaks thick with firs and deodars. Here was a wonderful refuge for men driven to the limit of their endurance by their labours in the baking inferno of the plains beneath. There was a delicious coolness in the air, and log fires in the evening. It was a place of incessant entertainment, of striving for social supremacy, of place-hunting, of petty intrigue and eager gossip. The fact that it was the summer seat of Government, and the distinction of the Viceroy's presence, which lent it something of the atmosphere of a court, raised Simla in the eyes of the English to a supreme social position among all the Indian hill-stations.

The Mall was like some street in an English resort torn from its natural setting and perched incongruously among the everlasting snows. Down it, at the fashionable hour, adoring subalterns walked at the rickshaw wheels of the ladies of their choice, and the flower of Simla society paraded. There was polo at Annandale, a vast plateau scooped out of the hills and surrounded by deodars, and amateur theatricals of embarrassing mediocrity in which Trix excelled, and for which her brother wrote the prologues. There was Pelitis, the café where all Simla met, and the public assembly room at Benmore.

The whole *ambiance* of the place might have been created to slake the appetite of a young writer hungry for material – the grass widows, the faded garrison hacks staking all on a last fling for a husband, the ambitious young officers and officials eager for advancement, ingratiating themselves with their superiors, the furtive adulteries, the pathetic suicides, the provincial *femmes fatales* – it was a rich seam to work.

The Indian Empire was administered in the hot months from this place of steep streets and awe-inspiring views, when the Government transferred itself lock, stock and barrel to the Hills. It was Lord Dufferin's first year of office. The hideous palace which was to be created during his viceroyalty was not yet built, and he lived in a mean and uncomfortable shooting lodge called 'Peterhoff'. The Kipling family, once the ice had been broken, were exactly the people to appeal to the sophisticated Viceroy and his fabled wife, herself the grand-daughter of Sheridan and one of three sisters famous for their beauty. Having met them, the Vicereine soon began to invite them to the more intimate parties at 'Peterhoff', which she so greatly preferred to official entertainments, and quickly came to enjoy their company. No surer proof of a growing intimacy could be found than the fact that the Viceroy's son, Clandeboye, soon began to develop an interest in Trix not altogether to Lord Dufferin's august liking:

One connection [wrote Carrington] was Lockwood's sketching class, which Lady Helen, the Viceroy's daughter, attended. The Viceroy would drop in to talk art and letters with Lockwood, and would stay to enjoy Mrs Kipling's conversation. 'Dulness and Mrs Kipling cannot exist in the same room,' he used to say. Furthermore, Trix in her second season was an acknowledged beauty, a breaker of hearts and an expert dancer. She had talent for writing both verse and prose, and was an accomplished amateur actress. When she also took the fancy of Lord Clandeboye, the Viceroy's son and ADC, it was rather more than the Dufferins approved. One day the Viceroy called on Mrs Kipling to discuss this dangerous development. 'Don't you think, Mrs Kipling, your daughter should be taken to another hill-station?' 'Don't you think, your Excellency, that your son should be sent home?' It was Clandeboye who went, and Trix who remained. The Viceroy, though defeated, was no less friendly. One day he dropped in unheralded at 'The Tendrils', the Kiplings' Simla lodging, and was turned away by the servants because the family was out, a rebuff which this autocrat accepted meekly enough.[17]

Thus the Kiplings entered the magic circle of the Viceroy of India, and Rudyard was brought squarely to his attention. We may imagine the resentment that the progress of these dark horses induced in others who had been outstripped in the race.

By 1886 Stephen Wheeler had been replaced by E. Kay Robinson, and the arrival of this new editor brought a delightful change to Kipling's office life. He had first met Robinson, a man only a little older than himself, in 1885 when Robinson left Fleet Street to become assistant editor of the *Pioneer*, and by the spring of 1886 he had stayed with the Kiplings at Lahore, and the two men had become friends. Robinson's first impression of his brilliant subordinate was not favourable:

His face [he said] had not acquired the character of manhood, and contrasted unpleasantly with his stoop (acquired through much bending over an office table), his heavy eyebrows, his spectacles, and his sallow Anglo-Indian complexion; while his jerky speech and abrupt movements added to the unfavourable impression. But his conversation was brilliant and his sterling character gleamed through the humorous light which shone behind his spectacles. He had an unlucky eye for colour in the selection of his clothes, and a weakness for brown cloth with that suggestion of ruddiness or purple in it which makes some browns so curiously conspicuous.

The repressive discipline of Wheeler was finished. Kipling worked from the first with his new editor on terms of easy companionship. Robinson had been instructed, at all costs, to put some 'sparkle' into the paper, and Kipling found himself, at the end of their first day's work together, adjourning to the Sind and Punjab Hotel opposite the office, and cracking a bottle of champagne with his editor to the successful sparkle of the *Gazette* under its new management. Robinson tried hard to relieve Kipling of Wheeler's soulless routine, but, with the greatest dislike of using a razor to cut a grindstone, he could not help burdening Kipling with a good deal of day-to-day drudgery: 'My experience of him as a newspaper hack,' he said, 'suggests, however, that if you want a man who will cheerfully do the office work of three men you should catch a young genius. Like a blood horse between the shafts of a coal wagon he may go near to bursting his heart in the effort, but he'll drag that wagon along as it ought to go.'

There is a curious contradiction between Robinson's admiration for Kipling as a journalist, and the views of Clive Rattigan, son of the William Rattigan who had given him his first chance. In the 75th Anniversary Supplement of the *Pioneer*, Rattigan wrote:

As a journalist Rudyard Kipling was far from being a great success. His father had induced my own father and the other proprietors of the two papers to give the young Rudyard a post on the Lahore paper. But in the day-to-day business of journalism Kipling did not by any means shine. He had little taste for mere routine duties; he was apt to neglect the rather tedious assignments that inevitably fell to the lot of the junior members of a very small staff.

Robinson has left a strange picture of Kipling at work in the office, roaring with laughter and bathed in sweat, his white cotton trousers and vest spotted with ink until he looked like a Dalmatian dog. 'He had a habit of dipping his pen frequently and deep into the ink pot, and as all his movements were abrupt, almost jerky, the ink used to fly.' When he bustled into Robinson's room, Robinson shouted to him to 'stand off', otherwise, as he knew by experience, the abrupt halt he would make and the flourish with which he placed the proof in his hand before the editor would send a penful of ink flying over him. 'Driving or walking home to breakfast in his light attire plentifully besprinkled with ink, his spectacled eyes peering out under an enormous mushroom-shaped hat, Kipling was a quaint looking object.'

The office, under the tolerant Robinson regime, was full of dogs, getting in everyone's way: Joe, Bux, and Kipling's Vixen, to whom he was absurdly devoted, and who looked like a 'nice clean sucking pig'. The paper changed its shape under Robinson, the new feature being the daily turnover of a column and a quarter, and the sleeplessness caused by these changes gave Kipling a breakdown from which he rallied with his usual buoyancy and courage. Kipling possessed considerable physical resources; apart from the various scenes in the Club, he fought successfully a large drunken photographer who invaded the office; later he was disturbed in the small hours by a hilarious party bent on ragging his rooms. 'As a rule,' said Robinson, 'when a man is favoured by a surprise visit of his friends in the dead of night, he is at first alarmed and afterwards effusively friendly. But Kipling was out of his bed in an instant, and before the foremost of the intruders had mastered the geography of the room in the dark, he felt the cold barrel of a revolver at his temple.'

In 1886, in the cool weather, Kipling began to write the satirical verse and the short stories which were published daily in the *Civil and Military Gazette* and brought him instant fame all over India. He was modest about his first volume of verse, saying: 'It's a tiny little book, but we hope to get it decently reviewed, and as it's anonymous no harm will be done.' He had been contributing verse to the paper for some time, verse born out of the life about him, of the backslidings of Government officials and their jockeying for position, of the scandals of Simla life, of the bazaar and the places he visited. He burned twice as many poems as he published. 'They were made,' he said, 'to ease off the perpetual strife between the manager extending his advertisements and my chief fighting for his reading-matter. They were born to be sacrified.' But Rukh-Din, the Muslim foreman on Kipling's side of the office, approved of them greatly, and when he had used one to fill an awkward space would say: 'Your potery very good sir; just coming proper length today.' In this way his verses had come to be printed week by week in the paper. The whole Indian press in those days was pock-marked with indifferent verse: 'Sometimes a man in Bangalore would be moved to song, and a man on the Bombay side would answer him, and a man in Bengal would echo back, till at last we would all be crowing together like cocks before day-break when it was too dark to see your fellow.'

Men in the Army, the Civil Service and the Railway wrote to Kipling saying that the rhymes should be made into a book. They had been sung to the banjo round camp fires and bivouacs, and had penetrated as far as Rangoon, Moulmein and Mandalay. A real book was out of the question, but Kipling had Rukh-Din and the office plant at his disposal at a price: 'So there was born a sort of book, a lean oblong docket, wire-stitched to imitate a DO Government envelope, printed on one side only, bound in brown paper and secured with red tape. It was addressed to all heads of departments.'

Kipling also took reply-postcards printed on one side with the news of the birth of the book, and on the other with a blank order form, and scattered these postcards over the East 'from Aden to Singapore, and from Quetta to Colombo'. In November he was able to write home in the sudden thrilling knowledge that his star was rising:

By the way that book has been most favourably noticed all round India, and the whole edition is sold out. *The World* too was good enough to give me a nice little notice, and I'm proportionately pleased. There was only one paper – *The Indian Review*, which cut 'em up savagely, and by way of showing that I bore no malice I cut out the slashingest parts and put them in the advertisement – the consequence was that all the world and his wife when they heard that the poems were vicious sent in orders for the book, and we scored hugely.[18]

By December 1886 the name of Kipling was known all over India, and he wrote to Aunt Edith with exultation:

Then a strange thing happened. The little booklet just hit the taste of the Anglo-Indian public for it told them about what they knew.... I got some lively reviews comparing me to ... all sorts of people whose shoe-latchets I am not worthy to unloose. Then I had the book published by a Calcutta firm. *Vanity Fair* reviewed it; Andrew Lang in Longman's said some of the work was worthy of Bret Harte, and again the public bought. And Thacker Spink & Co. write to say that the second edition is nearly exhausted. The Viceroy and divers other great people have written and said all sorts of sweet things to me about the book.

The fact remains that I have made a mark – I say it with all the modesty that a youngster who has had a fill of butter can say so. Everyone in the sets I knew had read or heard about the *Departmental Ditties*, and strangers in trains, and hotels and all manner of out of the way places come up to me and say nice things. Also, last proof of notoriety – people turn their heads and look, and ask to be introduced to me when I dance or dine in strange places beyond my district.

In the same year he began a series of stories in the *Civil and Military Gazette* which were to be called *Plain Tales from the Hills*, the stories which made Oscar Wilde feel, as he languidly observed, as if he were 'seated under a palm tree reading life by superb flashes of vulgarity'. These tales, Kipling said with modesty, were used as padding when space required it. It is probable that Trix also had her fingers in this particular pie, and it was even suggested that she wrote several of the stories that appeared in the *Civil and Military Gazette*, but were not republished. Trix knew Simla better than her brother, and was able to give him a great deal of information about personalities, and it was generally thought at the time that a number of old scores were faithfully paid off. But Kipling made fewer enemies than he might have done with these stories, owing to his habit of creating composite characters.

Although Kipling's name was now known in India, he failed, for the moment, to impress those critics in London to whom specimens of his work had been shown. Sir Ian Hamilton, who was a friend of Kipling and had quickly realized his genius, had sent a manuscript of *The Mark of the Beast* to England in 1886, to be shown to Andrew Lang and William Sharp, and to the editors of two magazines, in an attempt to launch Kipling in London. Lang returned the manuscript as abruptly as if he had picked up a snake, with the comment: 'I would gladly give Ian a fiver if he had never been the means of my reading this poisonous stuff which has left an extremely disagreeable impression on my mind!' Sharp reacted even more violently: 'I would strongly recommend you instantly to burn this detestable piece of work. I would like to hazard a guess that the writer of the article in question is very young, and that he will die mad before he has reached the age of thirty.' The story then returned to India but was published in *Lloyd's News* in 1890. Nor did *Plain Tales from the Hills* make an immediate impact on London. When it was received there in 1886, Thacker Spink & Co., to whom the book was sent by the parent firm in Calcutta, hawked it round the trade putting personal pressure on editors, but the subscription sheet only numbered sixteen copies, and it was not until a column notice in the *Saturday Review* created a demand for it that the book began to move.

In 1887, unwelcome orders reached Kipling to move to Allahabad to serve on the *Pioneer*, hundreds of miles to the south-east, under the vigilant eye of the proprietor, a very different matter from his distant personal outpost at Lahore, and one which involved a transfer from Muslim to Hindu India. He was now twenty-two, but so mature that he could have been taken for forty. His new position made it necessary for Kipling to make a number of visits to Northern India. And in Rajputana, in November 1887, he found the material for *Letters of Marque*, a series of articles which afterwards appeared in the volume *From Sea to Sea*, and for the background of *The Light that Failed* and other stories.

Throughout 1888 he poured out fiction in the *Week's News* and the *Pioneer Mail*, grossly overwriting, the work varying from good to execrable, and it was the stories emerging from this effort that were to appear in paperback editions. On the *Pioneer* he was entrusted with more outside work and made editor of the weekly edition of the paper designed for home consumption. At first he lived at the Allahabad Club but left it in June 1888 and went 'chumming', as it was called in Anglo-Indian slang, with Professor Hill and his wife, to whom he had been introduced by Sir Edward Buck, the author of a monumental book on Simla.

Aleck Hill was a quiet man, a scientist interested in photography; his wife Edmonia was a lively young American from Pennsylvania who was to play an important part in Kipling's life. He lived with them in their bungalow which stood in a large, untidy garden, sharing expenses on a *per capita* basis, and it was here that he wrote *Baa Baa Black Sheep*, a short story based on his sufferings at 'Lorne Lodge'.

Mrs Hill noted: 'Mr Kipling looks about forty, as he is beginning to be bald, but he is, in reality, just twenty-two.' Elsewhere she described him as 'a short, dark-haired man of uncertain age, with a heavy moustache, and wearing very thick glasses. He does not play tennis, but is quite good at Badminton.' She was astonished that he was the recipient of so many confessions, as he used every detail confided to him for copy. But she was impressed and 'gave him the Blue room for his study, and the guest room with the big four poster mahogany bed'.

Here he wrote at night to the sound of noisy *ekkas* jingling down the avenue and anklets tinkling to the twanging of the sitar. When he was writing *Baa Baa Black Sheep*, he was filled with bitterness and retrospective anger, and Mrs Hill found something disturbing in the hatred with which he raked over the past: 'It was pitiful to see Kipling living over the experience, pouring out his soul in the story as if the drab life was worse than he could possibly describe it. He was in a towering rage at the recollection of those days.'

Kipling now began to consider a move from India and journalism, strongly influenced in his desire to be a full-time writer by a book by Walter Besant called *All in a Garden Fair*. He was also, no doubt, encouraged to leave by the astonishing success, in India, of *Plain Tales from the Hills*, which was published by Thacker Spink & Co. in January 1888. He discussed the question with Mrs Hill in June of the same year: 'I have left myself no space to refer to the Scheme. *Am* I still for it? You know that, if it is possible, I most assuredly *am*. By all means and every means, yes, a hundred times, and let what may be, be.... I want rest somehow.'

At the end of 1888 he rearranged himself and took stock. He had already had encouraging notice taken of his work, the Viceroy writing to him in July 1888 to draw attention to a flattering notice of *Plain Tales from the Hills* in the *Saturday Review*. He possessed one book of verse, one of prose, and a set of six small paperback railway-book-stall volumes. The head of the firm controlling the railway bookstalls was Emile Edouard Moreau, senior partner in A. G. Wheeler & Co. Kipling owed a great deal to this man, and although he afterwards considered the negotiations to be incompetent, his failure to mention Moreau's name in his autobiography is a strange and ungracious oversight.

Moreau had known Kipling for some time before they came to their arrangement, as they were fellow-members of the Club and often played poker together. Moreau one day proposed to Kipling that he should publish some of the stories that he had read in the *Week's News*. Moreau had the insight to realize that here was a genius imprisoned in a newspaper office, thousands of bubbling words of his output coldly impaled on an official file, and it occurred to him that there was a chance of introducing Kipling to the world outside India and doing a good stroke of business into the bargain. Kipling responded at once to Moreau's offer of publication. He said that the idea appealed to him, but that he had no money. Moreau, however, proposed to take all the risk and to pay Kipling $1000 and a royalty of $20 per 1000 copies, after the sale of the first 1500, for the rights of publication of *Soldiers Three*, *Wee Willie Winkie*, *Under the Deodars*, *The Story of the Gadsbys*, *In Black and White* and *The Phantom Rickshaw*.

Kipling agreed to this offer, and the two men drew up their memorable contract, which Moreau kept all his life and would take out of a black japanned box to show his friends. The books were published in India in green paper covers with designs by Lockwood Kipling at one rupee per volume, and in England in 1890 by Sampson Low, Marston & Co., where they were also an immediate success.

Kipling was now looking forward to leaving India. Certain changes in his friendships and in the lives of relations added to his restlessness. His cousin Margaret Burne-Jones was to marry an Oxford don of liberal persuasion called Jack Mackail, with whose political views Rudyard could have no sympathy. The correspondence between him and Margaret ceased, and Trix's engagement to John Fleming, a soldier working in the Survey Department, also threatened a precious relationship. Alice Kipling noticed that long periods of solitude had caused a deterioration in her son's manners, and that he had become morose and prematurely old. 'You'll have to be civil, Ruddy,' she warned him.

There was a tradition in the *Pioneer* office regarding Kipling's departure. When he was assistant editor of the *Pioneer* he was given the assignment of reporting a meeting of the Congress Party in Allahabad. In his report he made some offensive references to a sour-faced captain called Hearsay. Hearsay hurried round to the *Pioneer* office with the conventional equipment of a horse-whip, and succeeded in getting to grips with the editor before being thrown through the *chic* on the veranda by another member of the staff.

An action was brought against the *Pioneer* for libel, and a cross-action was brought against Hearsay. Sir George Allen, manager and part-owner, thought that it would be undesirable for Kipling to give evidence, and proposed that he should take some leave and see the world. Another reason for his departure was that Mrs Hill, to whom he had become devoted, had been seriously ill with meningitis and had decided to recuperate at home in America. It occurred to Rudyard that he might travel eastward en route to England, and stay with his friends in Pennsylvania. He decided to leave India at once, not even waiting for Trix's wedding, and in February 1889 paid his last visit to Lahore to make his farewells to the family. He was to sail in company with the Hills on ss *Madura* bound from Calcutta to Rangoon.

He left Lahore on 3 March 1889, and embarked on a leisurely journey to England. Blissfully free from care, he found life on board ship delightful, steaming from one new exotic place to another – Rangoon, Singapore, Hong Kong, Japan. His eyes absorbed the new scenes, and his writer's senses were alert. He played paper games with the Hills, and studied his fellow-passengers narrowly. From Japan they sailed across the North Pacific on an American ship, *City of Pekin*, and after twenty days at sea passed through the Golden Gate to San Francisco.

In spite of his intellectual development, Kipling was still callow and insolent. He infuriated Americans in San Francisco by his intolerable remark after entering the harbour: 'I saw with great joy that the block-house which guarded the mouth of the "finest harbour in the world, Sir", could be silenced by two gunboats from Hong Kong with safety, comfort and despatch.' He gave brash interviews to journalists, and lost his temper with the American porters at the Customs House, who responded to his demand for service with far less alacrity than his In-dian bearers. When he discovered in San Francisco that his books had been pirated, his anger flared forth again at this act of effrontery.

When he left San Francisco he showed no disposition to hasten. No anxieties about time or money appeared to vex him. He embarked on leisurely expeditions–Portland, Tacoma, Montana, Salt Lake City, Washington and Boston – and fulfilled his intention of visiting the Hills, staying with them in Pennsylvania for a full two months.

Kipling described this journey in *From Sea to Sea*, and, according to Trix, surprisingly became engaged at this time to Mrs Hill's younger sister Caroline. The engagement was broken off, and she returned to India with her father, a Congregational minister, who objected to Kip-ling's creed. This engagement was rendered all the more singular, thought Trix, by the fact that Kipling, probably subconsciously, had given a perfect description of this lady in the person of the very un-attractive girl who won the diamond-bracelet archery prize in *Cupid's Arrows*. Kipling felt remorse about this abortive engagement, and later, in Villiers Street, told Trix that he had broken the heart of the 'noblest woman in the world'. Trix had had feelings of apprehension in the old days that Kipling might marry Mrs Hill herself after Hill's death, as he had a distinct leaning towards women older than himself. This, she considered, would have been a disaster, because Mrs Hill would not have been able to give him any children, and Kipling's mar-riage in such a situation would certainly have ended fatally.[19]

Kipling at last decided to make tracks for England. Aged twenty-four, he arrived in London in October 1889 to make his great assault on the capital.

CHAPTER VII

THE EARLY WORK

BEFORE following Kipling to London we should take some account
of the work he had accomplished in India, and on which he intended
to establish his literary career. It was by a fortuitous triumph of timing
that these poems and stories came to England, bringing to thousands,
for the first time, the dusty enchantment of India. 'He went up in the
sky like a rocket' – it was said – 'a rocket out of the magic East, scatter-
ing its many-coloured jewels in the bowl of the Night.'

The vast circle which was soon to worship this youth was as wide
as that which had revered the greatest literary figures of the century.
He was to be embraced in a general and astonishing veneration. Men
of every kind succumbed with an equal thrill to the sorcerer's incanta-
tions – clerks and sailors, clergymen, doctors, ministers, authors,
farmers and engineers. They found in him something strange and
beyond their normal ken, a beckoning to mysterious unvisited places,
a violent stirring of the senses, and a rich commotion of the blood.

Nor did he come to them as a mere dream substitute, but in such
a manner as to quicken their zest for everyday life and the pursuit
of their own callings. And it was not only ordinary men who felt the
potency of the spell. On Edmund Gosse he was to produce a 'peculiar
thrill, a voluptuous and agitating sentiment of intellectual uneasiness
– it excites, disturbs and attracts me; I cannot throw off its disquieting
influence'.[1] 'This man ought to be another Shakespeare, and something over,' said William Archer.[2] 'Who else, except Whitman,' asked
George Moore, 'has written with the whole language since the
Elizabethans?'[3] To Henry James he was 'a strangely clever youth
who has stolen the formidable mask of maturity and rushes about
making people jump with the deep sounds that issue from its painted
lips'.[4]

To some he was, and remained, repulsive, and the most notable
of these was a young man who arrived in London a few years after
Kipling. For Max Beerbohm's fastidious soul was stirred to its depths

by this new realism, and he attacked it from the first with a savagery far removed from his normal suave derision. To him there was always something revolting in the vulgarity, the synthetic violence and the mutilated dialect of much of Kipling's work. With a reluctant appreciation of his genius, he was yet repelled by what he believed to be its deliberate and insensitive prostitution. His object became Kipling's destruction. His hatred grew as the years passed and he could detect no repentance or change, and his criticism would be seen at its most biting in the days ahead when he was to review the dramatized version of *The Light that Failed*. We should recall this devastating notice not only because it came from the heart, but because it accurately describes the side of Kipling offensive to many who were otherwise conscious of his power:

Miss Fletcher, the adapter, has caught the 'way of a man with a maid' as conveyed by Mr Kipling. 'I want you Maisie, I want you badly' sounds rather like the echo of a coon song, but it is also good Kiplingese. And 'You're a woman Maisie, from the top of your dear little head to the toes of your blessed little boots' is Kiplingese of the purest kind inconfusable with any other kind of vulgarity. . . . It is a pity she has omitted Dick's immortal description of his inamorata as a 'bilious little thing'. You remember that he was walking in Kensington Gardens, meditating on Maisie's lonely life, wondering whether she took proper care of herself. It occurred to him that perhaps she did not eat regular meals. For some girls, he reflected, this would not matter, 'but', he cried in an agony of tenderness, 'Maisie's a bilious little thing'.

Beerbohm concluded his review: 'Some of the other actors in the cast, by dint of much growling and grunting and scowling and lumbering, come within measurable distance of the ideal.'[5]

Kipling's reception was assisted by unique circumstances. The fiction of the Anglo-Saxon world had become strangely feminized, and a vacuum had opened. Between excess of psychological analysis and excess of superhuman romance there was a great void in the world of fiction. It was into this gap that Kipling stepped with his exotic realism, aggressive and triumphant. Politically, too, he arrived in the nick of time. He came at the moment when the national imagination had suddenly grasped the vastness of the British Empire, and the responsibilities it involved.

The poets of the previous generation had written of England up to 1885 much as they might have written of her in 1815. 'The idea of Greater Britain as no mere mechanical appendage to our island, but flesh of her flesh, and blood of her blood,' said William Archer, 'did not emerge in the national consciousness until this moment, and Kipling emerged with it. Fate had fixed his horoscope.'[6] And his style, in spite of frequent lapses into an abyss of vulgarity and bad taste, then and afterwards proclaimed his genius and dominion over words, flashing out in many a golden and unforgettable phrase:

Come back with me to the North and be among men once more. Come back when this matter is accomplished and I call for thee. The bloom of the peach orchards is upon all the valley, and here is only dust and a great stink. There is a pleasant wind among the mulberry trees, and the streams are bright with snow-water, and the caravans go up and the caravans go down, and a hundred fires sparkle in the gut of the pass, and tent-peg answers hammer-nose, and pony squeals to pony across the drift-smoke of the evening. It is good in the North now. Come back with me. Let us return to our own people. Come!

Just as the lightning shot two tongues that cut the sky into three pieces, something wiped his lips of speech as a mother wipes the milky lips of her child [of a man struck dumb].

Nothing save the spikes of the rain without and the smell of the drinking earth in my nostrils.

The leisurely ocean all patterned with peacocks' eyes of foam.

I heard a scufflin' in the room behind, and Dinah Shadd's hand dropped into mine like a rose-leaf into a muddy road.*

To Gosse he appeared like 'the master of a new kind of terrible, and enchanting peep-show' which all crowd round, begging for 'just one more look', although Gosse recognized much that can be said against Kipling's early work – the callow self-conceit, the noisy newspaper bustle of the little peremptory sentences, the cheapness of the satires.

Another critic acutely dissected the technical elements of this style:

The rhythms run with a snap from stop to stop; every sentence is as straight as a string; each has its self-contained tune. Prise one of them out of its place, and you feel it would fall with a clink, leaving a slot that would never close up as the holes do in woollier work. Replace it and it locks back like type

* Some of these quotations are taken from work written later than this period, but are included as characteristic of the early style.

in a forme, fitting into the paragraph as the paragraph fits into the tale. There are no glides or grace-notes, or blown spray of sound.[7]

This miniaturist's ability was already a source of weakness as well as strength. His characterization was weak because it was difficult for him to escape from his own subjectivity, so that his characters were inclined to melt rapidly in the mind, a fault which continued with him to the end. He sacrificed a great deal to this unconscious individuality with sometimes absurd results. Can we believe that the little cockney private soldier Ortheris would have quoted to a boozing chum:

> Go forth, return in Glory,
> To Clusium's royal 'ome:
> And round these bloomin' temples, 'ang
> The bloomin' shields o' Rome.

Is this passage credible on the lips of an Irish private soldier? –

'And fwhat has happened, ye lumbering child av calamity, that you're low-ing like a cow-calf at the back av the pasture, an' suggestin' invidious excuses for the man Stanley's going to kill. Ye'll have to wait another hour yet, little man. Spit it out Jock, and bellow melojus to the moon . . . discourse Don Juan! The Moors av Lotharius Learoyd!'[8]

Like Byron, description was Kipling's forte, and many consider that he ventured far too often into the vernacular. Cockney, in any case, was a foreign language to this Anglo-Indian boy – and the educated man of letters is always discernible behind the façade of the mutilated dialect. A true Cockney would notice the alien note at once, and the spurious elements in Kipling's repertoire of mangled words ('ave, 'er, chanst, gawd, bloomin' orficers an' lydies).

It is indeed arguable that the use of these phrases is often a violent offence against good taste. Mr Somerset Maugham in *Cakes and Ale* described how his heart sank when the eminent Victorian novelist Edward Driffield led him in spirit into the foc'sle of a sailing vessel, or the taproom of an inn, and he knew he was in for twenty pages of dialect, and there are those who regard Kipling's early soldier stories in the same manner. In the opinion of one of these critics, George Orwell:

Kipling idealizes the army officer, especially the junior officer, but the private soldier, though lovable and romantic, has to be a comic. He is always made to speak in a sort of stylized cockney, not very broad, but with all the aitches and final g's carefully omitted. Very often the result is as embarrassing as the humorous recitation at a church social.

His early work, then, was by no means free from blemish. The characters often leave little impression on the mind. His taste is frequently bad. But Andrew Lang said:

His faults are so conspicuous, so much on the surface, that they hardly need to be named. They are curiously visible to some readers who are blind to his merits. There is a false air of heartiness; there is a knowing air; there are mannerisms, such as 'But that is another story'; there is a display of slang; there is too obtrusive knocking of the nail on the head. Everybody can mark these errors; a few cannot overcome their antipathy, and so lose a great deal of pleasure.[9]

Indifferent to these defects, Kipling was launching a magical appeal perfectly in tune with his times, and he was doing so with extraordinary power and flashes of unforgettable descriptive virtuosity. It was a strange world that he created then, almost as strange as the later world that he described, which came to be filled with odd shapes, animals that talked, machinery that argued – and, over it all, an impression of the author's omniscience. His remarkable range was to increase with the years, until he soon appeared to know everything, the organization of armies in battle, the habits of wild animals in the jungle, and the function of tappet valves, in a detail as numbing as that in which he described the government of India, the building of bridges or the rutting wrath of the great Man Seal in the Behring Straits.

One of his enemies saw the world thus depicted as a cruel world – 'filled with sudden and sinister shapes – not men, but the baleful caricatures of men; not women, but Maenad sisters; he knows much of hate, but he knows little of love'.[10] Others were repelled by his passion for detail. 'He cannot,' they argued, 'have any true knowledge of all these subjects. However convincing it may sound it can be nothing more than a maddening affectation of knowledge, a crammed barrister's brief', a criticism which would merely suggest that Kipling was a thorough and conscientious craftsman.

His first book of verse, *Departmental Ditties*, appeared in 1886, and his prose stories were collected in 1888 when *Plain Tales from the Hills* appeared in Calcutta. In the same year appeared the Railway Library books, *Soldiers Three*, *The Gadsbys*, *In Black and White*, *Under the Deodars*, *The Phantom Rickshaw*, and *Wee Willie Winkie*, the collection that Kipling brought to London.

The literature of the sub-continent of India had been curiously sparse before Kipling's advent, its English conquerors seeing little in their exotic surroundings to kindle the imagination, and being intent upon governing, making war and love, and compiling official reports. For an author India was an unworked seam; the novels of the author of *Tara*, Cunningham's sketches, and Sir Alfred Lyall's poems – there was little else: 'That old haunt of history, the wealth of character brought out in the confusion of races, of religion, and the old and new, has been wealth untouched, a treasure-house sealed: those pagoda trees have never been shaken.'[11]

At last by rare fortune came a young Englishman of genius and minute observation, unhampered by an official position, who had the power to make men see what he saw; who poured out for an enraptured audience those little masterpieces in prose and verse which seemed to embrace the whole of India, from the garrison hacks of Simla to the stinking alleys of Lahore; from the jewels and treacheries of her Maharajahs to the bellowing sergeants on parade grounds shimmering in the intolerable heat of a day in May. There was a strong element of mischievous aggression in these stories:

It was Beetle's way of enforcing respect at Westward Ho! It was young Kipling's way of adjusting things at Simla. He would prove that ink could be thicker than blood and the pen even more daring than the sword; and that a certain small spectacled sub-editor fond of poetry was not quite the innocent lamb that he looked, and so he picked up tales in the bazaars and the barracks, and sedulously Bret-Hartened them, and pointed them with Poe; and then wrote them out, with infinite cunning, in a hand like an indifferent drawl. One of the most effective ways of out-Heroding Herod is to yawn wearily when the head is brought in. Mr Kipling's yawn was a masterpiece.

The stories were widely read in India and considered clever but ephemeral. The *Plain Tales*, containing many vicious side-kicks at real people, were sure of a ready audience, but the subjects were so familiar to Anglo-Indians that the true technical brilliance and colour of the stories were not recognized. In England, remote from these scenes, it was quickly perceived that a new master had arisen. He, like Pierre Loti, had made his countrymen see a new world; a continent which before had been a boring abstraction became an enchanted land full of wonders and magic. Such pioneers as Kipling and Loti 'have, at least, seen new worlds for themselves; have gone out of the streets of the overpopulated lands into the open air; have sailed and ridden, walked and hunted; have escaped from the fog and smoke of towns. New strength has come from fresher air into their brains and blood; hence the novelty and buoyancy of the tales they tell.'[12]

The side upon which Kipling most roused English curiosity and sympathy was in his description of the soldier's life in India. A large body of Englishmen was being constantly drafted out to the East on active service. Something was known of life in the officers' Mess, but of that of the other ranks in this strange sun-baked country, of their vices and virtues, and sweltering barrack-room existence, the English public knew nothing; and although Kipling, as we have seen, over-idolizes the subaltern and sentimentalizes the private, he has left us an unforgettable picture of the old enlisted Army in India as it existed in his day. Nor can there be any doubt as to his profound sympathy with the private soldier and the horrible rigours of his existence, so largely dependent on indigenous resources, which he did much to improve.

The main weakness of these stories – *Soldiers Three* and the other Mulvaney tales – is, as already mentioned, that of putting in the mouths of his characters remarks that they could not possibly have made. A good example of this occurs in *Only a Subaltern* when Private Conklin makes an opprobrious remark to another soldier about his officer:

'Ho!', said Private Conklin. 'There's another bloomin' orf'cer da-ed.'
The bucket shot from under him, and his eyes filled with a smithyful of sparks. A tall man in a blue-grey bed-gown was regarding him with deep disfavour.
'You ought to take shame for yourself, Conk! Orf'cer, – Bloomin' orf'cer? I'll learn you to misname the likes of 'im. Hangel! Bloomin' hangel! That's wot 'e is!'

This preposterous sentence in the mouth of a private soldier is syn-thetic and embarrassing, but in extenuation we must remember that Kipling was a very young man when he wrote these stories and it would be grossly unfair to dwell upon these errors of taste if they had been more quickly eliminated from his art. Such a lapse as this lingers jarringly in the mind like an unresolved discord.

Nevertheless Mulvaney, Learoyd and Ortheris are memorable figures, and they quickly gathered an enormous circle of admirers in such stories as *The Big Drunk Draf*, *The Madness of Private Ortheris* and *The Taking of Lungtunpen*.

We see [said Gosse] the ignorant and raw English youth transplanted, at the very moment when his instincts began to develop, into a country where he is divided from everything which can remind him of home, where by noon and night, in the bazaar, in the barracks, in the flowing scrub jungle, in the ferny defiles of the hills, everything he sees and hears and smells and feels produces on him an unfamiliar and unwelcome impression! All around is the infinite waste of India, obscure, monotonous, immense, inhabited by black men and pariah dogs, Pathans, and green parrots, kites and crocodiles, and long solitudes of high grass. No writer had ever revealed all this to the British public before Kipling.

When we turn over the pages of *Plain Tales from the Hills* we are struck by the technical efficiency of these stories. Constantly disfigured as they are by the faults we have noticed, many of them are yet models of their kind, and it is one of the curiosities of literature that these little masterpieces were tossed casually each week into the columns of an Anglo-Indian journal by an overworked boy of twenty. He has already the power of the instantaneous snapshotting of a situation. In *Cupid's Arrows* the ugly Commissioner Barr-Saggot arranges an archery competition which will clearly be won by the girl of his choice, beautiful Miss Beighton, who is the best lady archer in Simla but who loves an impoverished young officer. She deliberately shoots at the target's legs and loses: 'Barr-Saggot looked as if the last few arrow-heads had been driven into his legs instead of the target's, and the deep stillness was broken by a little snubby, mottled, half-grown girl saying in a shrill voice of triumph: "Then *I've* won!"' One can almost see the episode.

The story of the Gadsbys shows the youthful Kipling at his two extremes. It contains the collector's piece of vulgarity by Miss D. that 'being kissed by a man who didn't wax his moustache was like eating an egg without salt' – but it also contains the conversation in the *Tents of Kedar*, and the pathos of the bride's delirium in the *Valley of the Shadow*, which moved Andrew Lang more strongly than the deathbeds of Little Dombey and Little Nell.

By general consent the stories of Indian society are the least effective of the early Kipling, yet they too have a strong interest for some of us today. They reflect Simla society in the 1880s with probably a far greater fidelity then the Mulvaney stories reflect the other ranks in the Army, because here Kipling was satirizing rather than romanticizing.

A grim but authentic picture is unrolled before our eyes, of balls and routs, and dated slang, of callow subalterns trotting beside the rickshaw wheels of faded provincial vampires, of picnics on ponies, of line officers showing off in the gymkhanas before the coy daughters of officials – all the snobberies and petty allegiances of a small second-rate society are petrified as in a stop-camera shot. This, we feel, has the authentic ring – for Kipling is describing it all with detached scorn. The scene is shot with contortions of envy and tragedy – tragedy because Kipling had fought his own way in the world and felt contempt for the sheltered life, and usually conducted its victims to a disastrous end in his early stories. There is a memorable suicide in *Thrown Away* – a grim scene even in Kipling's forbidding repertoire – when the Major and his friend try to find a lock of hair fit to send back to the boy's mother and are forced, in the end, to send a lock of the Major's.

In the groups of stories *The Phantom Rickshaw* and *Wee Willie Winkie*, we see a new and maturer Kipling emerging. The old faults are still there, now with almost perplexing stubborness, but the genius is hardening and the author is touching his instrument with surer fingers. These two books contain three of Kipling's finest stories, *The Strange Ride of Morrowby Jukes*, *The Man Who Would be King* and *The Drums of the Fore and Aft*. Had Kipling died at this point and written nothing else, these three stories might well have snatched his name from oblivion.

In *The Strange Ride of Morrowby Jukes*, a civil engineer with fever rides by accident into a ghastly bunker in the desert, a city of the living dead, from which he cannot escape up the walls of shifting sand. Life in this horrible settlement is described with brilliant skill and with a horror reminiscent of Poe. *The Man Who Would be King*, a longer and better work, was described by H. G. Wells as one of the finest stories in the world.

Kipling wrote many other admirable tales at this period, some of which deserve reference. *The Gate of the Hundred Sorrows* is a realistic version of *The English Opium Eater*, and *The Return of Imray* is another essay in the macabre. There are also the stories that deal, always from Kipling's political angle, with the fusion between Asiatic and European blood – *Namgay Doola*, story of the red-headed son of an Irish soldier and a Tibetan mother, and *His Chance in Life*, where Michel D'Cruz, the black telegraph signaller with what Kipling regarded as the saving dash of white in him, quells a riot – a story in which the author indulges his favourite theme of the relapse of the converted native. The sketch of Indian life, *On the City Wall*, came as a revelation to English readers, bringing to them again the fruits of Kipling's minute observation, his acute vision, and his easy confidence in his extraordinary powers.

Although it does not properly come within the survey of these early stories, *Without Benefit of Clergy* should be mentioned here, as it is

a startling correction of the accusations of cheap cynicism, heartless-
ness and brutality made against the author. It will stand for a long
time to vindicate that side of Kipling's character as a boy which has
most frequently been assailed.

It is a story of an Indian woman, the 'uncovenanted wife' of an
English civilian and mother of his son, a story which gave the middle-
aged critical admirers of his youth a sudden thrilling belief that there
were deeper things in store. It is easy to sympathize with Maurice Baring when, as an old man, he described a certain passage in this story
as containing the most beautiful words that Kipling every wrote.[13]
We have usually looked in vain among Kipling's dazzling talents for
signs of tenderness and compassion. Here, perhaps for the first time,
he himself is deeply moved as he describes the scene when Holden
and his Indian wife count the stars on the flat roof of their house during
their brief, happy honeymoon:

> Ameera climbed the narrow staircase that led to the flat roof. The child,
> placid and unwinking, lay in the hollow of her right arm, gorgeous in silver-
> fringed muslin with a small skull-cap on his head. Ameera wore all that she
> valued most. The diamond nose-stud that takes the place of the Western
> patch in drawing attention to the curve of the nostril, the gold ornament
> in the centre of the forehead studded with tallow-drop emeralds and flawed
> rubies, the heavy circlet of beaten gold that was fastened round her neck
> by the softness of the pure metal, and the clinking curb-patterned silver ank-
> lets hanging low over the ankle-bone. She was dressed in jade-green muslin
> as befitted a daughter of the Faith, and shoulder to elbow and elbow to wrist
> ran bracelets of silver tied with floss silk, frail glass bangles slipped over the
> wrist in proof of the slenderness of the hand, and certain heavy gold bracelets
> that had no part in her country's ornaments, but since they were Holden's
> gift and fastened with a cunning European snap, delighted her immensely.

And there was also the wonderful rhyme of *Are Koko, Jare Koko!*,
Ameera's lullaby to the child, which says:

> Come, crow! Go crow! Baby's sleeping sound,
> And the wild plums grow in the jungle, only a penny a pound.
> Only a penny a pound, baba, only a penny a pound.

But this beautiful achievement lay in the future. Now, armed with
his Railway Library books, Kipling came to London in October 1889.

CHAPTER VIII
LONDON OVERTURE

RUDYARD KIPLING soon found that the literary world of London,
which he intended to make his oyster, contained many different
schools and trends of thought. One of these, the Aesthetic Movement,
although its importance has been exaggerated, was in violent contrast
to all the values which Kipling had so far acquired, and, fresh from
doing a man's work in India, it is not surprising that he regarded it
with derision and contempt. In his attitude towards the decadent
school, his own limitations, educational background, and middle-
class prejudices are clearly revealed, and his feelings were perfectly
mirrored in the lines he wrote a few weeks following his arrival in
London, after an encounter with some of the despised 'intellectuals':

> It's Oh to meet an Army man,
>   Set up, and trimmed and taut,
> Who does not spout hashed libraries
>   Or think the next man's thought,
> And walked as though he owned himself,
>   And hogs his bristles short.

The Aesthetic Movement derived its impetus from France and
was inspired by such works of revolt as *Mademoiselle de Maupin*,
written by a Gautier disgusted by the mediocrity of the staid middle
class which had survived the butchery of the Revolution and the win-
nowing of the Napoleonic wars. It was a book designed '*pour épater
les bourgeois*'. It sounded the watchword and led the attack on the
new intellectual class, bringing a message of the dissolution of the
bonds of obligation and a belief that all passions and excesses were
justified in the creation of beauty. The artist in France in this society
was drawn into an aimless vagrant existence, despised by the settled
order, and reduced to a condition of anarchy and intellectual revolt.
This new contempt for conventional morality attained its lapidary
perfection in the *Fleurs du Mal*, in Baudelaire's satanism, in his pursuit

of self-destruction – the '*affreuses Juives*', and the naked mulatto woman, stretching herself in animal repose before the fire in his dark garret, which '*inondait de sang cette peau couleur d'ambre*'.

This pursuit of a *beauté maudite*, which was to influence some of Kipling's contemporaries so strongly, and to fill him with irritation and contempt, was carried a stage further by Verlaine and Rimbaud. These two strange children of genius screwed the cult of decadence to the topmost peg, and the mere fact of that genius appeared incredible to the smug Victorian world, 'ripening from precedent to precedent' – Verlaine sodden with drink and crawling with vermin, cadging from prostitutes and 'reeling between the Confessional and the lupanar'. The symbolist poets of Paris strongly influenced the London aesthetes. Arthur Symons came under the spell of Baudelaire, and Dowson was influenced by the '*Fêtes Galantes*' in his little bird-flights of passion.

'I love this word decadence,' wrote Verlaine almost with ecstasy. 'It is redolent of the rouge of courtesans, the games of the circus, the panting of the gladiator, the spring of wild beasts, the consuming in flames of races by their capacity for sensation.'

This doctrine had already crossed the Channel when Kipling arrived in London, and a group of men had come together who met at the Cheshire Cheese, with its sanded floor, pewter and churchwarden pipes, and at the Domino Room of the Café Royal, in an attempt to reproduce the French café life. They sought their inspiration in the London scenes, Symons writing of abandoned pillows scented with white heliotrope, and of rising from the arms of a lover as the grey dawn broke over the London chimney pots; Dowson gaping at a foreign girl in a café, and lashing himself into the agony of 'Cynara', the cadences of which still fall upon the ear melancholy with blighted promise in lines now dead and nostalgic as pressed flowers, and faded as an early-Victorian keepsake.

Crakanthorpe, Davidson, De Tabley and Wretislaw, and the frail and scholarly Lionel Johnson were also prominent members of this group. In Dowson are to be found all the attributes of the decadent school: the rotting lungs, the violent alternation of polar extremes of emotion, the pathetic frame, enfeebled by absinthe, too weak to house the energies within, the rat-infested wharf on the river front where he lived for a while alone, the meals in cabmen's shelters. The Second Empire atmosphere of the Café Royal well suited these men. There is an agreeable appropriateness about the red plush, the dominoes rattling on the marble-topped tables, in the mirrors and gilt cornices and the smell of cheroots. It was neutral territory which they could frequent without incongruity after the cabman's shelter and the dockside, and derive from it the same excitement as Toulouse-Lautrec found in the brothels of Montmartre, or Verlaine in the stews by the Seine.

Kipling found many other literary activities, besides this small band which he viewed with such distaste. High above *The Yellow Book* towered the twin peaks of Hardy and of Meredith, who would hum arias from Italian opera as he walked in his garden under Box Hill, but in an age singularly rich in literature there were also writing Stevenson, George Moore with his 'curiously blond face, very long and solemn and white, like a dripping candle', Conrad, Henry James, W. E. Henley, Yeats and Shaw. Matthew Arnold was still there, and Browning, his work becoming even more obscure and involuted. Newman's beautiful waning figure still adorned the Edgbaston Oratory, and Manning was still at Westminster. William Morris, 'Uncle Topsy' of 'The Grange', was making exquisite books at Kelmscott, selling wallpapers in Oxford Street and, with less success, Socialism to uncaring mobs in Trafalgar Square. Walter Pater, that strange don whose book on the Renaissance had so profoundly affected the Aesthetic Movement, was to extend that influence steadily as the 1890s unfolded.

Swinburne had begun his antiseptic imprisonment with Watts Dunton in a hideous yellow house at the foot of Putney Hill, which saved his body but stunted his genius. Barrie was in London and described his life with placid felicity in *The Greenwood Hat*. Ruskin, on whose road at Hinksey the undergraduate Oscar Wilde had briefly laboured, was there too, but he was to die in 1900, his massive intellect in pathetic decay, and filling those who loved him with embarrassment and grief.

Whistler, 'the Butterfly', had but recently left his famous peacock room in Chelsea, ruined financially by his litigation against Ruskin, but indulging in frequent and ferocious sorties from a temporary oblivion. Many of the Pre-Raphaelites were still alive, and most of the great Victorians were still enthroned, for, besides Ruskin at Brantwood, there was Herbert Spencer in Brighton and Tennyson in Haslemere or the Isle of Wight – 'The Master's yonder in the Isle,' said Andrew Lang with contemporary reverence. Besides these, Francis Thompson had written *The Hound of Heaven* in squalor and suffering; and the incomparable Max Beerbohm, who was stung into wounding controversy by Kipling alone, was weaving his delicate fantasies.

But the two boys, Kipling, and Aubrey Beardsley with his face like 'a silver axe with green hair', were perhaps the portents of the age, and sharply divided the schools of realism and aestheticism. Beardsley had left his dreary Guardian Insurance office, his mind haunted by Flaubert and Gautier, and quickly shaking off the early influence of Burne-Jones had arrived at his astonishing maturity in the designs for *The Rape of the Lock* and Aristophanes's *Lysistrata* with its strange figures unerringly drawn with superb line – the *loupeuses insatiables*, glowing with malignant life.

'It was an inner existence,' it was said, 'that Beardsley had put down on paper, of sexual images and fantastic literary reveries. He had a sort of innocent familiarity with evil; he communed with the leering dwarfs, the bloated figures that peopled the depraved landscapes and grotesque interiors designed by his pen, as a child might talk with fairies.'[1]

Like Des Esseintes, the hero of Huysman's *A Rebours*, he worked in a shuttered room by candlelight, the candles in two tall ormolu Empire candlesticks. His fame grew when he extended his creative talent to literature as well as art and produced his unfinished erotic masterpiece *Under the Hill*. This stricken prodigy was to die at the age of twenty-five, his name indelibly printed upon the age, his lungs eaten away by consumption, a convert to the Roman Catholic Church, scribbling desperately *in articulo mortis* to his publisher Leonard Smithers:

> I implore you to destroy all copies of *Lysistrata* and bawdy drawings. By all that is holy, all obscene drawings.
>
> AUBREY BEARDSLEY
> – in my death agony.

There was another figure, even more notable, in that literary scene upon whom Rudyard's eyes dwelled with instinctive repulsion. Oscar Wilde was still reckless and triumphant, but his secret graph was already describing a downward trajectory. He had become physically and morally coarsened by success, and was entering a world of illusion. His features had sagged through prolonged indulgence, and an ugly condition of *hubris* had supplanted his natural amiability. That swift epicene wit still enraptures today, and he has come, perhaps wrongly, to symbolize the *fin de siècle*. When most people consider the nineties it is to Wilde that their thoughts turn; Wilde with his silver tongue holding the dinner tables of the great in effortless thrall, Wilde in his astrakhan coat at Willis's, the green scarab ring, the ortolans, the hansoms rattling between Tite Street and the Savoy, the spring-like beauty of Alfred Douglas, the feline excursions after dark down Little College Street.

It is a career that moves to its close with the accumulating horror
of a Greek tragedy, and the central figure is invested with a sure
immortality by the drawn-out years of his imprisonment and the squalid agony of his lonely death. The impression he produced upon his
contemporaries was often far less pronounced, and it is surprising to
read today the words of Quiller Couch: 'Never, either then or later
in London, did I meet with anyone who held Wilde to be a writer
of importance. The legend of his influence in the nineties, though one
has watched it growing, is to men of my age a purely incredible myth.'

When Oscar Wilde fell the Aesthetic Movement fell with him, and
this uncontemplated destruction laid clear the path for such a writer
as Kipling:

> It caused a wholesale literary and social fumigation. An exaggerated
> robustness was one of the consequences. Poets, no longer velvet-collared,
> absinthe-sipping, were now a hearty and virile race, tweed-clad, pipe-smok-
> ing, beer-drinking, Sussex-Downs tramping. They broke into rousing
> choruses, discarded subtlety for a cheery lilt, and proclaimed that Philistines
> could also sing.[2]

The rout of Aestheticism was complete. Even Beardsley deserted
Wilde, whom he had never liked and whose *Salome* he considered
memorable only for his own illustrations, and caused Wilde to mutter
bitterly in his decline: 'It was *lâche* of Aubrey, a boy I made.'

Between Kipling and such a man as Wilde and his school there could
be no common ground. Rumours about Wilde were current in London
and if Kipling heard them must have stimulated his horror of homo-
sexuals. He did not understand the decadent school. Had he been more
sophisticated and experienced, this would have been to his discredit,
but as it was, his upbringing and character made it impossible for him
to view it with anything but a mixture of amusement and disgust. At
best it appeared to him silly, at worst revolting, and his own sudden
rise to a different kind of fame was soon to cut into it with a cauterizing
slash.

He had also been prepared unfavourably by a letter written to him
by Trix from London seven years before, when he was in India:

> 26, Warwick Gardens,
> March 18. 1882.
> ... This has been a specially amusing week, for I went to The Grange for
> half-term holiday – and Phil's* new adoration, Oscar Wilde, was there – only
> at Supper luckily, for he is a dish I love not, and I don't think you would

* Philip Burne–Jones.

either. To look at he is like a bad copy of a bust of a very decadent Roman Emperor, roughly modelled in suet pudding. I sat opposite him and could not make out what his lips reminded me of – they are exactly like the big brown slugs we used to hate so in the garden at Forlorn Lodge. He has a pleasant voice spoiled by a very affected manner – and his black bow-tie – the floppy sort – would have made a good sash for me. He talked incessantly, and at any pause Phil, who sat next to him, gasped: 'Oscar, tell us so & so', and set him off again. He hardly seemed to look at Margaret who was as white and beautiful as a fairy tale, and took very little notice of Aunt Georgie. Uncle Ned* was unusually silent, and winced, I think, when Oscar addressed him as 'Master'.[3]

Kipling had sailed from New York to England on the steamship *City of Berlin* on 22 September 1889, arriving in London about the first of October:

What can be more romantic than the arrival of a young man of genius to make good a reputation which had already preceded him but had excited almost as much distrust in authoritative quarters as astonished admiration? Another interesting thing is the angle at which he inserted himself into the London literary world and the aloofness he maintained from it. Although the 'Art for Art's sake' writers regarded him as a Philistine (Henry James used to refer to him as 'that little demon of genius') and as the enemy of their movement, yet, essentially, his passion for craftsmanship united him to them.[4]

It was not, however, an entirely unknown youth who was assaulting London. He had already reacted with delight in June 1889 when there appeared in Tacoma, Washington, a review in the *Spectator* of *Soldiers Three*, 'a splendid review', with long extracts from the speech of Mulvaney; and in September 1889 two more in the *World* and the *St James's Gazette*: 'Neither the *World* nor the *St James's* are moved to speak lightly – and yet you see what either says. Give us your congratulations, and not to me the praise.'[5]

Among the first to interest himself in Kipling was Andrew Lang, who took him to the Savile Club a few days after his arrival and advised the firm Sampson Low to publish the six volumes in the Indian Railway Library. Kipling, for the first and only time in his life, conducted the negotiations and made a sorry hash of the matter. The first volume, *Soldiers Three*, was published in 1890, bringing Kipling's stories for the first time to the notice of the English public. Two other early mentors were journalists he had known in India, now returned

---

* Edward Burne-Jones.

to London: Mowbray Morris, once art editor of the *Pioneer* and now editor of *Macmillan's Magazine*, and his old chief, Stephen Wheeler, the 'amber toad' of the old days on the *Civil and Military* and now on the staff of the *St James's Gazette*. As early as November 1889 Kipling was contributing to the *St James's Gazette* stories, poems and plays, and in December the superb *Ballad of East and West* was published in *Macmillan's Magazine*, and his brilliant ability was at once apparent to all.

He had resumed his childhood friendship with 'the three old ladies', now approaching the end of their lives, and had not forgotten Aunt Georgie. While looking for somewhere to live he had stayed at 'The Grange', North End Road, of blessed memory, and again rung the bell which had summoned him to brief felicity from 'Lorne Lodge'. When visiting the Hills at Beaver he had, as we have seen, transferred his volatile affections to Mrs Hill's younger sister, Caroline Taylor. During those early years in London there can be found in his letters the debris of yet another of his shallow love affairs which had even less substance and meaning than those which had gone before it.

Before long he had found a place to live. He installed himself in a dingy set of rooms in Villiers Street, Strand, on the third storey, overlooking the Thames. In those days it was a grim and primitive neighbourhood, and he described how he watched a man cutting his throat on the pavement outside:

> Once I faced the reflection of my own face in the jet-black mirror of the window-panes for five days. When the fog thinned, I looked out and saw a man standing opposite the pub where the barmaid lived: on a sudden his breast turned dull red like a robin's, and he crumpled, having cut his throat. ... A pot boy with a bucket of steaming water sluiced the blood off into the gutter, and what little crowd had collected went its way.[6]

Looking out of his window he could see through the fanlight of Gatti's Music-Hall entrance, almost to the stage. One one side he heard the whistling and clanking of the Charing Cross trains, and could see the switch-boxes lit up with yellow gas, on the other the traffic of the Strand. One of his windows looked over the Embankment Gardens, gay with crocuses in spring, and beyond he could see Cleopatra's Needle and the grey barge-thronged river. Further in the distance lay Waterloo Bridge, and the dome of St Paul's superb against a flushed horizon at sunset. The rooms were always untidy, littered with papers, manuscripts and tobacco ash, with a waste-paper basket full to overflowing. On the door of the entry was pasted a notice: 'To Publishers: A classic while you wait!'[7]

The two small rooms were connected by a tiny hall. The workroom was spread with Persian rugs and ancient prayer- carpets, and papered in a dull green and gold which had become dim with smoke. A tall Japanese screen, with a design of dancing skeletons, stood between two windows, and there was a large poshteen rug on the sofa, bordered by astrakhan and embroidered in yellow silks. On the walls were pictures of military subjects; above the mantelpiece a new magazine rifle and a box of black Indian cheroots; on the sideboard a mighty tobacco jar, and above it a rack of pipes and a map of Afghanistan. Littered round the room were old *Illustrateds* of the Mutiny and the Crimea, and a bundle of fishing rods in the corner.

In this room Kipling toiled with intense concentration by gaslight in his working clothes, a loose dark suit, buttoned high to the throat like a workman's blouse, and a tassel-less scarlet fez which he had the habit of thrusting backward. He suffered from bouts of depression. 'There are five million people in London this night, and saving those who starve, I don't think there is one more heartsick or thoroughly wretched than that "rising young author" known to you as: Ruddy.'

He sometimes varied his working dress by a Japanese dressing gown and monkey-skin slippers. He spent many afternoons with Aunt Georgie, and dined in the restaurants lining the Strand. 'Never was life so utterly isolated. I must confess I enjoy it, 'tho there are times when I feel utterly lonely. But then I can watch the fire, and weave tales, and dream dreams.'

On his arrival in England there was no need for him to hurl defiance at the capital and swear to conquer it like Rastignac from the Heights of Montmartre. He was soon besieged by editors and steadily over-worked on an average ten hours out of the twenty-four, his best time being at night when he sat up till two or three, writing to the sound of the traffic below, only stopping when the pulse of London ceased at last to beat. The very silence, he said, that fell discomposed his thoughts, as the stopping of the screw of a ship will awaken one at sea. He had no fear of writing himself out, and his head teemed with plots and rhythms. Rather was his greatest fear that of losing his head from praise, and committing some literary folly in consequence. He had not come to England, he said, to write himself out at first starting. He intended to go slowly and to do sufficient magazine work to get along comfortably while he turned his attention to the novels and the books. 'A man can fritter himself away on piece-work, and be only but a very little the richer for it. Whereas, if he holds his hand, the money, and what is of more importance, the power of doing fresh and original work comes to him.'

He wrote at a large businesslike desk between the two windows overlooking the life ebbing and flowing between the Strand and Charing Cross station. We find indications of the life Kipling led in Villiers Street in *The Light that Failed*, when Dick Heldar:

... leaned into the darkness, watching the greater darkness of London below him. The Chambers stood much higher than the other houses, commanding a hundred chimneys – crooked cowls that looked like sitting cats as they swung round.... Northwards the lights of Piccadilly Circus and Leicester Square threw a copper-coloured glare above the black roofs, and southward lay all the orderly lights of the Thames. A train rolled out across one of the railway bridges, and its thunder drowned for a minute the dull roar of the streets.

Kipling had come to London with only £200, and in spite of his success quickly ran out of money. He found himself with certain sums owing to him, but no available cash, and rather than borrow from his aunt or one of the three old ladies, thus admitting failure at the outset, put himself on a strict regime of economy. Below his rooms, he tells us, was the

establishment of Harris the Sausage King, who for tuppence gave as much sausage and mash as would carry one from breakfast to dinner.... Another tuppence found me a filling supper. The excellent tobacco of those days was, unless you sank to threepenny shag or soared to sixpenny 'Turkish', tuppence the half ounce: and fourpence, which included a pewter of beer or porter, was the price of admission to Gatti's.[8]

Here, in the company of an 'elderly but upright barmaid', he listened to the songs of the Lion and Mammoth Comiques, and he loved the smoke and the din and the vulgar good fellowship of the dingy old music-hall, while his ever-inquisitive mind mopped up impressions as he gossiped with the barmaid while she wiped off the zinc. There is no evidence that he led anything but a sober and careful life during this period, in spite of his fondness in later years of narrowly interrogating young men about the details of their amorous adventures, although he sometimes exchanged platonic banter with the prostitutes who frequented the neighbourhood.

In spite of hard work, Kipling was, as we have seen, often lonely in these rooms. London was strange to him and a trifle alarming. Sometimes, he said, he felt like a hermit crab. His main refuge from loneliness was with his relations: Aunt Georgie and Edward Burne-

Jones; their son Philip, a rising painter; Aunt Aggie Poynter and her son Ambrose, a writer *manqué* who would read his unmarketable poetry to Rudyard until the small hours; Aunt Edie Macdonald, to whom he had so often written from India; his cousin Margaret, now Mrs Mackail, who had raked under his bed to dispel the terrors of childhood, and a new cousin, Hugh Poynter.

Kipling had been elected a member of the Savile Club in 1890, and his sponsors included some of the best-known literary men of the day. But he regarded famous men of letters with profound suspicion mingled with a terror of patronage, and was often at his arrogant worst when confronting them. It was a point of honour to him not to be impressed by the great. When John Addington Symonds wrote to him: 'Thank you for feeding me on the wine and bread of the word', Kipling sardonically endorsed the letter: 'Does he mean *Soldiers Three*?'; and a maddening invitation from Grant Allen starting: 'Dear young chap of genius, come and cut your mutton with us sometime', failed to receive an answer.[9]

Of Sidney Colvin he wrote contemptuously: 'The same is an all-fired prig of immense water, and suffers from all the nervo-hysterical diseases of the 19th Century. Went home with him as far as Charing Cross in a 3rd smoking which made him sick. He recounted all his symptoms, and made me sick. A queer beast with matchstick fingers and a dry unwholesome skin.'[10] Of John Addington Symonds he had added: 'He's a sugary Johnnie, but I fancy I see his tender fist in some of the reviews of my performances.'

His account of a visit to George Meredith at Box Hill is a good example of his insolent attitude towards the leaders of his own profession, and of the uneasy Westward Ho! aggressiveness that affronted so many who met the young Kipling. Instead of expressing gratitude for the opportunity of meeting a great Victorian novelist, he wrote:

Show me no more celebrities for they disillusion me sadly. Imagine an old withered little man very deaf in one ear who, as did Dragonet in the *Morte d'Arthur*,
        'skips like a withered leaf upon the floor'.
He is full to a painful overflowing of elaborated epigrammatic speech which on the first fizz strikes one as deuced good. Five minutes later one cannot remember what on earth it was all about. And neither time, tide, Heaven nor Hell, nor the sanctities of five o'clock tea seem to be able to stop that flow of talk. The raucous voice continues; the little old man balances himself on his toes like a Shanghai rooster to command attention, and that attention *must* be given or he sulks like a child.

And Kipling added loftily: 'I don't want to see him any more.'

After the 'House of Desolation', the drab schooldays, and his seven years' drudgery in India, Kipling passionately wished 'to own himself', to be independent of the patronage and control of others. He was later to cut adrift from Henley for the same reason. He said to his sister after W. E. Henley had begun to refer to him patronizingly as 'one of my young men': 'Henley is a great man; he is also a cripple, but he is not going to come the bullying cripple over me, after I have been in harness all these years.'

Kipling was reticent as to his religious beliefs and the only detailed reference to them in his papers at this period is of particular interest. Kipling believed at this time in the existence of a personal God to whom man is personally responsible for wrong-doing – that it was man's duty to follow, and his peril to disobey, the ten ethical laws. He disbelieved directly in eternal punishment, on the same grounds as he disbelieved in an eternal reward. He regarded the mystery of the Trinity and the Doctrine of Redemption 'most reverently', but could not give them implicit belief, accepting them rather as a dogma of the Church than as matters that rush to the heart. He summarized his beliefs by saying that he believed in God the Father Almighty, maker of Heaven and Earth, and in one filled with His spirit, who voluntarily died in the belief that the human race would be spiritually better thereby. He believed, after having seen and studied eight or nine creeds, in Justification by works rather than faith, and in retribution for wrong-doing, as he believed in a reward, here and hereafter, for obedience to the law.

This solitary confession was made to Caroline Taylor, the daughter of a minister of Puritanical tendencies, who seemed to suspect that her friend Rudyard was sliding towards conversion to the Roman Catholic Church. It was one of the few sincere passages in these stylized effusions, and concluded: 'There! You have got from me what no living soul has ever done before.'

Kipling was, in those days, approachable. He had not yet developed that hatred of reporters which caused such offence in later years, and willingly gave a number of long interviews to the press. He met many leading editors, among them Frank Harris, whom he described as 'the one human being I could on no terms get on with'.

Harris, although a congenital liar, was sometimes shrewd in his judgements. He was personally attracted by Kipling, but found him 'intensely eager to get the most forcible or most picturesque, or most musical expression for his passionate prejudices; he was fair-minded too, in accepting any and every good suggestion or emendation, but he was not willing even to consider the opposite side of the question. His mind seemed closed to any argument.'[11]

There was a hint, too, of this positive conviction of rightness on certain subjects, of a reluctance to argue, in his interview with the reporter of *The World*, who wrote: 'On all that concerns India, the land of his birth, he feels very strongly, and speaks with a calm assurance of knowledge, as you listen to his "I have seen", or "Here I know", that drives home an indictment of the ends and methods of the National Congress.'[12]

Harris was astonished by Kipling's powers of narrative, oral as well as written. As they were sitting together in Villiers Street, Kipling, smoking a pipe on his bed, began to describe to Harris how he had witnessed a series of wild beast fights staged by an Indian Prince. He described the fight between a tiger and a buffalo with extraordinary pictorial intensity:

You saw the great cat flattened out on the arena while the buffalo with lowered head and side-long eyes moved nearer and nearer. Suddenly the flaming beast shot through the air but was met firmly by the buffalo's iron front and horns, and flung bodily yards away to the side and rear; like a flash it sprang again, and again was met and thrown. At once it fled to the wooden wall, and began to lick its wounds. In spite of long red gashes on his head and neck the buffalo was always the aggressor; nearer and nearer he went; while the tiger drew itself together, every hair on end, and struck fiercely at his head with one paw laying the bone bare in long parallel slashes and ripping off part of the nose; the next moment the buffalo had nailed the tiger to the barrier with one horn and kept on butting and kneading the writhing beast against the wood until one heard the hooped ribs crack while the whole structure shook. The tiger bit and clawed as long as life lasted, and when finally the buffalo, bellowing with rage, drew off from the dead cat, his head was one dripping scarlet wound. He had to be shot.

By February 1890 Kipling wrote to Caroline Taylor explaining his financial position. His work for *Macmillan's Magazine* was bringing him in £300 a year, and to this could be added another £100 earned from other sources. Considering the tremendous impact he had made on London it seems a modest sum, but Kipling was as suspicious of publishers as of literary celebrities, and although being pursued by a number of them refused to close with their offers:

I reply with great sweetness, that my engagements are *complet*. Publishers are not used to being treated in this manner and they return to the charge like Jew hawkers with proffers of ready money down. See'st thou the drift of this? It is to make the new man write as swiftly and as largely as possible on the novel subject. Then when he is squeezed dry they heave him away and call the newspapers to witness that there is no originality in the present writers.

The eagerness of publishers to ensnare him must have been intensified when in March 1890 *The Times* paid Rudyard the extraordinary compliment of devoting the whole of its leading article to his work in the Calcutta editions. The article began:

India has given us an abundance of soldiers and administrators, but she has seldom given us a writer. There is no question, however, that she has done this in the person of the author of the numerous short stories and verses of which we give the titles below. Mr Kipling has the merit of having tapped a new vein, and of having worked it out with real originality. He is even now a very young man, in spite of his seven or eight small volumes.

To appreciate the full extent of Kipling's triumph we should remember that at the time this article was written he was only twenty-four.

An important influence now came into Kipling's life in the form of one of the most remarkable young Americans of his day, Wolcott Balestier, whose sister, Caroline, Kipling was later to marry, with fundamental effects upon his own character and work. Balestier's grandfather came originally from Martinique, but the family had long settled in Brattleboro, Vermont, a little New England town that was soon to be the scene of an agonizing episode in Rudyard's life. Wolcott's father, a lawyer of international fame, became legal adviser to the Mikado, and in this capacity was regarded by some as being 'practically Secretary of State for Japan'.[13] After a desultory education and a course in Early English at Cornell, and with three obscure books to his credit, Wolcott was sent to England in 1888 by John W. Lovell, the publisher, to represent his firm and open an office in London. He was twenty-seven with dark sharp-cut features and an air of eagerness and restless energy. The bloodless conquest of literary London by this unknown youth from New England is one of the most extraordinary events of the period. Like Kipling, he took London by storm, a city of which he knew nothing and in which he could turn to no single friend for assistance.

Balestier came to England with ambitious schemes of publishing in his head. Towards the close of the last century the long struggle for international copyright in the United States was coming to an end. It was now evident that British and foreign authors would soon be

protected by law from the piracy that had always disgusted the more
decent elements in the American publishing world. Even the pirates
themselves, after a particularly blatant robbery, would sometimes
send small sums of money to the despoiled author to ease their conscience.[14] Collaboration with an American citizen was the only
method by which an English author could secure copyright in the
United States.

Balestier had contrived two schemes by which this inequitable position could be adjusted. A novelist himself, he proposed to arrange
in England the collaboration of some established author, thus providing that author with the protection of American copyright. He also
proposed to offer English authors considerable advance payments
for the use of early sheets of their forthcoming books, and to issue
American editions simultaneously with their publication in England.

Thus he hoped to forestall the pirates and secure the best books,
calculating that when international copyright became a reality, the
authors would remain faithful to the House of Lovell. Balestier was
also to form a close association with a young publisher called William
Heinemann, a firm which soon became Heinemann & Balestier, and
was to set in motion the English Library, an association for the distri-
bution on the Continent of English and American books, in competition with Baron Tauchnitz. He established himself in a peaceful office
in Dean's Yard, Westminster.

Caroline did not at first accompany Wolcott to London. He brought
with him his younger and far prettier sister Josephine, who described
Wolcott's triumph to her mother in a series of letters breathless with
girlish excitement. Edmund Gosse was one of the first to go down
like a ninepin before the Balestier charm: 'Wolcott and Edmund call
each other by their Christian names. I don't think you and I ever realized what very dear friends they are. Have you seen the exquisite new
book by him? He sent it to Wolcott the other day with "Wolcott
Balestier from his affectionate friend the author", on the fly-leaf.'[15]

Henry James was soon equally in thrall, and was to write to Mrs
Balestier after Wolcott's premature death:

Your letter each year continues to be a kind and touching memento to
me, and gives me now my only occasion to *name* dear Wolcott articulately
and feel that I still hold on firmly, in the cold rush of time which makes
a wind as from the passage of an ice-flow, to the reality of his brief presence
here. His ghostly photograph is on the wall of my room and looks down
at me as I write you late at night in this silent sleeping little town – as with
a melancholy consciousness of what I am doing.[16]

Gosse described with equal fervour his first meeting with Balestier, and the 'thrill of attraction' that came to him when he contemplated that sharp and eager face, 'a mixture of suave Colonial French, and the strained nervous New England blood. After seeing him almost daily for almost three years I never could entirely lose the sense of capricious contrast between this wonderful intelligence ·and the unhelpful frame that did it so much wrong.'

This extraordinary magnetism, so evanescent, and now impossible to recapture, brought to Balestier as admiring friends such people as Kate Greenaway, Jean Ingelow, Austin Dobson, Alma Tadema, and the current best-selling novelist, Mrs Humphrey Ward. He visited Whistler in his house in Cheyne Walk, where the artist drew a butterfly for him in the fly-leaf of his book. 'Whistler', Josephine told her mother, 'was talking of his wife's never walking anywhere but in the garden, and said that for exercise she sat in the summer-house.'

The progress of the two invaders is recorded by Josephine with naive but engaging triumph: 'Mr Gosse came up to me and said "do let us go over to that corner and have a good talk" – but just at the most delightful point up walks Mrs Thomas Hardy'; and Wolcott walks through the correspondence, an eager ever-rushing figure in an Inverness Cape. 'I forgot to tell you that Wolcott spent last Sunday afternoon and evening with George Meredith. They talked about seven hours on a stretch.'[17]

The rest of the Balestier family soon followed to London to participate in these triumphs. Mrs Balestier was there, and her elder daughter Caroline, small, plain, businesslike and determined – 'a good man spoiled', as Lockwood Kipling rather spitefully called her, while Rudyard's mother with swift intuition said: 'That woman is going to marry our Ruddy', and showed a marked lack of eagerness for such a consummation. It is probable that Rudyard first met Caroline when, competent and managing as always, she had taken over the domestic arrangements at Dean's Yard, and had arrived one day to set them in order. The Balestiers were first accompanied to England by Caroline's raffish but irresistible brother Beatty, whom we shall see later playing a decisive and tragic role in Rudyard's life, but he left such a trail of havoc behind him in London that it was thought prudent to repatriate him to Vermont before some irremediable disaster overtook him.

Wolcott Balestier was soon on Kipling's trail. Edmund Gosse had been deeply impressed by *Soldiers Three*, and advised Balestier to watch Kipling's progress closely. 'Rudyard Kipling?' replied Balestier with elaborate indifference. 'Is it a man or a woman? What's its real name?' But three days later when Gosse entered the office in Dean's Yard he found a pile of Kipling's grey-blue Indian books on the desk, and from that moment Balestier set out to draw Kipling into his net.

Kipling put up a slightly longer struggle than the others against Balestier's formidable personality. There was a brief but definite pursuit, and Arthur Waugh described how Balestier sent him to Villiers Street with an urgent note, begging to have a glimpse of an unfinished story, *The Book of The Hundred Mornings*. Kipling was sitting in a darkened room on a bed littered with manuscripts. 'Extraordinarily importunate person, this Mr Balestier,' he complained. 'Tell him that *The Book of The Hundred Mornings* is all over my bed and may never get finished. Tell him to enquire again in six months.'[18]

But Kipling made only a token resistance, and in July 1890 Josephine wrote to her mother: 'After the authors' dinner the other night Wolcott and young Kipling talked until four in the morning. They are growing fast friends; they are very congenial, dove-tail finely. I think it rather picturesque that the two London literary infants should play so prettily together.' The intimate friendship that followed was to lead to an important publishing *coup* for Lovell and to the event decisive in the development of Kipling's character and work – his marriage to Caroline Balestier.

Although in the first year Kipling's days in London were often lonely and his recreations few, his spirits were much sustained by his friendship with Mrs W. K. Clifford, widow of William Kingdom Clifford, the scientist, who exercised on him the kind of influence he needed. Mrs Clifford was herself a writer, the author of many novels including *A Flash of Summer* and *Aunt Anne*, and of the isolated arresting phrase: 'A life so flat that you can see your own tombstone at the end of it.'[19]

Although she wrote herself for six hours a day, she was always anxious to help young writers. Mrs Belloc Lowndes remembered Mrs Clifford showing her the little green book of short stories which a friend had sent her from India. She was at once struck by Kipling's genius and was one of those who made great efforts to make his work known and appreciated at its true worth.

No doubt Mrs Clifford's support was useful to Kipling at the outset, although he cannot have needed this help for long as within a few months of his arrival he had become a literary lion. But he found her house a soothing refuge. There were two pretty daughters, and a kitten called Scuttles to whom Kipling gave a collar inscribed: 'My name is Scuttles. I live at 26 Colvin Road. Please take me home.'[20]

Mrs Clifford was able to introduce him to important figures in the literary world, editors and publishers, and later helped him to negotiate the dramatization of *The Light that Failed*. That she helped to set the door of London ajar for Kipling, enlarged his narrow outlook, and did something to diminish his social uncouthness, seems probable. There was much to be done in this direction. His manners were little better than they had been in India; his casualness, if anything, was worse. He seldom answered invitations, and Mrs Clifford was forced into a number of awkward and irritating apologies on his behalf. There was a painful moment in their association when Mrs Clifford, struck by a thought, suddenly asked him at dinner: 'But Ruddy, aren't you supposed to be dining with ——?' Kipling replied: 'Oh yes, but I sent them a wire.'

Mrs Clifford must have been impressed by the indifference with which Kipling spoke, and the episode must have lingered unpleasantly in her mind, causing her to warn him later: 'You mustn't do it, or one day you will send one to me'; and so, in the end, he did.[21]

His friendship with this charming woman was ruptured in a sudden and embarrassing manner. Mrs Clifford and Kipling were in the stalls of a theatre, and in a box sat Wolcott Balestier and his sisters Caroline and Josephine. Wolcott and Rudyard were at this time unknown to one another. Some remarks made on this occasion about Caroline, to whom Kipling later became engaged, made it impossible for him to see Mrs Clifford again. This misfortune caused her the greatest pain, and in Mrs Belloc Lowndes's recollection: 'Not long before she died, she told me that when she came across Mr Kipling, as was inevitable now and then, a sensation of such pain filled her heart that she had at once to leave the room where he happened to be.'[22]

CHAPTER IX

LONDON CONQUERED

By the year 1890, then, Kipling's reputation was assured. By February of that year he had begun his association with W. E. Henley on the *National Observer*. Henley was one of the less endearing giants of the day. Crippled and ill, he is now chiefly memorable for the poem written on what he believed to be his deathbed, with its concluding stanza:

> It matters not how strait the gate,
>   How charged with punishment the scroll,
> I am the Master of my fate,
>   I am the Captain of my soul.

The periodical had formerly been the *Scots Observer*, and was published weekly at Edinburgh from November 1888 to 1889. It was then transferred to London, and the name changed. Henley was one of those editors who knew everyone worth knowing in the literary London of the closing years of the century. His taste in letters was catholic, and he collected round him a group of writers of whom Stevenson, Yeats, Barrie and Kipling were the most notable, to which were later added Wells and Conrad. Henley's writers were men mostly of the Anglo-Saxon tradition, knit together by a strong *esprit de corps* and a tenacious loyalty to their editor, 'old Pan playing on his reed with his crippled hooves hiding amid the water-lilies of the purling stream'.

Some time in February 1890 Henley had received a package addressed in an unknown hand, containing a manuscript headed *Barrack Room Ballads. 1 Danny Deever*. Before finishing it, Henley was said to have flung himself about the room, stamping on his wooden leg and shouting in an ecstasy of delight. Later Henley's patron, Fitzroy Bell, and Herbert Stephen arranged to call on the author to discuss *Barrack Room Ballads*, and were surprised to find a *farouche* boy of twenty-four, who stood on the hearth rug with easy assurance and recited another of his ballads, 'Fuzzy Wuzzy'.

He told them that he had also written a slashing satire on the Liberal Party, the declared idealism of whose aims always filled him with anger and repulsion. The report of a special committee appointed to inquire into what Kipling described as 'some unusually blatant traffic in murder among the Irish Land Leaguers' had cleared the Irish leaders of complicity in the crimes. But Kipling was more concerned in flaying English Liberalism than with exposing Irish murder, and the real object of his satire was to castigate Gladstone for his humiliating dependence, like Asquith after him, upon the Irish vote in the House of Commons. It was a blistering document. Frank Harris was said actually to have set it up in type for the *Fortnightly* before losing his nerve. *The Times* regarded it as too dangerous to touch.

'Where is it now?' asked the visitors. 'In the waste-paper basket,' said Kipling, and picked it out. In this way it came about that in the *Scots Observer* of 8 March 1890 appeared not only 'Fuzzy Wuzzy', but also the flaming indictment 'Cleared!' In this poem can be found the almost pathological hatred of Liberalism, which was to fester and spread as Kipling grew older and his opinions petrified:

My soul! I'd sooner lie in jail for murder plain and straight,
Pure crime I'd done with my own hand for money, lust or hate
Than take a seat in Parliament by fellow-felons cheered,
While one of those 'not provens' proved me cleared as you are cleared.

The poem concluded bitterly:

We are not ruled by murderers, but only – by their friends.

The decision by Henley to risk publishing the poem, when others had drawn back, delighted Kipling, who afterwards wrote of him: 'Henley's demerits were, of course, explained to the world by loving friends after his death. I had the fortune to know him only as kind, generous, and a jewel of an editor with the gift of fetching the very best out of his cattle.' He further endeared himself to Kipling by 'an organic loathing of Mr Gladstone and all Liberalism'.

For Henley's eclecticism in literature did not extend to his politics. He was an Imperialist and Tory of the most inveterate character, and was only exceeded in these respects by his bibulous assistant Charles Whibley. It must have seemed to these two men as though political as well as literary manna had dropped from heaven when Kipling appeared upon the scene and was enticed into their fold.

The *Barrack Room Ballads* fell one by one upon a shocked but enraptured public. After that macabre masterpiece 'Danny Deever' came 'Tommy', 'Fuzzy Wuzzy', and 'Loot' in March; 'The Widow at Windsor' in April; 'Gunga Din' and 'Mandalay' in June. Their success was immediate but, with the exception of 'Danny Deever', these verses have now lost their magic. Most of them, to modern readers, represent that aspect of Kipling which is most ugly and repellent to their ears – the cocksureness, the vulgarity, the synthetic cockney accent. 'Loot' is a revolting little piece, and the undoubted charm of 'Mandalay' has been dulled by a thousand reproductions.

Some of these reactions were no doubt felt in 1890, but then with a delightful shock. Kipling was presenting to the public an entirely new *genre* of poetry, and his ballads fell upon them like a series of hammer-blows. Henley, who soon came down from Scotland to meet him, was entranced by their success and with his new author, and it seemed to some that Kipling filled the gap left by Henley's estrangement from Stevenson in the previous year. In the great Scottish writer Kipling found a literary master whom he could at last admire without reservation. He never had the good fortune to meet Stevenson, although they occasionally corresponded, but that his admiration was, for a time, reciprocated by the older man is apparent from a letter to Kipling which was treasured among his papers:

Terence Mulvaney, Esq.

Dear Sir,

Well and indeed Mr Mulvaney but it is as good as meat to meet you, Sir. They tell me it was a man of the name of Kipling made ye; it was the Lord God Almighty that made you and the best day's work that he ever did. So here is wishing you a long life and more power to your elbow, Sir.

Your obadjint
ROBERT LOUIS STEVENSON

Memorandum

'This umbrella purchased in the year 1878 by Robert Louis Stevenson and faithfully stabled for more than twelve years in the halls of George Saintsbury – is handed at the suggestion of the first and by the loyal hand of the second to Rudyard Kipling.'[1]

Kipling's natural delight in his success was considerably eroded by the depression and eyestrain brought on by overwork and by the emptiness of his private life. When Trix, who had married and now become Mrs Fleming, came to England at the beginning of 1890, one of her first acts was to climb the stairs to the workroom at Villiers Street. She was greatly disturbed by Rudyard's condition. He was ill and dejected, and apparently indifferent to his glittering progress. He told her, 'his face beginning to work', that his liaison with Caroline Taylor was over. It was yet another false dawn. Perhaps the rupture in this anaemic relationship was due to the fact that he had recently met Flo Garrard in the street by accident. In an instant that nagging mysterious infatuation had been reawakened, and had encountered the old coldness and indifference. His fame had struck no spark in her, and her only desire was to be left alone to her painting.

Again we are baffled by Kipling's emotional relations. They were protected by a profound and almost morbid reticence. When he refers to this subject in his letters, it is still buried, as in India, in the irritating jargon he adopted, that language Biblical, facetious, and sometimes coy, which revealed nothing of the heart beneath. These secret regions of his nature are left unexplored, and the mere thought of their candid discussion would have filled him with an almost physical disgust. We therefore cannot tell how severe a contribution unrequited love made to his present malaise, and may conjecture that the main cause of it lay in his fantastic labours.

But there can be no doubt that his depression existed, and for such a condition there was, for Kipling, only one certain cure. In India, at moments of exhaustion and despair, there had been a safe anchorage to which he could return to rest and recruit his strength. This was the happy family circle to which he could turn at times of stress with the certainty of affection and understanding. At this appropriate moment his mother and father arrived in London and established themselves in Kensington. Their presence had its usual therapeutic effect upon his spirits; he felt reinvigorated, and ready for further literary effort, and even went so far as to make one of his rare appearances as a 'Great Man', accompanying Lockwood on a visit to Westward Ho!, when a half-holiday was declared in his honour.

Eighteen ninety was an *annus mirabilis* for the young Kipling. It not only saw the appearance of *Barrack Room Ballads* and the reissue of many of his Indian books, it was also marked, as we shall see, by a series of new stories of supreme literary merit, far surpassing anything he had accomplished before. He was now contributing to periodicals such as *Harper's Monthly*, *Lippincott's Magazine* and *Macmillan's Magazine*, and in the opinion of Charles Morgan it was the influence of Mrs W. K. Clifford which first brought him to the House of Macmillan.

The new series of stories which so greatly enhanced his fame began in January with the publication of *The Head of the District*. On 1 March *The Courting of Dinah Shadd* appeared in *Macmillan's Magazine*, and later in *Harper's*. *The Man Who Was* followed it in April; *Without Benefit of Clergy* in June. The chilling and masterly Indian story *At the End of the Passage* appeared in *Lippincott's* in August, and another, equally macabre, *The Mark of the Beast*, was also published that summer for the first time in England. The only rotten apple in this teeming orchard was the novel *The Light that Failed*, apparently finished in August, but it was redeemed by one of Kipling's finest stories, *On Greenhow Hill*, which was published in September.

Reading these stories one feels that Kipling's touch upon his instrument was now that of a master. *Without Benefit of Clergy*, as we have seen, contains one of the most beautiful and tender passages that Kipling wrote during his whole literary career, when Holden and his native wife, Ameera, count the stars in the velvet Indian night on their brief and doomed honeymoon.

The Man Who Was, the story of an English officer in India, captured and tortured by the Russians, who crawls back by instinct to his own Mess, where a Russian officer is being entertained, is a masterpiece of sparse narration, vivid, faultless, and pared to the bone. In *At the End of the Passage* the terrors of hallucination in the Indian heat are brilliantly explored, and as a study in the macabre the story is the equal of that other classical tale of horror, *The Mark of the Beast*, which had produced such a feeling of scandalized agitation in the bosom of Andrew Lang. Beside these, many critics consider *The Courting of Dinah Shadd* to be one of Kipling's most perfect short stories.

In *On Greenhow Hill* the three soldiers, Mulvaney, Ortheris and Learoyd, are gossiping in the lull of an operation on the North-West Frontier, and Learoyd speaks of the memories of his Yorkshire boyhood. Here, again, Kipling is triumphant in recapturing atmosphere; the peaceful green valleys round Skipton, and the tragedy of Learoyd's passion for a dying woman, are in strident contrast to the harsh outcrops of rock and the whining bullets among which the story is unfolded.

Criticism was made of the accuracy of Learoyd's Yorkshire speech as compared to Mulvaney's Irish, which was frequently described as that of a stage Irishman, and the cockney words of Ortheris. In the latter cases Kipling can only have had comparatively few originals from whom to fashion his characters, for he had never been to Ireland, and his experience of London in youth had consisted of holidays from

Westward Ho! But he was on surer ground when handling the character of Learoyd. He always showed his manuscripts to Lockwood, who would pick on the Yorkshire phrases and say: 'No lad, this won't do', and tell him what a real Yorkshireman would have said. Indeed Trix believed that in this story Lockwood went much further than mere advice, and that such was Rudyard's confidence in his father's judgement that he allowed Lockwood to write the whole of *On Greenhow Hill*, except the somewhat bloodthirsty introduction and the conclusion, which, according to her, were Rudyard's sole contribution to this story.[2]

It is unnecessary to dwell on *The Light that Failed*, in which the hero, Dick Heldar, is overtaken by blindness. It need only be said that this work was largely autobiographical, that the 'House of Desolation' is closely described, and the character of Flo Garrard thinly disguised as 'Maisie'. This unsatisfactory and ill-knit book suggested to a discerning eye a fact that was afterwards confirmed by *Captains Courageous*, that the short story, not the novel, was Kipling's forte, and the less he ventured into this *genre* the better for his own reputation.

As it was, a shower of dangerous adulation descended upon him. Again an author had woken up to find himself famous, and his rise had been one of the swiftest and most spectacular in literary history. 'I hear that he is only twenty-four years old,' said the *Weekly Times*. 'Even if he were twice that age his talents would be remarkable; but as matters stand they look something akin to genius.' His fame spread to Australia, where the *South Australian Gazette* described him as 'the literary sensation of the day', and to America, where the *New York Mail and Express* inquired in a banner headline: 'Will success turn his head?'

There were a few discordant notes in an orchestra of praise, most of the adverse critics laying just emphasis on the debit side of Kipling's work, and the faults that were never wholly eradicated in maturity. They spoke of that incorrigible vulgarity that was to be such a clinging companion to Kipling's genius. The *Pall Mall Gazette* expressed the opinion that 'the phonetic dialects with which Mr Kipling essays to show us the very form and presence of Tommy Atkins are as bad a bore as the nigger jokes of the American comic papers.' But such voices were lost in the general hero-worship.

Potent wine, all this, for a twenty-four-year-old head. But the head was strong, and Kipling remained aloof from the crasser forms of seduction, although he duly pasted the tributes of his adorers into press-cutting books. He resisted the intoxication of success with the same deliberate resolve as Dick Heldar in *The Light that Failed*, his constant dread that of being another flash in the pan. It was a fear that haunted him, and, as he said grimly to one of the few reporters who was lucky enough to receive a civil word from him: 'Up like the rocket, down like the stick.'

'I was plentifully assured, viva voce and in the press-cuttings – which is a drug I do not recommend to the young – that nothing since Dickens compared with my meteoric rise to fame etc. But I was more or less inoculated, if not immune, to the coarser sorts of prints.'

In March 1890 he wrote to E. Kay Robinson a letter which throws an interesting light on Kipling's estimate of himself, and the settled and sometimes sombre conclusions he had reached:

It's the amazing selfishness of the White Man that ruins your counsel of perfection. 'Money, fame and success' are to remain unto me? Surely 'tis as selfish consciously and deliberately to work for that Trinity as to lay siege to a woman or a glass of gin and porter!

Where I come from they taught me (with whips of circumstance and the thermometer at 110 in the shade) that the only human being to whom a man is responsible is himself. His business is to do his work and sit still. No man can be a power for all time or the tenth of it – else would some of my friends who have died at their posts be those powers. Least of all can a man do aught if he thinks about it, and tries to add cubits to his stature, mental or physical. It's as bad as waltzing and counting the steps 'one, two, three, one two three' under your breath. Surely the young man does best to be delivered from 'the public demand that walketh in the noonday and the cheque book that destroyeth in the study'. For the rest his business is to think as little about his soul as possible for that breeds self-consciousness and loss of power. The event is in God's hands absolutely and no hawking or clutching for fame or any other skittles is the least use.

Recollect I've tasted power – such power as I shall never get this side of the water – when I knew all the heads of the Indian government – rulers, administrators, and kings – and saw how the machinery worked. Sunshine, colour, light, incident and fight I've had poured into my lap, and now the chastened amusements of this bleak place don't bite. . . . Wait till you've been shot at and bossed a hundred and seventy men and walked 'with death and morning on the Silver horns' in the Himalayas if you wish to know how far the smoking room, the club and the music hall and the cheap ormulu amourettes taste good.

He continues in a sentence with ironical significance:

This only do. Pray for me, since I am a lonely man in my life, that I do not take the sickness which for lack of understanding, I shall call love. For that will leave me somebody else's servant instead of my own.*

My business at present, so far as I can feel, is to get in touch with the common folk here, to find out what they desire, hope or fear, and then after the proper time to speak whatever may be given to me. Also to do just enough fairly decent work to keep me going until I have found my calling and my voice. From this ideal I make no doubt I shall lamentably fall. Then I shall have to walk slowly through a Hell that I have been through once already. It's an awful thing to think that each Soul has to work out its own salvation, and more awful to know that if it sits down to think about that salvation it is in deep danger of losing it.

If the success comes my father's delight will be greater than mine. If the money comes my mother will be more pleased than I.

The two together may spoil my work and make me think less of waiting than getting more little pieces of newspapers and little cheques. Wherefore once again, let us pray. Here is *my* key-note. Don't believe in me one inch further than you can see. What's the use of pinning faith on things that one uses to write about? Please don't, for I must do my work my own way, and if my notions clashed with yours you'd be hurt for nothing. Look on it as an interesting study and let it go: I'm not going to set the Thames on fire so I hope I shan't have occasion to get mired in the mud on its banks.[3]

With such preoccupations and doubts in mind it was perhaps natural that Kipling refused to be lionized. It usually required the magnet of Wolcott Balestier to draw him reluctantly from his desk to a social occasion. Such a moment occurred on 11 July 1890, and Josephine Balestier hastened to describe the scene to her mother:

When Wolcott heard that I was to be at Dean's Yard that afternoon, he sent a note over to Mr Kipling asking him to come for tea as he wanted him to meet his sister. Now, you know Mr Kipling never goes anywhere and least of all among ladies, but wonder of wonders! he wrote that he would be delighted. As Wolcott was standing with Mrs Gosse and me on the balcony, he said quite casually 'Ah, there's Kipling'.

He is not at all a woman's man and young girls are always afraid of him, so of course I was on the defensive and declared to myself that if I hadn't been afraid of Henry James I certainly was not going to be afraid of Rudyard Kipling. So I chatted away with him and he came and sat down beside me. He is very clever. It was exciting and great fun keeping the ball rolling; you can't fancy anything more delightful than it all was. Sitting out on that West-minster balcony, the most perfect day we have had this summer, under the

* It would appear that Robinson's prayers proved of little avail for, within twenty-two months of writing this letter, Kipling was a married man.

shadow of the Abbey where it is as still and peaceful as the country, with no passers-by save the Bishops and the old Dean of Westminster and the boys in their caps and gowns.[4]

In spite of the warm refuge of his family, Kipling had driven himself so hard in 1890 that by September he had come to the end of his tether. After a bout of influenza he broke down completely, 'when all my Indian microbes joined hands and sang for a month in the darkness of Villiers Street'. He was not restored by a visit to Italy, where he stayed with Lord Dufferin, and listened to him talking of India in a twilit garden near Naples. Nor was his health likely to be improved by the turmoil over the copyright of his books which he found awaiting him on his return to London.

Kipling, not for the first time, had become a victim of the American literary pirates. Taking advantage of the absence of copyright protection, which had not yet been established, a large New York publishing house collected a number of Kipling's stories and published them in a volume without his permission and without showing him the proofs. On 4 October 1890 the *Athenaeum* recorded this event, adding that the American publisher had sent Kipling 'a bald announcement of the fact', enclosing the sum of ten pounds, which was promptly returned.

This was only the culminating act in a series of bare-faced thefts, and it reduced Kipling to a state of savage but futile indignation. The 'Literary Note' in the *Athenaeum* added that a year earlier he had offered this house the opportunity of publishing his work and had been 'speedily shown the door', and concluded that the policy of the firm was: 'When an author is unknown to fame they content themselves with insulting him; when he is celebrated they insult and rob him.'

This sturdy protest was answered six weeks later in a letter signed by Sir Walter Besant, William Black and Thomas Hardy. The letter deprecated the tone adopted by 'the greatest literary journal in the country', and claimed that the American publisher in question had always treated the signatories in a 'just and liberal fashion, showing itself willing and desirous to do what is possible for the foreign author'.

Kipling's festering anger was detonated by this servile apologia. He retorted with a poem so savage that it almost defeated its own object – the 'Rhyme of the Three Captains', with its play on the names of the three men who signed the letter – 'the bezant is hard – aye – and black'. Perhaps we may see in this early satire the same outraged protest that would sharpen his pen in later years, a sort of violent desperation with which he was to plead for forlorn causes, and entreat the uncaring world to heed his words. Now, it was only a personal grievance. In ferocious lines he described what the pirate's fate should have been:

I had nailed his ears to my capstan-head, and ripped them off with a saw,
And soused them with the bilge-water and served them to him raw,
I had flung him blind in a rudderless boat to rot in the rocking dark,
I had towed him aft of his own craft, a bait for his brother shark;
I had lapped him round with cocoa-husk and drenched him with the oil.
And lashed him fast to his own mast to blaze above my spoil;
I had stripped his hide for my hammock-side, and tasselled his beard in the mesh,
And spitted his crew on the live bamboo that grows through the gangrened flesh;
I had hove him down by the mangroves brown when the mud reef sucks and draws,
Moored by the heel of his own keel to wait for the land crabs claws;
He is lazar within and lime without; ye can nose him far enow,
For he carries the taint of a musky ship – the reek of the slavers' D'how.

All this blood and thunder was in vain. The pirate flag was not struck, and the offensive book continued to circulate. It was the first of Kipling's many failures to influence the course of events by the magic of his pen. But this public castigation by the young Kipling, and the references to Hardy and Besant, who 'dip their flag to a slaver's rag to show that his trade is fair' – caused a great stir, and again Balestier brilliantly seized his opportunity.

After a few cables to New York it was arranged that John W. Lovell & Co. were to publish the authorized edition of all Kipling's books with an introduction by Henry James, and the volumes were to include a new collection of poems and of short stories. This collection of stories was prefaced by the words:

A little more than half of these stories have been printed in America in book form without my authority, and under a name not of my choosing. I have been forced in self-defence to include these tales in the present volume, which has my authority. I owe it to the courtesy of my American publishers that I have had the opportunity of myself preparing the present book.

This unhappy affair confirmed the suspicion which Rudyard, like many authors, already felt for publishers: 'Kipling,' said Charles Morgan, 'was more suspicious of publishers than Byron himself, but had not the grand manner which ennobled Byron's affability towards Murray.' But although Kipling knew his own value, as afterwards did his wife and his literary agent A. P. Watt, he always remained on the best terms with his publishers when he met them privately.[5]

The episode of the American pirates evidently left a foul taste in Rudyard's mouth for some time. Even the sophisticated atmosphere of the Savile Club, where so many authors gathered, seemed to his overheated nerves to be charged with hostility and criticism:

> London is a vile place. The long-haired literati of the Savile Club are swearing that I 'invented' my soldier talk in *Soldiers Three*. Seeing that not one of these critics has been within earshot of a barrack, I am naturally wroth. But this is only the beginning of the lark. You'll see some savage criticisms of my work before spring. That's what I'm playing for.[6]

He was spared further personal negotiations with publishers when Walter Besant persuaded him to transfer his business affairs from his own uncertain management to that of A. P. Watt, the leading literary agent in London. Watt managed his affairs with skill and an acute eye to their mutual financial advantage, and on his death his son, a man of Kipling's age, continued their association. Towards the end of his life, Rudyard, looking back, could recall no serious difference between them in forty years. Besant also advised him to avoid literary squabbles and factions, and he followed this advice, scrupulously refraining till the end from public criticism of the work of a fellow-author, and holding himself generally aloof from literary cliques.

Rudyard had been working, at the end of 1890, on a poem of greater significance than any that had gone before. George Orwell, in an essay on Kipling, has drawn attention to the extraordinary number of his phrases that passed into general use, and were widely quoted by ordinary men and women, sometimes ignorant of their source. Such a phrase was minted in the first stanza of his new poem 'The English Flag', and was soon ringing round the world:

> Winds of the World, give answer! They are whimpering to and fro –
> And what should they know of England who only England know?

For the first time, in this poem, the young Kipling strikes a note of Imperial grandeur and obligation; the wild scenes and strange distant places over which the flag waved, thrilling to those with little realization of the extent of their Empire, are described with wonderful virtuosity in the language of the Four Winds, savage and menacing by North and East, crooning and seductive by the South. And one

of its stanzas, in particular, seldom quoted, gives evidence of the
artistry at his command:

> The South Wind sighed: – 'From the Virgins my mid-sea course was ta'en
> Over a thousand islands lost in an idle main,
> Where the sea-egg flames on the coral and the long-backed breakers croon
> Their endless ocean legends to the lazy, locked lagoon.

'The English Flag' was published in the *St James's Gazette* in April
1891, and its immense popularity was assured by its inclusion in Henley's anthology of English Verse, *Lyra Heroica*, in the position of
honour.

But Kipling's health remained bad, and there were recurrences of
his Indian fevers which had before lain dormant. He had worked too
hard, with almost the intensity of Balzac, and he had written too
quickly. Perhaps some hint had reached him of the doubts felt about
him by men whose judgement he respected. His admirer, Edmund
Gosse, 'sensitive as a cat to all atmospheres', had stated publicly that
he was writing too much and saturating the market, and that his creative powers should be replenished by travel: 'Go East, Mr Kipling,
go back to the Far East. Disappear!... Come back in ten years
time with another precious and admirable budget of loot out of
wonderland.'

His idol Robert Louis Stevenson echoed these warnings: 'He alarms
me by his copiousness and haste.... He is all smart journalism and
cleverness; it is all bright and shallow and limpid. No blot of heart's
blood, no harmony to the music.'

But it was James Barrie who put his finger on Kipling's trouble:
'His chief defect is ignorance of life. This seems a startling charge to
bring against one whose so-called knowledge of life has frightened
the timid. But it is true.... He believes that because he has knocked
about the world in shady company, he has no more to learn.'

Partly, perhaps, because he too felt that his talent should be
enriched by further experience, and partly because his parents and
doctor urged a long sea voyage, Kipling decided to leave England
again. In June 1891 he was in America with his uncle, Fred Macdonald, on a flying visit which proved to be the worst form of recuperation he could have attempted, for he was reduced to frequent rages
by his encounters with the American press.

Although often terse and rude to London reporters, he had arrived
at a certain *modus vivendi* with them. But here, in the United States,
still smarting under American piracy of his books, he began to form

a lifelong detestation for journalists. He might write of 'the old black art we call the Daily Press', and how it got into a man's blood, but henceforth he would regard it with increasing hatred, and bitterly resent its intrusion upon his life. No one had sought fame more avidly than Kipling, but illogically he refused to accept its consequences, and this estrangement from his old calling became almost an obsession of the mind.

He returned from America still restless and unwell, and travelled to the Isle of Wight, where Wolcott was staying with his mother and sisters recovering from an illness. The torpid atmosphere of the island did not raise his spirits. The summer had become grey and oppressive, and he was filled with a desire for distant places. He decided to go round the world and started his voyage, no doubt with a feeling of freedom and exhilaration, by sailing to the Cape in a ship of the Union Line from the grime and smoke of the London Docks.

Speeded on his way by the great J. M. Cook himself, he came to Capetown, quiet and untidy in 1891, with cows roaming down the main streets, women selling flowers outside the mosques, and Malays talking in low voices with the tireless fluency of their race. Here he soon recovered in the pure, invigorating sunshine. He spent much of his time in the naval society of Simonstown, visiting the Admiral of the Cape Station, and regarding with interest two live turtles tied to a wooden jetty awaiting their turn to be made into turtle soup; and there was a picnic on white wind-blown sands when a grimacing baboon slipped down from the rocks and stood gibbering waist-deep in a bed of arum lilies.

He remained in this dusty little town for nearly two months until the end of September 1891. Then to Tasmania in the ss *Doric*, the vessel wallowing like a sea beast for twenty-four days and nights in a dreary and monotonous passage to Hobart; and after that, another, equally rough, across the bleak wastes of the Tasman Sea to New Zealand. Of the time spent there he could remember little, but it is known that he travelled from Auckland, 'soft and lovely in the sunshine', to Wellington, Christchurch and Dunedin. According to his own confused memory, the tin-can boat which carried him was met at Wellington by Pelorus Jack, the white-marked shark which escorted all shipping to the harbour, and enjoyed official protection as a sacred beast. Whether accurate or not, a memory lingered in his mind of striking north from Wellington to Auckland, and bumping through the rain-washed Bush country in a buggy drawn by an old grey mare. The wild horses of the plains came out to gaze at him, and stamped their hooves, and at one of the halts he was given a roast bird 'with a skin like port crackling', but no vestige of wings – a kiwi or apteryx.

After New Zealand he made his way to Australia, but his visit was brief, and his memories of Australian travel 'mixed up with trains transferring me at unholy hours from one too-exclusive State gauge to another, of enormous skies and primitive refreshment rooms, where I drank hot tea and ate mutton, while now and then a hot wind like the loo of the Punjab boomed out of the emptiness'.

Kipling had hoped to sail from Auckland to visit Robert Louis Stevenson in Samoa, and the enchanted islands of the south, but the master of the little Samoa-bound fruit boat was too continuously drunk to offer any reasonable hope of safe arrival. He decided instead to revisit India, sailing first to Colombo. General Booth of the Salvation Army was a fellow-passenger, and Kipling remembered boisterous weather on departure, and dusk falling when he saw Booth walking over the uneven wharf, 'his cloak blown upwards, tulip-fashion, over his grey head, while he beat a tambourine in the face of the singing, weeping, praying crowd'.

They soon ran into appalling weather. The vessel was battered from stem to stern, and there was a foot of water in the saloon. 'The General's cabin,' said Kipling, 'was near mine, and in the intervals between crashes overhead and cataracts down below he sounded like a wounded elephant, for he was in every way a big man.'

At Colombo he left his ship and made his way to Lahore by train, travelling through southern and central India on a journey that lasted for four days and nights. He reached Lahore at the end of December 1891, a little before Christmas. He must have felt a tremendous elation at this hero's return. In India he had been a brilliant young writer and journalist, but it was a profession low in the rigid hierarchy that determined a man's position. Now, on this sentimental journey, he returned to his old haunts a figure of international renown, of whom Henry James wrote a month later: 'Kipling strikes me personally as the most complete man of genius ... that I have ever known.' In the changed circumstances they were now anxious to load him with attention in Lahore, and these demonstrations of respect for the wandering lamb from such a caste-bound family must have assured him, had he been in any doubt of it, of the reality of his triumph.

Kipling was staying with his parents in Lahore when, to his unspeakable grief, he received a telegram from Caroline Balestier telling him that Wolcott was dead. He had died in Germany from a virulent typhoid germ brought with him from London.

Balestier had been writing hard during Kipling's absence, and it soon became known in the office that a collaboration was on foot, and that Wolcott had once again accomplished the apparently impossible. It was a story of East and West centring round a fabulous jewel called the 'Naulahka'.* Balestier was writing the American scenes, Kipling the Indian, and Balestier had reported progress from time to time by cable. The work was nearly finished when Balestier went to Leipzig on the business of the English Library. He fell desperately ill in Dresden, and died on 6 December. *The Naulahka* was one of Kipling's least successful books. An alien hand lay heavy on him, and reading the dry, stilted chapters contributed by Balestier about life in the Middle West one is again astonished by the spell that this man exercised.

Refusing to stay in India, Kipling at once returned to England. Even by modern standards his sea journey home would have been thought a reasonably swift one. He spent Christmas Day with his people in Lahore and yet was in London on 10 January 1892.[7] Miserable as he was at Wolcott's death, it came as no surprise when he announced his intention of marrying Caroline, who had been keeping house for her brother in London. They had been through so much together, were united by a common love of the dead man, and drawn yet closer by the pangs of bereavement. Kipling wrote to his Aunt Louie (Baldwin) on 17 January 1892:

Langham Hotel,
Portland Place w.1.

Dear Aunt Louie,

By this light prepare yourself for what is coming in your own family! I am, for rare and singular merits which I cannot at this moment realize or detail, to be married tomorrow to the sister of the man with whom I wrote *The Naulahka*, now running in the *Century*. The affair has been going on for rather more months than I care to think about in that they were sheer waste of God's good life but – unless Miss Balestier or myself go down with influenza before tomorrow noon – we are launched on the threshold of things from All Souls Church. That I am penetrated with the solemnity of things in general is true. That I am riotously happy is yet more true, and I pray that out of your own great store of happiness you will bless us, because we have gone through deep waters together.[8]

We cannot doubt that Kipling's decision to marry Caroline was deeply involved with his love for Wolcott Balestier, one of the

---

* So spelled, perhaps by Balestier, in the title of the book. The correct spelling, 'Naulakha', was used by Kipling as the name of his house in Vermont.

strongest passions in a life not marked by close personal relationships. Nor can we doubt that Wolcott himself ardently desired this match, and the fact that when dying he charged his friend Rudyard with the care of his family planted a strong sense of obligation in Kipling's mind.

They were married on 18 January at All Souls, Langham Place, 'the church with the pencil-pointed steeple'. There was a dense fog, and a grim influenza epidemic was raging. The death-rate was high: the undertakers had run out of black horses, and brown ones were pressed into the hearses which were much in evidence on the streets. The wedding was quiet, almost surreptitious. Henry James stood for Caroline, Ambrose Poynter for Rudyard. Henry James, who had never liked Caroline, noted: 'She is a hard, devoted, capable little person, whom I don't in the least understand his marrying. It's a union of which I don't forecast the future though I gave her away at the altar in a dreary little wedding with an attendance simply of four men.' The only guests were William Heinemann, Philip and Tessa Gosse, and Edmund Gosse. Caroline arrived in a four-wheeler. Afterwards they separated at the church door, Caroline to administer medicine to her mother, Rudyard to a wedding breakfast with Ambrose Poynter at Brown's Hotel, where there took place the signing of Rudyard's will on a piece of hotel notepaper. The following day Caroline noted briefly in her diary: '*Jan. 19.* We continue to be married.'

They left Brown's on 26 January for 101 Earl's Court Road, Brown sending them their bill for £22 receipted, as his wedding present, begging them 'to allow him the privilege as a slight repayment for the pleasure Rud has given him'.[9]

CHAPTER X
TRAVEL AND AMERICA

KIPLING had now but one idea in his head, to get out of the pest-ridden city as quickly as possible. He had his nest-egg, some £2000 in Fixed Deposits, and the vagrant spirit again fretted in him. He bought two Cook's tickets for a voyage round the world, and another Odyssey in his restless life began. On 2 February 1892 they left London for Liverpool. The faithful Henry James, full of forebodings, we may conjecture, was on the platform to see them off, supported by Heinemann and Bram Stoker.* Next day they sailed on the *Teutonic* for New York, and during the voyage Kipling thought out the end of *The Naulahka*, and began to arrange verses and chapter-heads. The sixteenth found them in New England deep in snow, at the Balestier home at Brattleboro. Here Kipling first met his formidable brother-in-law Beatty Balestier, leathery, tough and sardonic, who was to play a momentous and painful part in his life.

The thermometer marked thirty below freezing when Kipling stepped from the train, catching his breath in the midnight air as though he had plunged into icy water, and entered a waiting sleigh piled high with blankets and buffalo robes, driven by the muffled figure of Beatty Balestier.

Kipling was new to snow scenes, having only seen the eternal snows from afar on the peaks of the Himalayas, and he found this moonlight sleigh ride, through the snow-covered country, beautiful beyond expression, like a dream. The snow-muffled hills were silent as graves, and the only sound on the ear beside the sleigh-bells was the Connecticut river, a ribbon of black, chuckling through the packed ice.

It was all new to him and filled him with excitement – this strange place at which he was arriving before he could properly see it, the bitter air, the piled snow, the gentle hiss of the sleigh runners on the crust, the jingling bells and the new beauties that his first daylight there was to reveal: deep blue sky over a white landscape, pine trees,

* Now remembered mainly for his story *Dracula*.

branches laden with snow, and a distant sweep of mountain peaks
dominated by Mt Monadnock 'like a giant thumb nail pointing
heavenward', at which Kipling stared by the hour, remembering Emerson's striking phrase about the mountain, 'the wise old giant busy with
his sky affairs'. 'There was never a cloud in the sky that rested on
the snow-line of the horizon as a sapphire on white velvet. Hills of
pure white, or speckled and furred with woods, rose up above the solid
white level of the fields, and the sun rioted over their embroideries till
the eyes ached.' He saw a mountainous wooded landscape divided into
small farms of barren acres, roads sketched in dirt, white clap-boarded
farmhouses, a country so wild that bears and deer roamed its woods.

After a few days reconnaissance the Kiplings resumed their wedding
tour. From New York they set out again for St Paul, Chicago, Winni-
peg, and Vancouver, where they embarked on 4 April in the *Empress
of India* for Japan.[1]

In Vancouver Kipling made a pathetic speculation in real estate,
buying twenty acres of a wilderness called North Vancouver. After
paying taxes on it for years he discovered that it belonged to someone
else. The people of Vancouver smilingly consoled him: 'You bought
that from Steve, did you? Ah-ah, *Steve*! You hadn't ought to ha'
bought from Steve. No! Not from *Steve*!'

On 20 April they reached Yokohama Bay, and began to explore
a Japan exquisite in the season of wistaria and peonies. The garden
of the house in which they stayed looked down upon the waters of
the harbour, shimmering in the heat, and the fishing boats at anchor.
It was full of azaleas in bloom, cherry trees and bamboo grass, willows
with their pale green trailers, and swallow-tail butterflies fluttering
among the blossoms. Kipling was filled with a deep sense of repose:
'Little warm sighs come up from the moist warm earth, and the fallen
petals stir on the ground, turn over, and go to sleep again.' Outside
the garden and beyond the roofs and fluted temples lay the chequered
rice fields where men with blue and white cloth twisted round their
heads toiled under the pitiless sun, bare feet sunk in viscous mud. An
earthquake in Nikko alarmed the visitors and sent them scurrying into
the garden at seven in the morning, where 'a tall cryptomeria waggled
its insane head back and forth with an "I told you so" expression,
though not a breath was stirring'.

Disaster came to them on 9 June. Kipling went in the morning to
arrange about their passage in the *Empress of China*, and to draw
money from the Yokohama branch of his bank. When he had cashed
a modest cheque, the manager said: 'Why not take more? It will be

just as easy.' Kipling answered that he was too careless to carry large sums of money on his person. He might return in the afternoon. He did so, to find that in that short period the bank had failed.

He returned with this staggering piece of news to his bride of three months, now carrying a child, but Caroline with her sturdy New England courage and keen business instinct took the blow bravely, writing gloomily in her diary: 'Rud goes in the morning to arrange about the passage on the *Empress of China*. In the afternoon he goes to draw money for the passage and finds the New Oriental Banking Co. have failed. As all our savings were with them we are without a cent in the world excepting $100 in the New York Bank.'

It rained steadily all the next day, and Kipling's gloom increased. They sat by the hour playing Casino, at which Kipling was no match for his wife, and was forced to go for a walk in driving rain 'to conceal his rage'. They formed what he called a 'Committee of Ways and Means', and decided on flight. Cook returned their money for the unexpended vouchers, and Kipling later attended a meeting of the bank, at which it was decided, on Kipling's motion, that creditors should accept twenty-five per cent of their deposit in deferred shares and give the bank one year in which to pay.

They sailed from Yokohama, much chastened, on 27 June in the *Empress of China* for Vancouver, Kipling taking a surprising part in the life of the ship, appealing for subscriptions for the widow of a sailor who fell overboard, and reading aloud *The Taking of Lungtungpen* at an entertainment in the Saloon. He was already occupied with 'The Rhyme of the Three Sealers', and was sending back accounts of his travels to *The Times*. 'Back again, then, across the cold North Pacific, on the heels of the melting snows, and to the outskirts of a little New England town where my wife's paternal grandfather (a Frenchman) had made his home and estate many years before.' The stormy American period had begun.

They arrived in Vermont on 9 August 1892, leaving New York behind them 'with her roar and rattle, her complex smells, her triply overheated rooms, and much too energetic inhabitants'. On his marriage to the beautiful Mai Mendon, Beatty Balestier had been given 'Maplewood', an old farmhouse on the Balestier estate 'Beechwood' This estate, which was occupied by Carrie's grandmother Madame Balestier, was a tract of land with wooded hillsides overlooking the Connecticut River Valley. At 'Maplewood' Beatty lived in raffish contentment with his wife and daughter Marjorie, and it was there that the Kiplings had stayed on the first visit.

Later in the summer Kipling found a building known as 'Bliss Cottage', a storey and a half high, and seventeen feet to the roof-tree, which he rented for £2 a month. They furnished this house with squalid simplicity, putting a large hot-air stove in the damp cellar, and cutting holes in the thin floor for the eight-inch tin pipes, so that they lived not only in hideous discomfort but also in constant danger of fire. When the lead pipes froze they would put on their coon-skin coats and thaw them out with a lighted candle. Kipling's output of work during this honeymoon year was well below his normal average, his most important achievement during this time being one of the most powerful of all his short stories, *Love o' Women*. Meanwhile he had acquired from Beatty, on his first visit, a pasture of eleven and a half acres on which to build a house.

Kipling had no roots in any particular country, and it is probable that he intended to spend his life in this place. He could feel no longing for home, and he soon realized that the atmosphere of Vermont was propitious to his talents, for he was quickly writing with zest in the crisp invigorating climate, working long hours without consciousness of effort. In 'Bliss Cottage' his ill-starred daughter Josephine was born on 29 December 1892, and the event endeared the property so much to him that he wished to buy it, but the Blisses were not prepared to sell.

Josephine was in every sense a child to entrance, with fair hair and blue eyes, sensitive, imaginative and precocious, and her death in 1899 was the first of a series of paralysing blows that were to shatter the serene progress of Kipling's career. She was his idol, but he had always felt a strange distrust in her destiny. He had a passion for children, and although he became increasingly unpredictable in his behaviour to adults, he could refuse nothing to children, playing with them for hours, inventing fascinating stories and games. 'We worship,' he said of Josephine, 'a baby in a snow temple' – and again, 'there is nothing in the world so beautiful as a babe's small foot.'[2] So he could deny nothing to Josephine. He even wasted precious time inventing letters she was supposed to have dictated at the age of twenty-two months:

18 Oct. 94.

Dear Miss Julia,

I have not been allowed to write before because my Father and Mother don't want to stimulate my brain but as I have just been spanked for throwing a brush into the fire after I was told to leave it alone they think it would be safer for me to take to pen and ink. I want to thank you for my White Seal slippers. They are good to eat though hairy, but this, I am told, is not what they were meant for. I use them to walk about in my nur – bedroom and they become my complexion. But I am not allowed to lift my skirts up to my waist when I have them on so I am afraid no one has seen them properly yet though I have done my best – such as lying on the floor and kicking and offering them to visitors. Two people, a man and a woman, stayed here the other day. They said they belonged your way but I was busy cutting some eye-teeth and did not notice them much. I am still cutting my eye-teeth and they do not let me sing in the night as much as I should like. I am always being spanked these days for making noises and taking things that don't belong to me but I am always Your most affectionate

Josephine Kipling.

Years later he was to write to a father who had lost his son in the same year that Josephine died: 'People say that kind of wound heals. It doesn't. It only skins over; but there is at least some black consolation to be got from the old and bitter thought that the boy is safe from the chances of the after years. But it is the mother that bore him who suffers most when the young life goes out.' When another child in Vermont died, Kipling wrote a letter of the most tender and comprehending sympathy to the father, and he told Mary Cabot that if it were Josephine he would never be able to think or speak of her again.[3]

The death of those he loved struck him with a shattering force. Wolcott Balestier's name could never be mentioned; no photograph of him was allowed in the house, and when the news of the death of Stevenson, whom he scarcely knew, came over the wires, he was prostrated with grief and unable to write a line for nearly three weeks.[4]

It was a happy and uneventful life at first. They bought horses and drove down dusty lanes between the maple woods, a riot of glorious colour in the autumn. Kipling described in mellow retrospect in his autobiography how he worked with his hands at household tasks, but in truth he was without resource in the simplest practical matters. A neighbour found him sitting in a buggy trying to turn round so awkwardly that she offered to help. He did not know how to cramp the wheels, and handed over the reins with relief. 'At luncheon,' the neighbour added, 'he told me of a dinner of eight in India, everyone of whom, except himself, had killed his tiger; the fact then flashed on my consciousness that the fearless author was an uncommonly timid man.'[5]

Kipling was long remembered affectionately by the farmers in Vermont, whom he was fond of visiting on walks in his odd clothes, and he loved to ride with oxen ploughing out the roads, two pairs of oxen on one sled. He never drove them, but he liked to touch them with the whip.[6] He was fond, too, of wandering through the woods in search of anemones, and he was soon to learn to appreciate their significance as heralds of the spring, which came as balm to the dwellers in this harsh northern climate, and he refused to go away when they were in bloom.

He began to take a deeper interest in the countryside and in the cycle of the seasons, which come in New England in violent contrasts of beauty: summer with its ripening corn and tobacco, and sudden whiplash winds from the north-west, overturning barns and strewing the dusty roads with fallen trees, making him feel that the New England summer 'had creole blood in her veins'; the sudden summer storms, turning into rivers roads which before had been sunbaked and thick with grey-yellow dust.

Then autumn and the turning of the leaves –

the insurrection of the tree-people against the waning year. A little maple began it, flaming blood-red of a sudden where he stood against the dark green of a pine-belt. Next morning there was an answering signal from the swamp where the sumacs grow. Three days later, hill sides as far as the eye could range were afire, and the roads paved with crimson and gold. Then a wet wind blew, and ruined all the uniforms of that gorgeous army; and the oaks, who had held themselves in reserve, buckled on their dull and bronzed cuirasses and stood it out stiffly to the last blown leaf, till nothing remained but pencil-shading and bare boughs, and one could see into the most private heart of the woods.

He learned the flowers that came with each season, the wind-flowers of spring, Solomon's seal, and the trailing arbutus whose scent is the very essence of May, and autumn with its golden rod and asters. He saw white pine, hemlock and spruce mingled with the dominant maple trees, and beneath them mosses and lichens with the ruffled grouse picking his way delicately among them. He was sickened by the slaughter of the wild birds and animals that roamed these woods; there were hawks sometimes, and eagles with majestic wing-beat, foxes, deer and bear, but the marauding bands of hunters saw to it that the woods were often silent.

Twelve hours journey by railway brought one to wilder country still where the moose roamed in solitude, and twenty miles to the virgin timber country, and the haunts of the trappers. Kipling grew to love it all, and he learned much on his walks past the white clapboarded farmhouses, down dusty byways where he met tinkers and quack pedlars in painted wagons, and by the river in spring where the gypsies pitched their camps, lit their fires and tethered their horses.

He even loved the rigours of winter, when the snow was master of the countryside, when for months on end the farmers saw no one but the doctor in his hooded sleigh, and the air was filled with stinging hail or blown snow. He remained deeply immersed in his private universe of creation, and incompetent in practical affairs. When his odd-job man had difficulty in putting the screens in the windows and asked Kipling's advice, he replied: 'You'll have to ask Mrs Kipling, I don't know the first thing about it.'

He had grown somewhat timid with horses, and took little interest in his pair, Nip and Tuck, a spirited couple closely matched, each with a slight mottling on the haunches of dull mouse colour, and he seemed to know nothing about them. Although he wrote with enthusiasm in retrospect about the making of the garden at his new house 'Naulakha', named after the book written in collaboration with Wolcott, he seems to have taken little personal part in laying the stones in the garden wall or planting the flowers. When asked about this, August Rhode, a cabinet maker who was often called in by the Kiplings, almost shouted: 'No! he wouldn't have known how to take hold of a stone to lift it!'[7]

Watching the building of 'Naulakha' was, however, a great delight to him. It was built by Jean Pigeon from Quebec on a high foundation of solid rocks, with its roof and sides covered by dull green hand-split shingles. They laid out a long drive to the road, using dynamite to diminish the gradients. Power was supplied by a low-power atmospheric pump which it was Kipling's messy duty to oil.

Here, at last, was home, his first and his own, and how different it was from the bungalow in India with its tamarisks and eucalyptus trees. He referred to the house as a ship, with the propeller the material provision of the furnace and kitchen at the stern, and his own study as the captain's bridge at the bow, opening on the south and east. The architect, Henry Rutgers Marshall, did what he could with the treeless hillside. He placed the living-rooms on the side of the view, looking across the valley to Wantastiquet, and you saw from the balcony a splendid vista of mountains with Monadnock surmounting all – its very name, Kipling said, bewitching him like 'Mesopotamia', its austere beauty the inspiration of his first American writing. The wooden house was painted a pale green to achieve protective colouring, and avoid being seen from the Chesterfield Road. There was a sense of remoteness about the place that pleased Kipling. Maples, birch and pine cut off all but leaf-fringed glimpses of 'Maplewood' to the north and all sight of 'Beechwood' a half-mile to the south, so that you felt alone in a tranquil land until the eye reached the toy houses and play trains on the track by the river.

It cannot be said that the house reflects credit on the Kiplings' taste, a bare, wooden oblong with chilling interior decoration. When the author visited it in the 1940s, the house stood silent and deserted, its garden choked with weeds, and an atmosphere of tragedy seemed to brood over it. The interior furnishings were at first meagre, and were later unhappily augmented by cotton hangings of oriental colouring, Benares brass and carved teak, producing a melancholy ensemble, but the garden was made beautiful by Caroline, and the air stimulated mind and body.

Kipling's spirits soared, and he told his wife that he was conscious of the return of a sudden surge of great strength, such as he had felt when he first went to London to conquer the capital.[8] Although she referred to 'Naulakha' as 'Liberty Hall', Mrs Kipling, said a neighbour, 'provided only bare necessities and slender allowances for her life, made much of the difficulty of conducting a household so far from the source of supplies, and kept the machinery of life always in evidence. An unexpected guest at luncheon would have been an impossibility.' There was none of the easy informality of Beatty Balestier's house, where his friends came in for meals at any hour and were always welcome.

They moved in the summer of 1893, and the omens were good. They had a home as well as a family, and a few intimate friends. Kipling had never felt more confident in his powers. He worked to a regular routine from nine to one each morning. Absolute silence reigned throughout the house, sometimes pierced by a helpless call for Caroline to help him find a word or unearth a rhyme.[9] Mrs Kipling sat busy with her accounts or needlework in an ante-room, the only avenue of approach to the sanctum, a vigilant and unrelenting Cerberus.

Before the house was finished Lockwood Kipling, now retired, but with many active years before him, arrived in Vermont, to the delight of Rudyard and Carrie. He took an immediate interest in 'Naulakha', and soon, as he sat writing, Rudyard could look up and read the words from St John's Gospel inscribed by Lockwood on the mantelpiece: 'The Night cometh when no man can work.'

In the afternoons Rudyard would walk or drive, picking flowers, observing the country as he had at Westward Ho!, putting his companions through minute and tedious cross-examinations. Lockwood, whose alien appearance soon made him a familiar figure trudging the dusty roads round Brattleboro, was able to give Rudyard timely advice with work in hand at this time, such as *The Bridge Builders*. He had always valued advice from this source more highly than from any other. It was this period, too, which saw the birth of *The Jungle Books*, begun at the Bliss cottage with the story of *Mowgli's Brothers*. And after his father's departure, the new creative impulse of which he had spoken to Carrie produced the poems collected in *The Seven Seas*, the two *Jungle Books* and the short stories assembled in *The Day's Work*.

He was also working on 'McAndrew's Hymn', in which he extolled the glory of steam, a poem which was to lead on to other works which were to fascinate some and repel others, in which machinery talked in complex jargon – stories that were to reach their perfection in *The Ship that Found Herself* in 1895. Many will find in delightful and refreshing contrast to this obtrusive expertise the *Jungle Books* that appeared in 1894 and 1895, and will turn with relief from locomotives and tappet valves to these enchanting and immortal stories, and to the denizens of this magic world.

As in all his writing for children, Kipling gave these stories a particular loving care, his daemon soaring to new heights of inspiration. And his reward has been that generations of children have since been enthralled by them, so that they have become the greater part of many an adult's memories of childhood. For there is a unique magic in the *Jungle Books* from the moment the infant Mowgli enters the wolf's lair, and the moonlight is blacked out at the mouth of the cave by the great head of the tiger Shere Khan, and his roar fills it with thunder. There is magic too in the jungle, so glowingly portrayed, with its danger-haunted thickets, and the monkeys threading its frail liana ways, the enchanted land of which Mowgli is to become the master; and in the animals who are his friends and mentors – Bagheera, the sleek and terrible panther; Baloo, the wise old bear; Hathi, the elephant; Kaa, the gigantic python who makes a nest for Mowgli in his coils; Akela, the leader of the wolf-pack; and the bandarlog, chattering outcasts of the tree tops, whose only wish is to be noticed, and who immediately abandon every task they have begun.

But there is terror too in the jungle, in the ruined honeycombed city where the monkeys live, and where Mowgli is taken by Kaa to see the old white cobra, baleful underground custodian of the treasure of kings; terror in the red dogs, so devastating and ferocious in their pack that even tiger and panther turn aside at their approach. With what glowing inspiration Kipling conceived his animals and their mysterious world; Bagheera and Kaa are awe-inspiring, but they are sublime, and the mind still wonders at the genius of the imagination that created them and Mowgli, their friend, uncertain whether he was man or beast, torn by his dilemma, but in the end remorselessly guided by his creator away from the jungle and its animals to assume his duty as a man. Perhaps it is significant too that there should be a Law of the Jungle, immutable and hard as a pikestaff, which demands obedience, a law which particularly established Mowgli's brothers, the wolves, as the 'Free People'.

> As the creeper that girdles the tree trunk, the Law runneth forward and
> back –
> For the strength of the Pack is the Wolf, and the strength of the Wolf is
> the Pack.
> The jackal may follow the tiger, but, Cub, when thy whiskers are grown,
> Remember the wolf is a hunter – go forth and get food of thine own.
> Keep peace with the Lords of the Jungle – the Tiger, the Panther, the Bear;
> And trouble not Hathi the Silent, and mock not the Bear in his lair.
>
> Now these are the Laws of the Jungle, and many and mighty are they;
> But the head and the hoof of the Law and the haunch and the hump is –
> Obey!

Well might Kipling have told his wife that he had received an access of power, 'the return of a feeling of great strength', for into the *Jungle Books* are poured the full glory of his imaginative genius, untainted by bitterness, and unalloyed by special pleading. Had he written nothing else, these inspired stories would have made a powerful claim to immortality. They may have been in the direct line from *Aesop's Fables*, and have owed something to the *Jataka* tales familiar to the Kipling family, but they should be enjoyed rather than interpreted. We should succumb to their enchantment without question or analysis, in the same way that we accept the dream world of *Swan Lake*.

In the Bliss cottage he had also written some more 'soldier verse', much of it now vulgar and jarring on a sensitive ear – such pieces as 'Shillin'-a Day', 'The Widow's Party', 'Bobs' and 'Gentlemen Rankers'. These were to be followed by others, some far superior, from 1894 to 1896, the most notable perhaps 'The Sergeant's Wedding'. Memorable also were 'For to Admire' and 'Follow me 'Ome' in 1894. Supreme among his verses at this time was the poem 'The Mary Gloster' – similar in form but far more successful than 'McAndrew's Hymn' – in which a villainous shipowner on his deathbed berates his effeminate son.

Surprisingly, Rudyard became interested in athletics, becoming adept on ski and snow-shoes in the winter, and playing golf with a neighbour, the Reverend C. O. Day, cutting holes in the soft snow which was more than two feet deep, and losing the balls until it occurred to him to paint them red. Playing on a steep slope, the ball rolled for ever on the crust, and it was possible to make a drive of two miles.[10]

Kipling confined himself to a few friends, but with these he was entirely free from the sullen reserve he often showed with people he did not wish to meet. He could not see too much of Mary Cabot, who had been a friend of Wolcott Balestier, Mrs Holbrook, who also lived in Brattleboro, Henry Rutgers Marshall, his father's old friend Charles Eliot Norton, also a friend of Ruskin and Burne-Jones and now a professor at Harvard, Pen Browning, Robert Browning's son, Arthur Conan Doyle, the de Forests, and a few others. From Brattleboro came his dearest friend Dr James Conland, who had been rescued from a shipwreck as a baby, and did not know his parents' name, his own being given to him to signify that he was a waif of the sea. It was Conland who helped Kipling with *Captains Courageous*, going so far as to bring a dead haddock into the house, which he deftly eviscerated to show Kipling how the cod-fishers worked off the Newfoundland Banks. Kipling's downhill coasting on his bicycle and crashing into a haycart outside the Conlands' house first brought them together, and their acquaintance was renewed when Conland attended Caroline at her first confinement. He proved to be the best friend that Kipling made in New England.

His small circle would assemble for tea at 'Naulakha', tea made by the hostess, and served on a Benares brass-topped table. Kipling's manner at these parties was hearty, and even rollicking. Mary Cabot has left us a picture of him smoking a pipe, one leg over the arm of his chair, talking 'in a soft mellow voice strangely at variance with his choice of words, which was strong and picturesque, but anything but refined'.[11] He welcomed with cordiality anyone introduced by one of the habitués of the house, but was liable to take refuge in mutinous silence when confronted by strangers. He was apt to withdraw completely into himself in the presence of persons uncongenial to him, in a manner closely verging on rudeness. At a supper party he refused to speak to an agreeable woman who had been invited to hear him talk, and was equally cold to the other man present, whom he did not know, but among his friends there were no such awkward lacunae.

He bubbled with vivacity and inventive wit. At parties in his barn, lit by smoky kerosene lamps and illuminated by texts in Kipling's writing and, in his most immature vein, a notice: 'Here are the marble pillars, here is the gilded divan!' – with a fiddler from Slab Hollow, he was relaxed and free from constraint. At the Christmas celebrations for Josephine and Marjorie, daughter of Beatty Balestier, he talked with a wonderful freshness and vigour, and in a *tour de force* extemporized seventy-five verses in unhesitating sequence, never wanting a rhythm, never pausing, drumming on the desk in accompaniment to the rhyme, illustrating the subjects as he improvised with drawings in pencil, on and on with tireless virtuosity until the audience cried out for quarter.

It now becomes possible to observe more clearly cut the relations of Rudyard Kipling and his wife. From this moment their functions were sharply divided, Kipling's share in the partnership being almost entirely confined to writing. Every aspect of business was, from now on, taken off his shoulders by Caroline, no bad thing perhaps for a creative writer. Her character was strong and possessive; she had a passion for the domination of others which she did not attempt to control, and greatly disliked being crossed. She was in many ways the ideal wife for a man of genius – jealously guarded his health, supervised every detail of his daily life, arranged the publication of his works and the terms of his contracts, acted as his copyright agent, and fiercely interposed herself between him and jarring interferences with his work.

Kipling, his mind teeming with ideas to be put on paper, and already sick of minor anxieties, gave in abjectly to this control of every detail of his personal life, with the result that one who had before been independent and resourceful soon became childishly reliant upon his wife's management. Many years later he said to Lady Milner: 'Even if I wanted to run away from Carrie I couldn't do it, because she would have to look out the train and book the ticket.'[12] And Mrs Cabot at a railway station, while Mrs Kipling was checking the luggage, asked Kipling which hotel they were staying at. 'Why God bless you, I don't know,' he answered, 'I am no more than a cork on the water when Carrie is with me.'

They made a mixed impression on the inhabitants. The farmers were fond of Kipling, who put on no frills with them and enjoyed visiting their white houses on his walks down the dirt roads through the maple woods, and talking to them about ploughing and the price of crops. Some of the Brattleboro people began by distrusting Kipling as an Englishman, and were further affronted by the slovenly clothes in which he appeared on Main Street, ancient knickerbockers tucked into top boots, an old brown coat thrown open, and a sombrero hat: garments that they considered unsuitable for a man with such a great reputation. They were surprised when they saw him coasting downhill with his feet on the handlebars of his bicycle, coat-tails flying. His clothes were indeed so eccentric that he was mistaken for the berry man when attempting to call on Miss Cabot's mother, whose eyesight was failing.[13]

A section of Brattleboro also considered it unseemly that this Englishman, under pretext of having lost money, should have settled the 'Balestier girl' among her own folk. These feelings were accentuated for some by the *folie de grandeur* that grew upon Mrs Kipling, who soon became far more English than her husband. She instituted a heavily conventional routine at 'Naulakha'. Stiff shirt and full evening dress were the rule, even when the pair were dining alone, a procedure explained by Mrs Kipling on the grounds that it was necessary to keep the respect of the English servants. That Kipling disliked this practice, but saw no way out of it, is suggested by his rueful remark to the farmer John Bliss: 'When your work is over you can go into the kitchen and have supper. I have to dress up in evening clothes.'

A similar formality quite alien to the New England community was demanded in the servants. Their groom, Robins, was succeeded by a man named Matt Howard. Kipling had advertised for a coachman, married but without family, and Howard applied for the situation and obtained it, saying that he had worked for an English peer, but omitting to add that his wife and eight children were in England. He confessed to two children and was told to bring them to Vermont, which he did, leaving the other six in England whence they filtered over in discreet driblets. When winter set in Kipling bought a smart basket sleigh with a tiger-skin rug thrown over the back. The inhabitants were then further regaled by the spectacle of Howard, clad in livery, top hat and cockade, driving Josephine and the nurse round the 'Circle', a six-mile drive via Croxby Pond to Waits and back to 'Naulakha'.[14] 'Matt Howard,' said a farmer, 'sat up straight as a major when driving them. Didn't bend his back even when the horses ran away and tipped over the carriage on a corner.'[15]

The desire for privacy that has so often been referred to as neurotic and unnatural had begun to grow. It is true that Kipling resented what he regarded as intrusions, but his reserve has been ridiculously distorted by the clinical probings of psychological critics. It is easily forgotten how immense this man's reputation was in the 1890s. When he lay desperately ill in New York in 1899 the whole world waited in breathless suspense for the bulletins of his progress. He received a telegram – to his deep subsequent annoyance, for his mistrust of German intentions was already alert – from the Kaiser. He was clearly fair game for any kind of intruder, particularly members of the American press, who badgered him in such a manner that, had he yielded to all their demands for interviews, his output, serenely proceeding, would have come to a standstill.

He believed fiercely that he was entitled to a private life, and he did not think it part of his public life to be interviewed. He and Caroline also placed an extremely high value on anything that he wrote or said, and intensely resented giving away valuable copy for nothing, unless to some person he wished to help. What he had to say, he preferred to write himself, and his own prejudice in this direction, strong as it was, was nothing compared with Mrs Kipling's fury at the interruption of his jealously guarded creative routine. Furthermore, although virile in the written word, he was timid under the harassing fire of American reporters, and greatly dreaded the ordeal of their interrogations, so that they usually went back unrewarded, angry with Kipling for a fruitless journey, expensive in time and livery hire.

It is sad to observe his growing estrangement from his own once beloved profession, and his resentment of reporters that sometimes verged on hatred. He went to hide in John Bliss's barn from visitors who, he said, he was sure were reporters. 'Why don't you tell them to go to hell?' asked Bliss. 'Can't do that, they would write it all up in their papers.'

Kipling's attitude was strongly resented by the American journalists, accustomed to easy access to everyone from the President downwards, and they vindictively bided their time. Kipling's judgement, when he was irritated or nervous, was by no means a sure one, and he undoubtedly committed some very foolish actions. Had he been a better mixer, had he made up his mind to neutralize a potentially hostile force with *bonhomie* and tact – had he in fact been a different man – he might well have been able to preserve most of his existing freedom. He would also have avoided the occasion, intensely lacerat-

1 Rudyard with his mother, 1866.

2 As a small boy.

3 At the time of his stay at Lorne Lodge.

4 Lorne Lodge, Southsea, 'the House of Desolation'.

5 Letter from Rudyard to his aunt Louisa Baldwin with drawing of himself and cousin Stanley cleaning a picture for their uncle Burne-Jones.

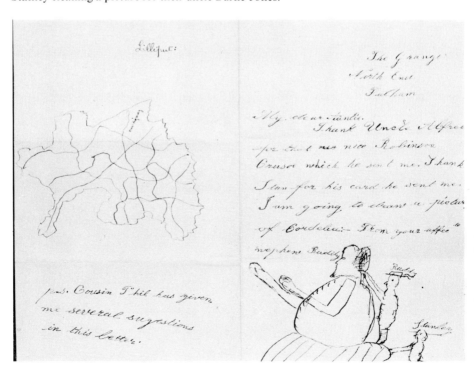

6 Masters and pupils at Westward Ho!: Beresford ('M'Turk'), Kipling ('Gigger'),
Dunsterville ('Stalky'), M. H. Pugh ('Prout'), the headmaster, Cormell Price
and William Crofts ('King'). Contemporary sketches by G. C. Beresford.

7 Group at Westward Ho! c. 1882; Kipling in centre.

December 30.
[Bombay 1865]
[London 1890.]

Mock Turtle.
à la Gadsby.

Turbot & Oyster sauce.
(avec plain tail.)

Roast Turkey & sausage.
à la Bin(a)lia

Plum Pudding.
in black & white

Apricot Cream

J.L.K.

8 Menu-card designed by Lockwood Kipling for Rudyard's twenty-fifth birthday.

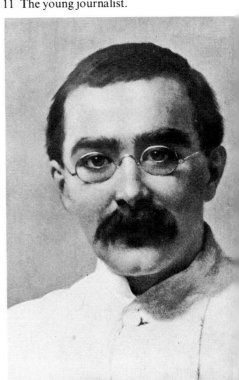

9 Trix Kipling.

10 Lockwood Kipling.

11 The young journalist.

12 Lockwood Kipling's sketching class, Mayo School of Art, Lahore.

13 Kipling outside Professor and Mrs Hill's bungalow, 'Belvedere', at Allahabad, 1888.

14 Wolcott Balestier.

15 Madame Balestier with her daughters, Josephine (*left*) and Carrie.

16 'The Old Self and the Young Self' by Max Beerbohm.

17 Naulakha, Kipling's home in Vermont.

18 Carrie Kipling in her 'office' at Naulakha, 1895.

19 Beatty Balestier on his farm near Brattleboro.

20 Mrs Kipling in the carriage much criticized by Brattleboro neighbours.

ing to his nerves, when, the moment ripe for revenge, pressmen from every State in the Union descended like vultures on the little Court House at Brattleboro, and tore him to pieces before the world at the trial of Beatty Balestier.

Already, as early as 1892, he had goaded a Montreal newspaper into the following castigation:

Montreal has had a snubbing such as it is little used to from the eccentric and conceited Indian novelist, Rudyard Kipling. The latter notoriety arrived here on his first visit with his wife from Vancouver yesterday and immediately closeted himself in his apartment in the Windsor Hotel. Although a number of prominent citizens wished to make the novelist's visit pleasant and called on him, Kipling haughtily refused to receive even their cards, and would see no one. The Pen and Pencil Club, one of the most exclusive in the city, decided last night to tender to Mr Kipling a reception, and sent him an invitation. The expected guest did not even deign to answer the invitation. The members of the Club, of which Mr W. C. Van Horne, the Canadian Pacific Railroad magnate, is President, feel exceedingly put out at the ungentlemanly behaviour.

He was hardly more successful with the *Springfield Republican*:

Rudyard Kipling has bought a house lot in B'boro near his wife's home. If the young man improves the privileges of the place he will find the society quite otherwise than he appears to fancy it. It must really be hoped that Mr Kipling will become acquainted with the B'boro people. It would broaden and deepen his mind and greatly improve his manners.

The truth is that Kipling, in his contempt and resentment for anyone who tried to get something from him for nothing, could never realize that it was impossible for him to preserve intact both his fame and his seclusion. He stubbornly refused to see that he belonged to no one person, and that the public which was so faithful to him, and provided his ever-growing income, had some right to know about him. He forgot, too, the innumerable occasions when, as a reporter, he had interviewed others in India at inconvenient moments and in a ruthless manner.

The result of this attitude was that many Americans unnecessarily disliked him, and felt no compunction about disregarding his feelings. What he regarded as curiosity was, in many cases, nothing more than a desire to be friendly. The ignorant flow of destructive criticism of England, which most English visitors supported with what patience they could summon, stung him to fury and caused him to accuse

Americans of a 'savage parochial pride that squeals under a steady stare or a pointed finger'; and a mere comment which angered him appeared to Americans to distort his entire view of a subject, particularly in international affairs, in which he was becoming more and more convinced of the unassailable virtue of his own opinions.

Yet it would be wide of the mark to conclude that Kipling disliked Americans. Rather was he baffled by the new complex problem presented by American politics, and prone to over-simplify his analysis of it. He had started with favourable impressions:

Let there be no misunderstanding about the matter. I love this People, and if any contemptuous criticism has to be done, I will do it myself. My heart has gone out to them beyond all other peoples; and for the life of me I cannot tell why. They are bleeding raw at the edges, almost more conceited than the English, vulgar with a massive vulgarity which is as though the Pyramids were coated with Christmascake sugar-work. Cocksure they are, and as casual as they are cocksure, but I love them, and I realized it when I met an Englishman who laughed at them.[16]

His impression of America was not further elevated by a visit to Congress with Cecil Spring Rice. Here he saw an enormous room devoid of any sort of dignity. Some of the Members were lying full length on sofas at the back of the hall. Many were smoking. Some were chewing, and each had thoughtfully provided himself with a spittoon, frequently employed. A confused babbling noise prevailed. Occasionally the Speaker pounded his desk, and the babbling continued with increased volume. Kipling saw with amazement one man on his feet, with five or six men standing opposite him, and a little man nearby with a roll of papers on which he was writing. The first was the Member speaking, the latter the official reporter. Kipling could not hear a word that was said, but he could see the floor crowded with milling Members trying to get recognition from the Speaker, newspaper reporters and errand boys, and littered with torn papers and cigar ash, a spectacle which no doubt increased his growing mistrust of representative assemblies.[17]

Nor was he reassured when he looked round him in Vermont and saw many things that filled him with wonder and distaste. He saw a labyrinth of judicial offices and titles, but no law-abidingness. He saw immigrants coming into the States at the rate of about a million a year and treated with a callousness that horrified him.

'The Irish,' he remarked with the venom that was to grow when that race was mentioned, 'had passed out of the market into "politics"', which suited their instincts of secrecy, plunder and anonymous denunciation.' To him the eternal theme of the American people was that England was still the terrible enemy to be feared and matched. This was guaranteed by the Irish, 'whose other creed was hate', the textbooks in the schools, the Senators and the press.

He discussed these matters with John Hay from the State Department, who replied in a phrase which remained indelibly in Kipling's mind: 'America's hatred of England is the hoop round the forty four staves of the Union. So, when a man comes out of the sea we say to him: "See that big bully over there in the east? He's England. Hate him, and you're a good American."'

It was the only standard to apply to such a heterogeneous population, explained Hay, and it caused Kipling to refer to 'the overwhelming vacuity of the national life', the desperate activity that masked a hideous boredom – 'the dead weight of material things passionately worked up into Gods, that only bored their worshippers more and worse and longer'. Many of his outbursts sprang from the conviction, often impregnable against argument, with which his views were held. He was incapable of meekly accepting attacks on British imperialism delivered by the nationals of a country whose own past he considered by no means immaculate. He had an uncanny knowledge of American history to reinforce his violent replies to criticism.

Kipling's attitude towards America and Americans was always curious, not to say touchy and explosive [wrote an American friend]. One minute he would load us down with compliments; in the next, attack with vicious precision. If I said something about the ruthless measures which produced the British Empire, he would turn on me like a bull, and bellow that Americans had no cause to boast. Who fell upon decadent Mexico, after she had been beaten by a 10,000 handful of Texans on their own, and marched victoriously over her prostrate armies, snatching New Mexico, Arizona and the Southern half of California with scarcely the decent pretence of a fair purchase? Who tore the Philippines and Porto Rico from a Spain too poor to fight a single battle? Who ran into a hornet's nest of revolution in the Philippines, and made an unholy mess of governing even miserable little Porto Rico?

'Even before this,' he would add in scorn, 'look at the rape of Hawaii, as plain an example of imperial brigandage as any similar blot on British history! That also had its origins in the Bible-propagating Missionaries. So black was the record made by President Harrison that his successor Cleveland promptly gave the island back to its people.'

'Who,' he would add, 'in the end, shamelessly and with an arrogance which could not be equalled anywhere in history, stole the Panama Canal Zone from the Republic of Columbia and for years even declined to pay reasonable compensation?' Then he would add: 'You may talk of the white man's burden, as I did for my sins a year ago. Well, you may yet get, and richly deserve, – a bellyful of the subsequent pains and burdens.'[18]

The following letter throws an interesting light on the stage that Kipling's political development had reached in 1893, and we may safely assume that these are the conclusions that he took with him out of India, the convinced belief in executive ability, the admiration for experts, the distrust of 'politicians' and vague generalizations.

As for the Tory spirit. What would you have? It's a question of raising and training again. All I've been taught to see is that carelessness in administration, sloppiness of speech, vague appeals to the sentiments of great multitudes and tampering with the Decalogue, because a lot of people don't like to play consequences logically, ends in sending up the murder statistics, and murder is no good thing. There's nothing in the 'People' and the talk about the 'People' a jot more to be reverenced than in Kings and the Divine Right of the same. They are only men anyway – not Gods above the law of wrong doing and, so it seems, much of the windy talk in England about the inherent rightness and righteousness of lots of folks in a lump is skittles – nothing more than the old bunkum about the Divine Right of Kings transferred to an ungetable fetish which isn't responsible for its own actions.

You can't indict the People and cut off their heads for evil practices, and for myself I like a responsible person whose head I can help to cut off if need be. I suppose all this is mildly out of date but I've had the horror of seeing the result of a few 'popular' movements, when the regular administrators received a mandate to do certain things and the 'People' lost interest in the show as they always do, and the luckless administrators were left alone to fight out all the sorrow and sin and dirt and filth and disease that 'The People' (who are above the law) so light-heartedly scattered for others to reap.

There are in life such things as special knowledge, training, obedience, order, discipline, and views that extend beyond the eyes of the seer. How the deuce can you expect a million men keenly interested in their own domestics to have these things? 'The People' is Mrs Harris. There ain't no such person. There are men and women and interests and communities but there's no clear-eyed impeccable overseer of all interests as the papers pretend. If there were we should have no need of the Almighty.... The 'People' hate being made fun of even worse than ever Kings did. I've tried and it called me awful names – on both sides of the water, regular bone-breakers of names, but the bones didn't break.[19]

The year 1893 ended in success and happiness. Kipling noted in his wife's diary: 'Another perfect year ended. The Lord has been very good to us. Amen, R.K.' It had been a year of steady literary output, and the extracted figures for the twelve months ending November show that his income was approximately £3000.

They were on the move again at the beginning of the next year – to Bermuda, where Kipling picked up a sergeant in the street, and made like a homing pigeon for the barracks and dinner at the Mess, and then, in April, on a visit to England, where his parents had now settled in a Wiltshire village. In London, in May, he attended a dinner where he sat between Mr Astor and Lord Roberts, whose toast he proposed, together with that of the British Army. It was just after the publication of 'Bobs', and when Kipling and Roberts entered the Banqueting Hall the company stood two rows deep in homage at their passing. The dinner resolved itself into an extraordinary personal ovation for Kipling, whose star was now so brightly agleam that he could content himself with the laconic comment: 'It was some fun, as I am only twenty-nine.'

In July he revisited Westward Ho! and contemplated once again with the wistful nostalgia of the *revenant* the familiar scene. There was the gymnasium with its memories of 'Foxy', the study greatly altered, but bringing back vivid recollections of Dunsterville and Beresford, the Pebble Ridge and the serene, ample sweep of Bideford Bay.

But it was no longer 'Gigger' who surveyed these scenes of his boyhood not long distant, and who refreshed his memory of the past in mouldy locker-rooms or tradition-hallowed furze patches, but Rudyard Kipling, the great man of the hour, who was given a stirring official reception. The occasion was a sad one, for Cormell Price was at last retiring, and a subscription was raised for him to which Kipling contributed £20. The school was soon to fall on evil days, and to be moved from Westward Ho! But poor Uncle Crom could not forsake the place, and for years he was to haunt it like some ghostly sacristan who could not abandon his charge. Kipling's genius was with children, rather than with adolescents. With the former his affinity was natural and complete, but the latter he sometimes embarrassed with dated schoolboy slang. The head prefect and another boy were detailed on this occasion to escort Kipling. The head prefect, later General A. S. Little of the Royal Marines, recalled rather apologetically:

'I was accompanied by a pal and oddly enough we were not impressed with some of his conversation as it partook of the immature schoolboy slang, and we were rather of the blasé age, as we had just been up for the Sandhurst exam and didn't feel schoolboyish. I do recollect that at times he seemed to be silently looking into the past, and didn't speak for longish periods. Then he would burst into quite boyish behaviour, and rush off to the tuck-shop and do us in a princely manner. In the tuck-shop he would always attach himself to the younger boys. I am afraid we, as high and mighties, rather stood aloof from these interviews.

'I recollect his decidedly boyish outlook on things and enthusiasm for recalling amusing incidents about old Pugh (Prout in *Stalky and Co.*). The last time I saw him was at the OUSC lunch the year before he died. He was then in a sad mood, and told me that it was the last Old Boys' gathering he would see. I really only knew him as a grown-up schoolboy renewing the exploits of his youth, and I am bound to say that as a swollen-headed head prefect he at times bored me – what a confession!'[20]

While he was in London Kipling transacted an important piece of business, closing a contract with Wheelers by which he bought back the English copyright of his first six Railway Bookstall books for £1200, while Wheeler retained the Indian sales for himself. They sailed for America on 5 August 1894. Entry in diary, 6th: 'All hands collapsed but me (Rud). I am a noble mariner. 7th. I (Rud) am the only person alive and well and strong. I am a *most* noble mariner.'

In December 1894 he made an entry in Caroline's diary: 'C. tots up the books and finds I have this year earned $25,000 – $5,000. Not exactly a bad record. Not that mine be the praise, but C. deserves it all.' The success continued in the following year, 1895, and two American towns were named after him, Rudyard and Kipling. Work went easily but with moments of simulated regret at the freedom from suggestiveness which he had always imposed upon his writing:

I have a yearning upon me to tell tales of extended impropriety – not sexual or within hailing distance of it – but hard-bottomed unseemly yarns, and am now at work on the lamentable history of a big fat Indian administrator who was, in the course of duty, shot in his ample back-side by a poisoned arrow, and his devoted subordinate sucked the wound to the destruction of his credit as an independent man for the rest of his days. One can't be serious always.[21]

He remained active in local affairs. Having failed to dissuade the Road Commissioners from their intention of building a trolley line through the Main Street of Brattleboro, he was successful in establishing his own personal post office, which he named Waite after the postmistress Anna F. Waite, at the cross-roads leading from the Putney road to his house. It was also his intention to develop a country store and supply depot at the railroad siding, so that he might be free of Brattleboro for ever, measures which indicate that he intended to remain permanently in Vermont. They again visited London in July 1895, staying with Lockwood at Tisbury, and calling on the 'dear old ladies' of Kensington High Street.[22]

On his return to Brattleboro in August an idea came to Kipling for a story of a dream. He first proposed to call it *The Infants of Bohemia*, but later altered the title to *The Brushwood Boy*. Caroline's diary shows the characteristic progress of a Kipling story running smoothly, and the speed at which he worked. It was begun on 23 August and was finished with all its verses on 19 September. It was then published in the *Century Magazine*, which paid £354 for it.

Kipling's attention in 1895 was concentrated upon *The Second Jungle Book* up to the time of his visit to England and, after *The Brushwood Boy* was also off his mind, on his 7000-word article on the Victoria Cross, which had been commissioned by the *Century*. Again it had been a good year, although at its beginning he had been disturbed by Caroline's health, never robust, which had been further affected by severe burns on the face from a stove which turned her brown hair grey, soon to become completely white. It was to recuperate from this accident that Conland had sent her to Washington with Rudyard at the beginning of 1895.

During his holiday in Washington Kipling had made friends with one of those rare spirits to whose criticisms and arguments he was prepared to listen with patience and respect. This was Theodore Roosevelt, then head of the Civil Service Commission, and afterwards President of the United States, an ardent disciple of the robust and virile life, and a despiser of cant and humbug in public affairs.

Kipling, who was at once attracted to this man little older than himself, described with humour how Roosevelt would come to his hotel and 'thank God in a loud voice that he had not one drop of English blood in him'. They went to the Zoo together, and Kipling gazed with infantile excitement at the grizzly bears. When he asked Roosevelt how he proposed to raise the money for a new navy, he answered unexpectedly: 'Out of you' – by explaining to America how perfidious Albion was only waiting to descend on the unprotected coasts of Liberty.

After this early-flowering friendship in Washington, the two men saw little of one another, but we shall see them corresponding in brilliant letters which show two powerful minds in frequent collision.

Kipling declined a curious invitation during this visit from the wife of a Senator to visit the Senate and listen to her husband 'twisting the lion's tail', but such episodes made him even more thoughtful. He browsed unhappily in the Smithsonian, reflecting that:

Every nation, like every individual, walks in a vain show – else it could not live with itself – but I never got over the wonder of a people who, having extirpated the aboriginals of their continent more completely than any modern race had ever done, honestly believed that they were a Godly little New England community, setting examples to brutal mankind. This wonder I used to explain to Theodore Roosevelt, who made the glass cases of Indian relics shake with his rebuttals.[23]

At the end of the year 1895 Kipling's spirits were revived by two events. His old editor and friend Kay Robinson, who was travelling in the Middle West, came to Vermont to stay with his most illustrious employee. He was followed by a man who was to become a lifelong friend, and who now presented himself on behalf of the publisher Scribners, who wished to undertake a complete edition of Kipling's works. His name was Frank Doubleday, and owing to his initials FND was soon to be known facetiously as 'Effendi', a joke after Kipling's heart. At first received by Rudyard and Carrie with the churlish suspicion they reserved for publishers and reporters, his charm and personality quickly brushed aside their defences, and one of the most enduring friendships of Rudyard's life was established.

On 31 December he added his usual end-of-year note to Caroline's diary: 'And so ends our fourth and best year. The Lord has been good to us beyond telling, and we have taken delight in all the days of our life.' This confident note of happiness was, unfortunately, premature.

CHAPTER XI

THE END IN VERMONT

ON 10 October 1894 Mrs Kipling had already made an ominous entry in her diary: 'A Glory of a day turned wrong by a miserable Beatty complication', and this is the first reference she makes to the deteriorating relations between 'Naulakha' and 'Maplewood'. There was already a cold autumnal blight in the air.

What manner of man was this, who was to cause such havoc in the ordered prosperity of his brother-in-law's life? Here was the problem child of the Balestier family, upon whose future that paragon Wolcott had spent many unprofitable hours of reflection – a robust sinewy figure, fine features, glacial blue eyes in a leathery countenance which, when age and dissipation had eaten into it, resembled 'an ailing eagle',[1] a mouth of surprising gentleness, an indescribable strutting swagger of mien, and a conversation shot with a profanity robbed of offence by a devastating and unsimulated charm. This was no mere Vermont hayseed, but a man of formidable personality, at once baleful and endearing, who, when fired by drink or anger, had 'a tongue like a skinning knife'.[2]

Oddly allied to the wild manners of the Western Prairie were a fastidious intellect, a love of good books, and a passion for conviviality and companionship which made men go miles out of their way, on a trip northward or southward, to spend an afternoon in the remote white farmhouse where Beatty lived with his wife Mai and daughter Marjorie in a happy confusion of dogs, bottles and agricultural implements. He had had a vagrant boyhood, his mother, a widow, having no fixed abode, living first in one town then another, the children with her. In each of these places Beatty left a trail of havoc. 'We are all a little crazy,' he said, 'it's the only normal way to be.'

When the sober Wolcott was writing his first books and mastering his trade, Beatty could not settle down to any steady work. A desultory process of gentleman-farming was his nearest approach to it. Sometimes, when the fit seized him, he would be seen, a strapping figure in cowboy hat, the sunburned arms with their swelling biceps tossing hay into the wagon. He was a hard man with his cattle and with his horses, which he loved to drive at a crazy speed down the dusty Vermont roads, lashing them round the blind corners.

He was hopelessly incompetent in finance, and often heavily in debt, yet it was years before anyone had the heart to serve a writ on him. The farmers remembered his reckless generosity, and no winter night was too foul for Balestier to answer a neighbour's call for help, whether it was to rally an expectant father, or free an animal caught in the snow. His open-handedness often bordered on folly. When he had harvested some superb peaches, a friend, aware of his financial state, asked how much they had realized: 'Oh,' he said, 'they were much too beautiful to sell, I gave them all away.'[3]

Beatty's main passion was for offering hospitality to others, and his only serious enemy drink, under the influence of which the darker side of his character would emerge with sudden and alarming violence, and he could become an ugly customer. A great bronze bell hung from the top of his front porch, and when he saw someone in the distance he would tug the bell rope and bawl across the valley, 'God damn it, come and have a drink!'[4] The visitor would sometimes see meat being cooked over a great outdoor grill, from which came a delicious smell, and Beatty standing at a long wooden table carving a dripping tenderloin steak, heaping the plates of his guests, plying them with more. It was of no consequence to him how many unexpected guests arrived; room must be found for them. The plates were loaded and the glasses filled and refilled.

He was a brilliant talker and raconteur, and a dangerous man to argue with, quick as lightning on to a weak point, swift and brutal in repartee. It was a character delightful and naive in its deep instincts for affection, but darkened by a capacity for sustained and vindictive hatred. Above all, he intended to lead his own life and would not tolerate advice or admonition – a life of hard manual work in hot sun or driving snow, broken by mad sleigh races with lathered horses across the frozen Connecticut River for wagers he could not afford, bouts of wild dissipation, and acts of neighbourly kindness.

Wolcott had always worried about this scapegrace brother, so different from himself. When Beatty became engaged to Mai Mendon he wrote musingly:

But Beatty would choose nothing but the best, the best and most expensive, so she is probably charming. In fact I have his word for it. But they both need a guardian appointed. Do pray talk seriously to Miss Mendon. They will be for driving a four-in-hand through life, both of them I'm afraid; and they will be lucky if this inclination does not bring them to a donkey cart. If Miss Mendon would swear a solemn oath before her marriage never to buy anything for which they cannot pay at the moment, or let Beatty have a bill anywhere, she may be sure that she will have a solider foundation for happiness than in any single resolution she can take.[5]

But Beatty was not impressed by these cold admonitions, and preferred to dispense altogether with the prudential virtues. His anxious brother had tried to keep an eye on Beatty by bringing him to London, 'and,' said Alexander Woollcott, 'there are uneasy recollections of his striding through the Savoy, stewed to the gills, dragged by several leashed wolf-hounds'.[6] The words once used by Lloyd George about Michael Collins float back to the mind, strangely applicable to Beatty Balestier, although one man achieved much and the other nothing: 'Vivacious, buoyant, highly strung, gay, impulsive, but passing readily to grimness and back again to gaiety, full of fascination and charm – but also of dangerous fire.'

It was not merely the need for thrift, or Caroline's homing instinct that had caused the Kiplings to settle in Brattleboro. There had been another consideration – Beatty. Wolcott, who babbled about Beatty in his dying delirium, had charged the capable and managing Caroline with the care of the *enfant terrible*, and Rudyard, through his love of Wolcott, felt himself involved in the responsibility.

At the very outset we can see all the necessary ingredients for bitter domestic strife, and the disaster moves forward to its climax with depressing certainty. Two persons of exceptional strength and determination, and precisely antipathetic character, were now opposed to one another: Caroline with her strong will and love of power over others, always before satisfied, her strict conventions and respectability – the cockaded groom, the changing for dinner – and Beatty, equally strong and far more wilful, contemptuous of snobbery and convention, and fiercely resolved to preserve his raffish independence – prepared, indeed, to do so when really angered with complete indifference to public opinion, vicious relish in the scandal, and methods of callous brutality.

Beatty's finances were disgraceful, and he would come and whistle outside the Kipling house, when Kipling would steal furtively out and pay off the sheriff who had come to collect payment of a debt. On other nights Beatty would call on his grandmother, who had a weak spot for him, to wheedle cash out of her. On such occasions he would be driven out by the maid, Kate, their voices rising through the house in loud argument and Madame Balestier dissolving in tears.

The fatal quarrel, then, between Kipling and his brother-in-law had its origins in a Balestier family feud, beginning in childhood with an early collision between Beatty's wayward character and his sister's love of domination. As we look back upon this pathetic fracas it is easy to see glaring faults on both sides. Caroline's sharp tongue was a source of constant friction, and she did not hesitate to give Beatty the rough side of it. To her trim and businesslike mind he was a worthless scamp and a disgrace to the family, and wounding comments soon found their way back to him. And these were merely a repetition of the past, for when Beatty had been courting Mai Mendon, Wolcott's reactions had been anxious but paternal, whereas Caroline had not concealed her opinion that no girl would marry Beatty owing to his addiction to drink and his idle feckless habit of life.

When Wolcott had taken Beatty and Mai to England in 1890, it was not only with the object of keeping an eye on his brother, but also to enable the couple to exist physically and to draw upon Wolcott's business resources in London. This unmanly dependence further angered Caroline, who received the bride so frigidly that the Balestiers returned to America in a few months' time to set up house in 'Maplewood',[7] and a lasting resentment of Caroline was from that moment planted in the mind of Beatty's wife.

The atmosphere was further clouded by a rumour that Beatty was a forger, spread by a malicious servant at Madame Balestier's house, and which in spite of its tainted source he resented so bitterly that eventually he severed all connections with 'Beechwood'.

When the Kiplings decided to build 'Naulakha', they employed Beatty to superintend the workmen and outdoor work and arrange for the purchase of building materials, imagining that they were thus carrying out Wolcott's wishes and giving him much-needed employment. Rudyard's relations with his brother-in-law were excellent. He warmed to the strange creature with his weatherbeaten face and volcanic oaths, and enjoyed the easy-going flexible hospitality of 'Maplewood', so different from that of his own house. He saw Beatty as reckless and attractive, an American version of the army officer whom he had venerated in India in those days that now seemed so long ago.

Caroline's dislike of Beatty steadily increased as her brother's financial backslidings continued. Determined to live a grand life with a famous husband, she was incensed at this albatross round her neck, at her relationship with this ne'er-do-well brother with his drinking bouts and incorrigible idleness, and she was appalled by his slovenly business habits. She felt, with reason, that he was disgracing the Balestier family, and she made the fatal mistake of trying to discipline him through financial control, thus further humiliating him by the abuse of her position.

No action that could have been taken to excite the cruel side of Balestier's character was omitted. Caroline had not the slightest idea how to control such a wayward horse, nor any suspicion that the snaffle might be more effective than the curb. The gentle Mai was antagonized by the suggestion that Marjorie was a bad influence on Josephine, and strongly resented what she considered to be Caroline's patronizing manner, while Beatty's murderous temper was further roused by the impression current in the village that he was being kept by Kipling out of charity, 'held up by the seat of his breeches', statements that soon found their way to Mai's ears.

Meanwhile, Beatty's conduct had been equally reprehensible, and he increased the tension by a series of ridiculous offences. He was caught sneaking into 'Naulakha' before the Kiplings were up, and helping himself to various household articles, including the baby's malted milk, an action unlikely to improve his standing with Caroline.[8] Nor had he performed his side of the 'Naulakha' contract satisfactorily. He remained a spendthrift, with a hopeless ineptitude for finance, and although Kipling gave him the money to pay all the bills, many of them came back unsettled. 'Maplewood' was heavily mortgaged and there were notes owing to the bank, backed by Mrs Balestier and Caroline.

At last affairs were taken out of Beatty's hands and given to Matt Howard, the coachman, whom he had always disliked. Beatty nearly landed himself in another fight when driving the same way as Howard, by weaving back and forth across the road to prevent the angry Howard passing.[9] This deplorable situation was brought to a head when Caroline directly accused Beatty of appropriating the money he had been given to pay the workmen. She tried to persuade her mother to join her in removing their names from Beatty's notes to the bank, thus foreclosing the mortgage and reducing him to bankruptcy.[10]

The purpose of this desperate manoeuvre was to confront Beatty with the alternative of going away and doing an honest job of work, or starving, and she appears to have ignored the fact that such an action would also have left Mai and Marjorie destitute, or dependent on charity. Old Mrs Balestier refused to consider it. 'Beatty,' she said, 'is a gentleman, drunk or sober.'

When Beatty heard of this move he hurried round to 'Naulakha' in great perturbation, with the intention of answering the charge, but found the house closed to him, while an agitated letter which he left, asking for a meeting, remained unanswered. There were other sordid causes of dispute. Beatty had conveyed to Caroline a parcel of meadowland of nine acres, reserving the right of changing the highway and of crossing the meadow in such places as might be agreed upon. They had a furious quarrel about his right to cross the meadow in front of 'Naulakha', and her right to plough up the garden area.[11]

This trouble had estranged the households, and after it there was no further intercourse between the two wives or the daughters. Caroline was further vexed when her mother tried to be impartial in the dispute, and lost no opportunity of instilling a general derogation of Beatty into her husband, perhaps causing him, after three years, to feel a certain social dread of him, and even physical apprehension. Beatty had taken to coming up to 'Naulakha' and talking atrociously to Kipling. It appeared that he made a point of drinking before these visits. In the end he was drunk every time he came, and so disturbed and upset Kipling that he could not write.[12]

We may leave the sorry affair for a moment, and turn to some of the other events of Rudyard's life in this year. On 2 February his daughter Elsie had been born. 'I have been a sorely tried man and anxious,' he wrote to Norton, 'but I write now to tell you that at 3.20 yesterday (Sunday) afternoon a very fat and healthy she-girl-babe, ridiculously like her mother, was born to us.' His earnings steadily increased. On 6 March 1896, the editor of the New York *Sunday World* wrote to an agent: 'I wish you would try and get me a story from Rudyard Kipling at a dollar a word for a thousand words on the idea "America could never conquer England".'

He remained indulgent and sympathetic towards young people, relaxing even the iron rule of no work without a contract and copyright. On 1 May, he was approached by the undergraduates of Yale University, who had just founded a Kipling Club, to attend their first banquet, designed to be a gay meal at Heublin's Café across the green from the campus. He was not prepared to go, but, unwilling to disappoint them, gave them this generous send-off, which arrived in a small square envelope and was read out at the dinner:

Attend ye lasses av swate Parnasses
   An' wipe my burnin' tears away
For I'm declinin' a chanst o' dinin'
   Wid the bhoys of Yale on the fourteenth May.

The leadin' feature will be literature,
   (Av a moral nature as is just and right)
For their light and leadin' are engaged in readin'
   Me immortial worracks from dawn till night.

They've made a club there an' staked out grub there
   Wid plates an' napkins in a joyous row,
An' they'd think it splindid if I attinded
   An' so would I – but I cannot go.

The honest fact is that daily practice
   Av rowlin' inkpots, the same as me
Conshumes me hours in the Muses' bowers
   An' leaves me divil a day to spree.

When you grow oulder an' skin your shoulder
   At the World's great wheel in your chosen line,
You'll find your chances, as Time advances,
   For takin' a lark are as slim as mine.

But I'm digressin'; accept my blessin',
   An' remimber what ould King Solomon said,
That youth is ructious an' whiskey fluxious,
   An' there's nothing certain but the mornin' head.[13]

                         Rudyard Kipling.

He made several journeys with Conland to Gloucester, Mass., and Boston, to collect material for *Captains Courageous*, and learn how the cod fishermen worked off the Grand Banks. At Gloucester Kipling attended the Annual Memorial Service to the men lost in the cod-fishing schooner fleet. Haunted, as ever, by the terror of recognition, he had himself and Conland registered in the hotel as 'Dr Conland and friend'. They went to the old T wharf of Boston Harbour, and frequented the sailors' eating-houses, boarding every craft they saw, and acquired charts and the crude marine instruments of the day.

Kipling looked at the bustling scene with boyish wonder: 'I had a sight of the first sickening up-rush and vomit of iridescent coal-dusted water into the hold of a ship, a crippled iron hulk, sinking at her moorings.' Conland took the great slippery cod, and gutting them with deft surgical fingers, showed Kipling how the fishermen prepared them for the hold, and Kipling listened intently while he mused over old bygone ships he had loved. Carried away by his enthusiasm, Conland sent Kipling out in a pollock-fisher where he was horribly sick, and the crew tried to revive him with stale pollock.

Captains Courageous was finished in October but by this time the Kiplings were in England. 'It seems very odd to me,' Oscar Wilde remarked languidly of this book, 'that a man should write a whole novel about cod-fishing – but then I suppose that is because I do not like cod.' Kipling, at the time of writing, was delighted with *Captains Courageous* and thought it a major achievement, but it afterwards dawned on him that the novel was not his forte. He wrote later to a friend:

> You're dead wrong about my 'sustained fiction'. There ain't two cents worth of plot in the blessed novel – it's all business – cod-fishing on the banks; and no love at all. Wish I hadn't told you now in such enthusiastic terms, but I was bung full of it when I wrote. It's in the nature of a sketch for better work: and I've crept out of the possible holes by labelling it a boy's story.[14]

On 6 May 1896 Kipling was riding his bicycle in the wooded country called the Pines, between 'Naulakha' and 'Maplewood'. He had just posted a manuscript to London. Suddenly Beatty Balestier's team rounded a bend, cruelly driven as usual, and pulled up with a jerk. Kipling saw at once that Beatty was demented with rage, and he fell off his bicycle. Balestier roared at him: 'See here – I want to speak to you!' Kipling was alarmed by Balestier's wild appearance and said: 'If you have anything to say, say it to my lawyers.' Beatty, after this remark, 'seemed crazy, waving his hands about, his cheekbones blue with passion' and shouted: 'By Jesus, this is no case for lawyers, I want you to understand that you have got to retract those God-damned lies you've been telling about me. You've got to do it inside a week or I'll kick the God-damned soul out of you.'

'Let us get this straight,' said Kipling, 'do you mean personal violence?'

'Yes, I'll give you a week, and if you don't do it I'll blow out your God-damned brains.'

'You will have only yourself to blame for the consequences,' said Kipling.

'Don't you dare to threaten me, you little bastard!' roared Beatty.

Then he spat out the words: 'Liar, cheat, coward!'

He lashed his horses and drove on to where the road forked forty yards on, leaving Kipling standing on the road with his bicycle. Matt Howard was close behind, and approached quickly, taking Kipling by the arm and seating him in the carriage, which was then driven home.[15]

This preposterous episode had a deplorable effect on Kipling's nervous system. He detested any form of scene, and the encounter had made him feel physically ill. He was also extremely alarmed. Convinced that Beatty would kill him in some future state of frenzy, from now on he kept a pistol, which was afterwards offered to and declined by Howard, who said that he preferred to use his fists. To everything else was added the bitter mortification that owing to the physical disparity between the two men, the Laureate of the Deed, in a situation when he was clearly right, was compelled in the face of the menace of this enraged American farmer to confine himself to stilted talk about lawyers. The doctrine of power had failed in application. Instead of splendid purification by action there was a visit to a magistrate.

Back at 'Naulakha' he held a conference with Caroline, and in their extreme agitation they made the fatal decision, in the interests of Kipling's safety, to send a sheriff to arrest Balestier for assault. The folly of this decision is sufficient proof of how shaken Kipling had been by his brother-in-law's outrageous behaviour. Further scandal was the last thing that he wanted, but in his bewildered mind was a picture of a country magistrate in his library, lecturing Beatty gravely on the error of his ways. Certainly there was no remote idea in it that this ill-considered step was setting spinning the wheels of the criminal law, and providing an opportunity for which the oft-rebuffed reporters had so long waited, sharpening their pencils in vain.

A preliminary hearing took place on 9 May, in the office of Judge Newton, where Beatty was summoned, charged with breaking the peace by making an assault on Rudyard Kipling 'with opprobrious and indecent epithets, and threatening to kill'. Kipling was alarmed by the interest taken in the case, by the crowded room, the atmosphere of Bank Holiday levity in the proceedings, and Beatty's ominous assurance. He was in his element, delighted by the mud he had stirred up. He admitted having threatened Kipling, but only with a beating; he admitted his violent language. Newton decided that he must hold Balestier pending a further hearing, which was fixed for the following Tuesday. Was Mr Balestier prepared to furnish bail for his release? Balestier gave a leathery smile, and intimated that he was not prepared to do so.

It was at this point that Kipling suddenly perceived the position in which his impetuosity and Beatty's revengeful tactics had placed him. He saw himself branded in America as the great man of international fame and princely earnings, who had hounded his penniless brother-in-law into prison and ruin, and his mind ranged over the appalling vistas of publicity he saw opening before him. He fluttered a cheque book, and offered to supply Beatty's bail. It was disdainfully refused. Kipling lost his head and made a number of statements far from the facts, until at sunset the hearing was adjourned.

The Balestier hearing was reopened on 12 May, and room was made in the Town Hall for those who wished to attend. The news had flashed to all parts of the world that Rudyard Kipling had arrested his brother-in-law. The exultant reporters streamed into the little town by night and day, scarcely believing that they were at last to witness the public baiting of the man who had so often repulsed them.

They came from New York, from Boston, Springfield, Philadelphia and Washington, glowing with anticipation. It was a moment for Kipling of despair, for Beatty of malignant triumph. For some reason at liberty, he met the reporters at the railway station, and drove them in relays past Kipling's windows to 'Maplewood', where they were filled with whisky by the attentive Mai. Afterwards he sat in court watching Kipling wincing under the glare of publicity that now held him like a burning glass, under the roars of laughter that swept over the packed Court House.

The torture continued all day. C. C. Fitts, the State Attorney, prosecuted; an attorney called Haskins appeared for Kipling; Beatty was represented by George Hill. Judge Newton, having the time of his life, allowed the fullest latitude. The audience was regaled by the spectacle of Kipling floundering under a racking cross-examination by Hill. He said that he had settled in Brattleboro mainly to help Balestier – 'I came here for that purpose – to help that boy all I could: if Beatty would stop drinking and go to work. It's what I stayed here for, the reason I settled here in preference to anywhere else in America.'[16] He made occasional sarcastic sallies: 'This was the first time I ever had my life threatened, and I did not know just what was etiquette under such circumstances.'

The cross-examination tried to extract from Kipling the admission that he had put about certain rumours, for Beatty's counsel indicated that his claim was that the threat was simply one of a thrashing, and the provocation consisted in stories which he believed Kipling had set in circulation, that Balestier was living on his bounty. Kipling swore that he did not know what Balestier meant when he demanded a retraction. Although Beatty's side of the case was not given in court, he adroitly cornered his friends the reporters, who liked him and went fishing with him, and focused his *farouche* charm squarely upon them. 'I don't look like a tough, do I?' he asked plaintively.

Kipling's testimony was so contradictory that the gallery frequently roared with laughter, and the sympathy that had first been given to him by the townspeople ebbed towards Beatty, the hero of the hour. Kipling insisted that he had been in danger of his life: 'I honestly think he will kill me some time, if he loses his head again,' he said earnestly. The cross-examination dragged through the morning and afternoon, probing and taunting, a period of sustained agony to the plaintiff. He had claimed to have been supporting Balestier, but was forced to admit that for the last year he had not been doing so. When he said that his main reason for settling in Brattleboro was to help 'that boy', Hill asked sarcastically: 'Was it out of kindness that you served out this warrant?' and Kipling snapped: 'I have a distinct aversion to being shot at.' When Hill asked if taking care of Balestier had been his chief occupation, he answered coldly: 'I have also written a thing or two.' Finally he raised his voice and said: 'I would not retract a word under threat of death from any living man.'

Kipling had, on the whole, not impressed, but his failure in court has been exaggerated. The reporter of the *Brattleboro Reformer*, fresh from the scene, wrote: 'Mr Kipling's appearance on the stand was one to reveal the qualities that so attract people who come into close relation with him, while a superficial acquaintance is apt to repel. There were not only flashes and sparkles of brightness, but there were glimpses of the depth and tenderness of feeling that contribute to his power.'[17] The case was put off for the September term of court, Beatty being ordered to give bail of $400 to keep the peace and another $400 for his appearance at the County Court.

The case left Kipling prostrate for days. Caroline wrote in her diary on 12 May: 'Beatty's trial comes on in the a.m. and lasts until 5 p.m. leaving Rud a wreck. The lawyers play to the reporters. May 13: Rud a total wreck. Sleeps all the time, dull and listless and dreary. These are dark days for us. May 14: Rud very miserable and I most anxious.' In vain did his friends, Day and Conland, call on him on the evening of the trial to assure him of the respect of the community, which would tolerate no threats or annoyance to him. He seemed past caring.

Kipling had next to endure the dreary ribaldry of the press. Even the *Brattleboro Reformer* could not refrain from an oafish parody of 'Danny Deever':

> 'What makes the Kipling breathe so hard?' said the copper ready-made.
> 'He's might scart, he's mighty scart', the First Selectman said.
> 'What makes his wife look down so glum?' said the copper ready-made.
> 'It's family pride, it's family pride', the First Selectman said.

The American period was nearly over. Pan was soon to be driven from Vermont. Kipling knew that he could never again recapture the tranquil happiness of those first years, and Vermont must for ever remain for him a place of evil associations. He could not face the triumphant Beatty again in September. Emotionally and physically he was incapable of confronting the ordeal. He did not wish to go to England, where he found the climate enervating and the privacy inadequate. It was with profound sadness that he prepared to leave 'Naulakha', where his children were born, and where the *Jungle Books* had been fashioned in a mind working at the height of its wonderful creative power.

His spirits further ebbed as the full consciousness of what had happened slowly penetrated his numbed mind, and he spent his last three months in a state of morose convalescence, never moving now, even within the limits of his own land, without the protection of a friend –Lockwood de Forest, or Matt Howard. The atmosphere at 'Naulakha' was one of abysmal gloom, while hard by at 'Maplewood' reigned almost indecent triumph.

Kipling's attitude towards America was hardened by his experience there. Already before the case came on, during the Venezuelan crisis, he told an American lady that if the Great White Squadron appeared on the coast, New York, Boston and Philadelphia would be wiped out in three days, becoming so angry that he could only recover his composure after a long walk in the woods.

When the time came to go, Caroline was in tears, and Kipling seemed broken-hearted. He said: 'I love "Naulakha",' and as he spoke of the touch of autumn already on the distant hills, tears filled his eyes. He was leaving the only home he had known, through a farcical misunderstanding with a man who should have been his friend. Never in the years ahead was he to talk of Brattleboro, or read anything that reminded him of that dreadful year. No sudden contrition softened Beatty's malignant triumph. The Kiplings should never return, he said, except to litigation and humiliation in the Court Room.[18]

It is, at least, a melancholy satisfaction to have heard from Beatty's second wife that in the later years all hatred of Kipling had vanished from his mind, and that his restless spirit was at last cleansed from revengeful thoughts. Indeed it is doubtful if he had ever really harboured them. He never relaxed his hostility to his sister, to whom he attributed the whole disaster. When he was dying, worn out by the mad impetus of his life, with the writs at last pouring in, he said with pathetic impotence that if ever Kipling came back he would be his best friend – he would get all the bands in Brattleboro to play for him.[19] He told his doctor, Hogle, that he was sorry for the fight with Kipling, and referred to it as between two hot-headed young men. Hogle's father, an old-fashioned minister, came up to see Beatty, and the old man suggested that he should say a prayer. Beatty nodded, sat with tears streaming down his cheeks, and quietly thanked the minister. It was probably the first time in his life that he had been affected by religion, but he knew that he had not long to live.[20] He died in poverty and debt at Brattleboro in 1936, the same year in which Rudyard Kipling was buried in Westminster Abbey.

And so at the end of August 1896 Kipling left America with a heavy heart, leaving much behind him that he loved and would never see again: Monadnock 'busy with his sky affairs', anemones in the woods in spring, and the fresh mornings of blue sky and keen air when he walked to the scattered clapboarded farms, and talked to the farmers while the milk rattled into the bucket in the cowshed; the roads heavy with dust in summer, and horses at pasture in the heat, swishing flies under the shadow of the maples, the blackberries hot and vinous in the sun. Of this cruel episode in his life he makes in his autobiography a single characteristic remark: 'So far as I was concerned, I felt the atmosphere was to some extent hostile.'

CHAPTER XII

ENGLAND

THE Kiplings returned to England in the Norddeutscher Lloyd steamer *Bremen*. They ran the Banks in brilliant sunshine, and passed within half a mile of the living image of the schooner *We're Here* of *Captains Courageous*, slatting about under her riding sail and the dories bobbing on the swell round her. They passed more ships than Rudyard could ever remember seeing, a sullen tramp plunging so near to them that they burned rockets for her, and for the first time in all his voyages he saw a whale jumping clear of the water.

The summer was ending, and on 8 September 1896 they began to run into the climate of England – a thick greasy sky, wind from the south-west and a sullen choppy sea. Already Kipling's heart sank, and he began to think with longing of the fine tingling September mornings on the hillside at 'Naulakha', coming keen with a tang of frost.

The ninth of September found them at Maidencombe, a village near Torquay, where they leased 'Rock House', a building of stone and stucco that had been inhabited for thirty years by three old ladies, a house 'large and bright, with big rooms each and all open to the sun, the grounds embellished with great trees and the warm land dropping southerly to the clean sea under the Mary Church cliffs'.

Kipling looked from his work-table on to the decks of the fishing boats which came in to tend their lobster-pots, and upon the sea, sometimes aquamarine in the sun and so clear that he could see the smooth white stones upon the bottom, sometimes ruffled dark purple when a rising wind stirred the listless palms, and always, as he wrote, was in his ears the monotonous rise and fall of the 'lazy, plunging sea'.

Their beach was a tiny cove, reached by an almost perpendicular lane – a place, he thought, for the smuggling days – and a flight of rude stone steps. Three miles south was the rocky nose that covered Torquay harbour, and there were dangerous shoals outside, half-tide rocks slimy and razor-toothed, where the whiting and pollock congregated in shoals. No one went to the little bay except the fishermen and Kipling, but now and then he found footprints in the sand and the mark of a row-boat's keel.

Down in the cove, where the cliffs towered on either side, the air was heavy as in a greenhouse, and it was as lonely as Land's End, the silence broken only by the forlorn scream of sea-birds and the beat of the waves on the sand. Over all the place was a lush redness. The grass and trees grew to the water's edge, but the dominant note was red: the soil was a deep red and there was a splendid mixture of red, green foliage, and blue sea and sky.

At first it seemed that Kipling would be happy here, in this sub-tropical 'un-English' place, which resembled rather some wooded cleft in the Italian coast asleep in the noonday heat. He had arrived auspiciously in the splendour of a storm, an equinoctial, when the glass fell an inch and oscillated wildly, and the wind took hold and whipped the Channel into lather. Kipling exulted, as always, in the sudden anger of the sea and wind. He watched the top twisted out of a big poplar on his lawn, then an elm torn up by the roots. He saw a trawler blown out to sea, a rag of brown sail in the flying spume, and heard the whistle of a steamer. The scud was thick over the sea and from a secluded corner in the kitchen garden he looked down on the waters boiling like a tub of yeast. Off Brixham the fishing fleet were holding on under the lee of the land with everything down that could bite bottom, and a brig was dying down the Channel. It was an exhilarating welcome.

He was quickly in touch with the Navy.

I was invited down to Dartmouth – half an hour down the line – to sleep on the *Britannia* – the old three-decker training school for officers in our navy. I had a great time among the naval cadets while the wind whistled and tore down the Dart, the tiny little river where she is moored. All the instructors are naval officers – and their tales were beautiful. And it blew and it blew and it blew! Then a grey smudge shot up the river and moored. That was a torpedo-boat destroyer of 200 tons made to go 26 knots. She just jumped her soul out and went under the water for the most part.

Meanwhile the *Britannia*'s tender – *The Racer*, which goes out every week with a load of cadets for practical seamanship, was about ten hours overdue somewhere up-channel. She turned up on Sunday, a steam sloop, barque-rigged, and her Lieutenant arrived on the *Britannia* with the news that he had spent Sunday night in Portland harbour, both anchors down, and steaming to keep his place. All the cadets had been deadly sick, but, he told me, his great secret was 'never let 'em get their heads down'. 'Once a boy's head goes under a blanket,' said he, 'he's no good for the rest of the trip. So I kept 'em at it.' But I never saw such a gale. The torpedo boats were scuttling into port wherever they could find one. Next week I go down to Plymouth ... to see a steam trial – if it's fine.'[1]

The collection of verse *The Seven Seas* was published in November 1896, and was an immediate success both in sales and in critical praise, while the fact that Kipling was the author of 'McAndrew's Hymn' was not lost on his new naval friends. He found himself a familiar figure, indeed a hero, to officers and ratings alike. They were not lonely in Torquay. Relations and friends came and went. 'The Pater' came from Tisbury and turned the coach house into a studio, for he was planning to illustrate the complete edition of Kipling's works with figures in low relief. And at the beginning of 1897, Frank Doubleday, 'Beloved Effendi', arrived in England and came to 'Rock House'. He was about to leave Scribner's to set up in publishing on his own, and would henceforth publish all the American editions of Kipling's work for the rest of his life.

Apart from his contacts with the Navy, Kipling had followed his usual practice of attaching himself to the local characters in the pub, and soon found himself at the head of a strange menagerie, consisting of a Sergeant Instructor of Volunteers, a Volunteer Sergeant of Engineers, and a Roman Catholic priest. He spent much time with the fishermen, indulging his passion for technical detail, comparing the English methods with those used by the cod-fishers off the whiting grounds, and noticing that the fishermen's forefingers were gashed and scored with the friction of hand-lines he wrote to Conland: 'I want to astonish the natives with "nippers". Please mail me a pair of 'em – small size – they'll save me a good deal of discomfort.'

He soon became restive in the strange climate, mild, damp and enervating, the roses and fuschia bushes in full bloom in November, their red petals hardly trembling in the close air: 'It has played the cat and banjo with all my teeth.' 'Our weather,' he wrote, 'is and has been – British. "Bloody British" is the only word for it.'[2]

The returned wanderer also surveyed the surrounding English gentry with distaste:

I have been studying my fellow-countrymen from the outside. Those four years in America will be blessed unto me for all my life. We are a rummy breed – and O Lord the ponderous wealthy society. Torquay is such a place as I do desire acutely to upset by dancing through it with nothing on but my spectacles. Villas, clipped hedges, and shaved lawns; fat old ladies with obese landaus – the Almighty is a discursive and frivolous trifler compared with some of 'em. But the land is indescribably lovely and I am making friends with the farmers.

Everyone was learning to ride the latest novelty, the bicycle, and there was a circular cinder-track in Torquay where men and women rode round in special costumes supplied by the tailors for this sport. On a tandem machine with double handlebars and in quaint clothes the Kiplings rode down the winding high-banked lanes past grinning villagers, each under the false impression that the other enjoyed it.

In good weather Kipling would do ten miles a day, with his rod strapped on the frame and his lunch on his back, for a day's luce-fishing, ending up in a delightful inn he had discovered six miles down the road, kept by a fat old woman and her two daughters. Here he relaxed on a sofa in the parlour while they brewed him hot whisky and water 'with the air of duchesses'.

Kipling's military enthusiasm prompted the local Volunteer Company to invite him to give away their prizes at the yearly prize-giving, and to make a speech. The Captain of the Company owned the fifty-acre farm next to Kipling, who would go ferreting with the son, working the ferret, 'a cream-coloured weasel with blood-red eyes', in the afternoons in a rabbit warren that backed on the old abandoned smugglers' cave. Just within gunshot the land went down to the sea in two-hundred-foot bluffs; 'and what with the screaming of the gulls, the echoes of the shot, and the sea booming and churning in the caves below as the twilight fell, it was a curious experience'. All the land had been slowly bitten into by the sea, which covered a sunken forest, and after the gales blackened tree-stumps were thrown on to the beach.

Kipling now began to set himself a higher literary standard, probably on Caroline's advice, and the waste-paper basket received even more than its usual quota of prematurely discarded manuscripts. For a while he felt happier and better than he had for the past year, and largely recovered the energies that had been so unworthily dissipated. He felt the creative impulse moving again, and he knew that there was a rich, unworked vein latent there, but he was doubtful about his powers as a poet, and when Charles Eliot Norton wrote an article in the *Atlantic Monthly* on this subject, Kipling replied with unaffected humility:

True it is, most sadly true that I have not been true to my duties, but I did not know that I had been so untrue. As you know I love the fun and the riot of writing (I am daily and nightly perplexed with my private responsibilities before God), and there are times when it is just a comfort and delight to let out with the pen and ink – so long as it does not do anyone any moral harm. I don't believe very much in my genius. Then there is the danger it seems of a man running off into William Watson's kind of wordy rot if he at a comparatively tender age considers himself a poet.[3]

'It is not easy,' said Mrs Kipling to Norton, 'to make Rud take what you are good enough to call his genius seriously: he does not believe in it, in the very least.'

On 13 December Kipling began a story of schoolboy life which was to become *Stalky and Co*. He was delighted with this book, which was continued when he moved to Rottingdean, but it offended many others, including 'Stalky' himself.[4]

In Kipling's own breezy phrase: 'I crowed over it like a hen with one chick.' He was fond of reading it aloud to his friends as it progressed, with terrific gusto, laughing, as his cousin Mrs Mackail remembered, so loudly at his own jokes that she could not hear what he said.[5] Another cousin, Florence Macdonald, was one of those privileged to sit in his study while he was writing these stories. Both would burst into frequent roars of laughter, and Rudyard would say: 'Come on, Florence, what shall we make them do now?'

Kipling's own relish in this book is an indication that his humorous literary bent was, for the time, set broadly on slapstick. The effects are contrived with the blatancy of a percussion instrument, and the stage properties are conventional and juvenile, dead cats stinking under dormitory rafters, drunken yokels, and fatuously oafish schoolmasters. It was the *genre* which was later to pervade such famous stories as *Brugglesmith*, *My Sunday at Home*, *The Village that Voted the Earth was Flat* and *The Puzzler*.

It is a heavy, earthy humour with a strong whiff of *Schadenfreude* in the revengeful comic climaxes, sometimes set curiously in a background of mellow pastoral description, as in *My Sunday at Home*, where the preposterous brawl with the navvy is in strident contrast with a beautiful and languid picture of an English shire in an afternoon of high summer. While this method is the delight of many admirers of Kipling who know these stories by heart, there are others who will sigh in vain for a lowering of pressure, a feathery touch of irony, and the economy of understatement.

We should not overlook the courage which Kipling showed in writing *Stalky and Co*. There was much in the public-school system that dovetailed perfectly with his own conception of the perfect administration and executive. In *Stalky*, as in the couplet in 'The Islanders' about the muddied oafs at the goals, he was metaphorically spitting into the faces of his own bewildered supporters, in an honest castigation of aspects of public-school life that roused his anger and impatience. 'In *Stalky and Co.*,' wrote Edward Shanks, 'he took his life as an author in his hands. It could not have been other than a violent shock to readers brought up on *Tom Brown's Schooldays*. The venture succeeded because the stories were superb of their sort.'

Yet in spite of its merits and originality there remains much in *Stalky and Co.* that jars upon a sensitive ear. Nor is it a book that could have been written by Kipling as a schoolboy. Superimposed upon his memories of Westward Ho! lies an alien layer of acquired Indian and subaltern hero-worship, which was still burning steadily nine years after he had left India.

The mild, egalitarian Price has become a flagellating disciplinarian, referred to with awe as 'Head Sahib', whose draconian barrack-room discipline is so much to the taste of the boys that they cheer him hysterically for flogging the whole school *en masse*. The parson has become 'Padre Sahib', who encourages Stalky and his friends to turn the tables on a group of bullies by bullying them in turn with almost equally repulsive ingenuity. The school, the agreeable laxity of whose rules Kipling had liberally exploited in diversions far from military, is now represented as a forcing house for the Colonial and frontier officers whom he had so much admired in India.

On Old Boys' Day the heroes return to the Alma Mater, hallowed by the pursuit of dacoits and other natives hostile to the British Raj, and sit in the dormitories relating their exploits with gruff modesty to an adoring circle of future officers of the Queen, in whom is thus planted a fundamental submissiveness to authority. There is, too, in *Stalky*, as in other Kipling stories of violence, a strong indication of what would now be called 'wish-fulfilment'. Those who venture to disturb the demigods in Study No. 5 are invariably handed over to condign humiliation and reprisal. No such events, of course, happened in reality. The author is in the position of a man lying awake at night and courting sleep by telling himself stories in which he is the dominant central figure in protean form, dream stories, splendidly remote from terrestrial reality, and pleasantly suspending the laws of probability.

Kipling did not forget to keep alive his military contacts, and his interest in military matters. In 1897 we find him writing to thank Lord Roberts for sending him his book *Forty-one Years in India*.

Rock House,
Maidencombe,
St Marychurch.

My dear Lord Roberts,

I have been away a few days staying with my Father and Mother and have just returned to find your book and the two friendly letters which accompany it. I don't think you can realize what a source of pride and gratification they are to me. Practically I knew the gist of the book before it came, because I took some dozen papers with reviews of it, but not till I read it in full, as I did last night and this morning, did I understand the wonderful skill of it, from an artistic point of view.

In its utter simplicity and directness it reads like the detached account of some interested by-stander who chanced to have been present at the making of the world's history, and even I, who know, I think, every step of your career by heart, was amazed by it. The papers have been so taken up with the *matter* of the book that, so far as I have seen, they had not in the least done justice to its perfection of *technique*; and that is the side on which it appeals to me.

Now, if you will forgive me the suggestion, what I want is a cheap sixpenny précis of the book for barrack-reading-room and bookstalls. Already some of your men, – time-expired soldiers, who are picking up livings as gardeners and grooms, have said to me that they too, as one man put it, 'want to know what Bobs 'as been writing about us'. My work takes me among this stamp of man and I am prepared to believe that never did living leader of men have so many passionate worshippers among his rank and file. . . . With my best salaams to Lady Roberts, believe me

Sincerely and gratefully yours,
Rudyard Kipling.

With March came weather that better suited Kipling. He found that it was the great spring month in Devonshire, with the countryside as forward as May in Brattleboro. The white limestone roads glared and shimmered under the sun, the hedges were green, and the spring flowers almost over. The sun had warmed this corner of southern England into a torpor on which burst sudden heavy tropical showers of rain. Kipling remained hard at work, refusing to write a Jubilee poem, saying: 'It's rather outside my beat and if I tried, I am afraid I should make a mess of it, but surely London is full of loyal poets who are all getting odes ready against May.'

On 2 April he was elected to the Athenæum, greatly to the gratification of Caroline, who entered in her diary: 'Rud is elected a member of the Athenæum in committee. Great honour. Many congratulations.' The ever-ready Philip Burne-Jones drew a picture of Kipling in the club window of the Athenæum reading *The Times* and wearing the kind of hat that Philip considered suitable to his new dignity.[6] Kipling was undoubtedly flattered by this further tribute to his success, but attempted to make light of it in a letter to Marshall:

You are entirely wrong in your estimate of the Athenæum. Tisn't a club to be found dead in – unless you're a bishop ... you keep out of it on account of the lowness of the Company and its variegated boredom. You can't even take a stranger across the door mat: and – as for drinks – you'd be cast out of the British Constitution by the Archbishop of Canterbury in person. We'll go to the Savile as of yore.[7]

In April 1897 Kipling wrote a poem which made a sudden and inexplicable return to his early manner as a cocksure youth in India. The verses, of which Kipling thought nothing, were written to accompany a problem picture by Philip Burne-Jones. They did his reputation considerable harm and are still quoted today by those who find something repellent in the man and his work:

A fool there was and he made a prayer
(Even as you and I!)
To a rag and a bone and a hank of hair
(We called her the woman who did not care)
But the fool he called her his lady fair –
(Even as you and I!)

All was not well with the Kiplings at Torquay. For the first time, but not, unfortunately, for the last, an intense gloom gradually descended upon the household, and Kipling's exuberant correspondence soon concealed a hideous boredom. It was a malaise of the soul which he described as a gathering blackness of mind and sorrow of the heart, that each of them attributed to the strange soft climate and struggled against in silence. Gradually, the lotus-island atmosphere became unendurable to them: the smugglers' cove, blotted in the fine rain, was no longer a place for joy and exploration, and the roses and nodding fuschias had become charged with intolerable melancholy.

Even the gales that broke the calm had lost their zest – roaring Sou'-westers chopping round to tearing North-easters – those days of wind that blew over naked grass, days of flying sand and sheets of foam shutting in the horizon, with the glimpse of a coaster flying for life up Channel, days that passed as suddenly as they came, giving way to warm, languid spring weather. It was, he thought, the *Feng-Shui* – the spirit of the house itself – that quenched the sunshine and fell upon them every time they entered it, freezing the very words upon their lips. His own depression was increased by the first stirrings of the internal illness that was to be the bane of his life, and it is in 1897 that we find the first entries that darkened the long chart of his clinical history.

Among other things – such as a grievous cold which I now am enjoying the end of – I've been rather out of sorts. Hipped and depressed from day to day, and this climate does not help to put a man on his legs again when he once feels sorrowful. So I went up to see a doctor. He reduced me to a state of highly improper nudity, and whacked and thumped and tested and did all the old tricks we know so well.

'Liver', says I. 'Liver and ghastly depression.'

'Liver be sugared', says he. 'You haven't a trace of a liver but you've got a colon rather distended with wind. Also you smoke too much.'

Somehow it seemed to me I had heard that last remark before. Well the net result was that with a tonic, and knocking off tobacco, he pulled me out of the darkness and the gloom that had been enveloping me. Being pretty much of the same dark temperament as I am you will understand what I suffered. Well, now I have felt serene – really at ease – for some weeks.[8]

They had decided to leave Devonshire some time before Kipling wrote this letter. Using a broken cistern as an excuse, they fled to London, and in the spring of 1897, Jubilee Year, were living in a hotel overlooking Hyde Park. Caroline was again pregnant, and they soon moved to a house near Brighton, lent by a friend, to begin the dreary process of house-hunting. Thirty years later, drawn by a desire to recapture the past, they went again to Devonshire, down the high-banked winding lanes spangled with convolvulus, through the stone villages where swarthy children sat on the doorsteps, past the gaunt hills ablaze with daffodil fields, and at last down the steep little road to 'Rock House'. Nothing had changed. The gardener was standing in the open sun-splashed stable yard, the lethargic cattle swished flies in the meadow, and 'quite unchanged, the same brooding Spirit of deep, deep Despondency within the open, lit rooms'.[9]

They left Torquay for good on 11 May 1897. Aunt Georgie had said to them: 'Let the child that is coming to you be born in our house,' and had prepared to efface herself until the event took place. Kipling said that he felt like a houseless gypsy. He went to the banquet of the Royal Academy and sat between Irving and the Poet Laureate, Alfred Austin. Here he met Thornycroft, the sculptor – 'brother', as he explained like an eager schoolboy, 'to *the* Thornycroft who builds the torpedo-boats'.[10]

His interest in the Royal Navy was again violently stimulated. Thornycroft invited him to attend the steam-trials of a new thirty-knot destroyer. Such a proposal was irresistible to Kipling. The world of action presented an intoxicating excitement to this sedentary man of letters, and it was a thrilling moment when Kipling found himself in oilskins on the throbbing deck of the unfinished prototype. Naval officers were co-equal with Army officers among Kipling's heroes. When in America he had already addressed one of them, Captain Robley D. Evans of the warship *Iowa*:

> Zogbaum draws with a pencil
> And I do things with a pen
> But you sit up in a conning-tower,
> Bossing eight hundred men.
>
> Zogbaum takes care of his business
> And I take care of mine,
> But you take care of ten thousand tons,
> Sky-hooting through the brine –
>
> Zogbaum can handle his shadows
> And I can handle my style,
> But you can handle a ten-inch gun
> To carry seven mile.
>
> To him that hath shall be given,
> And that's why these books are sent
> To the man who has lived more stories
> Than Zogbaum or I could invent.[11]

At such moments, when deeply excited, Kipling could pack his letters with a descriptive virtuosity normally reserved for his short stories.

Well, Sir, this is about all there was to the boat. She was 91 ft. beam 7 draft aft and 5 forward and 210 overall. She was filthy black – no bright work anywhere; and covered with oil and coal dust – a turtleback forward to turn the worst of the seas: a conning tower plated with $\frac{1}{4}$ inch steel to turn rifle-fire: but her skin was $\frac{3}{16}$ of an inch everywhere else! Her deck was covered with some sort of compo, like floor cloth but she tumbled down so that her widest available beam wasn't over ten feet. We pulled out of the Medway into the mouth of the Thames at an easy twelve knots to get down to our course – from the Mouse Light to the Lower Hope Reach – a lumpy sea and a thirty knot breeze. Then I was introduced to one George Brown – Thornycroft's head man, who had attended more than 2000 trials! He had a goatee beard and a head like a Yankee – was tremendously interesting: a born engineer. We talked about steam trials.

'Yes,' said George Brown, 'we've had every damned thing happen to torpedo boats that could happen. We've shed our propeller blades, we've carried away everything that could carry away: we've twisted our rudders off; and we've next to waltzed the engines off the bed-plates. There's nothing can surprise us now – unless some boat got out of the water and began to fly.'

By that time we'd freshened up to 17 knots – jogging along easily. They wrapped my neck up in a comforter, gave me heavy oilskins; and tied a sou'-wester over my ears. The wind was pretty keen and now and again the top of a sea came aboard. She was steered from the bridge forward and we all huddled under the protection of the turtleback – practically the break of the foc'sle. Then we struck a twenty two knot gait – and very nice it was. They began to rig up the indicators, to know how many revolutions we were doing and I went down into the engine-room. Two engines of 3000 h.p. apiece were making about 230 to the minute – maybe a trifle less. Our stoke-hold was open.

Then I heard someone say to the Captain: 'We'll shut down as soon as you say sir' and they screwed down the stoke-hold hatches and a fan (700 revolutions a minute) began to pump forced draft into the fires. Then the Captain said: 'Let go!' or words to that effect and – well do you know the feeling of standing up in a car when the thing starts up quick, I nearly fell down on the deck. The little witch jumped from 22 to thirty like a whipped horse – and the three hour trial had begun!

It was like a nightmare. The vibration shook not only your body but your intestines and finally seemed to settle on your heart. The breeze along the deck made it difficult to walk. I staggered aft above the twin screws and there saw a blue-jacket, vomiting like a girl: and in the ward-room, which is right in the stern of her, I felt my false teeth shaking in my head!

All we could do was to get under the lee of the conning-tower and hang on while this devil's darning needle tore up and down the coast. We passed 17-knot passenger boats, flew ten miles past 'em, turned and came back and overtook them.... The wake ran out behind us like white-hot iron; the engine-room was one lather of oil and water; the engines were running 400 to the minute; the gauges, the main-steam pipes and everything that wasn't actually built into her were quivering and jumping; there was half an inch of oil and water on the floors and – you couldn't see the cranks in the crank-pit.

It was more like Hell on a ten foot scale than anything you ever dreamed of, and through the infernal din of it George Brown shouted in my ear 'Isn't she a darling!' I went up on the bridge by the Captain. You never saw a boat steer as she did. One grey-haired old quartermaster held her at the wheel; and her two heavy drop-rudders swung over the face of the waters. She shaved a brig coming up the Thames just to show how near we could go; and our wash threw her up and down as though we had been a liner. We skimmed past buoys with about two yards to spare, running all along the edge of the Maplin Sands.

Just for fun the skipper said: 'We'll take her over the mile', that is marked by the two red Admiralty buoys – and is the official testing mile for all ships of the navy. The first time we had the wind at our back going almost as fast as we were; so I wasn't blinded. Well, we all timed her and away we went. The buoys simply seemed to be flying to us and we covered the mile in 1.50½, or something over 32 knots to the hour. Just try to think of it. That's faster than any trotter or bicycle – and most trains.

Then we turned her round. We faced into that thirty knot gale and for the honour of the thing I *had* to stay up on the bridge. This was pure hell. The wind got under my sou'wester; and I was nearly choked by the string round my throat. But we did the mile in the face of wind and tide in 2.5– 6 or 8 the timings did not agree. Then we went on and on till we all turned white with fatigue. At last those awful 3 hours came to an end, but not before the speaking tubes to the Captain's bridge had been smashed off by the vibration.

Then we drew breath, and everyone said 'Thank God.' She'd done ninety knots in those three hours, but if it had been straightaway in deep sea, we'd have done 31. Everything was quite cool and nothing had smashed up and they all said I was the Mascotte. Every engineer aboard knew 'McAndrew's Hymn' by the way and enjoyed it. Well, then we jogged back to Sheerness at 20 knots an hour. We were all as black as sweeps; and utterly played out. It took me two days to get the 'jumps' out of my legs. But I wouldn't have missed the trip for anything.[12]

They came in June to 'North End House', Lady Burne-Jones's home in the little fishing village of Rottingdean, where Kipling had spent his last days before sailing for India fourteen years before. In 1882 there had been one daily bus from Brighton taking forty minutes to Rottingdean, and the village green was deserted, with only the white ducks sailing on the village pond. He found it little altered. The Downs swooped sheer into the village street, and stretched eastward, noble and unbroken from the cross-roads to Russia Hill above Newhaven. It was peaceful to walk on the sheep-bitten turf under a blue sky with the sea dancing with a thousand diamond points below and the black windmill stark on the hill, over Downs as yet not pock-marked by the obscene debris of the speculative builder. A fresh salt-laden breeze fanned the ridges and the bent gorse bushes of which the blossom smelled of coconut in the sun.

Kipling's cousin, Stanley Baldwin, had married the eldest daughter of the Ridsdale family who lived in 'The Dene', the house on one side of the green. On the other was Burne-Jones's 'North End House', and in the centre, opposite the church, 'The Elms', the house into which Kipling was soon to move. It was an old depot for smugglers as its cellars showed, a red-tiled, stucco-fronted house with worm-eaten stairs, low-ceilinged and warm, with a beautiful garden. There was a blue-lamp with a 'leprous distilment of white blobs over it' and there were brackets and pictures of the sixties which were soon consigned to an attic.

The house stood, surrounded by flint walls, under the shade of ilex trees. Kipling was happy when the Burne-Joneses returned to 'North End House', in spite of the fact, which he admitted, that his uncle's world was no longer his.[13] He refers, still with affection, to Burne-Jones's boisterous laugh, his delight in small things, and the war of practical jokes that raged between them. 'Uncle Ned,' he said, 'has been down here a good deal this autumn, and he and I have browsed about in couples. It has been gorgeous and refreshing – a life to me that I shall never forget. The things that the big man does not know, and cannot help in, might be written on a postage stamp.'[14] In turn Burne-Jones wrote to his nephew with cumbrous affection: 'O my beloved Ruddy, I am so glad to be going back to you tomorrow. I am growing tame and like a curate – like an over-anxious curate. So tomorrow to little Rottingdean, to laugh and roar, and throw care to the dogs – which is a beast I hate.' Heavy frolicking, perhaps, but indulged in with true affection. These were good days for Kipling, and the work came full and easily. The cousins, Stanley Baldwin and Kipling, were much together, and would go to the beach in the hot weather, bringing back descriptions of fat bathers, their weight inflated by Herodotean fancy, and Burne-Jones would draw them, indescribably gross-bellied, wallowing in the surf.

Meanwhile, as we have seen, the Lockwood Kiplings had some time before left India for ever and settled in a small stone house near Tisbury in Wiltshire. Here Lockwood erected a building for his portfolios and architectural books, modelling tools and varnishes, and lived happily, immersed in his work and visiting his neighbours – Arthur Morrison at 'Fonthill', where he was made free of the exquisite collection, and the Wyndhams, a few miles away at 'Clouds'.

Kipling remained active, visiting Oxford, where this thirty-two-year-old man was mobbed by adoring undergraduates in Balliol Hall, so that grace could scarcely be rendered audible. He wrote some of the *Just So Stories*, told long ago to four-year-olds in Brattleboro, and stalked the Downs in strange attire, a broad-brimmed South African hat which he took off with a flourish, and patches of leather all over his suits, on both elbows and the seat.

He engaged in angry discussion in the cool taproom of the Plough Inn with the host, Bleyber, who was a Little Englander and fiery in argument. Kipling, who was fond of the man, would begin with quiet reasonableness, but quickly lost his temper with Bleyber's sacrilegious onslaughts on the British Empire and the methods which had produced it. So acrimonious did these discussions become that Bleyber would be left gasping with a dangerously quickened pulse, while Kipling strode angrily out of the house, warned in the end by the local doctor to cease these conversations 'unless you want to murder him'.[15]

Relieved from this particular strain, the ailing publican became the victim of another form of Kipling's insatiable curiosity.

There has been a rather interesting case [Kipling wrote to a friend] of blood-poisoning in our village – the local liquor dealer, and strong politician, got a cut on his hand and a scrape on his shin from the edge of a cask. You know how with that type of man recovery is slow in all cases. The local doctor is very young but very enthusiastic. I'm glad the patient got better because the local doctor and I (I was egging on the doctor to it) wanted to try a new form of germ killing remedy, and oxygen gas (local) treatment. I went down and sat with the invalid once or twice; expecting erysipelas and all sorts of complications; but as I have said, he bulled up. Curious how saloon-keepers' flesh is always unhealthy. There were blebs and pus, and all sorts of larks on a merely abraded surface that with normal health, a strip of plaster would have mended.

It was as early as this year, 1897, that Kipling expressed the first of a series of prescient comments about the aggressive intentions of Germany, and we shall see this theme running like a red vein through all his political thinking, that one-way street of conviction, insight and bigotry. Once formed, ideas were usually petrified in marmoreal permanence, and from this intense dread he never deviated, that England could save herself only by her own exertions and, if she failed to make them, must become a melancholy addition to the submerged races of history. One cannot but be amazed at the foresight that urged these irksome opinions in 1897, but Kipling, like his later French friends, was a connoisseur in the study of Germanism.

You see [he wrote to Charles Norton] we are girded at and goaded by Germany, and there is an uneasy feeling that the continent is getting ready for the big squeeze. We have only ourselves to trust, but the people won't move (you know our way) en masse, till they consider it's a just war. For that war will be for life. My memory is short but I don't remember anything that has made me more polite than Sherman's statement that England quarrels oftener than she fights. When Armageddon comes, remember that whatever our sins may have been since America won her independence, we shall have been kicked into this war – England is still engaged in saving the peace of the world, pretty much as the lady-passenger saved the Cunarder – by offering her virtue to the excited man who was about to sink the ship if he didn't get it, and the common people are slowly growing wearied of it all. I wonder when the big break will come.[16]

1897 was the year of Queen Victoria's Jubilee. Kipling felt strangely uneasy about the news that came to him from abroad. There had been trouble in South Africa after the Jameson Raid, and he was warned of further disturbance ahead. He had a sense of 'a sound of going in the tops of the mulberry trees', of things moving into position as troops move, and he was disturbed by the casual, sleek optimism with which people on all sides prepared to welcome the great Queen's Diamond Jubilee.

It was in this mood that he sat down to write 'Recessional', as a *nuzzur-wattu*, he tells us, or averter of the evil eye.[17] The Jubilee celebrations apparently began on 21 June, but Kipling did not start work on the poem until 22 June, and then abandoned it for three weeks, a fortnight of which he spent on a cruiser during naval manœuvres. Dr Bell, keeper of manuscripts at the British Museum, to which the late Lord Baldwin presented the original manuscript, has described how the poem was finished.

Charles Norton's daughter, Sarah, was staying with the Kiplings, and on the morning of 16 July the three were sitting together, Kipling at his desk, running through the papers and from time to time throwing one into the waste-paper basket. Miss Norton asked if she might look at the basket, and picked out a sheet of paper on which was written a poem on the Diamond Jubilee called 'After'. She protested against its being thrown away, and Kipling agreed to refer the matter to the arbitration of Aunt Georgie across the green, who insisted on it being preserved. Kipling then began to revise it, reducing its length from seven to five stanzas, and it was Miss Norton who suggested the repetition of the last couplet of the first stanza –

> Lord God of Hosts, be with us yet,
> Lest we forget – lest we forget! –

as a refrain in the second and fourth. Kipling accepted this suggestion, borrowing her pen to write opposite the first insertion 'written with Sallie's pen – R.K.' Then he altered the last line to 'Thy mercy and forgiveness Lord!', a change afterwards abandoned in favour of the original version. Then, after an Amen and his signature, he wrote beneath:

> 'Done in Council at North End House, July 16.
>   Aunt Georgie
>   Sallie
>   Carrie and me.'

He made a fair copy of the hymn, and Miss Norton and Aunt Georgie took it to London in the afternoon when they sent it by express messenger to Printing House Square, and on 17 July *The Times* printed the poem and gave it part of a leader. The draft signed by Kipling was given to Miss Norton, and it passed, after her death, to her sister, Elizabeth Gaskell Norton, who, at the coronation of King George VI, presented it to the British nation through Lord Baldwin of Bewdley, from whom it was accepted by the trustees of the British Museum.[18]

A mild controversy in the correspondence columns of *The Times* bears upon the authenticity of this account of the birth of 'Recessional', and the circumstances in which it was sent to *The Times*. The account given in this book was endorsed by Sir Roderick Jones, but Mr Shanks reminded *Times* readers that two other accounts exist: 'In *Something of Myself*, he [Kipling] says that he composed the poem as a "nuzzur-wattu" (an averter of the Evil Eye). It was not until he had been away on the naval manœuvres of that year he considered that the time had come for publication.' Kipling was represented, however, in what may have been a newspaper interview, quoted by Thurston Hopkins, as saying that *The Times* had commissioned him to write a poem on the Jubilee; that he found it extraordinarily difficult; and that only when letters of entreaty became imploring telegrams did he shut himself up with the resolve not to emerge until the poem was done. The result was 'Recessional'. Unfortunately, Mr Thurston Hopkins's collection of Kiplingiana was no longer in his possession, so that he was unable to verify the source of this quotation.

The Times comment on this letter was:

On April 13, 1901, *Literature* (the predecessor of the *Literary Supplement*) published the following statement in its *Notes of the Day*: So many accounts of the way in which *Recessional* reached *The Times* have been published on 'the very best authority' that it may be as well to dispose of them by the publication of the following letter which enclosed the MS:
Dear——
Enclosed please find my sentiments on things – which I hope are yours.

We've been blowing up the Trumpets of the New Moon a little too much for White Men, and it's about time we sobered down. If you would like it it's at your service – on the old conditions that I can use it if I want it later in book form. The sooner it's in print the better. I don't want any proof. Couldn't you run it tonight so as to end the week piously?

If it's not your line, send me a wire.

Ever yours sincerely,
R.K.

The poem appeared next morning. Mr Kipling was asked to name his own price, but absolutely declined all payment.

The 'Dear——' was presumably the late C. F. Moberly Bell, Manager of *The Times*. The above quotation may be taken as disposing of the statement, alleged to have been made by Kipling in a newspaper interview, that *The Times* was pressing him for a poem on the Jubilee. No record of any such request to him has been found in the archives of this office, though there is a reference to the alleged interview. This newspaper cutting is dated December, 1898, but unfortunately there is no note of the name of the paper from which it comes. The account given by Kipling in *Something of Myself* does not appear irreconcilable with that given in *The Times* of Dec. 20, 1937 and by Sir Roderick Jones in his recent letter.

Finally amended the poem read:

RECESSIONAL
1897

God of our fathers, known of old,
    Lord of our far-flung battle-line,
Beneath whose awful Hand we hold
    Dominion over palm and pine –
Lord God of Hosts, be with us yet,
    Lest we forget – lest we forget!

The tumult and the shouting dies;
    The Captains and the Kings depart:
Still stands Thine ancient sacrifice
    An humble and a contrite heart.
Lord God of Hosts, be with us yet,
    Lest we forget – lest we forget!

Far-called, out navies melt away;
    On dune and headland sinks the fire:
Lo, all our pomp of yesterday
    Is one with Nineveh and Tyre!

Judge of the Nations, spare us yet,
    Lest we forget – lest we forget!

If, drunk with sight of power, we loose
    Wild tongues that have not Thee in awe,
Such boastings as the Gentiles use,
    Or lesser breeds without the Law –
Lord God of Hosts, be with us yet,
    Lest we forget – lest we forget!

For heathen heart that puts her trust
    In reeking tube and iron shard,
All valiant 'dust' that builds on dust,
    And guarding, calls not Thee to guard,
For frantic boast and foolish word –
    Thy mercy on Thy People, Lord!

Kipling received many telegrams of congratulation, and an offer from Arthur Sullivan to set 'Recessional' to music.[19] The hymn was an instant success, and many years later was sung in 300 churches at the Nelson celebrations.

But it was not wanting in detractors. It was pointed out that the basic idea owed much to Cardinal Newman's 'England'. Nor did Kipling's probable indebtedness to the verses of Francis Quarles escape hostile attention. Critics observed the curious coincidence in metre between them and 'Recessional':

> Lord God of Gods, before whose throne
> Stand storms and fire, O what shall we
> Return to Heaven that is our own,
> When all the world belongs to Thee?
> We have no offering to impart
> But praises and a wounded heart.

It was suggested that the lines 'We have no offering to impart/But praises and a wounded heart' immediately called to mind Kipling's

> ... ancient sacrifice
> An humble and a contrite heart.

It was further suggested that another famous line:

> Beneath whose awful Hand we hold
> Dominion over palm and pine –

derived from Emerson who had written:

> And grant to dwellers with the pine
> Dominion o'er the palm and vine.

'Recessional', which has so often been criticized as typically arrogant and brutal, was in fact, at a moment of national apotheosis, an unusually humble admonition to the English people to keep the law as a special obligation. Of the line 'Or lesser breeds without the Law', which stirred some of the progressive intelligentsia into a frenzy of distaste, George Orwell wrote years later:

This line is always good for a snigger in pansy-Left circles. It is assumed as a matter of course that the 'lesser breeds' are 'natives', and a mental picture is called up of some pukka sahib in a pith-helmet kicking a coolie. In its context the sense of the line is almost the exact opposite of this. The phrase 'lesser breeds' refers almost certainly to the Germans, and especially the pan-German writers who are 'without the law' in the sense of being lawless, not in the sense of being powerless.

The whole poem, conventionally thought of as an orgy of boasting, is a denunciation of power-politics, British as well as German. . . . [Kipling] still believes that Pride comes before a fall, and that the gods punish *hubris*.[20]

On 17 August came an event even more satisfying to Kipling than any literary success. He wrote in his wife's diary: 'The boy John is born at 1.50 a.m. of this day. C. and he doing well ... inundation of letters, cables, p.c.s. and advertisements. I think she is more cheerful than ever before, and the boy John he says nuffin', and takes his vittals.'

To Sallie Norton he wrote with self-conscious pride: 'Yes, she is coming on all right – better in fact than I've ever known her to do before and is just now starting the campaign of nursing John. Reserved young person John: but considerably better looking than he was two days ago.'

'John, the beetle-browed John,' he told his uncle Alfred, 'does nothing but grunt and yawn. He is getting a shade more presentable and in a week or so will be fit to look at.'[21]

Shortly before Carrie's confinement they had moved from 'North End House' to 'The Elms', where they settled on a temporary basis, still continuing the process of house-hunting. Kipling was still pierced by sudden darts of longing for 'Naulakha' and Vermont, and anything American painfully reminded him of them. There was a man named Winans at Brighton, son of an American millionaire, whose weakness was trotting horses, and who drove up and down the sea-front behind

first-class trotters. Kipling passed him on his bicycle and was soon
cross-questioning the man about gaits, breeds and shoeing. Although
Kipling had little interest in horses and was indeed physically
frightened of them,[22] nothing could quench his thirst for technical
knowledge and his zest in its accumulation. 'He has one trotter with
a 2.17 record – an ugly brute but a good one. Well, England isn't the
place to race horses in unless you get a track of your own. Winans
let the animals out to a four minute clip and before he had gone a
quarter of a mile the police wanted him for furious driving.'

One of Winans's training carts was an old piano-top buggy. Kipling
and Caroline met it one sunny December day, hood up, and the horse
with a breast strap jogging along. They were quite silent for about
ten minutes; then they began to talk about 'Naulakha'. Josephine
would keep quiet about it for weeks at a time; then they would hear
her describing to Elsie the summerhouse under the trees, and the fun
of going about barefoot. Filled with such yearnings, Kipling scoured
the countryside for a house, but his heart was not in the task; he had
struck roots, and he wrote sadly to Conland: 'I wonder when we shall
come back. There are times when I feel like taking the first boat and
getting you up to dinner straight off. I tried to offer it for sale once
but I took damn good care to put a prohibitive price on it. Howard
seems to be going ahead quietly. I fancy he'll be rather wealthy a
citizen by the time we return.' But instead of returning they had begun
to pack for departure for their new home across the green, 'The
Elms'.

Of Kipling's work during this year, 'Recessional' was outstanding.
The school stories, some letters on the Naval Manœuvres, and a few
verses formed the remainder of his output, which seemed to slacken
off considerably in the latter half of the year. They kept open house;
no sooner did one set of guests depart than their places were immediately filled by others. It is noticeable that for the year in which he
fled from America no postcript in Caroline's diary was forthcoming
from Kipling's pen, but the year that gave him his son gave him also
the inspiration to add the last word for 1897: 'Here endeth the 6th
Vol – which is within three weeks of the sixth year of our life together.
In all ways the richest of the years to us two personally.' 'She shall
do him good and not evil all the days of her life.'

On 8 January 1898 they sailed for South Africa, taking their children
and Lockwood Kipling with them. It was choppy weather in the Bay
of Biscay and until they reached Madeira, where they were impressed
by the unearthly beauty of the island, rising in its volcanic tiers from

the sea in the violet light of dawn, the lights twinkling in the mountains and the first balmy kiss of the tropics in the air.

They arrived in South Africa on 25 January and went by train to the 'Vineyard' at Newlands,[23] a boarding-house kept by an Irish woman whom Kipling sourly described as following 'the instincts of her race and spreading miseries and discomforts round her in return for good monies'. He tells us that 'the colour, light, and half-oriental manners of the land bound chains round our hearts for years to come'.[24] And the heat of the Cape brought back vividly his childhood in India:

> We shall go back to the boltless doors,
> To the life unaltered our childhood knew –
> To the naked feet on the cool, dark floors,
> And the high-ceiled rooms that the Trade blows through:
>
> To the trumpet-flowers and the moon beyond,
> And the tree-toads' chorus drowning all –
> And the lisp of the split banana-frond
> That talked us to sleep when we were small.

They went for a ride on a mountain road and met Cecil Rhodes, who asked them to lunch. Kipling at first found the Empire-builder inarticulate and tongue-tied, with a habit of coming out suddenly with the kind of devastating questions that render children so unpredictable in adult society.

'What is your dream?' he asked Kipling abruptly, and Kipling replied resourcefully that Rhodes himself was part of it. Rhodes showed him the new fruit farms, the old Dutch houses 'stalled in deep peace', and explained to him his plans for starting a fruit-growing industry in the Colony. Kipling's views on the Dutch were already hardening into strong disapproval:

The racial twist of the Dutch (they had taken the title to themselves and called the inhabitants of the Low Countries 'Hollanders') was to exploit everything they could which was being done for them, to put every obstacle in the way of any sort of development, and to take all the cash they could squeeze out of it.... It was against their creed to try and stamp out cattle-plagues, to dip their sheep, or to combat locusts, which in a country overwhelmingly pastoral had its drawbacks.[25]

Caroline remained all the four months of their visit at the Cape, but Kipling struck out in various directions, visiting Kimberley, Bula-

wayo and Johannesburg. While they were together at the Cape, they
spent their time walking, or riding their cycles. In April they returned
home and spent the rest of the year at 'The Elms'. On his return Kipling found that America was at war with Spain, and it was not long
before she, who had so often fulminated against British Imperialism,
found herself a Colonial Power with the Philippines and Cuba on her
hands, defeated, and seething with resentment. It was not to be
expected that Kipling would fail to improve the occasion, or to extol
the glories of Empire to the American people:

> Take up the White Man's burden
>   Send forth the best ye breed –
> Go bind your sons to exile
>   To serve your captives' need.

It was a call to that great sister-nation, the United States, to join in
the vast civilizing movement which in Kipling's eyes England had
spread across the world. Their time had also now come to

> ... wait in heavy harness
> On fluttered folk and wild –
> Your new-caught sullen peoples,
>   Half devil and half child.

It was exhortations of this kind, always less offensive when carefully
analysed than at first sight, that so enraged men and women of liberal
habits of thought, and were the main cause of the steep decline in
Kipling's reputation. Then, and afterwards, they appeared to many
blatant, arrogant and odious.

On his return from South Africa, Kipling also added to the *Stalky*
stories, wrote an article on his African tour, produced *The Fleet in
Being*, and spent a great deal of time on *Kim*. In June he received and
read the dramatized version of *The Light that Failed*, 'a vivid and
agonizing play, but better than we had supposed'. Max Beerbohm did
not share this opinion. It brought his hatred of Kipling to the boil,
and drew from him the devastating review already quoted. A collection of stories called *The Day's Work* was published in October.

The first of September 1898 found Kipling on HMS *Pelorus* for
naval manœuvres off the Irish coast as the guest of Captain Norbury.
His interest in the Navy was now deep, and the squat, short-sighted
figure was to be seen in every part of the vessel, from the bridge to
the stoke-hold. The ship's company, from the Commander down to
the ratings, were put through the usual grilling cross-examinations on

their duties, and their answers duly recorded on Kipling's absorbent mind. When on board he wrote for his host, Captain Norbury, an amusing and ingenious *tour de force*, introducing the name of every ship in the squadron:

Written on HMS *Pelorus* for Capt. Norbury:

On the first appearance in the wardroom of the *Pelorus* of the *Victorious* Norbury in his new treble-plated Harvey Steel automatic self-reefing Monkey Jacket, it was decided that in it by *Jupiter!* he would win *Renown*: in spite of the fact that the *Latona* of the *Magnificent* creation was merely a naval outfitter. When approached *Sirious*ly on the subject he admitted in confidence that the gift was his *Ma(r)'s*, so *Powerful* is the effect of well-directed chaff in eliciting truth, even from one so *Majestic* as the owner of the jacket in question, when fairly cornered at the *Tribune* of public opinion. The *Terpsecor*uscating garment is now in its *Halcyon* prime but will *Speedy*ly lose its lustre when it will cease to attract the eye of any *Naiad* of Gosport Hard. But why anticipate that *Terrible* day? *Thetis*sue paper has barely been unwrapped from the gleaming buttons, and by general *Resolution* it is agreed that *Prince George* in his most *Brilliant* toggery was not attired like Norbury.[26]

R. Kipling.

He remained, through the firm control of Caroline and the vigilance of A. P. Watt, an author well defended from the commercial angle. Contracts were strongly fought out, and infringements of copyright dropped on with alacrity. Yet Kipling was always charmingly indulgent to the young. Approached in 1898 by two boys of Horsmonden School in Kent for a contribution to the school magazine, for which they offered three pence per page, Kipling at once responded with 'A few Hints on Schoolboy Etiquette', a breezy snippet which produced an abnormal sale, and enabled the editors to dispose of the few unsold copies at 7s 6d each.[27]

In the same year, when asked by editors of the *Cantab.*, a magazine published by Cambridge undergraduates, for a contribution, he replied good-temperedly:

The Elms, Rottingdean, nr. Brighton.
September 17th, 1898.

To the Editor of the *Cantab*.

There was once an author who wrote:
'Dear Sir: In reply to your note
    Of yesterday's date,
    I am sorry to state
It's no good at the prices you quote.'

Rudyard Kipling.

When the editors were emboldened by this reply to ask for a photograph, Kipling answered with docility: 'As to photos of myself, I have not one by me at present, but when I find one I will send it; but not for publication, because my beauty is such that it fades like a flower if you expose it.'[28]

CHAPTER XIII
AMERICAN TRAGEDY

THE tranquil and successful course of Kipling's life began now to be overshadowed by a series of disasters. They began in 1898 when he was disturbed by the beginning of a serious illness of his sister Trix, whose brilliant mind had been temporarily disordered, and Caroline noted: 'Rud does not work; the children amuse him a bit, but he is very anxious.' He was further saddened by the death of 'Uncle Ned', Edward Burne-Jones. Their views on politics and life were no longer the same, and Kipling's affection for his uncle had become coloured by a good-natured contempt. But his passing was none the less a severe blow – the removal of a firm link with childhood, which must have brought back memories of 'The Grange', that heavenly refuge from the 'House of Desolation', and of his happiness in lifting its door-knocker so many years ago. An even worse blow was to fall upon him in the following year which left an aching wound, and may be said to have brought about his maturity as a man, if not as an artist.

Caroline wished to see her mother again, and she and Rudyard sailed for America on 25 January 1899. Kipling, who was tired of England, embarked on his holiday in a mood of juvenile zest. 'I've had enough of grey skies and boiled potatoes. I'm going to where the sun shines and oysters is cheap. I shall have 'em on toast, likewise stewed *and* roasted and fried; and I shall have grapefruit for breakfast and nineteen different sorts of bread.'[1]

They docked at New York on 2 February and Kipling was at once surrounded by his old enemies, the reporters. When asked for an interview, he is said to have contented himself with a short and not very colourful statement of his credo as an artist: 'Every effort of art is an effort to be sincere. There is no surer guide, I am sure, than the determination to tell the truth that one feels.' This arid glimpse into the obvious caused even the American reporters to despair at last of their long-sought quarry. They left, said the *New York Mail and Express*, singing softly:

We've met with many men from overseas,
An' some of 'em was shy and some was not.
The Frenchmen and the Germans and Chinese,
But Kipling was the hardest of the lot.
Some of 'em talked in English an' the rest
Would talk from early winter to the fall,
But the Mowgli-man we found the greatest pest,
For the bloomin' sod 'e wouldn't talk at all.[2]

In sanctuary at the Hotel Grenoble, Kipling sat down with relief to compose a letter to his old friend Dunsterville. He had been writing to OUSCS (Old United Service Collegers) all over the world, and endeavouring to find out their news and fortunes. This was a task which he enjoyed, and his style with his old friends is breezy, and rather reminiscent of a hearty middle-class tradesman talking in the bar of a golf club:

Dear Old Man,
    Hurrah! I'm raising 'em one by one like a scientific trout-fisher – OUSCS from all parts of the world. I want you to get a staff billet, where your peculiar talents will have a full field. I think you're a bit too good to be stuck always with a native regiment – even with so crack a lot as the 20 PNI. I wonder how you would have got on with the Gippy Army? Old (Satan) Young is a full-blown *Bimbashi*. But I am annoyed with one thing. I saw the balance sheet of the old Coll. the other day. It's in an awful condition – only 70 or 80 boys and the bulk of 'em day boarders. A fat man of God called Harris is in charge and *they-let-the-Coll.-buildings-in-the-holidays-for-a-holiday-resort*! That just enables 'em to pay their way.
    Well that isn't all! The Chronicle still goes on, and a recent issue discussing the Stalky tales claimed *me* as an old OUSC and wondered why I didn't write for 'my own paper!' Cheek! Don't you ever own that you belong to the Coll. after Price left it. I have tried to make my position clear, and I think I have. We are the original OUSCS but remember, we don't know anything of the Coll. since Price left. I was present at the last prize-giving in 1894 and I made a speech to the Coll. You ought to have heard the boys cheer. It was in the old Gym, and I nearly broke down.
    We came over here for a few weeks a fortnight ago with our three kiddies – two girls and a boy – so as to enable the wife (I married an American) to see her mother. It's a great nuisance to be a notorious and celebrated literary man. It makes me laugh a good deal, but the bother and fuss of talking to a hundred people a day isn't good enough. I hear that old Beresford has joined the Fabian Society (he was always a bit of a Socialist) and he also got a scar while in India. Gilbert May was also down at Brighton. I got a note in from White (he had the study below us and we poured fried bacon

fat on his head); as soon as I can turn round I shall go and have a Coll. bukh with him.

The 'Weazle' is the only one of the original staff left at Westward Ho! I'd dearly like to go down and see the place again but I'm afraid that the beast Harris would use it as an advertisement!

All this time I haven't congratulated you on your marriage. I can only hope that you'll be half as happy in that relation as I've been, old man. It's a good and honourable position and it makes a man's character – let alone the deep and abiding joy one gets out of the kiddies. I've a small son a year old who is all the world to me.

Remember me to all OUSCs of our rank and standing. Convey my best salaams to your wife and believe me,

Thine as ever,
Gigger.[3]

On the day of their arrival in New York Caroline had made a worried entry in her diary: 'We feel the greatest anxiety about the children who all have colds.' Three days later: 'The children ill and miserable; cause us much anxiety. Josephine the worst.' On 8 February Caroline took to her bed with *grippe* and all next day was dazed with fever. On 20 February, when worried to distraction about Josephine, another blow fell upon her, and she wrote miserably in the diary: 'Rud feels dull and has fever in the night.'

On 21 February Kipling was too ill to get up. He had developed a cough with rusty expectoration, the onset of acute lobar pneumonia. Dr Dunham, who had recently married Caroline's sister Josephine, was in charge of the case. He called in consultation Dr Edward G. Janeway. Dunham gave up everything else, and spent every night with Kipling, while Janeway also spent several nights by the bedside. The chief nurse was Miss Helen M. Warner. The doctors expressed the view that Kipling's simple life and habits would count in his favour, but a lifelong tendency to fever made him a difficult patient, and it was clear that he was desperately ill. The case was a long one. The lung on one side progressively solidified. Then that on the other also began to solidify by degrees. As this second lung was approaching complete solidification, resolution began in the lung first affected, and it started to take on again its function of respiration, making it possible for life to continue. Fever was continuous, and Kipling talked much of the time.

This talk had the alien quality of delirium, but was coherent and fascinating. Many times he pictured the 'dog-tread', underground passages where multitudes of dogs congregated and went to and fro.

Delirium appeared to have given his fantastic imagination licence to roam where it wished. Thirty years later, at Burwash, Dr Dunham asked Kipling if he remembered the 'dog-tread' of his delirium. He said no. Then, a few hours later, he told Dunham that the memory of the 'dog-tread' had come back to him.[4] He remembered too

leading an enormous force of cavalry mounted on red horses with brand new leather saddles, under the glare of a green moon, across steppes so vast that they revealed the curvature of the earth. We would halt at one of the camps named by Alikhanoff in his diary (I would see the name of it heaving up over the edge of the planet) while we warmed ourselves at fires of sax-aul, and where, scorched on one side and frozen on the other, I sat till my infernal squadrons went on again to the next fore-known halt.[5]

At least one aspect of his delirium remained with him after the fever subsided. As soon as he reached the stage when his disabled brain was able to collect its thoughts, the journalist that was ever-present in Kipling asserted itself. He summoned a stenographer who took down at his dictation the rambling adventures that he had experienced in the land of shadows. Fortunately this account was preserved in the Kipling Papers and is given in full in its original untouched condition in Appendix A.

Caroline was cheered during her ghastly double vigil by the good friends who lent helping hands, and recorded: 'I feel how everyone he has ever spoken to loves him and is glad and happy to help.'[6] The crisis brought out to the full Caroline's dogged courage. Her fortitude was extraordinary. She never lost her nerve, never gave way; ate well, and took all the rest that was possible. By 23 February Kipling's temperature was lower, but he was restless and unable to sleep. Meanwhile Josephine had developed a high temperature and fever during the night and it was decided to remove her from the hotel and take her to be cared for by their old friends the de Forests at their house in Long Island. 'Dr MacDonald fears complications and I take her to Julia de Forest and leave her – a moment of conscious agony to stand out from the average,' wrote her mother in her diary.

Kipling met his crisis on the night of 28 February–1 March. On the twenty-seventh Caroline had wired to Norton: 'No material change. We are making a strong fight and may win or lose any hour. Caroline Kipling, 1.35 p.m.' The crisis brought terrible suffering, and these were the most painful hours he passed – when an agonized sobbing for breath made it seem that life was almost extinct and he was only rallied by the superb skill and devotion of his doctors, Dunham and Janeway. Finally, one day the patient ceased to talk and fell into a deep sleep. The doctors scrutinized him with anxiety. Was it terminal coma, or was it sleep at last? Opinions were divided, but the thermometer answered the question, his temperature showing a marked drop. It was sleep, and recovery had begun. In the meantime the world outside held its breath. Telegrams poured in and were filed by his publisher, the admirable F. N. Doubleday. The Kaiser sent an anxious inquiry, and far away in London Arnold Bennett, who was giving a musical party and reading the programme aloud to his guests, ended by saying 'God save Kipling' instead of 'God Save The Queen.'[7] The bulletins were indeed devoured with an anxiety that might have been accorded to the King of England.

On 5 March Caroline found herself at the limit of anxiety about Josephine, whose condition appeared to be critical, and wrote in the diary: 'I saw Josephine three times today, morning and afternoon, and at 10.30 p.m. for the last time. She was conscious and sent her love to "Daddy and all".' And on 6 March: 'Josephine left us at 6.30 this morning.'

And so while Kipling still lay desperately ill and necessarily ignorant of this awful blow, Caroline, accompanied by Conland and other friends, took the little coffin containing Josephine's body to the cemetery at Fresh Pond, Long Island. They decided to keep the news from Kipling as long as possible, as he was making good progress and was already stronger and more cheerful. Allied to Caroline's agony of mind at Josephine's death was the necessity, some time, of informing her husband about it.

No more devastating news could have been brought to him than the death of this child, and we can only be amazed at the courage which enabled Mrs Kipling to do her duty so firmly. Miss Norton called on her on 25 March and wrote to her father:

> She told me a great deal about Ruddy's illness but she said very little about little Josephine. I could see it was all too painful in its detail, too heartbreaking for her to talk of now. She said the days between little Josephine's death and Ruddy's knowing of it, were 'dreadful', and that at last she *had* to tell him though the doctors said, perhaps she had better wait another day, 'and at first', she added, 'he was too ill to realize it quite, but now every day he feels it more.'[8]

F. N. Doubleday had been a tower of strength in the trouble. He had taken charge of the enormous mail, had worked under the doctors, cooked Kipling's food, and looked after all the business details connected with the illness. He understood how to rouse Kipling from the black despondency into which thoughts of Josephine plunged him, took the nurse's place when she went out and, relieving Caroline of so much of the burden, probably saved her from a total collapse.

By 26 March Kipling was allowed to see a few friends. He lay, changed and thin, and his voice was hoarse. Sallie Norton sat by the bed with his hand in hers and saw a look of profound sadness about his mouth and eyes. He talked first of trivial things, and then his own illness, which was full of interest to him, of the wonderful devotion of his doctors and the deadly weariness of convalescence. Caroline believed that the doctors had not estimated what Josephine's death meant to Kipling, and that the stronger he became physically day by day the more the comprehension of his loss would strengthen and conspire against recovery. Miss Norton saw him again on 30 March and was surprised by his mental poise into writing:

Oh! that blessed English temperament, so steady, so matter of fact even, and capable of achieving so much and expressing so much when the time comes. I could not but think of the contrast with Carrie's temperament, as I observed Mr Kipling. Carrie so splendidly restrained and self-controlled, but vibrating with sensitiveness, and bodily worn by it. It is hard to know which at its best is the best, but it is not hard to know which is the most comfortable for the human being, the nature which is unconsciously steady, or the highly organized nature which keeps its balance by conscious effort.[9]

The generous and devoted Miss Norton was deceived if she imagined that any exercise of the English temperament could palliate Kipling's despair. This was the man who was so stricken by the death of Stevenson, whom he had never met, that he could not write a line for three weeks. No mention of Josephine could be made to him from now on. Perhaps one could say that this cruel blow was the beginning of his intellectual maturity, when Death, whom he had seen come so often to others, had for the first time cast its javelin into his own house.

The return to 'The Elms' was to prove harder and more painful than either of them could have imagined, and their only refuge, as on their second bereavement, lay in an almost inhuman restraint and application to the work in hand.

They were to find the house and garden at 'The Elms' full of the lost child. Rudyard told his mother that he saw her every time a door was opened, every time a place was empty at table, saw her in every green corner of the garden, radiant and heart-breaking, and it was slowly that this grim restraint was broken and they began again to talk of her. Talk of Josephine to others he seldom did to the end of his days, but at least he could write about her for himself alone, and through this catharsis expel an intolerable sorrow. It is not in his letters, but in such works as *They* and 'Merrow Down' that we shall find the intensity of Kipling's passion and dereliction. Staying near Guildford with Lockwood's friend, St Loe Strachey, two years later, and wandering about the countryside, he could not look at Merrow Down or any part of the Surrey landscape without thinking of the dead child:

> But long and long before that time
> (When bison used to roam on it)
> Did Taffy and her Daddy climb
> That Down, and had their home on it.
>
> Then beavers built in Broadstone brook
> And made a swamp where Bramley stands;
> And bears from Shere would come and look
> For Taffimai where Shamley stands.
>
> The Wey, that Taffy called Wagai,
> Was more than six times bigger then;
> And all the tribe of Tegumai
> They cut a noble figure then.
>
> Of all the Tribe of Tegumai
> Who cut that figure none remain, –
> On Merrow Down the Cuckoos cry –
> The silence and the sun remain.
>
> But as the faithful years return
> And hearts unwounded sing again
> Comes Taffy dancing through the fern
> To lead the Surrey spring again.
>
> Her brows are bound with bracken-fronds,
> And golden elf-locks fly above
> Her eyes are bright as diamonds
> And bluer than the skies above.
>
> In moccasins and deer-skin cloak,
> Unfearing, free and fair she flits,
> And lights her little damp-wood smoke
> To show her Daddy where she flits.

> For far – oh, very far behind,
> So far she cannot call to him
> Comes Tegumai alone to find
> The daughter that was all to him!

Kipling's cousin, Angela Thirkell, wrote of Josephine's death:

Much of the beloved Cousin Ruddy of our childhood died with Josephine and I feel that I have never seen him as a real person since that year. There has been the same charm, the same gift of fascinating speech, the same way of making everyone with whom he talks show their most interesting side, but one was only allowed to see these things from the other side of a barrier and it was sad for the child who used to be free of the inner courts of his affection.[10]

On 17 April Kipling was taken by private car to a small hotel at Lakewood for the first stage of his convalescence, and here, ten miles from the sea-shore, he began to go for drives through the pine woods. His recovery was very slow and pulse far too high, and there was an atmosphere of gloom over 'The Laurel House': 'I have only scraps of mind left me', said Caroline, 'and so no memory except of these black weeks just passed.'[11]

On 9 May Kipling was well enough to move to Morristown to stay with Mrs Catlin, whom the Kiplings had first met on their cruise to Bermuda five years earlier. By the twenty-second his doctor examined him and found his lungs greatly improved, and advised him to do no work for six months, and to rest for two hours daily. Caroline went in June for her last visit to 'Naulakha' to collect odds and ends.

It stood grey and deserted, the garden tangled with weeds. Beatty at this time had asked Matt Howard: 'Howard, when are you expecting the Kiplings?' but he did not disturb her. Perhaps Caroline was apprehensive, for she stayed only two days, putting up at Mrs Kirkland's lodging-house in Main Street.[12] They arrived home at Rottingdean on 24 June, and at first it seemed to provide a tranquil sanctuary. 'The village green is most beautiful. The streets are empty, and we come quietly to The Elms to take on a sort of ghost life. Aunt Georgie meets us at the garden gate.'[13]

Kipling settled down to the desultory pottering existence of a convalescent. He played inexpertly with a little domestic printing press, and spent much time with Philip Burne-Jones. The ill-assorted cousins were becoming more attached to one another. The strenuous activity of social advancement had begun to pall on Philip. He had lost interest in his superficial friends, and was by no means the happiest of men. He was now inclined to turn to Kipling, so sympathetic to men of his own age, so stimulating to a discontented mind.

In July Philip Burne-Jones began his famous portrait of Kipling: 'It's just me at my writing table, and as like as one pea to another down to the flap of my pocket and the pipe at my side.' The painting was a welcome break in Kipling's enforced idleness. The weather was perfect and the garden beautiful, but he could only lie low, sleep in the afternoons and go to bed at 10 p.m. Nevertheless his mind was again teeming with ideas, and he determined to resume work when he returned from Scotland.

They set out for Sutherlandshire in August, to a manse on Andrew Carnegie's estate half a mile from the trout loch, with smoky lamps and horse-hair furniture. Kipling got his rods and tackle into order, and included a collection of rainbow-coloured salmon flies. He was happy in the new surroundings: the broad valleys and harsh solitude of the hills, the silver lochs imprisoned in their clefts, and sometimes a golden eagle sailing on mighty wing-beats over the hills.

He was happy listening to Carnegie's diffuse exposition of his views – Carnegie looking like a quaint Japanese *netsuke* in yellow and time-worn ivory. They made a trip with Lockwood to Dunrobin Castle in Carnegie's steam yacht. The Castle stood nobly on the shore, looking out to sea from its pointed turrets. They walked through the superb gardens, along lawns and herbaceous borders to the wide sea prospects and 'moist courts of foliage' where fountains played.

Kipling was interested by the Duchess of Sutherland, 'a beautiful creature, but haunted by a worse than New England conscience – a great sense of her responsibility. She maintains a crop of nurses and medical women for the alleviation of the lot of the poor crofter women and tries to reconcile the beliefs of Christian Socialism and ardent philanthropy with great possessions and the life of a *grande dame*. Carnegie says that she will end by some dreadful feat of renunciation.' Kipling, Lockwood observed, 'steadfastly refused to dance on the hearth rug of the great, and spent much of his day listening with contempt to Carnegie summarily settling the fate of the British Empire, with particular emphasis on the futility of our Indian Dominions'.

Stalky and Co. was published on 6 October and was well reviewed in the morning papers, to Kipling's relief. The aged Dean Farrar, author of *Eric, or Little by Little*, was, however, offended by the schoolboys' references to his hero and his school. Kipling hastened to assure him:

It would be impossible to write any sketch of schoolboy life of twenty years ago without in some way alluding to their influence, and also that there are boys ignorant, vulgar-minded it may be, who take less interest in the moral teachings of the two books than in their divergencies from the facts of school-life as boys know those today.[14]

Kipling's sufferings made much further work in 1899 impossible. After his return he did little serious writing, only the Elephant *Just So Story*, which he completed on 17 October, and a little verse. He had become interested in the Volunteers, and a new car that he had ordered gave him amusement and distraction. The postscript for 1899 was: 'One year ended and I owe my life to Carrie. R.K.'

CHAPTER XIV
THE BOER WAR

━━━━━

BEFORE the end of 1899 Kipling was absorbed in the South African
trouble, where the situation had deteriorated during his long illness.
The British Government had declared war on 11 October, and already
the campaign was going badly for them. At first he had no doubts
or qualms about the matter, although the sympathy with the Boers
exhibited by Aunt Georgie and Jack Mackail, her son-in-law, must
have produced some uneasy moments. His views in October 1899 are
probably fairly reflected in this letter of Lockwood to Miss Norton:

> Of course one regrets the war, but ever since I was in the Transvaal I have
> been daily growing more certain that Kruger and Steyn have been preparing
> for it and intending it for years past. No effort of ours could have averted
> it. They say, at least the *one* English paper which champions the Boers, says,
> that Chamberlain meant war, and that some other Colonial Minister in his
> place could have prevented it. I am sure this is a mistake. The Dutch were
> bent on fighting and there was no help for it.

Rudyard did not believe that the Boers were fighting for liberty for
their own hearths, or even for a free republic. He thought that they
were a republic only in name, in reality a one-man despotism, feebly
tempered by a corrupt and ignorant oligarchy. He was confident that
once the tide had turned the prophets of evil would be disappointed
who predicted a perpetuation of race-hatreds and sanguinary petty
struggles. He would have agreed with his father's words: 'Since we
ₐave an Empire, needs must we hold it; it is our existence that is at
take – *rien que ça.*'[1]

In spite of this, Kipling was well aware of the disgraceful condition
in which British soldiers had been despatched to South Africa. Caroline recorded: 'Rud is absorbed with excitement and anxiety about
the troops in Africa . . . A bad night on Rud's part with anxiety over
the troops.'[2] He busied himself in the village organizing a volunteer
corps, colliding heavily with the authorities.

Some day [he wrote] we may even have an efficient army; about half the men I ever knew seem to have been killed, and the other half are wounded. I have an inferior pair of eyes, and a more inferior pair of lungs and so am out of it all. But I've raked in a little cash for my men. It's the first time I ever set out out of malice aforethought, to sell my name for every blessed cent it would fetch and the result so far as women and children are concerned is good.[3]

He was here referring to the verses entitled 'The Absent-Minded Beggar', a rhymed invitation, of singular vulgarity, to subscribe to a fund for soldiers' wives and children which appeared in the *Daily Mail* and became the most talked of publication of the hour:

Sir Arthur Sullivan wedded the words to a tune guaranteed to pull teeth out of barrel-organs and the *Mail* boomed, puffed and auctioned every saleable detail of it – so much for Caton Woodville's picture, so much for Sullivan's music – with the help of actors and actresses, printers, journalists and music-hall singers. Anyone could sing, recite or re-print, but all fees must go to 'The Absent-Minded Beggar Fund'.

Lord Newton in his autobiography gives us an interesting glimpse of Kipling's touchiness in connection with this poem. In the course of a debate on a military Bill, Newton had spoken disparagingly of Kipling's verse, which he described as being admirable in sentiment, but deplorable in poetry, with its 'Duke's son, cook's son, son of a belted Earl'. He was surprised to receive a few days later a letter from Kipling complaining that his friends deplored the attack and, far from being ashamed of the poem, he (Kipling) felt very proud to think it had helped to raise over £250,000 for soldiers in South Africa. Newton replied that Kipling had overestimated the importance of his criticism and that, while recognizing Kipling's patriotic sentiments, he was not an admirer of all his poetry. He also regretted having hurt the feelings of Kipling's 'friends', but was surprised to receive a second letter saying that the 'friends' were still dissatisfied, to which he made no reply as 'there is no law written or unwritten which compels one to admire poetry which is distasteful'.[4]

On 14 December Kipling was offered and refused a KCB. On this occasion Lord Salisbury's secretary came down to offer the distinction, but Kipling 'felt he could do his work better without it'.[5] He was never to abandon this position, and in the years to come some of the highest honours in the Government's or monarch's power to bestow were pressed on him in vain.*

* For Kipling's full record in respect of Honours see Appendix B.

On 20 January 1900 he and Carrie left for South Africa, and landed
at Cape Town on 5 February.[6] Next day he had an hour's talk with
Lord Roberts, who gave him a pass to go anywhere in South Africa.
He wasted no time in using it to visit military hospitals and see conditions for himself.

The Kiplings stayed at the famous Mount Nelson Hotel, 'the
Helot's Rest', with its strange riff-raff of Rand and Kimberley million-
aires, army officers, censors, war correspondents and dubious women.
Here he met a group of journalists – L. S. Amery, who had represented
The Times at Kruger's capital, Bennet Burleigh of the *Daily Telegraph*,
Julian Ralph, an American who was in Africa on behalf of the London
Daily Mail, and two men who were to become friends for life – H. A.
Gwynne of Reuter's and Perceval Landon of *The Times*. Lord Roberts
was one of the first generals to recognize the importance of the press
in war, and to give his confidence to journalists. On his last night,
before leaving to assume command of the army in the field, he sent
for Kipling, who spent the evening with him, and it is probable that
they discussed the establishment of the newspaper for the troops which
Kipling later helped to edit with Gwynne, Ralph and Landon.

In mid-February Kipling heard that the siege of Kimberley had
been raised. He was particularly pleased by this good news, as it meant
that his friend Cecil Rhodes, who had been in the beleaguered town,
was now released. Kipling hastened to meet Rhodes, and accompanied him on a visit to his estates. On the way Kipling unexpectedly
met an old acquaintance from Indian days. George Younghusband
was with Lord Methuen's Division, and had been visiting the outlying
pickets. On returning to the bivouacs Beresford Pierce, the Adjutant,
said that two civilians had come in and asked for him. One was very
tall, and the other a small man with glasses. As the visitors neared
the Mess Cart the Adjutant and Younghusband became aware that
the tall one was Cecil Rhodes and the other Rudyard Kipling. Younghusband had met Kipling at Simla and Lahore, and his appearance
was still the same – the thick black eyebrows over the double-decked
glasses, the top deck for viewing distant objects, and the lower deck
for objects nearer in. Kipling now focused Younghusband through
the lower deck, and the astonishing memory asserted itself. His first
words were:

'Who was the third who lived in Kashmire House? Younghusband,
Maud and –'

'Woon,' Younghusband said.

'Yes, of course, Woon, I remember.'

In the meantime Rhodes was standing in awkward silence in ill-fitting clothes, until he suddenly gave the reason for his visit:

'You have 500 English horses here. What did they cost you landed at Cape Town?'

'I should say an average of £60 a piece.'

'If you will let Mr Collins, my stud groom, come down and make his selection, I will give you £120 for every mare, when the war is over.'

Younghusband asked him when the war would be over, and he replied vaguely: 'Oh, in a few months.'[7] Two years afterwards they trekked over that same district, with the war still dragging on.

Rhodes told Kipling that while shut up in Kimberley he had made plans to build a house on the 'Groote Schuur' estate for the use of artists and men of letters. As a beginning he offered it to the Kiplings for as long as they wished to stay. The thought of working in this heavenly climate in such lovely surroundings appealed to Rudyard strongly. Carrie, too, welcomed the idea and went with Rhodes's architect, Herbert Baker, to choose the site for a house to be built in the Dutch Colonial style.

After Roberts's entry nearly a month later into Bloemfontein, capital of the Orange Free State, *The Friend* was established as a paper for the troops, taking over the name and office of a small local paper, and Kipling joined the staff in March. He was delighted to be back in the old routine, with the smeared galley-proofs, the chattering press, and the constant harrying of sullen, captured compositors. 'Oh, how good to be at work in a newspaper office again,' he exclaimed on the first day, with the smells and the atmosphere of the old *Civil and Military* office coming strongly back to him. His American fellow-editor, Julian Ralph, was astonished at the energy that kept him working all day on *The Friend*, and deep into the night to catch the mails with their despatches. With pen in hand and pipe in mouth, Kipling sat at the larger of the two tables in the poky editorial room bawling, 'Haven't any: go to Barlow's shop round the corner', to Tommies who were trying to get copies of the paper.

He was a guest of honour, with Milner and Roberts, at a dinner held at the railway station because it had the best room and cook in the new colony – a band playing outside, a carriage clattering up and the great men alighting, a room buzzing with talk under the flaming banner and the huge paper roses,[8] and Kipling speaking with unattractive exultation:

I propose to you tonight, gentlemen, the health of the man who has taught the British Empire its responsibilities, and the rest of the world its power, who has filled the seas with transports, and the earth with the tramp of armed men, who has made Cape Town see in Table Bay such a sight as she never saw before, and please God will never see again; who has turned the loafer of the London streets into a man, and called out him who led our forces to Kandahar, and knew not what he did; who has made the Uitlander of South Africa stand shoulder to shoulder with the boundary rider of New Zealand, and taught the man of New South Wales to pick up the wounded men who wear the maple-leaf – and all in support of the Mother Country. Gentlemen, I give you the name of the Empire-builder – Stephanus Paulus Kruger.

Kipling drove himself hard when Julian Ralph's son, Lester, succumbed to enteric and appeared to be dying. Kipling 'nursed him with consummate skill and the gentleness of a woman' until he could be got to hospital, sponging him down with alcohol until his temperature fell from 103° to 99°.

He was appalled by the sanitary arrangements revealed in the war, which had led to 8000 cases of typhoid in Bloemfontein, to which was added the sickening stench of dysentery, so that you could wind the dysentery tents a mile off. He saw a dead-beat Horse Battery come in at midnight in lashing rain and be assigned 'by some idiot saving himself trouble' the site of an evacuated typhoid hospital, and men drinking raw Modder-river water a few yards below where mules were staling. No attention whatever was given to the care and siting of latrines, with the usual deplorable results.

Kipling devoted himself to cheering the wounded in tours of the hospitals and trains from the front, and there appeared at Orange River Station 'a little kindly man with a dramatic wealth of passionate understanding hidden beneath an iron-clad protective surface'.[9] He tramped down the train and wrote letters home for the more severely wounded, signing them himself; shared his rations with the hospital cases, cheerfully going short of food. Two weary troopers who had been turned away from an officers' canteen from which came a heavenly smell of frying bacon heard a voice saying: 'These are friends of mine, Mr Logan, whom I wish to breakfast with me. Please let them in.' A small man with dark glasses then gave them the breakfast of their lives and listened in eager silence to their experiences in the field, with no hint to them of who he was.[10] From these experiences came the inspiration for one of the finest rhetorical poems Kipling ever wrote, 'The Dirge for Dead Sisters', an elegy to the nurses who died in the South African War.

It is just, in view of Kipling's violent and often unwarranted bludgeoning of the Boers, to quote a generous poem that he wrote at this time to the memory of the Boer General Joubert, whose death had just been made known to him. Hours after he wrote the poem, and tired of waiting to see the proof, he walked over to the printing office, broke in through a window, and set up the last lines of it himself at one of the printers' cases:

> With those that bred, with those that loosed the strife,
>   He had no part whose hands were clear of gain;
> But subtle, strong and stubborn, gave his life
>   To a lost cause, and knew the gift was vain.
>
> Later shall rise a people sane and great
>   Forged in strong fires, by equal war made one –
> Telling old battles over without hate,
>   Not least his name shall pass from sire to son.
>
> He shall not meet the onslaught of our van
>   In the doomed city where we close the score;
> Yet o'er his grave – his grave that holds a Man –
>   Our deep-tongued guns shall answer his once more!

At one of the daily meetings of the editors Kipling suggested that they should have a club with a ritual something like that of Masons. He had a passion for Masonic ritual and ordered a set of gold and enamel medals with the initials of each editor in Greek capitals. It is not certain when Kipling wrote the ritual itself, but if it was written in South Africa, which is probable, it is yet another indication of the industry of that restless teeming mind. In a fat notebook, written in Kipling's neat hand, it came afterwards into the possession of his friend, H. A. Gwynne.

The opening of the ritual indicates its form, but its great length and the fact that throughout it is in Kipling's own handwriting throws a strong light on the character who could devote so much thought and labour to a mere triviality.

QUESTION: Halt! who comes there?
CANDIDATE: A man trying to join the Main body.
QUESTION: Long delayed it has at last gone forward, but what do you seek therein?
CANDIDATE: Friends who bade me follow so soon as I was sure of my road.
QUESTION: And why do you seek them?
CANDIDATE: First to discuss.

QUESTION: And after?
Here shall the candidate holds his peace tho' twice entreated ...

And so on for 100 pages.[11]

On 29 March 1900, Kipling for the first time in his life came under serious fire in the field. This was at the Battle of Karee Siding, which was attended by the staff of the Bloemfontein *Friend*. It was a minor and inconclusive engagement in which the British General attempted with the usual lack of success to encircle a Boer force, which slipped away on their ponies like ghosts before the jaws of the trap could be closed. But it was at least a genuine experience of action, and Kipling was intensely thrilled by having taken part in it. He went up to the front in a Cape cart, driven by a native driver and accompanied by the correspondent of the *Daily Telegraph*. Passing through the vast, pale landscape they came to a farmhouse in a valley with five white flags flying over it, and from beyond the ridge they heard a rattle of musketry and now and then a bark of field artillery:

That farmhouse (you will see in a little why I am so detailed) held two men and, I think, two women, who received us disinterestedly. We went on into a vacant world full of sunshine and distances, where now and again a single bullet sang to himself. What I most objected to was the sensation of being under aimed fire – being, as it were, required as a head. 'What are they doing this for?' I asked my friend. 'Because they think we are the Something Light Horse. They ought to be just under this slope.'

I prayed that the particularly Something Light Horse would go elsewhere, which they presently did, for the aimed fire slackened and a wandering Colonial, bored to extinction, turned up with news from a far flank. 'No; nothing doing and no one to see.' Then more cracklings and a most cautious move forward to the lip of a large hollow where sheep were grazing. Some of them began to drop and kick. 'That's both sides trying sighting-shots,' said my companion. 'What range do you make it?' I asked. 'Eight hundred, at the nearest. That's close quarters nowadays. You'll never see anything closer than this. Modern rifles make it impossible. We're hung up till something cracks somewhere.'

There was a decent lull for meals on both sides, interrupted now and again by sputters. Then one indubitable shell – ridiculously like a pip-squeak in that vastness but throwing up much dirt. 'Krupp! Four or six pounder at extreme range,' said the expert. 'They still think we're the —— Light Horse. They'll come to be fairly regular from now on.'

Sure enough, every twenty minutes or so, one judgmatic shell pitched on our slope. We waited, seeing nothing in the emptiness, and hearing only a faint murmur as of wind along gas-jets, running in and out of the unconcerned hills. Then pom-poms opened. These were nasty little one-pounders, ten in a belt (which usually jammed about the sixth round). On soft ground they merely thudded. On rock-face the shell breaks up and yowls like a cat. My friend for the first time seemed interested. 'If these are their pom-poms it's Pretoria for us,' was his diagnosis. I looked behind me – the whole length of South Africa down to Cape Town – and it seemed very far. I felt that I could have covered it in five minutes under fair conditions, but – *not* with those aimed shots up my back. The pom-poms opened again at a bare rock-reef that gave the shells full value. For about two minutes a file of racing ponies, their tails and their riders' heads well down, showed and vanished northwards. 'Our pom-poms,' said the correspondent. 'Le Gallais, I expect. *Now* we shan't be long.'

All this time the absurd Krupp was faithfully feeling for us, *vice* ——— Light Horse, and, given a few more hours, might perhaps hit one of us. Then to the left, almost under us, a small piece of hanging woodland filled and fumed with our shrapnel much as a man's moustache fills with cigarette-smoke. It was most impressive and lasted for quite twenty minutes. Then silence; then a movement of men and horses from our side up the slope, and the hanger our guns had been hammering spat steady fire at them. More Boer ponies on more sky-lines; a last flurry of pom-poms on the right and a little frieze of far-off meek-tailed ponies, already out of rifle range. '*Maffeesh*,' said the correspondent, and fell to writing on his knee. 'We've shifted 'em.' Leaving our infantry to follow men on pony-back towards the Equator, we returned to the farmhouse. In the donga where he was waiting someone squibbed off a rifle just after we took our seats, and our driver flogged out over the rocks to the danger of our sacred bottles.[12]

Kipling, who from youth had thought so much about warfare and concentrated so much of his violent imagination in creating scenes he had never witnessed, was naturally exhilarated by this first-hand experience, but the exultation, mingled with the fear that comes to all under fire for the first time, did not distract his critical attention from the manner in which the British had fought the action. Indeed it is hard to believe that the author of the following letter was also the author of the bombastic speech about Table Bay filling with transports and the world learning the might of the British Empire.

About as merry a day as ever I spent. However, I wasn't hit, which was the main thing; and I certainly managed to pick up a good deal of mixed and valuable information. War is a rummy job – it's a cross between poker and Sunday School. Sometimes poker comes out on top, and sometimes Sunday School – but most often poker. The Boers hit us just as hard and just as often as they knew how; and we advanced against 'em as if they were street rioters that we didn't want to hurt. They spied on us at their leisure, and when they wanted a rest they handed up any old gun and said they'd be loyal subjects. Then they went to their homes and rested for a week or two; and then went on the war-path again with a new coat and a full stomach.

They are an elegant people; and we are the biggest fools, in the way that we wage war, that this century has produced. If America messes about in the Philippines as we muck around in the Transvaal, the Day of Judgment will find both nations with their wars still on their hands.[13]

But it had been a great experience. It stirred his pulses to watch the troops marching into Bloemfontein, 'the ragged bearded fierce-eyed infantry plodding along under their cloud of dust'. It was astonishing to think that the smart soldiers of peace could be so suddenly transformed into these grim barbarians: 'Bulldog faces, hawk faces, hungry wolf faces – every kind of face except a weak one. Here and there a reeking pipe – here and there a man who smiled, but most with their swarthy faces leaned forward, the features impassive; and by the columns the baggage wagons creaking through the dust, the mules all skin and ribs, with the escort tramping beside the wheels.'

Kipling found intense excitement in all this, and in the routine of the veldt: soft little whistles an hour before dawn, blown by the squadron sergeant-majors, a stamping and sneeze from the horse lines, breakfast in the dark, the loaded wagons and the saddling up. Then at first light the march till mid-day across the vast open rolling country over which a bugle-call could be heard for miles, the off-saddling, and the horses turned out to graze. Memories of the country sank deep into his mind, the endless veldt, the stubborn *kopjes*, and here and there a wrecked bridge; sweeping expanses pock-marked by trenches and block-houses. It was all in his mind when he returned to South Africa after the war with the Duke and Duchess of Connaught, and in these little-known verses which he gave them[14] are reflected the harsh country and the scarred battlefields:

THE SILENT ARMY

From the corn and wine of the Lowlands to the stubborn hills of the North
The word that heralds your coming shall call your army forth,
With the voices of many cannon where the ordered legions pace,
They shall give you welcome befitting the House of the Kings of our race.

We may not answer that Summons, we may not arm and ride,
We have done with our loved battalions, with the squadron's pomp and
    pride,
Our ears are deaf to the bugles, our eyes are blind to the day,
But we do not forget our duty, and we watch beside your way.

When you steam from the cheering platforms, when the guards of honour
    are gone,
And the Veldt returns to her dreaming, silently we take on.
From end to end of your journey with never a break in the chain,
The men of the last Divisions are guarding the Royal Train.

On either side of the Railway, where the tins and bottles are,
You can trace by trench and blockhouse the scars of the three years' war,
And clear on the stony hillsides, or hid where the young grass waves,
On either side of the railway, always and always our graves.

In the fierce fantastic sunset, when earth takes colour and glows,
Till the moonlight turns it to silver, and the dawn to silver and rose,
In the breathless noon-day silence when the mountains swim in the heat,
Look – look out of the window, for behold we lie at your feet.

Oh, you that have loved us a lifetime, that loved us the wide world o'er,
We may not mount with our comrades to do your honour once more,
But after the dust and the thunder, when the silence settles again,
From end to end of your journey we are guarding the Royal Train.
                Written January 1906
                and given to the Duchess on 6 January 1906.

On 3 April Kipling returned to the Cape. His active service had thus consisted of sixteen days' absence from the Cape, from 19 March to 3 April. Back in England, he heard at Rottingdean on 18 May the news of the relief of Mafeking. Kipling did his best to reproduce in the peaceful village the frenzy that was raging in London. He had already greeted three men home from the South African War by firing a cannon over the cliff;[15] on Mafeking day he roused the strongly Tory village, and produced tin cans to make strident noises of victory, while across the green at 'North End House' Margaret Mackail sat in misery and shame behind drawn shutters. If not actually pro-Boer, she felt passionately that the war had been a stain on British honour, and a callous flouting of the rights of small nations. She, Aunt Georgie, and Jack Mackail had argued often and bitterly with Kipling, who had closed his mind to their protests with the finality of an iron shutter descending. He loved these relations, but could not regard their politics except with pity and contempt. They belonged, he thought, to that vague washed-out brand of idealism which recked nothing of war or its necessity, 'in which the Fabian Society was spawned' – the sort of talk he had heard for the first time under the mulberry tree at 'The Grange'.

CHAPTER XV

A WANING CONFIDENCE

MANY of Kipling's memories of the war were bitter. After his experiences of it his themes were mainly the courage of the common soldier and regimental officer, and the disgraceful bungling of the higher authorities. He described the tramp of weary men on the march with brilliant skill in 'Boots'.

> Don't – don't – don't – don't – look at what's in front of you.
> (Boots – boots – boots – boots – movin' up an' down again);
> Men – men – men – men – men go mad with watchin' 'em,
>   An' there's no discharge in the war!
>
> Try – try – try – try – to think o' something different –
> Oh – my – God – keep – me from going lunatic!
> (Boots – boots – boots – boots – movin' up an' down again!)
>   There's no discharge in the war!

He lashed at the men responsible for their misery, and it was by no means only 'politicians' who felt the lash, but also the leaders in the field:

> (Panicky, perishin' old men)
> That 'amper an' 'inder an' scold men
> For fear o' Stellenbosch!*

In a delightful poem, redolent of Australia, about the New South Wales contingent, he paid tribute to the men of the Empire:

> Smells are surer than sounds or sights
>   To make your heart-strings crack –
> They start those awful voices o' nights
>   That whisper, 'Old man, come back!'
> That must be why the big things pass
>   And the little things remain,

* Generals who had failed in the field were sent in disgrace to the town Stellenbosch.

> Like the smell of the wattle by Lichtenberg,
>   Riding in, in the rain.
>
> I have forgotten a hundred fights,
>   But one I shall not forget –
> With the raindrops bunging up my sights
>   And my eyes bunged up with wet;
> And through the crack and stink of the cordite
>   (Ah Christ! My country again!)
> The smell of the wattle by Lichtenberg,
>   Riding in, in the rain.

But the bitter feelings predominated, and persisted into old age. Years later he was still musing angrily about the Boers:

> We charged ourselves step by step with the care and maintenance of all Boerdom – women and children included. Whence horrible tales of our atrocities in the concentration camps. Eventually the 'war' petered out on political lines. Our men did not see why they should perish chasing stray commandoes, or festering in block-houses, and then followed a sort of demoralizing 'handy-pandy' of alternate surrenders complicated by exchange of army tobacco for Boer brandy which was bad for both sides.
>
> At long last we were left apologizing to a deeply indignant people, whom we had been nursing and doctoring for a year or two; and who now expected, and received, all manner of free gifts and appliances for the farming they had never practised. We put them in a position to uphold and expand their primitive lust for racial domination, and thanked God we were 'rid of a knave'.[1]

The rigidity of Kipling's thinking and the unyielding nature of his prejudice were most pronounced during and immediately after the South African War. Afterwards, the trajectory describes a descending curve, but for this period we have searched his papers in vain to find one qualm as to the rightness of the British action, in what was at least a highly controversial issue. The Jameson raid which 'upset Rhodes's applecart', and now appears to most as a ruthless and incompetent piece of power politics, excites not a word of censure. These are reserved for the Dutch, and applied with no sparing hand – 'unutterable shiftiness', 'astounding conceptions of loyalty'. What is left is consumed in mordant diatribes on the gross incompetence of the British High Command in the conduct of the war, and on the lethargy and frivolity of his own countrymen, upon whom he now turned the full jet of his indignation in a passionate but vain attempt to inspire a *risorgimento*.

We have noted the impressions that Kipling brought away with him
from India, and he had continued to hold these beliefs till the South
African War, which gave a rude shock to his political thinking. In
India he had seen the administrators of the Indian Civil Service grap-
pling with their tasks in the baking oven of the Indian summer, spanning rivers, quelling epidemics, surveying jungles, and restraining
native princes. From this had sprung his admiration for the type of
Orde and Tallentyre, 'the strong man ruling alone'. A passionate
admiration for everything 'military' accompanied his zeal for efficient
administration. He had developed an early mistrust for democratic
government, and Members of Parliament visiting India in the course
of their Parliamentary duties were exposed to such bitter sneers as
'Pagett MP':

And I laughed as I drove from the Station; but the mirth died out on my lips
As I thought of the fools like Pagett who write of their 'Eastern Trips',
And the sneers of the travelled idiot, who duly misgoverns the land;
And I prayed to the Lord to deliver another one into my hand.

He barely noticed, and then only with derision, that strange band of
BAs (failed) and other products of the Inns of Court, who formed
the Congress Party, and conducted stilted debates in the language of
Burke.

In Tokyo he had argued with his Japanese hosts about the new
Constitution:

'You've a Parliament, have you not?'

'Oh yes, with parties – Liberal and Radical.'

'Then they will both tell lies to you and to each other. Then they
will pass bills, and spend their time fighting each other. Then all the
foreign governments will discover that you have no fixed policy.'

When dazzling success had come upon him in the dingy chambers
in Villiers Street, Kipling began to regard himself as a man with a
mission. Just how great that success was, we are in danger of forgetting. It would not be an exaggeration to say that Kipling enjoyed a
position given before only to Dickens and Tennyson among English
writers. Although the chill cloud of oblivion was to fall upon him for
a while, he was in fact already immortal, and he was not going to
squander his opportunity for moral leadership by either accepting
honours or allowing success to go to his head.

Kipling, as we have seen, was authoritarian in his conception of
civil government. He believed that the 'job belongs to the man who

can do it'. He believed his experts. He had a passion for technical proficiency and, indeed, for any form of craftsmanship. The man who, after years of diligent apprenticeship, could make the lock of a shot-gun, the poacher who unerringly set his snares, the mariner who had mastered the science of navigation, the engineer who could calculate a girder-stress, all these were to him objects of admiration. He could do none of these things himself, but his own craftsmanship, that of words, was equally intense; and nothing gave him more pleasure than to write about it – the fishermen gutting the cod on the Grand Bank, engineers coaxing recalcitrant marine engines, Burne-Jones and Morris mixing their pigments, and, later, the placid craftsmanship of the husbandman.

This absorption in technical detail sometimes led him into passages of spurious erudition which infuriated many people. In his story *The Devil and the Deep Sea* he writes of an engine-room accident on board ship:

What followed is worth consideration. The forward engine had no more work to do. Its released piston rod, therefore, drove up fiercely, with nothing to check it, and started most of the nuts of the cylinder-cover. It came down again, the full weight of the steam behind it and the foot of the disconnected connecting-rod, useless as the leg of a man with a sprained ankle, flung out to the right and struck the starboard, or right-hand, cast-iron supporting column of the forward engine, cracking it clean through about six inches above the base, and wedging the upper portion outwards three inches towards the ship's side. There the connecting-rod jammed. Meantime, the after-engine, being as yet unembarrassed, went on with its work, and in so doing brought round at its next revolution the crank of the forward engine, which smote the already jammed connecting rod, bending it and therewith the piston-rod cross-head – the big cross-piece that slides up and down so smoothly.

He had a bitter hatred for the Radicalism displayed in the Sunday newspapers, 'which would always support a German artisan against an English nobleman, a negro against a white overseer, a mutinous soldier against his officer; which has done its best to arouse hatred of Russia, our great ally, because ... she is not governed on a mock-democratic system'.[2]

He had shaken his head ruefully over Japan, 'the second oriental country which has made it impossible for a strong man to govern alone'.[3] He had regarded the shrill chatter of the Congress Party in India with contempt, and the vulgarity of Congress in the USA with horror. In the future, he was to be one of the many who at first sight genuflected before the unlovely shrine of Mussolini. Democracy to him was a system conducted by unpractical people who tended to obstruct those who were properly equipped in the art of government.

Kipling was not, as he has often been called, a slavish idolater of British rule. Again and again, a note of mordant criticism flashes out, as in *The Masque of Plenty* and *The Head of the District*. He was convinced, however, that in spite of many shortcomings, to which he drew scathing attention, the British had an innate genius for government and that their rule in India had been a far better one than any that had preceded it, or could follow it at any conceivable time in the future. He was convinced that a British withdrawal from India would lead to civil war, hideous carnage and universal corruption. It is important to observe the genesis of these opinions. They were formed in India, and their essence was that the English must govern, since they alone were capable of doing so.

That is why in *The Jungle Books*, those inspired stories of animal life, there penetrates into the enchanted glades of the forest the antiseptic discipline of the public school. Mowgli is the district officer, or the prefect; although a child of the Jungle, he is a white man, and must therefore have predominance over even the most capable native colleagues – Bagheera the Panther, or Kaa the Python; in a later story Mowgli is pressed into the service of the British Raj in the Forestry Commission.

One of Kipling's most important books, *Kim*, was finished during the South African War. He had been working on it, at intervals, for more than seven years, frequently consulting his father at Tisbury, and it is still regarded by many as the most perfect of his longer works, perhaps the only one that fully succeeds. Kipling made his farewell to India in *Kim*, which was published in 1900. Years before, at 'Bliss Cottage' in Vermont, an idea had stirred in his mind of an Irish boy born in India and immersed in native life. But he decided that the idea must wait for a while, until his daemon was ready to put flesh upon its bones. It was not until 1898 that he began concentrated work upon the book and, after much discussion with Lockwood, saw it published two years later: 'In a gloomy, windy autumn Kim came back to me with insistence, and I took it to be smoked over with my Father. Under our united tobaccos it grew like the Djinn released from the glass bottle, and the more we explored its possibilities the more opulence of detail did we discover.'

Kim is the only major work of Kipling to be praised with small reserve by normally hostile critics. It is indeed accepted as his only successful full-length story, enchanting, intensely moving, and authentically great, in which he allowed the imagination and sympathy full rein to remember and to explore. Bitterness and prejudice were forgotten, or at least suspended, and a warm understanding shown of all creeds and races. And it is precisely this profound insight into the ways and beliefs of others, this absence of homily and special pleading, that makes *Kim* unique in Kipling's work. He had attempted no such tolerance and understanding before, and he never did so again.

Kim is white. The son of an Irish soldier and Irish nursemaid, he has grown up as an orphan in India, as immersed in the native life as Mowgli was in that of the Jungle, even thinking, as the young Kipling had, in Hindustani. He is different from the other children in the bazaar who merely parrot the opinions of their parents: as an orphan he is a child of the whole city of Lahore, 'the little friend of all the world', a bridge between opposing creeds and a stranger to caste prejudice.

The English overlords have earmarked Kim as a potential recruit for the secret service, 'the Great Game', and he has already been entrusted with some minor tasks. From the beginning of the story, with his future uncertain and his loyalties undefined, Kim moves between the opposed worlds of the Pathan horse dealer Mahbub Ali, a virile adventurer who works for the English secret service, and the Tibetan Lama whom Kim first meets in the 'Wonder House', Lockwood Kipling's museum in Lahore.

The Lama in the beginning is childlike and helpless, pathetically vulnerable to the chances of ordinary life, and Kim becomes his *chela*, his disciple, guiding him and protecting him from the malignity of the world. To the Lama the earthly life is the domain of *Maya* or Illusion, and he must separate himself from it in order to be released from what Buddhists call 'the wheel of things'. But this detachment means the denial of the most potent human emotions, and in the end the Lama and Kim recoil from these cold admonitions from the cloister.

Meanwhile this demand creates a tension between the strange pair which becomes acute during their journey on the Grand Trunk Road in search of the Lama's fulfilment. This section of the book is perhaps Kipling's masterpiece of descriptive writing on India. He is totally absorbed by the different races and castes who are revealed as this 'River of Life' flows by, and describes it in a prose as glowing and many-hued as the garments of the passers-by. There is all of India in this inspired *tour de force* – her stridency and harshness, splendour and squalor, noises and smells. Kim is filled with rapture by the bustle and excitement, but to the Lama stalking along with downcast eyes it is all illusion, and he can feel only pity for these noisy hurrying people who are all on the wheel.

On the journey Kim falls into the hands of two chaplains in his father's old regiment, and is sent to an English school. Here he is taught much that will be useful to him if he is employed by the English, but his identity is still uncertain. Although he absorbs much 'Sahib's' knowledge, when his holidays come he resumes native dress and disappears again into the sea of Indian life. His dilemma is whether he is a Sahib or a member of the race in which he has been embraced since infancy.

Some critics, notably Edmund Wilson, believed that at this point the reader expects Kim eventually to realize that if he joins the secret service he will be delivering into bondage to the British invaders those whom he has always considered his own people. Wilson also believed that in the *dénouement* of the story Kipling allows Kim to dissociate himself from the Lama and his mysticism, and commit himself to a role in the secret service:

> Kim must now exploit his knowledge of native life for the purpose of preventing and putting down any native resistance to the British; but it never seems to occur to his creator that this constitutes a betrayal of the Lama. A sympathy with the weaker party in a relationship based on force has again given way without a qualm to a glorification of the stronger.

Read in this way, Kipling's handling of the *dénouement* of his story might seem to justify this interpretation – that Kim discovered, like Mowgli and the Brushwood Boy, that his future belonged to the world of action and not to that of dreams. But another, and less obvious conclusion can also be drawn. At the end of the book Kim and the Lama, reunited, journey on into the Lama's mountains, where in the icy air the Lama's endurance increases, as does his certainty of success in his quest for spiritual release. His salvation is earned by penitence for a moment of murderous passion. He has been tempted to kill a Russian agent working against the British who has torn his sacred chart, and the anguish of his repentance is described in a scene probably unmatched elsewhere in Kipling's writing.

Kim's identification and sympathy with the Lama become complete as they make their perilous escape from the mountains. He now feels the old sense of conflict. He rejects any mention of his Sahibhood, and 'the Great Game might play itself for all he cared'. Love and its responsibility fill his mind, as the Lama now fills his whole horizon. It is never expressly stated, although it might be inferred that Kim, realizing his obligations, resolved his dilemma by choosing the secret service:

We should need very strong evidence however [wrote a discerning critic] to support the idea that Kim could return to the Game, against the whole current of the book's disabling criticism – and there is no such evidence. We must not mistake the last direction of the novel's imaginative exploration; for the remaining conflicts of Kim and the Lama are essentially complementary, and the issue leaves them finally united. When Kim staggers from his sickroom with the last and worst loss of his sense of identity, it is because as *chela* he has been involved not only with the old man's loving soul, but also with his Buddhist ideology.[4]

It is because of the inhuman strain in this ideology that Kim felt,

'although he could not put it into words, that his soul was out of gear with its surroundings . . . "I am Kim. I am Kim. And what is Kim?" His soul repeated it again and again. He did not want to cry . . . but of a sudden, easy, stupid tears ran down his nose, and with an almost audible click he felt the wheels of his being lock up anew on the world without. Things that rode meaningless on the eyeball an instant before slid into proper proportion. Roads were meant to be walked upon, houses to be lived in, cattle to be driven, and men and women to be talked to.'

So his restoration is completed full-length on the earth, drawing strength from it. As the 'gear' imagery makes clear, this is commitment not to the Game, with which we are no longer concerned, but at a far more fundamental level, to the wheel of earthly and human life, against the view which holds that all these things are illusion, and that one must keep oneself apart from them. Yet this means no final conflict with the Lama, because in the end the Lama rejects apartness too. At the moment of achieving the final extinction of his humanity . . . he turns back 'with strivings and yearnings and retchings and agonies not to be told'. At the very last moment, love and human relationship are more important than Nirvana for oneself.[5]

The characters in *Kim* are drawn with far more than Kipling's usual faint emphasis and impatient observation: Mahbub Ali, the Babu Huree Chunder, the Ressaldar, the old soldier who speaks for the side of Kipling occupied with military preparedness on the North West Frontier, the *sahiba*, that lively old Indian lady fascinated by the 'River of Life' on the Grand Trunk Road; the wily Creighton, and Lurgan, 'healer of sick pearls', Kim's teachers in the art of spying – all are memorable. And it is highly significant of the mood in which Kipling wrote this book that the timid and garrulous Babu, an example of a type of Bengali he despised, should be shown capable of high courage and endurance when put to the test, and that the cruel and barbarous Pathan should reveal depths of tenderness and emotion. For Kipling here showed himself capable of understanding attitudes fundamentally different from one another, and profoundly different from his own.

And there is to be found in *Kim* 'the triumphant achievement of an anti-self so powerful that it became a touchstone for everything else' – the creation of the Lama. This involved imagining a point of view and a personality almost at the furthest possible remove from Kipling himself; 'yet it is explored so lovingly that it could not but act as a catalyst towards some deeper synthesis.... It is an artistic triumph that occurs only by virtue of its own conditions, and it never happened again.'[6]

Kipling was, as we have seen, no blind idolater of the Indian Civil Service. He had been in the habit of slipping wounding gibes about it into the columns of the *Civil and Military Gazette*, which greatly disturbed the editor. He believed, however, that the conditions of modern life had grown to such complexity as to make it impossible for any government whatever to fulfil its task perfectly, and that the Indian Civil Service with its long tradition of the leadership of 'a strong man governing alone', unencumbered by democratic interference, was as good an administrative organization as the world had ever known. Although he frequently castigates the venality and incompetence of departmental heads, he always admires the man in the field who is working under their orders and has to pay the penalty for their blunders – the bridge-builder, the doctor struggling with a cholera epidemic, the district officer, the lonely administrator of an enormous area. 'A strong man governing alone': again and again the thought recurs. Alfred Milner, who with his 'Kindergarten' had undertaken the reconstruction of South Africa after the war, seemed to satisfy this ideal, and when later his recall from that country was under question Kipling was to write in angry protest:

When the first flush of talk is over he is very likely to make the resettlement of South Africa a sane and orderly success. Theoretically, of course, this matter, as one affecting the Empire, should stand outside politics, but the trouble is that Milner is an administrator, and therefore detestable to a certain type of politician. I do hope you'll be able to make the people your way realize that this silent capable man worrying out his path alone, down south, in the face of all conceivable discouragements, is not a steward to be got rid of on the threats or wire-pulling of a rebel commando.[7]

Although at the time of the South African War the imperialism at moments of emotional excitement was shot with jingoism, and the voice strident and angry, the basic conception remained logical. He still believed in the British Empire precisely in the way in which Cecil Rhodes believed in it, as an engine of progress and general happiness for the ordinary family. He believed that the fierce clashing creeds of India were held in place by the cement of British rule alone and that a withdrawal from India would lead to violence, mass-murder and anarchy. Because he viewed with profound mistrust the capacity of Indians to govern themselves, to him the 'good' Indians were those who faithfully discharged positions of trust under British administrators, and not those to whom he referred as the 'hybrid university-trained mule', who, as he thought, indulged in political agitation directed to undermining the British position.

Kipling's hatred of liberalism was returned in full measure, as can be seen in these blistering sentences:

The rocket that rose in the East completed its arc in the Transvaal. Mr Kipling in a word was the poet of the great reaction. Through all the amazing crescendo of the nineties, with its fever of speculation, its Barney Barnatos, its Whitaker Wrights, its swagger and its violence, its raids and its Music Hall frenzies, the bard of the banjo marched ahead of the throng, shouting his songs of the barrack-room, telling his tales of the camp-fire and jungle, proclaiming the worship of the great god Jingo. What did they know of England, those pitiful mean-souled Little Englanders, prating of justice, slobbering over natives, canting about the 'righteousness that exalteth a nation'?

> For the Lord our God most High
> He hath made the deep as dry,
> He hath smote for us a pathway to the ends of all the Earth.

Was not this fair earth ours by way of purchase and right of race? Had we not bought it from Jehovah by blood and sacrifice?

> We have strawed out best to the weeds' unrest.
> To the shark and the sheering gull.
> If blood be the price of admiralty,
> Lord God, we ha' paid in full.

And should we not do as we would with our own? The Indian in India, the Boer in the Transvaal, the Irishman in Ireland – what were they but food for our Imperial hopper? 'Pagett MP was a liar', a wretched emissary of Exeter Hall, prowling round the quarters of gentlemen and cackling about the grievances of Indians. What did he know of India? What were the natives that they should have grievances?[8]

Another critic saw no mention of, or allusion to, the social move-ments of the natives, who were viewed in the light of 'a huge mass of raw brown naked humanity to be manipulated by the civil and mili-tary officials for the arcane purposes of the great Indian Empire, or by the male Anglo-Indians for more or less animating, if monotonous, sexual experiences without benefit of clergy'.[9]

It has been said that there was a strain of sadism in Kipling, mani-fested, for instance, in the poem about beating a 'nigger' with a clean-ing rod to get money out of him, and in the way in which he described dog fights with relish and lingered affectionately on the more horrible details of war.

There was unquestionably a violent strain in his writing and an in-tellectual interest in cruelty. But it could be argued that the violence was consciously projected by an effort of the imagination. George Orwell went so far as to write: 'Kipling *is* a jingo-imperialist, he *is* morally insensitive, and aesthetically disgusting,' but this absurd generalization is far removed from Orwell's usual cold surgical prob-ings. It is true that Kipling's passionate belief in the Empire often degenerated into unseemly arrogance, and that he was guilty of fre-quent lapses of taste, but to dismiss him as 'aesthetically disgusting' is an almost meaningless commentary on the author of *They*, *Kim*, 'Merrow Down' and 'Recessional'.

And war? Much has been made of Kipling's addiction to war in an effort to emphasize the sadistic strain. We have seen Kipling's passion for the military, and it is probable that in his younger days he regarded war as a necessary instrument of policy. He was brought up in a period of frontier wars and local skirmishes, of which for a long time he had no first-hand knowledge, although he had a profound interest in them. The authoritarian side of his nature is revealed in the fact that he was extremely angry that the English people never took kindly to his suggestion that the 'greasy idols' of cricket and football should be replaced by the practice of the art of war, from youth upwards, in a series of mock battles which were to be entered upon in a spirit 'almost like cricket', an idea which he developed in *The Army of a Dream* and 'The Islanders'.

He was incapable of understanding the deep British hatred of mili-tarism, which has always rendered the OTC camp the most detested aspect of public-school life, and which makes it far preferable to Englishmen to spend a hot day in high summer listening dreamily to the clack of ball on bat, than to go on a ten-mile route march, or crawl up a hillside on the belly, an attitude which has no doubt cost us dear, but is an amiable characteristic of the race.

The casualties in the wars of Kipling's youth were not heavy and it was possible to consider warfare as an exercise tending to develop valuable personal qualities and at the same time tending to spread the rule of law. Whatever the shortcomings of his early attitude, this preoccupation with war was to wreak a hideous revenge on him. As he wrote his miserable foreboding under the shadow of the war of 1914, which he had long foreseen and in which his only son was to be killed, they were not words of exultation or arrogance:

> Once more we heard the word
> That sickened earth of old:
> 'No law except the sword
> Unsheathed and uncontrolled' ...
>
> Comfort, content, delight,
> The ages' slow-bought gain,
> They shrivelled in a night.
> Only ourselves remain ...

As has been well observed:

Mr Kipling's ferocity on paper is not to be explained as a natural delight in violence and blood. On the contrary it is distinctly a literary ferocity – the ferocity, not of a man who has killed people, but of a man who sits down and conscientiously tries to imagine what it is like to kill people. It is essentially the same kind of ferocity in imaginative fiction as the ferocity of Nietzsche in lyrical philosophy, or of Malthus in speculative politics. When Mr Kipling talks of men carved in battle like the nasty noise of beef-cutting upon the block, or of men falling over like the rattle of fire-irons in the fender, and the grunt of a pole-axed ox, or of a hot encounter between two combatants wherein one of them after feeling for his opponents' eyes finds it necessary to wipe his thumb on his trousers, or of gun wheels greasy from contact with a late gunner – these things are disagreeable.

But let us be clear as to the reason. These things are disagreeable not because they are horrible fact, but because they are deliberate fiction ...

It is indeed not altogether true to say that Kipling delights in war. The delight is partly delight in the subject, and the gusto that of the craftsman for doing his job thoroughly and effectively:

Professors have gloried in blood and iron, who would probably faint away in the nice clean operating theatre of a London Hospital. Philosophers who cannot run upstairs have preached the survival of the physically fittest. Mr Kipling's savagery is of this essentially cultivated kind. They are the kind of battle story which is usually written by sedentary poets who live in the country and are fond of children.

It was this romantic attitude to war that led Kipling into the error that soldiers enjoy fighting: in *The Drums of the Fore and Aft*, the Lancers were 'chafing to deliver a dainty charge'. When the Gurkhas are called upon to attack the Afghans, 'a happy sigh of contentment soughed their ranks', and they felt that the land smiled as they gripped their *kukris* and looked longingly at their officers for the word to charge. Thurston Hopkins served for four years beside the Gurkhas and advanced with them into action, but found them no more enthusiastic over the horrible business than the men who had arrived on the last draft.

An intellectual brutality of this kind came over Kipling when he wrote *On Greenhow Hill*, in the scene when the friends were waiting for the kill. 'They were talking in whispers, for the stillness of the wood and the desire for slaughter lay heavy upon them.' In *Many Inventions* there is a description by Kipling of Ortheris surveying a new draft of recruits, arrived in India. It is a revolting passage:

'Well, you are a holy set of bean-faced beggars, *you* are,' he said genially to a knot in the barrack square. Then, running his eye over them – 'Fried Fish an' whelks is about your sort. Blimy if they haven't sent some pink-eyed Jews too. You chap with the greasy 'ed, which o' the Solomons was your father, Moses?'

'My name's Anderson,' said a voice sullenly.

'Oh Samuelson! All right, Samuelson! And 'ow many o' the likes of you Sheenies are comin' to spoil B. Company?'

Kipling's comment on this disgusting dialogue is: 'There is no scorn so complete as that of the old soldier for the new. It is right that this should be so. A recruit must learn first that he is not a man but a thing, which in time, and by the mercy of Heaven, may develop into a soldier of the Queen.'

There is intellectual brutality again in *The Head of the District*:

They tickled him gently under the armpit with the knife point. He leaped aside screaming, only to feel a cold blade drawn lightly over the back of his neck, or a rifle-muzzle rubbing his beard. He called on his adherents to aid him, but most of these lay dead on the plains, for Khoda Dad Khan had been at some pains to arrange their decease. Men described to him the glories of the shrine they would build and the little children clapping their hands cried: 'Run, Mullah, run! There's a man behind you!' In the end, when the sport wearied, Khoda Dad Khan's brother sent a knife home between his ribs. 'Wherefore,' said Khoda Dad Khan with charming simplicity, 'I am now Chief of the Khusru Kheyl!' No man gainsaid him; and they all went to sleep very stiff and sore!

But foremost in Kipling's mind was always the apprehension of danger from without, and the agencies that must be used for protection against such perils – the 'Law' and the 'Wall'. It is a fundamental demand for strong government, an almost atavistic demand for security. His law is the Law of Civilization and of progress, and at least part of his interest in inanimate objects (locomotives, machinery and so forth) which sometimes so exasperates us lay in the fact that he saw them as agencies for strengthening the Law and assisting orderly and peaceful progress.

Locomotives and rolling stock help to break up epidemics, and in removing victims to hospital; dams chain the river and prevent it bursting its banks, inundating villages and crops and drowning men: both are servants of administration. The 'Wall', which appeared first in *Puck of Pook's Hill*, became symbolic in Kipling's mind of the preservation of the Law. Once a breach is made in the Wall by the barbarian without, the Law is in danger. At all costs it must be held against the forces of anarchy and rapine, for should it fall, the world would relapse for generations into drab barbarism. It is untrue to say that Kipling's later malignant hatred of the Germans, which produced such murderous stories as *Mary Postgate*, was wholly due to the death of his son. As we have seen, his mistrust of them had begun long before, when he first realized that an assault on civilization was coming and that the Wall was in peril, and for years he had winded the Prussian menace sweeping across the North Sea like the smell of a sewer.

What is it that makes Kipling so extraordinary? [wrote W. H. Auden]. Is it not that while virtually every other European writer since the fall of the Roman Empire has felt that the dangers threatening civilization came from *inside* that Civilization ... Kipling is obsessed by a sense of dangers threatening from *outside*? Others have been concerned with the corruptions of the big city, the *ennui* of the cultured mind; some sought a remedy in a return to Nature, to childhood, to Classical Antiquity. Others looked forward to a brighter future of liberty, equality and fraternity. . . . In Kipling there is none of this, no nostalgia for a Golden Age, no belief in Progress. For him civilization (and consciousness) is a little citadel of light surrounded

by a great darkness full of malignant forces and only maintained through
the centuries by everlasting vigilance, will power and self sacrifice.[10]

One can only comment that the course of history amply justified
Kipling's fear of external danger.

But it was not indifference to internal progress that caused Kipling's
preoccupation with defensive vigilance. It was because he realized that
for every single thought for the embellishment of Life, there must be
ten for its actual preservation. And he knew that this vigilance must
be eternal:

> As it will be in the future, it was at the birth of Man –
> There are only four things certain since Social Progress began: –
> That the Dog returns to his Vomit and the Sow returns to her Mire,
> And the burnt Fool's bandaged finger goes wobbling back to the Fire.

He soon realized after the Boer War that nothing had been learned
from 'the Imperial lesson that might make us an Empire yet', and it
was with a sense of growing despair that he surveyed the scene afterwards – the Little Englanders and Radicals blind to the menace to
their existence: 'To them the Empire seemed only a financiers' ramp
for exploiting the backward races, or at least an invention of the
Tories. That others were toasting "the day" when the age-long security
and Empire of the English should end, and that their own way of life
in the crowded cities might unfit them to stand in battle against the
armies of young and jealous nations never troubled them for a
moment.'

Intent on sport and frivolity they went their feckless way to football
field and cricket pitch and 'cheered the cheapjack politicians of the
hour who offered to plunder the rich and distribute the next year's
seed corn. And a despairing poet, feeling in his heart the imminence
of doom, lashed his indifferent countrymen.'[11]

> Now we can only wait till the day, wait and apportion our shame.
> These are the dykes our fathers left, but we could not look to the same.
> Time and again we were warned of the dykes, time and again we delayed:
> Now it may fall we have slain our sons as our fathers we have betrayed.

We may see this period of Kipling's life as a watershed between the
buoyant hopefulness of youth and the disillusionment of maturity.
Experience planted in him a revulsion from his early passionate belief
in the mission of the British Empire. 'India's full of Stalkies,' he had
once written, 'Cheltenham and Haileybury and Marlborough chaps
– that we don't know anything about; and the surprises will begin

when there's really a big row on. Just imagine Stalky let loose on the South side of Europe with a sufficiency of Sikhs and a reasonable prospect of loot – consider it quietly.'

But alas, too many of the 'General Sahibs' he had so revered, had failed ridiculously in the field, and been sent to Stellenbosch; the world had watched with a rich amusement, not unmixed with more acquisitive emotions, the spectacle of this mighty Empire struggling desperately to defeat a handful of Boer farmers. It was even clear that the 'Stalkies', 'Brushwood Boys' and 'Bobby Wickses' were no great shakes at their own job. Kipling did not abandon his ideals, but his confidence was sapped: 'Kipling,' said a critic, 'lost his optimism and did not regain it. It cannot have surprised him when in 1914 the Stalkies of that time were sent into action armed with swords, and distinctively dressed so that they might be the more easily picked off by the enemy.'[12]

CHAPTER XVI

FROM WAR TO WAR

THE Kiplings came to South Africa again on Christmas Day 1900, to the house Rhodes had built for them, 'The Woolsack' on the 'Groote Schuur' estate. They were to return there every winter until 1907. The long sea journey was as invigorating an adventure for Rudyard as for his children – the first moment of excitement when he saw the great vessel at the quayside with the gulls screaming round it, caught a whiff of oil from the engine room, and listened to the ship's noises; and then the liner seething through the dark past Ushant into the wastes of the Bay of Biscay. Again they would pause at Madeira, which seemed to glow with a purple luminosity just before dawn broke, with the lights still twinkling on its volcanic slopes, and then would come the long steam to the Cape – steadily and delightedly southward, the heat growing each day, flying fishes heralding the tropics, and the Southern Cross flaming above the bow.

Kipling always worked during these voyages, usually in a small cabin opening on to the noisy promenade deck, but sometimes seated at a high folding-table on the deck itself. He was oblivious to the noise and movement round him, and would pace the deck, return to the table for a few moments, and pace the deck again, as if he had been in his own study. He was unconscious of the interest aroused by his presence among his fellow-passengers. One chilly evening, going below to find his overcoat, he vaguely put on the first garment that came to hand, which happened to be a brown camel-hair dressing gown. Someone on deck diffidently pointed out his mistake, but Kipling replied that the dressing gown kept him warm, and that was all that mattered. His friend muttered in admiration: 'Fancy being the sort of man who can do a thing like that and not have it matter.' As the ship steamed south a circle of children would gather round him in a quiet corner, while he told them the tales that afterwards became the *Just So Stories*.[1]

Kipling's spirits were quickened, each voyage, by his first glimpse of the paradise that Rhodes had placed at his disposal, 'The Wool-sack', a low white house surrounded by a *stoep*, lay lapped in deep peace with oak trees casting their shade over the patio and squirrels leaping among the foliage. 'In the stillness of hot afternoons,' he said, 'the fall of an acorn was almost like a shot.' A heavy mixed scent came from the pine and eucalyptus grove, while flowering shrubs grew like weeds in the garden, and myrtle and plumbago hedges, oleander and fig trees, wild cannas and arum lilies, roses and violets grew under the lazy eye of Johnston, the Malay gardener. Behind all towered the flank of Table Mountain and its copses of silver trees flanking scarred ravines, the mountain of which he had written as he saw it throbbing in the heat:

> Under hot Constantia, broad the vineyards lie.
> Throned and thorned the aching berg props the speckless sky.

In front of the house one looked across a flat fifteen miles of pines, aromatic in the sun, to the foothills beyond. 'No one seems to explain the fascination of Africa,' he said. 'We unite to curse it root and branch and yet we love it. I wish you could ever have seen the sunlight and the space of it and the great breadth of wine-dark sea where I am going to lunch today with Carrie.'[2]

Wild animals roamed the Rhodes estate, lion, zebra, emus, and a llama who spat at his visitors through the wire fence. There was a vast bull – a Kudu of eighteen hands, who would jump the seven-foot fence round the little peach orchard, 'hook a loaded branch in the great rings of his horns, rend it off with a jerk, eat the peaches, leaving the stones, and lift himself over the wires, like a cloud, up the flank of Table Mountain. On coming home after dinner we met him at the foot of the garden, gigantic in the moonlight.' There was a baby lion, whose life Caroline saved by feeding it with mutton-broth on a dipped finger from which his tongue removed the skin, and who, when recovered, stalked butterflies among the flowering bushes in the garden.

To reach Rhodes's house, 'Groote Schuur', one walked down a path through a ravine choked with hydrangeas, which in autumn was one solid-packed blue river. Here lived Rhodes, now in the last year of his short life, grimly striving to fulfil his fantastic vision before he was stricken by the aneurism which he carried with him as a constant death-sentence. Its premonitory throbbings would compel him to re-cline on a huge couch on the cool, marble-flagged verandah 'facing up Table Mountain towards the four-acre patch of hydrangeas, which lay out like lapis lazuli on the lawns'. In 'The Woolsack' hard by, in the dark teak-panelled study with its slatted shutters closed against the outside glare, the *Just So Stories* were written, and read to the two children, whose reactions were keenly observed. He listened gravely to their criticisms of the stories, but would not tolerate criticism of his own illustrations, a curious foible which never left him.[3] By April the weather would turn cooler, and fires of great pine cones were burned in the evenings in the open fireplaces.

Sir Herbert Baker, Rhodes's architect, tells us that the side of Kipling presented to the world was not well understood by Rhodes, but was suited to the agile wit of Jameson. 'It was not the man of smart satire, as he sometimes superficially appeared to be, to whom Rhodes gave the house he built on the mountain-side. It was the poet and prophet Kipling, who could be generous to his enemies ... and who understood the kindly relation that might exist between conquerors and conquered who had to live together in the same land.'[4]

Kipling's veneration for Rhodes was profound, as was his gratitude for Rhodes's generosity, but Jameson's wit matched his own and could draw a spark from him, and he adopted the character of Jameson for the poem 'If'. Rhodes had no such gifts; clever conversation bored him, and he preferred the method of quiet confidences. He was also inarticulate, and used Kipling as a conduit for words stuck in his groping mind. He would ask: 'What am I trying to express? Say it, *say* it.' Kipling paid this tribute to the Empire-builder in a letter to Baker, in which he gives Rhodes almost Divine status: 'I don't think that anyone who did not actually come across Him with some intimacy of detail can ever realize what He was. It was His Presence that had the Power. Same as Jameson's held all the magnetism. And of all people it would seem to me that home-keeping Englishmen would be among the last to feel the power of a man as inarticulate as He was.'[5] Baker remarked shrewdly that Kipling and others, who knew Rhodes in his later days only, overrated Jameson's part in the combination. 'Had there been no Jameson,' he said, 'there would still have been a Rhodes; but had there been no Rhodes, Jameson would have been only a very distinguished surgeon.'

The Kiplings often dined at 'Groote Schuur' when Rhodes was at home, jingling in a shabby horse-fly through the pinewoods to those evenings of endless talk about the development of the country, and Caroline, dark-haired, in a pale yellow silk dress flounced with black lace, often found herself the only woman sitting at the long table. The conception of the Rhodes Scholarships was born at these dinners, and endless plans put forward and discarded. It was due to Caroline's practical mind that the proposed allowance to Scholars was raised. She pointed out to Rhodes that having no homes to go to during vacations the Scholars' expenses would be higher than those of ordinary students.

It was at this time that a lunatic conceived the idea that Kipling was the reincarnation of someone he did not like, and that it was his duty to shoot him. He followed Kipling from England to the Cape, and broke into 'The Woolsack' late one hot summer night with a revolver held in a shaking hand. Kipling enticed him into the house, where they sat talking for hours and drinking whisky until the lunatic fell asleep. At intervals, for several years and in various places, the lunatic reappeared, finally taking a pot-shot at Kipling as he emerged from the Athenaeum. After this he was locked up, and when he died Kipling sent to his funeral a large wreath, with his card attached.[6]

Back at Rottingdean in 1901 he discovered a new enthusiasm. Shaken by the revelations of inefficiency in the South African War, he noticed with strong disapproval that none of the young men in the village were grounded in the elements of military training or musketry. He started a rifle-range and club, setting out a thousand-yard rifle-range at a place called the Lustrals on the swelling chalk downs, and a miniature range where the convent later stood. The club comprised thirty or forty members, who shot against the Volunteers and against other rifle clubs. They were drilled by the petty officers of the coastguards, and by Johnstone, the Sergeant Instructor at Rottingdean preparatory school. They used the Lee-Enfield rifle with a tube for the miniature range, and Kipling presented the club with a Nordenfelt machine-gun that had been used in the South African War.

With his eye already on the next war, he regarded his club with deadly seriousness. He always shot in the competitions, adequately, in spite of his eyesight, coming over at three or four in the afternoon in his wide-brimmed hat and leather-patched clothes. The club members learned morse and semaphore in the gymnasium, and did gymnastic exercises. The four old windmill-type targets on swivels in the pit were replaced by modern types paid for by Kipling. When firing against the Newhaven Volunteers one of the Volunteers expressed interest in meeting the great man who growled: 'Well, now you can see the animal on his own ground.' He detested any kind of fuss or special treatment, saying, 'We must all muck in together.'

Kipling would preside at committee meetings of the club, which were held in an upstairs room at 'The Elms'. He would sit at a white table, endlessly drawing pictures on the agenda paper, all of which he carefully destroyed before the end of the meeting.[7]

Kipling's desperate seriousness is admirably shown in a letter to Sergeant Johnstone from South Africa in March 1901:

Instructions for use of shed in my absence

Men to have two evenings a week for MT practice and such other evenings
 as the Sergeant shall see fit for
  Gardner gun drill
  Signalling
  Guard drill etc.

Boys to have two evenings a week. One for MT practice and one for gymnastics.

Boys' evenings are *not* to be Monday and Wednesday.

Men and boys' evenings to be kept separate.

Men to be instructed in gym work if the Sergeant thinks fit.

Fatigue parties must be told off to clear up the shed, every night *as there
 will be no allowance for caretakers.*

All damage must be paid for by offender.

The Rifle Club may hold meetings and concerts in the shed under Sergeant's
 supervision. *No intoxicating drinks* allowed under any circumstances.

Smoking is permitted.

Cst. Gd. Wells is to be in charge of the Gardner Gun with right of way and
 free entry into shed for that purpose.

The Sergeant to be the officer in charge till my return.

             Rudyard Kipling.[8]

This illuminating letter indicates clearly Kipling's burning anxieties about military preparedness, but it suggests, too, the soldier *manqué* in its terse peremptory sentences and pseudo-military phraseology.

Kipling at Rottingdean was already greatly pestered by tourists. In these early days an ancient horse-bus used to draw up outside 'The Elms' when Kipling was working in his study, a man blowing a long post-horn: 'This 'ere is Mr Kipling's house, and if you look over the iron gate you may see him at work!' Kipling sent a furious letter to the owner of the buses who, with gratification, removed the signature and showed it to all his friends before pasting it into an album; after which Kipling stopped signing his full name on letters.

He was regarded by some as a good parishioner who took an interest in local matters, keeping the woodwork of the Domesday Mill tarred and sound, and preserving the chalky whiteway lane to the Downs. He and Stanley Baldwin would hire a wagon and go picnicking on food purloined from the larder to a patch of gorse in the valley called Honeysocks. Kipling's political convictions soon brought him into collision with the incumbent, Wynne, a man of liberal bent, who could not stomach Kipling's imperialism. Neither was prepared to yield an inch, and Wynne's feelings for Kipling soon became those of keen dislike,[9] while Kipling's detestation of the clergyman's politics caused him, after he had left Rottingdean, to refuse to subscribe to a heating apparatus for the church in a brief cold letter.[10]

How did Kipling review the scene after the South African War? In a letter to Norton in May 1901 he wrote:

> For us, this side, the experience has been wholesome. We were bung full of beastly spiritual pride as we were of material luxury and over-much ease. We went about despising things and people, unconsciously turning our ideals to mean an easy life ... soft rubber-tyred. Now we are slowly coming back to the primitives, and realising that a lot of what we call civilisation was another name for shirking. The mere war ... is the least part of the business. Everything we have – Church, School, and craft – has – so to speak – been challenged to show cause why it should continue on the old unthinking hide-bound lines; has been asked explicitly by circumstances and necessity whether all the trappings with which the centuries have adorned it do not cover the ordinary tendency of working to be – plain dog-gone idle. One can feel this in the air; and see it in people's faces. It makes for humility and common earnestness ... one may almost hope that England ... may in time learn to work, and be less of a fatted snob than she is at present.[11]

The paradisial atmosphere of 'Groote Schuur' had failed to cure Caroline's nerves. She suffered at intervals from those bouts of neurotic depression so often masked by a brisk managing exterior. She passed through a black period in July 1901 when Kipling was staying with his parents at Tisbury, and then went on Naval Manœuvres, and made an extraordinary jerky entry in her diary:

> *July 13*. Wires from Rud. *14*. Two letters from Rud from Tisbury. *15*. Four wires from Rud. *16*. Four wires from Rud. He returns to Tisbury which appals me. My nurse comes. A night of agony. *17*. Rud goes to see Willoughby Manor. I sink down leagues in my declining stride to reach my actual physical state when not braced by necessity. An awful ghost to live with. *18*. Down and down I go. Rud writes from Tisbury. *20*. Still down. Rud joins his ship and gets into her this evening. *21*. Still more down in body my mind doing a series of acts in a circus beyond words to depict in its horrors. Rud writes from Sandown Bay at anchor. *22nd*. Dreary enough. Rud at anchor off Brighton. *26*. Rud at Shillington. I remain empty at the bottom of my collapse I think. *27*. I remain stationary at the bottom depth physically. *31*. The children return, very pleased to see me as I am to see them. *Aug. 3*. Rud goes to Tisbury. I can not realize it – it has shocked me so. *4*. Dreadful night

trying to think out the black future. 5. Rud means to stop longer away. 6. A night of mental agony leaves me down in the bottom of the pit and well nigh hopeless for the black future. 7. Rud arrives at 6 p.m. Great rejoicings.

This strange passage is the first indication in Caroline's diaries of the emotional instability that was to grow upon her with the years, and finally to cloud the relationship between her and Kipling.

He was now much preoccupied with motorcars, being one of the early pioneers. It is greatly to his credit that he realized at once the future of the internal combustion engine, and persevered grimly with a series of these strange monsters emitting loud explosions and cascades of oil, their tyres puncturing every other mile, jeering little boys running beside them in clouds of yellow dust, and a heavily-veiled Caroline on the box.

He had begun in 1897 in the days of tube ignition, when six horse-power was considered sufficient for a touring car, and fifteen miles per hour an achievement. These ghastly vehicles were to Kipling as the rabbit is to the vivisectionist – 'The men to reverence, to admire, to write odes and erect statues to, are those Prometheuses and Ixions (maniacs, you used to call us) who chase the inchoate idea to fixity up and down the King's Highway with their red right shoulders to the wheel.'[12]

Kipling came to use his motors on voyages of discovery of England – 'Yesterday we went over to Aunt Georgie's – 56 miles of most bitter cold through a silver fog under a red wafer sun, and the trees all furred with diamonds.' He liked to reflect that in six hours he could leave 'the land of the Ingoldsby Legends by way of the Norman Conquest and the Barons' War into Richard Jefferies' country, through the Regency, one of Arthur Young's less known towns, and Celia's Arbour, into Gilbert White's territory'. In his ardent imagination the motor became a time machine on which he could slide from one century to another. He described how on one morning he had seen the Assizes, javelin-men and all, entered a Cathedral town, by midday skirted a new-built convent for expelled French nuns, watched the Fleet off Selsey Bill against a sinking sun, and, after dark, had nearly broken a fox's back on a Roman road. 'To me it is still miraculous that if I want petrol in a hurry I must pass the place where Sir John Lade lived, or the garden where Jack Cade was killed. In Africa one has only to put the miles under and go on; but in England the dead, twelve coffin deep, clutch hold of my wheels at every turn, till I sometimes wonder that the very road does not bleed.'[13]

He later described to Norton the Maladies of 'Amelia' [his Lan-
chester], when she was lying comatose at Henry James's house at
Rye:

Because we swaggered and boasted about Amelia (she being a virgin) and
told him how we would drive him all over Sussex, in two hours Amelia was
took with a cataleptic trance then and there – opposite a hotel – and she
abode in Rye stark and motionless till we wired to the place where she was
born (it happened to be Birmingham) – for an expert mechanician or obstetri-
cian or whatever the name is, and after two days Amelia came back to us.
But Henry James's monologue over her immobile carcase ... would have
been cheap at the price of several wrecked cars.[14]

When she had been repaired he wrote:

Dear Mr James,
    Don't say that I told you but Amelia is a bitch – the petrol-piddling des-
cendant of untold she-dogs. Today was divine. We waited for your chariot
wheels till we felt you weren't coming and then we went to see Aunt Georgie
at Rottingdean – 28 miles in an hour and 25 minutes. Amelia with a scientific
frontier, I mean reconstructed interior – did it like a kestrel, and one way
and another we put in 61 miles ere we came back for tea through woods
lovelier than a partridge's breast. Amelia is very female. If she thinks she
isn't giving pleasure but helping to improve the world she'll toil like a yankee
school ma'am.[15]

He continued to divide his life between England and South Africa,
and before he sailed for the Cape again in 1902 he published a poem
in *The Times* which gave bitter offence to many who had been his
staunchest supporters. This was 'The Islanders', a piece of violent and
intemperate nagging of the British people for the shortcomings
revealed in the South African War, and for their strange reluctance
to devote their leisure to military preparedness. But this time he had
gone too far. In brutal manner he had ridiculed the sacred cows of
cricket and football, and how superb was the scorn of the lines in
which he did so:

And ye vaunted your fathomless powers, and ye flaunted your iron pride
Ere – ye fawned on the Younger Nations for the men who could shoot
    and ride!
Then ye returned to your trinkets; then ye contented your souls
With the flannelled fools at the wicket or the muddied oafs at the goals.

These last two lines, which still stick in their target like a dart, show
clearly that Kipling's disapproval on this score was not, as some
thought, confined to the so-called lower-classes, being, as George

Orwell pointed out, aimed as much at the Eton and Harrow Match as at the Cup Tie Final. This blasphemy of the national idols by the Poet of Empire was bitterly resented, but Kipling was past caring. The inherited way of life of the British, he shouted into indifferent ears, could only survive if they learned how to fight for it. What did they propose to do if attacked by a powerful enemy?

Will ye pitch some white pavilion, and lustily even the odds,
With nets and hoops and mallets, with rackets and bats and rods?
Will the rabbit war with your foeman – the red deer horn them for hire?
Your kept cock-pheasant keep you? – he is master of many a shire.

On 26 March they heard that Cecil Rhodes was dead. Kipling was deeply stricken by the lonely agony of Rhodes's death-struggle, when with suffused face and bursting heart he staggered from room to room in his little cottage built on the rocks at St James's, gasping for air. 'So little done, so much to do.' He was forty-nine. Kipling was incensed by the evil influence exerted on Rhodes in his decline by his friend, Princess Radziwill. 'I wish you had dealt more hardly with that Radziwill bitch,' he wrote later to Sir Herbert Baker, when congratulating him on his book on Rhodes. The body was brought home to 'Groote Schuur' and a service was held when Kipling read some verses which he had spent the previous day composing. On 3 April he walked in the procession at the State funeral in Cape Town Cathedral and followed the coffin to the railway station, where Rhodes began the long journey to his last resting-place in the Matoppo hills.

At last peace was signed in South Africa on 1 June 1902. At Rottingdean it was a day of mourning for Aunt Georgie, who hung a black banner from the window of 'North End House': 'We have killed and also taken possession.' In the evening angry young men came to pull the banner down, and even to try to set fire to the hedge over which it was hung, and Rudyard hurried across the green to the rescue of his still-loved aunt. As to the war he now felt, like Churchill, that in victory there must be magnanimity. These verses, so much more graceful than his early jingoism, were his epitaph to the miserable business:

Here in a large and sunlit land,
    Where no wrong bites to the bone,
I will lay my hand in my neighbour's hand,
    And together we will atone

For the set folly and the red breach
And the black waste of it all;
Giving and taking counsel each
Over the cattle-kraal.

Rottingdean had become intolerable, and the Kiplings had long sought a home more remote from marauding trippers. On 10 June 1902 they bought 'Bateman's' at Burwash in Sussex, with thirty-three acres, for £9,300.[16] They moved in on 2 September, Kipling dissociating himself from this upheaval with the same adroitness he had shown at 'Naulakha' and leaving the whole responsibility to Caroline, who, while making heavy weather over it, accomplished the move with her customary efficiency, to a running commentary of peevish complaint in the diary: '*Sept. 3*. Go to Bateman's to meet chaos and black night. Hudson has not kept a single promise and foreman of removers is drunk. Labour and struggle to put things right. *4*. A hopeless day. *5*. Fought with workmen and cleaners all day long. A terrible day.' Had she known it, there might have been some consolation in the fact that this would be the Kiplings' last house-moving.

Rudyard was now the owner of a grey stone lichened house – AD 1634 inscribed above the iron-studded door, beamed and panelled, and with old oak staircases which had survived the havoc of mid-Victorian restorers. 'You walk up to the porch over a stone-paved path laid down in the turf and the cart road runs within fifty yards of the front door. The rest is all fields and farms and to the southward one glorious sweep of woods. We coveted the place for two and a half or three years, and have loved it ever since our first sight of it.'[17]

It lay in a deep cup in the ground, dark and oppressive in winter, but in mid-summer sheltered and peaceful with terraced lawns and a walled garden of old shell-pink brick. There were two oast-houses and a silver-grey oak dovecot on the roof. At the bottom of the lawn the River Dudwell flowed sluggishly through neglected alders. A little upstream stood the old Mill with the original dam holding back the mill-pond. The Kiplings' first action on buying 'Bateman's' was to harness the stream to turn the mill-wheel again to make electricity for the house. Inside there was a black and white tiled hall, panelled to the beamed ceiling, a window seat and a leaded window with green glass panes, an Elizabethan table and benches, and a stone fireplace backed by old Sussex iron-work, on which burnt logs five feet long. The house was built by a Sussex iron-master two hundred and seventy years before.

It was bitterly cold at 'Bateman's' in winter down in the damp hollow, and, settled in by November, Kipling vividly described it to Norton:

A cold wave has hit us and driven us within doors – a venomous snowing blowing frost – all the country looks like a Christmas card, but is one of the cold circles of the Inferno – the only one that Dante didn't describe. We are fighting the cold with logs – five feet long – in the hall; with stoves that cease not day and night; with two foot baulks; with hot water-pipes. We have conquered it indoors but outside it is untempered, and all the birds of the woods have come to beg rations. Figure to yourself a blackguard jay – a beautiful ruffian in blue – coming into our garden cowed and penitent, like a sort of half-frozen Villon – and being received with howls of indignation from the blackbirds and robins who stand in with the landed and household-ing classes. Tits, wagtails, and finches are all in the crowd and unless they migrate I don't despair of getting a sight of kingfishers. The moorhens daily feed nearer to the house. If the cold lasts they'll come in amongst the fowls. A great deal of England is explained by its winter climate. I used to think it was on the edge of decay – the national character – but now, I see that what I mistook for the rigidity of death (just before corruption begins) is frost – just frost and darkness.[18]

Kipling was, on the whole, happy in this house, although later on when his health declined and the grim winter mists settled over the hollow he would sometimes fall into profound melancholy and yearn for the tropics. William Rothenstein sometimes found him stiff and unapproachable at the Athenaeum, but happy at 'Bateman's' with its garden, fish ponds, and pleasant meadows. 'Only what would become of it all, Kipling asked, when he was gone? Probably it would be sold to some speculative builder. At which I wondered, thinking him rich enough to ensure its future.'[19]

Living now in a house at the back of beyond, and completely secluded from prying eyes, Kipling's creative imagination began to soar with astonishing vigour. *The Five Nations*, his book of South African verse, was finished in 1903. It was followed in 1904 by a strange story, *Mrs Bathurst*, which puzzled many of his admirers. In it he showed that tendency, which was to grow upon him, to concede less and less to the reader, to pare the material so ruthlessly down to the bone as to leave an impression of baffling obscurity, seeming almost to challenge the reader to place his own interpretation on it.

He next began work on *They*, an allegory deriving from his un-assuaged grief at Josephine's death, its background the fruit of his own experiences driving about Sussex in search of a house:

In the mind's eye, Rudyard saw the long procession of the dead who had
walked the Pilgrims' Way throughout the centuries, till time lost its significance. The transience of life was its one persisting feature and a year as long
to the grief-stricken as a thousand years. From Merrow Down to Brooklands
in Romney Marsh, there was no landscape, now, that did not recall to Rudyard that slight figure, dancing through the fern; and when, deep in woods
of stilly oak, he found his dream-house at last, it lacked one blessing only
for him, the child that might have taken his hand. It was not for him to beat
against the bars of space and time in so-called psychical research. So, in his
story [*They*], the blind woman in the haunted house, whose second-sight
reveals the presence of the dream-children, was no true guide for him....
She, too, recognized his vocation as craftsman not as mystic: 'For you it
would be wrong,' she said, 'you who must never come here again.'[20]

There was no pause now in the creative torrent. A few days after
They was finished Kipling's leaping imagination turned to a very different subject – the world of the future. In *With the Night Mail* he
described with brilliant perception an Atlantic crossing by air in the
year 2000. With a foresight equal to that of H. G. Wells he envisaged
in 1904 – when there was no radio-telephony – an air liner guided
by radio services giving weather reports, and allotting safety levels
and landing priorities. It was no mean feat to predict 'flying control',
seven years before Blériot flew the Channel.

He followed this story three years later, in 1907, with another
attempt to pierce the future, *As Easy as A.B.C.*, in which broadcasting
is described, and an international company of technicians, the 'Aerial
Board of Control', gradually takes over the administration of the
world, the old national states becoming eroded by the force of the
new technology. He had been fascinated by radio experiments since
his cruise with the Channel Fleet in 1898, and in 1903 had written
what many consider his most brilliant inventive story, *Wireless*, in
which time as well as the aether is penetrated, and thrilling contact
made with a past century. There are good grounds for the opinion
held by many that this is Kipling's finest short story.

Yet no sooner were these prophetic writings finished than he
returned suddenly to the past with a succession of stories from English
history which occupied him for the next five years. The immersion
in English and local history which led to *Puck of Pook's Hill* and *Rewards and Fairies* was not caused by a sudden inspiration on seeing
the country round his new house. As long ago as 1897 he had consulted
Burne-Jones on the best authorities for the end of Roman and the
beginning of Saxon Britain, and Burne-Jones had suggested the last

volume of Mommsen's *History of Rome* and other useful source books. The idea of writing about Roman Britain had been planted in his mind by Ambrose Poynter, who had urged him to describe a Centurion of the Occupation telling his experiences to his children. When Kipling asked Poynter what the name of the Centurion should be, he had answered: 'Parnesius.'

But the real inspiration came from Kipling's own children, John and Elsie, who were to become Dan and Una in *Puck of Pook's Hill*. We find him writing urgently to Gwynne in 1904 to procure him a paper donkey's head and a pair of gauze wings: 'Don't think I'm mad, but the kids are doing a little piece of *Midsummer Night's Dream* in the Quarry.' Their theatre was an old grass-grown quarry near the brook, and with John as Puck, Elsie as Titania, and Rudyard as Bottom, rehearsals and performances were happily carried out. The theatre lay at the foot of a grassy slope which they called Pook's Hill. It had been known before as Perch Hill, but the name was later changed in deference to the book.

There is something timeless about the country round 'Bateman's' which gave a strong impulse to Kipling's *daemon*. Down in the hollow you felt already far from the workaday world, which seemed to have come to a sudden end, and the country beyond – lush, wooded, completely undisturbed – might have belonged to another age. It was a place for magic; and his fantastic imagination was now to people its glades with a throng of ghosts. To him it was already redolent of the past:

Just beyond the west fringe of our land . . . stood the long over-grown slag-heap of a most ancient forge, supposed to have been worked by the Phoenicians and Romans and, since then, uninterruptedly till the middle of the eighteenth century. The bracken and rush-patches still hid stray pigs of iron, and if one scratched for a few inches through the rabbit-shaven turf, one came on the narrow mule-tracks of peacock-hued furnace-slag laid down in Elizabeth's day. The ghost of a road climbed up out of this dead arena, and crossed our fields, where it was known as 'The Gunway', and popularly connected with Armada times. Every foot of that little corner was alive with ghosts and shadows.[21]

By 25 September 1904 he was at work on *Puck of Pook's Hill*, and after several false starts the stories came readily to his pen. As we all know, their theme is that of the ageless Puck appearing from the thickets to Dan and Una, friendly yet immortal, and, by bringing before their enraptured eyes figures from bygone centuries, presenting to the children in a series of episodes the unfolding history of England.

It was a labour of love, for England was now to Rudyard 'my favourite foreign country'. He had already saturated himself in local history in the Sussex Records Office and in the parts of Domesday Book that referred to Sussex, and become deeply versed in the history and legends of the country round Burwash. Much of the writing of this book, and of its sequel, *Rewards and Fairies*, was done during the winter months at 'The Woolsack', and much of the research in the public library at Cape Town. In the summers he would take the stories to Tisbury to be 'smoked over' with Lockwood Kipling.

Some conception of the imaginative range of these stories can be gained from the words of one of the leading authorities on children's books of the twentieth century: 'Kipling is an intuitive historian, but generations of children have come to see through his eyes the moving pageant of England's story. In the *Puck* stories one sees Hal Dawes' "dear, dear land", the long process of change – the God of the Knife, the Roman soldier, the Norman knight, the Renaissance craftsman – and the unchanging country ways, "seely Sussex for everlastin' "'.[22]

But although the children are taken in these books on a breathless journey through time, and many characters from the past are brought before them in the familiar woods, we are conscious that Kipling's real intention is to leave in our minds an impression of the endless continuity of English life, the persistence of the land and its people through war and disaster. He had cast his mind back and tried to explore everything in her history that had contributed to this strength – the 'Glory of the Garden' – that he saw all round him. And for this reason it has been rightly said that the real hero of the two books is not Puck, not Dan nor Una, not the Roman Centurion nor the Norman knight – but old Hobden the hedger who knows all the lore of the valley and the stream, and, the list of his forebears stretching deep into bygone centuries, seems to symbolize the spirit of the place, brooding over it and filling his creator with humility:

> His dead are in the churchyard – thirty generations laid.
> Their names were old in history when Domesday Book was made,
> And the passion and the piety and the prowess of his line,
> Have seeded, rooted, fruited in some land the Law calls mine.

The stories were intended by Kipling to be read by children 'before people realized that they were meant for grown-ups', and they were written with this purpose in mind. But the tales in *Rewards and Fairies*, issued in 1910, must have given John and Elsie some moments of tedium and bewilderment. For the technique of some of the stories in this book is similar to that he was to employ in his 'late' manner, which so puzzled his most ardent admirers, and no child could possibly have understood the symbolic meaning of *Cold Iron*, or the sombre undertones of *The Tree of Justice*. Not only was he already composing stories in 'layers' so that four or five interpretations could be placed on each, but was also compressing them so tightly to fit into his normal length (fifteen to twenty pages) that some of the tales require several careful readings before the meaning can be grasped.

Dan and Una are again present in each episode: indeed each of Kipling's children was given a personal story in *Rewards and Fairies*; John's is a tale of craftsmanship set in a builder's yard, *The Wrong Thing*, while in Elsie's story, the delightful *Marklake Witches*, the narration takes place against the background of a lesson in cowmilking, a true fact in Elsie's life, and is written in the manner of Jane Austen, whom Kipling so deeply revered.

Apart from beguiling children and investing the past with a new and potent magic, the *Puck* stories produced other results perhaps even more to Kipling's heart's desire:

> In the whole range of Rudyard Kipling's work [wrote Carrington] no pieces have been more effective in moulding the thought of a generation than the three stories of the centurions defending Hadrian's Wall during the decline of the Roman Empire. 'There is no hope for Rome,' said the wise old father of the centurion. 'She has forsaken her Gods, but if the Gods forgive *us* here, we may save Britain.' The story of Parnesius the centurion's task is told as a panegyric of duty and service.... It strengthened the nerve of many a young soldier in 1915 and 1941, and, if that was its intention, it mattered little that Rudyard's Roman soldiers of the fourth century too much resembled subalterns of the Indian Army.[23]

Even more notable to many than the stories were the verses which accompanied them, perhaps the apex of Kipling's poetic achievement, the earlier tastelessness purified or discarded. *Puck of Pook's Hill* includes among other verses the 'Harpsong of the Dane Women', 'Cities and Thrones and Powers', and 'A Smuggler's Song'. *Rewards and Fairies* is even richer in the quality of the verse accompanying it – 'A St Helena Lullaby', the haunting 'Way through the Woods', and 'If'. He continued in this happy vein with the verses written for C. R. L. Fletcher's *History of England* which included 'The Glory of the Garden' and the magnificent 'The Roman Centurion's Song'. This, one of Kipling's most poignant and successful poems, is put in the mouth of a centurion born and bred in England so that

21 Josephine, Kipling's beloved daughter, who died in 1899.

22 Kipling at Naulakha.

23 The original manuscript of 'Recessional' showing Kipling's comments: 'Done in Council at North End House, July 16. Aunt Georgie, Sallie, Carrie and me.'

24 The Woolsack, built for the Kiplings by Cecil Rhodes in South Africa.

25 The editors of *The Friend*: (*left to right*) H. A. Gwynn, Julian Ralph, Perceval Landon and Kipling.

26 Kipling and his son John on the beach.

27 Bateman's at Burwash in Sussex, bought by Kipling in 1902.

28 At Vernet-les-Bains, 1910: (*left to right*) ?, Lady Edwina Roberts, Lord Roberts, General du Moriez and Kipling.

29 Kipling (*centre*) appeals for recruits at Southport, 1915.

30 Kipling with George v during the King's visit to British war graves in Belgium, 1922.

31 Leaving Buckingham Palace after a Royal Garden Party, 1921: Kipling, his wife and daughter Elsie.

32 After Kipling's installation as Rector of St Andrew's University, with Stanley Baldwin.

33 (*left to right*) Mrs Stanley Baldwin, Mrs Kipling and Mrs Irvine, 1923.

34 Rudyard and Carrie at Bateman's.

he feels that he belongs there and begs not to be moved, dreading
transfer to Rome:

You'll take the old Aurelian Road through shore-descending pines
Where, blue as any peacock's neck, the Tyrrhene Ocean shines.
You'll go where laurel crowns are won, but – will you e'er forget
The scent of hawthorn in the sun, or bracken in the wet?

But none of the poems were so widely acclaimed and quoted as
'If'. Those who had begun to wonder where Kipling's *daemon* was
leading him were reassured by this robust declaration of faith. It is
an ideal of masculine character, based on that of Dr Jameson. The
public-school rectitude which animates this piece has made it laughable and even nauseating to a later and more cynical generation, but
the poem struck the contemporary world with a tremendous impact,
restoring faith in their idol to a public who had been savaged by 'The
Islanders'. Even those who today look most askance at the sentiments
of 'If', must, if they know anything of prosody, be amazed by its metri-
cal and technical brilliance.

It was some time before the *Puck* books won recognition, for Kipling, owing to his political activities, was passing through an unpopular phase of his career. But the stories, particularly those of the first
volume, have always been loved by children, and modern critics now
look on them with a friendlier eye. In the words of one of these: 'Kipling's vision of the procession of the generations, centuries, epochs
and their millennial gravure upon the face of England is surely the
deepest, the strongest ever to have been achieved in terms of literary
art. ... It is a vision that to this day enriches England for us.'[24]

Certain incidents stand out as the placid years passed before the
next storm. The naval exercises and the speed trials had done their
work, and John, 'my man child', the apple of his father's eye, was
destined for the Navy, and swaggered round with a beautifully plaited
lanyard. In 1904 Kipling refused, for the first of many times of asking,
to stand for Parliament, for Edinburgh, declining Steel-Maitland's
offer 'to walk straight in, in place of some of our side wanting to retire
now'. Later, in South Africa, he went quietly with Caroline to see the
Rhodes Memorial in Cape Town, reading his own inscription upon
it, and afterwards driving in a Cape Cart to see the orchards and vine-
yards.

His hatred of Liberalism and politicians in general increased in intensity. When referring to the latter he sometimes reveals the narrow
bigotry of certain generals in the Great War who never referred to

politicians without prefixing to the word the adjective 'bloody'. 'I am glad,' he wrote to Gwynne in 1906, 'you have seen the politicians at close quarters. They are a macaroni-backed crew, even the best of them, and they will follow only winning causes.' Henry Wilson could scarcely have uttered a more unworthy gibe.

But Kipling's bitterness increased with the new turn in politics. The General Election of 1906 resulted in a Liberal landslide, when the House of Commons was filled by an enormous and exultant majority of that Party. He was outraged by one of their revengeful actions – an attack on his friend Milner, 'the strong man working alone', who had reconstructed South Africa, and was now formally censured by a vote of the House of Commons. But Kipling's nature was revengeful too, and his memory long and vindictive. He never forgave the young man whose duty it was, as Under Secretary of State for the Colonies, to register this decision – Winston Spencer Churchill. With a familiar sickening feeling of failure, he saw the past as sold and the war fought in vain. Self-government was pressed upon the Transvaal, and Milner disappeared into the shadows. But even worse was to come when Rudyard's idol, Jameson, who had been Prime Minister in Cape Colony for four years, lost his majority in the Election of 1907. It was time to cut his links with South Africa as he had done before with America. The Kiplings' last visit to 'The Woolsack' was in 1908, and it was somehow characteristic that much as they adored the place, they never returned there.

His vigilance about compulsory national service increased, and he sent detailed instructions from South Africa to Gwynne, who was now editor of the *Standard*. A series of peremptory directives passed between the eucalyptus-scented garden under Table Mountain and the humming newspaper office in London. Gwynne was to feel out the true atmosphere about compulsory service – start a referendum and reveal public opinion on it to the world. He was to put the one single question: 'Are you in favour of national compulsory military service in some form or other?' He must start with the mayors of all the towns, the ministers, and trade-union leaders and employers. He was to turn on a clerical staff of twenty clerks to tabulate answers, and make a feature of it, giving the replies week by week. He was to publish also a map of England, marking where sentiment for or against the project resided, and lastly he was to take the proprietor, Pearson, into his confidence, 'and tell him to work it as a scoop'.

The Bishop of London was to pronounce a benediction on compulsory drill, and the *Standard* ought to get it. 'You ought to run religion

for all it is worth.'[25] He indicated his displeasure curtly: 'I don't think
much of your leader summing up the sports correspondence. Too
damned impartial and wishy-washy. The future is with any paper that
takes a strong stand on compulsory training ... don't let the D.T.
[*Daily Telegraph*] cut in ahead. Start that plebiscite that I suggested
and get letters now from the head-masters and other leaders of the
young.'

When the Liberals came into power in England they were pledged to the
hilt to remove the blot of 'slavery'. Obviously the only way to do it was to
grant full representative government to the Transvaal in the hope that the
Dutch would at once repatriate the Chinese. But on the other hand it would
not look so well in the eyes of the home elector if the new government in
the Transvaal was openly and preponderatingly Dutch. It was necessary if
possible to get a government which, while numerically English, should please
the Dutch and do the behests of the Liberal Government.
   Wherefore the Liberal Government having told its lie, set out deliberately
to take a constitution and gerrymander the constituencies with the idea of
so equally balancing the Dutch and English representation in the Transvaal
that the control of the two parties should fall into the hands of one Sir
Richard Soloman, a sort of political pimp and go-between who had been
in Milner's administration but who was capable of doing anything and everything that might lead to his own advancement.[26]

Although Kipling continued to refuse all national honours, he was,
for some reason, willing to accept academic awards. He was given
a doctorate by Durham University, where the undergraduates dragged
him up and down hill to the University Green, and at Oxford, where
hurriedly assuming his gown at the station he took his D.Litt. degree,
dining with the Fellows at All Souls. He was also honoured by McGill
University in Montreal. In September 1907 he embarked on an
arduous tour of Canada, covering the country in exhausting train
journeys – Prairie Country, Regina, Calgary, Vancouver, Ottawa,
Toronto – speeches, reporters and receptions.
   Canada began to take shape in Kipling's mind as the new land of
promise, the cleanness of which he saw in sharp contrast to the peccant
United States: 'Always the marvel – to which the Canadians seem
insensible – was that on one side of an imaginary line should be Safety,
Law, Honour, and Obedience, and on the other, frank, brutal decivil-
ization; and that despite this, Canada should be impressed by any
aspect whatever of the United States.' From now on he was to remain
deeply interested in this country, and two remarkable Canadians,

Andrew Bonar Law and Max Aitken (Lord Beaverbrook), became intimate friends.

On his return from Canada in December he was offered the Nobel Prize for Literature, and he described his return journey from Stockholm, where he had received this high distinction, in a letter so packed with excitement and descriptive power that it deserves quotation in full:

Dec. 16. 1907.

We have come out of a small trouble in the shape of a crossing from Flushing to Queensboro on our return from Nobelling at Stockholm. The trip – Heaven forgive the advertisers – is recommended as giving you 'only three hours of open sea'. We had the felicity to take it in the middle of the worst gale, hurricane, or tornado, 'known on the North Sea, within living memory' ... we came by train from Hamburg, across Holland, which is so flat and treeless that I never realized, till I saw a little pond in a meadow, what a fell wind was blowing. The sight of that tiny patch of water all whipped into yellow foam in the middle of a green field made me feel uncomfy, and when the train discharged us at Flushing pier I felt worse than uncomfy. The very inner harbour was in a yellow yeasty lather, and all to sea-ward was flying water – not rain but a soufflé of wave tops whipped off by the wind. This was at 11 o'clock of the morning of Saturday 14th Dec.

Mercifully I had had intelligence enough to reserve a cabin on the boat. She was a fat and not energetic thing of about a thousand tons, a side wheeler with much superfluous gilt work. We moved about so far from the pier when she took her first dive (all this in harbour if you please), and an adequate and most English stewardess made C. lie down in the cabin; gave her pillow and blanket, and, with soothing equable words, went away.

Our cabin was a deck one, accessible only from the deck, and it dawned on me as soon as we reached the open sea it would be just about as much as anyone's life was worth to leave or enter it. These matters I hid from C. and devoted myself with a single mind and much disturbed stomach to the business of being sick. Please tell Theodore [Roosevelt] that though I am not a man of science, I am thankful human beings are not ruminants. One simple little stomach suffices me.

C. lay on the sofa and shut her eyes. These things befell while we were yet an hour from the sea itself and I have not been sick in many years. Through the cabin door I got a glimpse of a forlorn sandy coast and a belt of shaving-soap mixed up together in one wild flight of grey water and rain.

When we reached the open sea, she, the boat, simply stood still, and batted her paddles about as a fainting woman waggles her hands in a crowd. The water swept her from end to end, and between the regular swish of the downfall and the sucking rush through the scuppers, one felt vicious digs, kicks

and punts as various waves hit her on various sides. The wind was all but
dead in her teeth and each separate wave, as it came, had to be negotiated
singly. My sorrow was that I was not sick any more, but actually well and
interested and quite unable to go to sleep.

Once the paddles stopped altogether and I put my head out to look for
an instant. It was black dark evening full of flying white. Someone else looked
out of another cabin along the streaming upper deck and then we all surged
down into the water and banged the door home. This must have been about
4 o'clock – after an eternity of laborious climbing and kicking and being
kicked, and lying down, and creeping forward and reeling back again.

In the middle of the torture I heard the voice of a huge Cicada – not the
'katy-did' but the big buzzing chap who says *buzz-buzz-buzzer* all through
the hot summer nights. It was the Marconi Telegraph office under the bridge
sending off messages; and you have no conception how cheering and homely
the sound seemed. I said to myself: 'Well, if anything *does* happen, the latitude and longitude of the funeral will be decently recorded', and the thought
consoled me.

After that we just seemed to be handed over to all the demons at once and
I lay on two lively chairs and speculated about the paddles being smashed.
You see I know just enough about ship-building and so forth to make me
unhappy. My new fear was that the paddle-boxes would be stove into match-
wood (this actually happened to the Ostend boat that same night about 40
miles away), and naked paddle wheels are rather dangerous things. Then I
wondered about sailing ships tearing down channel out of control (several
were adrift) and ran my eye over all sorts of chances in a dreamy and detached
way.

After untold eternities spent watching the minute hand of my watch I got
up and looked at the sea. The rain had passed; the sky had blown clear,
and a panic-stricken piece of moon was running from one flying piece of
scud to the next, and the wind was up in earnest. But the extraordinary sight
was the sea, snow white, and unable to rise. It reminded me somehow of
a nest of serpents wriggling, or of an ermine cloak made of live weasels lying
on their backs and squealing because they couldn't rise. The malignity of
the thing impressed me beyond words; the rage and the lack of sense about
it; for the sea was running round in little whirl-pools, two waves beating
against each other, but all with this cowed and beaten-down air of a raging
captive. I guessed that anyhow this could not be open sea any more because
the big dives and lunges had loosened and we were simply being jerked about
like a corpse being dissected, and as I lifted up my eyes ... I saw the North
Foreland light, and a sparkle of jewels all along the black shore which meant
the lights of Margate and Ramsgate.

We were actually in the mouth of the Thames – the tide tearing against
the wind – and all the Thames seemed to be gone raving mad. There are,
as you know, shoals and sandbanks in the river and these showed as discs

of white (almost) fire, in the moonlight – against the general tumble of silver. Little ships cutting in for shelter … all lay over at impossible angles.

The storm pursued us right up to Sheerness. We ran between miles of anchored sailing ships all tossing together and at last turned into the Medway between lines of battleships looking like lighted hotels. Here our Marconi took in the news that a boat load of our bluejackets had been drowned crossing a ferry in a steam boat. A wave had turned the thing upside down at the very pier, as they were landing for their Christmas holidays. One of the men was going to be married next week. I think boats were out from the battleships dredging for bodies because here the water was calm. The wind could not get at it, and it only shook feverishly like a lunatic restrained from doing harm. I think of all experiences, the sight of that inky black water shuddering and yet not breaking into waves was the most striking.

Bangor and Bar Harbour may not be nice places to change at, but for sheer icy desolation give me Queensboro Pier Station at close on midnight. The customs wanted to look at my baggage, and we are a Free Trade country. I was dizzily conscious of delivering an allocution on Protection and Free Trade to the Officer who, I suppose seeing that I was insane through hunger, merely laughed and said: 'Oh that's all right Mr Kipling. We won't look.'

And at 12.30 o'clock we reached London, and headed for our own faithful, beloved, warm, affectionate Brown's Hotel, to whom I had sent a Marconi in the middle of the gale asking for supper. Even then the hated storm had one more whack at us, for as we were coming into Piccadilly a policeman wheeled the cab round and bade us go another way to Dover Street. A building derrick, perched on the top of a wall which was being pulled down, had threatened all day to fall. It gave one a sort of nightmarish impression to see the naked length of street like the dry bed of a river, and this black goblin of a derrick far and far up against the moonlight. So to bed at 1.30.[27]

At Stockholm Kipling had been presented to the new King, Gustav V, whose father had died while the Kiplings were on their way to Sweden. Kipling drove through the great squares of buildings, climbed echoing, empty stairs, and found himself before a shut door, which he opened at a venture and 'tumbled straight into Rupert of Hentzau, Stevenson's Prince Otto and all the rest of them. There was a faded ante-chamber, long, low, and narrow, full of court officials with clinking spurs and stars moving about in semi-darkness and whispering to each other. Doors opened and shut without sound and in the court below the snow lay on the cannon in the square and on the folds of a still sentry's cap.' He was led to the presence chamber, with blazing chandeliers and red carpet, and encountered a tall sad-faced man in a frock-coat, who received them with a grave set speech deploring his father's death.

Then to the Queen's apartments, an enormous room empty in the centre where there was a circle of carpet: 'I mean all the carpet was one circle about 30 feet across, and all I saw in that vastness was the single figure of a thin hospital nurse in uniform. Swedish mourning in a black dress, white apron, white bob or collar, black coif and white streamers.' She talked to Kipling quietly about animals and his *Jungle Books* and he thought her 'a sad-eyed very delicate woman whose court doctor comes boldly out of a transpontine melodrama'.[28]

At least one Liberal regarded Kipling's Nobel Prize with amazement and anger: 'He is the first Englishman to be crowned in the Court of Literary Europe,' said Gardiner, 'he is chosen as our representative man of letters, while George Meredith, Thomas Hardy, and Algernon Charles Swinburne are still amongst us. The goldsmiths are passed by and the literary blacksmith is exalted.'[29]

During his last visit to the Cape in the spring of 1908, Kipling took to golf once more, spending several afternoons a week hacking his way blasphemously round the links with Dr Jameson. Sometimes he would come across a snake, usually a cobra, and it was etiquette to play the snake the same way as the ball. Kipling observed one player negotiating this forbidding hazard and, after the stroke, the snake lying there coiled but without the head, which had been scythed off by the club.

The Nobel Prize had already turned to Dead Sea fruit in his mouth: 'I had a rather tumultuous year in the way of technically called recognition, and was disgusted to find how little it really touches one. At first I thought it might be my liver, but I think it must be temperament, or the horrid effects of early "success".' In 1908 his old friend Gwynne's mother died, and Kipling wrote tenderly:

Dear old man,

Your wife has just sent us the bad news from Wales. It is a sorrow that men can perhaps better understand than any other, because a son's relation to his mother must always be sacred and apart, and, when she goes – no matter how inevitable the departure must be – a man feels specially lonely – with the loneliness sometimes almost of a child again.[30]

An annual absence from England was necessary for Kipling, and he now chanced upon Engelberg in Switzerland, which he loved so much that he returned to it every year from 1908 to the outbreak of war. He found exhilaration in the mountains and the snow, the wind lipping over a pass, and the astonishing splendour of the sun. He loved the cold lakes and the slow tramway journey up the gorge, the icicles glittering from the rock-face and the racing mountain torrents that fed the sawmills. He loved the air, 'tasting like diamonds and ether mixed', and the little engine with the rack and pinion that hauled him up the last thousand feet into Engelberg, and the bright blazing blue sunshine, expiring into purple twilight.

Amid all these mountain joys, and back in the peace of 'Bateman's', Kipling never relaxed his fears of Germany. In 1908: 'You are dead right about the Teuton and I fear the time shorter even than we think.'[31] Two years later:

We in England are just camping comfortably on the edge of a volcano, and telling each other that the danger of a German explosion is over. What I admire about the English is what you might call their 'bloody optimism'. Meanwhile the Teuton is angry, and is taking measures and steps as fast and as hard as he can. I don't want to see a conscript army under small-arm fire for the first time ... but I expect I shall live to see it – for a few minutes at any rate.[32]

Meanwhile the Teuton has his large cold eye on us, and prepares to give us toko when he feels good and ready. We ought to see in a few years now. There was a lot of shooting round us yesterday and I couldn't help thinking how it would be if all the wounded birds now lying in the woods were wounded men.[33]

To Kipling the rantings of the Pan-Germans – Fichte, Treitschke, von Bernhardi – represented the true voice of the war-party in that country, and he was one of the few to appreciate their authentic menace.

He was further depressed in 1910 by a series of personal losses. The gentle Cormell Prince, to whom he owed so much, was the first to go, and his passage brought back across the years memories of that tobacco-scented library where he had read Hakluyt's voyages and mused with Omar. It was with a heavy heart that he took up his pen to write the inscription that is now engraved on the brass tablet under a stained-glass memorial window in the south wall of Westward Ho! Church:

To the Glory of God and in loving
Memory of Cormell Price, Esq., M.A., B.C.L., Oxon.
For 20 years the first Headmaster of the United
Services College, Westward Ho! Who died 4th
May, 1910. Aged 74 years.
Who with toil of his today
Bought for us tomorrow.
KIPLING.
This window is dedicated by some of his old boys.

In November 1910 another blow fell upon him with the death of his mother, whom Lockwood did not long survive, following her to the grave in January 1911 after a ten-minute heart-attack. With that morbid reluctance to preserve intimate records, Kipling remorselessly burned their letters – all his mother's burnished wit and his father's mellow philosophy, all the letters they wrote him as a child. 'If Rud had been a criminal,' said Trix, 'he could not have been fonder of destroying any family papers that came his way – especially after the parents died.'[34]

Many of his other old friends had gone – Ned Burne-Jones, Aggie Poynter, Alfred Baldwin, Henley, Conland, and Charles Eliot Norton. Trix had had several nervous breakdowns and was of little comfort to him, and from now on he would rely mainly on Perceval Landon, with whom he had worked on the Bloemfontein *Friend*, and H. A. Gwynne, who was to become editor of the *Morning Post* in 1911, and whose extreme right-wing opinions perfectly matched his own. There were friends, too, among his neighbours at 'Bateman's': Lady Edward Cecil, who had been with them at the Cape in the Boer War, Sir George Allen, and an old soldier Colonel Fielden, who was to enter Rudyard's life closely and even achieve a certain intimacy with him.

Kipling, tired and miserable, felt the need again for travel and change, and set out in February 1911 for Vernet-les-Bains, where he had his first massage bath and began to drink the waters. He sent back to Bateman's for half a dozen flies, for the Cadi was full of trout, provocative to him in the clear icy water. It had been a late winter and the snow was lying about in patches, but the wind, he thought, was Spanish, and stabbed through the gorges like a knife. The almonds were in bloom, and peacock and brimstone butterflies fluttered over the rocks.

His jaded spirits began to rise. He lay in the pleasant lassitude of the hot sulphur baths, made expeditions down the coastline in a 75 h.p. de Dietrich in blue weather and a keen wind, eating good food in little restaurants down the coast and drinking the wine of the country. 'Then the Mediterranean hove up, all sapphire, with a shark's fin of a lateen sail here and there and a rip or two of white wave-tops before the wind, and forty-foot palms waving in the hollows of the hills against the coast.' Under a striped awning he made a meal of *bouillabaisse*, relishing with *gourmandise* the sauce of pale yellow with slices of bread soaked in it, and the fish so fresh that they seemed to have been taken out of the sea less than an hour before, and with less pleasure snails that tasted 'like chopped rubber worms'.

He returned from this holiday in better spirits and full of vigour. The Daimler which had supplanted 'Amelia' was exchanged for a Rolls-Royce, which distracted him pleasantly for a while, but by December, with the floods rising in the misty hollow at 'Bateman's', and bare trees and forlorn cattle in the fields under a watery sun, he began to yearn again for the tropics. He attempted to eradicate this itch by devising an imaginary journey to the Philippines – he would sail to Singapore by P & O, touching at Colombo, and south into the enchanted archipelago of Malaya, with its hot, moist sunshine and bamboos, junks and pearling luggers, and quaint villages built on stilts above the green water. He saw himself reclining under an awning in white tropical clothes, eating bananas and pineapples and custard apples and jack fruit, and returning, surfeited with the sun and butterflies and lush tropical vegetation, by the Barrier Reef and Australia, eager again for the northern weather – its mist and bracing north-easters.

Kipling roused himself from this pleasant pipe-dream and again in 1912 directed a censorious eye on politics. His first salvo was at the expense of Haldane, whose true share in our military preparedness he misunderstood as grossly as many others of his contemporaries:

> When Haldane's Hound upon Haldane's hobbies
> Writes a book which is full of lies
> Then we find out what a first class job is
> And how Inspector Generals rise.

I think Swinburne wrote this.[35]

This individual sample of prejudice against politicians is worth examination. It sometimes appears as though Kipling's resentment of them as a class grotesquely distorted his judgement. Kipling, as we have seen, venerated soldiers, and it is therefore interesting to be presented with the views of a distinguished professional soldier, Field Marshal Lord Chetwode,* upon Haldane, whom Kipling so contemptuously dismissed. Lord Chetwode wrote to the author:

As you know, before he [Haldane] became War Minister, there was no proper staff in the Army in England, and, as always, we went to war without any preparation whatever. He was the first War Minister who really helped us, and was responsible for the 1914 Regular and Territorial Armies. He was the first War Minister who did not tell us soldiers that he knew a lot more about the Army than we did. I happened to be Military Secretary on Sir

* Commander in Chief of the Indian Army, 1930–35.

John French's Staff, when he came to see him, and began by saying that he knew nothing about the Army but he knew a great deal about Parliament, and what he could get out of them.

He came to a meeting at Government House at Aldershot, at which Sir John French, Haig, and Lord Esher were present. I had to take notes of the meeting. He began by saying that he wanted to know what the soldiers thought was the minimum strength of the Army and Territorials in order to be ready for the war which we all considered inevitable at that time – 1909.

He said, if the soldiers would say what they wanted, he would let us know what he could get out of Parliament.

The same meeting took place some time afterwards, and Sir John and Haig and Esher informed Haldane that they considered that eight Regular Divisions and fourteen Territorials was the minimum for peace-time safety. Haldane then went away, and summoned a meeting again some time after, and informed the soldiers that he could get six Regular Divisions and fourteen Territorials. He said further that if they would give up a certain number of Artillery Batteries, redundant to the six Divisions, he could guarantee that those six Divisions were perfect, and fully equipped in every respect.

I well remember that he was much abused in the Press for reducing the Artillery, and there was a lot of talk about a remark he made in a speech that Germany was his 'spiritual home'. The result of all this was that we went into the first Great War with six perfectly equipped Divisions, according to the standards of those days, and certainly the best trained, and the Territorials were ready long before anyone expected them to be. When Haig came back to England after our victory, he went straight to Haldane in London, and presented him with the first copy of his despatches, and he said it was owing to him that we had won the war.[36]

Of the coal strike which was then in progress, Kipling wrote savagely:

It looks to me at this distance that Labour will come out of it like a sort of singed Ishmael – with every man's hand against it ... if we don't knock under it means that Labour's brief and hectic reign is up, and we may even prelude the return of sanity along the line. We have had six years orgy of saying and doing what we dam well chose; and preaching folly to the ignorant, who, as is always the case, have acted upon the preachings. If it weren't for the misery, one could wish that the strike would go on till the very name of 'miner' stank like 'suffragette'.[37]

March 1912 found Kipling in Venice, his inquisitive mind eagerly registering impressions:

The Kaiser's yacht, the *Hohenzollern*, came in here the day before yesterday, coaled, washed herself all over, and is now painting and gilding like

a public prostitute. Yesterday there was a Te Deum at St Mark's in honour
of the King's escape from assassination. We saw it from the gallery – a wonderful sight, officers, consuls, cuirassiers, etc. and the Patriarch of Venice
(he comes next to the Pope and glowed in his robes like a rose tiger beetle
under a microscope) read a speech. Here's a question. The pigeons at St
Mark's have bred there for, say, 700 years. They are all one stock, curiously
mimicking the grey, white splashed, black shadowed masonry of the square.
Very good. For, say 300 years there must have been a 12 o'clock gun fired
in Venice – the easiest way of marking time. *Still* all those pigeons rise in
their thousands and fly hurtling round the square when the gun fires. Why?
What price hereditary instinct? Explain![38]

   Kipling had not yet regained the buoyancy he had lost when his
parents died. On politics he had reached settled and sombre conclusions. His secretary, Sara Anderson, remarked in this year: 'I fear
I do, with all my heart, echo Mrs Kipling's wish that politicians would
leave him alone; he is not made of political stuff which regards the
thing as a "game"; to him it is deep earnest, and he wears his heart
strings out over what to them is merely a move that must be
countered.' This is a revealing judgement. Kipling was in politics by
remote control, and his complete intellectual sincerity, coupled to the
fact that he so seldom entered the cockpit himself, invested his
opinions with a passionate conviction and made it impossible for him
to take refuge in compromise as professional politicians must do, like
actors who cannot physically allow the emotion of their role to con-
sume them. Every departure from what he regarded as principles made
him wince, and added to his mistrust of politicians in general and
Liberals in particular. In April 1912, he wrote to Gwynne: 'I don't
suppose you could prevent a Liberal from lying any more than you
could stop a little dog from lifting up his leg against a lamp post.'[39]
   Meanwhile he was exploring with fascination a new world, the
Royal Flying Corps. Here again his foresight was remarkable. He realized that he was standing on the threshold of a revolution, like primitive man when he first launched his canoe. He noted that the Flying
Corps had already developed a particular eye and face, and he was
struck by a new smell in the Service – 'not infantry (hot or cold), not
artillery (which is horse sweat and leather), not motor-transport which
is petrol and oil, but a fourth and indescribable stink – a rather shrill
stink if you understand – like chlorine gas on top of petrol fumes.
It's a bit disconcerting to see the air-generation coming along.'
   Kipling threw himself with almost despairing ardour into any cause
likely to promote national virility or military preparedness. A friend

and admirer of Baden-Powell, he was an early supporter of the Boy
Scout movement, for which he wrote 'Patrol Song' in 1909, and when
the Wolf Cub organization for younger boys was started, its indebtedness to the Mowgli stories was clear to all. And it need hardly be added
that he was a fanatical supporter of the National Service League,
through which Lord Roberts, in the twilight of his life, urged upon
unheeding ears the need for conscription.

But Kipling was restless at this period and did not remain anywhere
for long. In February 1913 he was in Egypt, where he lay at rest under
a bank of the Nile, which was sprinkled with a thick crop of beans
and castor-oil bushes. The desert began thirty paces from where he
lay and ran without break for three thousand miles. The Greek cook
sat on the bank in his shirtsleeves, roasting coffee.

There is not the faintest use in describing the temples. All I know is that
the spectacle of the dawn striking the Colossi outside the Temple of Abu
Simbel is the most wonderful and awe-striking I have seen. It *is* true, as many
assert, that the statues come to life. I saw them do it: but just as they are
ready to burst through the stone and the centuries and to stand up, the full
sunlight pins them down into their places again. When the Day of Judgment
comes, the dawn will be delayed long enough for them to escape from their
bondage and they will walk about the earth shouting.[40]

Meanwhile he had strongly associated himself with the cause of
Ulster, displaying the old rancid contempt for politicians, and in
December 1913 he wrote to Gwynne:

They say that the movement is led by politicians. So it is, but the politicians
did not make the movement. They only headed it, and as I see things the
movement can't be checked by politicians any more. You can't let 80,000
men arm themselves and spend time drilling and keeping their tempers while
they are being insulted, and then expect the whole lot to file back quietly
to quarters as soon as a 'compromise' is announced. It's like getting the Djinn
back into the bottle. There's the oath of the Covenant for one thing, which
pledges resistance to any form of Home Rule in Ireland. People who aren't
politicians will not lightly slide out of an oath of that sort. You talk of the
German danger. Does it occur to you that a betrayed Ulster will repeat 1688
in the shape of a direct appeal to Germany? Which is the most dangerous
enemy? The South playing a game it has not got its heart in, or the North
in a blind rage *led by its own leaders, not by politicians*? [41]

It appears to have escaped Kipling's attention in his hatred of politicians that Ulster's resistance to Home Rule owed a great deal of virility
and determination to the politicans, Bonar Law, Edward Carson and

F. E. Smith, none of whom had any intention of 'sliding out of their oath'. In April 1914 he wrote some inflammatory verses for the journal of the Ulster party in an effort to precipitate the crisis:

> We know the wars prepared
> On every peaceful home,
> We know the hells declared
> For such as serve not Rome –
> The terror, threats, and dread
> In market, hearth, and field –
> We know, when all is said,
> We perish if we yield.

A few days later he lashed himself into a paroxysm of rage at the conduct of the Liberal Government. In one of his rare excursions into the arena, in a speech at Tunbridge Wells, he excelled even the Conservative leaders in the virulence of his accusations. He compared the Government to 'a firm of fraudulent solicitors who had got an unlimited power of attorney by false pretences and could dispose of their client's estate how they pleased'. He said that the Marconi scandals had revealed them as common swindlers, and that they were now reduced to betraying Ulster to a gang of criminals 'for no other reason than that they might continue in enjoyment of their salaries'.

This crazy outburst marked the lowest point yet reached by Kipling's sagging reputation, and one is scarcely surprised by the response he received from a man signing himself O'Donnell of O'Donnell, beginning: 'You contemptible, lying slanderer, vomiting your foul stomach like a drunkard's spew, where you are safe from an Irish kick.'

But the Ulster crisis was submerged in the greater issue of the German War which Kipling had so long anticipated:

Yes [he wrote to Fielden on 4 August 1914], I feel like Jonah or whoever it was who went about saying: 'I told you so.' The whole thing seems to be working out with the usual even logic of fact, but, – and it's a big but, it strikes me as tho' the Teuton had a little bit lost his head. Wind in the head is an awful disease but I do think the Germans frankly and fully left us out of the show altogether. I think they err a shade in underestimating us as they do.

Caroline's sole entry in her diary for the tremendous day 4 August 1914 was: 'My cold possesses me', but Kipling added sardonically in his own writing – 'incidentally Armageddon begins'.

CHAPTER XVII

1914-1918

THE war which Kipling had so long foreseen had come at last, and, when the long years of miserable forebodings and unheeded warnings had passed and his predictions had come true, it seemed as if a great burden had been lifted from his shoulders. The tone of his letters becomes one of buoyancy and sober optimism:

I confess I feel rather proud [he wrote three days after the outbreak of war] of the way England has bucked up at this pinch and tho' not an optimist by nature I can't help feeling cheerful over this. Here's a bit of a bet. When Liège falls the German army will make such a ghastly 'example' of it (with a view to striking terror), as will send every available male in England scuttling into the ranks in order to get a gun to have a pot at the Germans. That's where the policy of 'striking terror' breaks down as applied to English folk.[1]

He prepared, with pride, to offer to the armies his only son John, a schoolboy still but sixteen, who was fretting to begin his training in the pathetic belief, common at the time, that the war would be over before he could take part in it. On 17 August, John's seventeenth birthday, Kipling took him to Hastings and then to Maidstone to procure him a commission, but he was rejected on account of bad eyesight. Kipling decided to ask Lord Roberts for a nomination to his own regiment, and on 10 September met his old hero at the Irish Guards HQ. John was ordered to report at once for duty, and on 14 September left for Warley Barracks, where he joined the Irish Guards.[2]

There was, at this time, some question of Kipling visiting America, and an interesting correspondence is quoted on the subject by Lucy Masterman in her *Life of C. F. G. Masterman*. It begins with a letter from Sir Edward Grey (14 September 1914, Foreign Office), in which he writes: 'I hear Rudyard Kipling is going to the United States. This is to give notice that unless I am in a position to say that his visit has no official character, is not authorized or in any way countenanced by HM Government, I shall resign. For otherwise all my efforts to keep the goodwill of the United States will be useless.'

This note was passed to Masterman at a Cabinet Meeting, and he scribbled back: 'You write me a very violent letter! I have no knowledge that Kipling is going to the US. I should do all I could to stop it if I heard of it. I will immediately enquire if it is true. My whole activities have been devoted to preventing the Kiplings, Xs etc. from doing this sort of thing, but the only hope would be to get powers to lock them up as a danger to the State.' Grey replied on the same sheet: 'My letter wasn't violent against you, but against Kipling. I thought it would have your sympathy. You practically give me the answer I want.' Masterman admired much of Kipling's work, but Grey could not abide him, and the correspondence is an interesting indication of the reaction that Kipling's ardent polemics could provoke in an eminent and high-minded Liberal.

Kipling's thoughts had indeed already turned to America. Although her neutrality had not at this early stage produced in his mind the venomous contempt that came later, he was already striking a note of urgent warning. Well aware how unreal European conflicts appeared to Americans, sundered by three thousand miles of the Atlantic, he had written on 11 September to his friend F. N. Doubleday:

> Bateman's,
> Burwash, SUSSEX.
> September 11, 1914.

Dear Frank,

Many thanks for your last note to Carrie. We are all settling down to the business of war now. John goes off in a day or two to join his battalion at Warley in Essex, and – the rest is as God shall dispose.

Now I want you to read carefully what I am going to say. Germany is running this war, of set purpose, without the faintest regard for any law human or divine. You've heard of course of the burning of Dinant and all the other things. They are done in order, as the Germans say, 'to strike terror into the world'. And, by the way, the United States represents about all of the civilized world which is unaffected by the war.

We have an American friend who has been living in France for years in a chateau which she converted into a 50 bed hospital, and had to abandon as the Germans advanced. Her record of the horrors committed is something ghastly. They cut the hands off a Surgeon whom they took prisoner in order that he might never practise again. A Belgian officer, a friend of hers and a man whom I know also, told her that women and girls were *publicly* raped in Belgium by the command of their officers.

I know it must be difficult to give you any idea of it, but – believe me – it is true, and the half of the truth has not yet been revealed – for obvious reasons. And so this Hell-Dance goes on: and the US makes no sign. Nobody wants her to take part in the war, but for her own conscience's sake, for the sake of her record in history, and her position as the one untouched civilized power, she ought to enter her protest against these atrocities. Be as neutral as you like, but do not pass these brutalities over in silence officially.[3]

He referred to the issue in passionate terms as one that touched the whole foundation and future of civilized life. The Americans could not remain dumb in the face of the negation of every idea and ideal they had stood for since their beginnings. He tried to stimulate Doubleday by describing the contempt with which Germany regarded unarmed, indifferent America, how she insolently refused to give information about the missing, even to the American Ambassador Page, and the agonies of those waiting in vain for news, a bitter cup he was soon to drain himself. 'I don't know whether *you* realize,' he ended, 'but we do clearly, that all and more than all the horrors of Louvain ... Dinant, etc. will be duplicated here, if we can't keep them out. Odd – isn't it? – in the 20th century.'

Kipling, from the outbreak of war until the early months of 1915, felt a burning enthusiasm for the cause which was never satisfied by the work he was able to undertake. He felt an honourable regret that in this war, the menace of which he had so frequently urged upon his indifferent countrymen, he was able to play only a passive, rather desultory part. Conscious of a certain unreality in his actions, he made recruiting speeches and appealed for funds for the troops, visited wounded soldiers, providing cigarettes and prizes for whist drives and autographing books – and declined an offer to visit GHQ in France to write a history of the Ypres battle from the statements of various generals.[4] But he gave much help to his friend Max Aitken, who had been appointed official war correspondent with the Canadian Army in Europe, and spent Christmas 1914 at Aitken's house 'Cherkley' near Leatherhead. He had been revolted by the terrorism, deliberately chosen, as he thought, by the Germans and had retaliated with two savage stories that winter – *Swept and Garnished*, written in October, and *Mary Postgate* in March.

But mostly he was back again, with a grim irony, in the days of the South African War, performing the same limited tasks, urging the same patriotic appeals – but with what a difference! The Boer War had been to him a necessary vindication of the Imperial position, but, in comparison with the present conflict, little more than an expensive football match played away from home. Even that Pyrrhic victory had turned sour. Now, with every illusion as to the glamour of war long stripped from him, he saw 'the Wall', ill-kept through the years of trance, its brickwork crumbling, its bastions sparsely manned, awaiting the greatest Barbarian onslaught since the Dark Ages.

Although Kipling had gone to exceptional lengths to get his seventeen-year-old son placed in the Army in spite of his bad eyesight, the thought of his actual departure for the front filled him with dread. Drafts were already streaming out from Warley to replenish the mangled Regiment, and the eager John was mortified at being kept at home. Meanwhile he would come on leave for short visits to his parents at Brown's Hotel. He was placed in the Second Battalion of the newly-formed Guards Division, and assured that he would be sent overseas. His father had first to give his permission owing to John's tender age. But 10 August 1915 saw his Battalion under orders from France, and Rudyard met his son in London to say good-bye.

On 12 August 1915 Kipling went to France to write an account of the war. As before, this approach towards the scene of conflict removed with one antiseptic wipe the malaise of the frustrated non-combatant, and sharpened his pen. He felt that he was coming near the heart of activity throbbing on the busy quays and railheads. His senses were alert and receptive: 'Then we left the pier with a quick stealthy turn and two destroyers came out of the warm grey sea ... and fell in alongside us on either side, sort of lounging along to keep pace with our modest 22 knots. The Channel was full-packed with traffic – and there were certain arrangements for the discomfort of roving submarines, which were very nice to watch.'

On the ship he talked to Princess Victoria of Schleswig-Holstein. She explained her feelings and those of her mother about the war, and enlarged on the excellence of Louis of Battenberg 'who saved the Nation'. She told the cold and unresponding Kipling that she considered it cruel that people should write insulting letters to her mother, and she enlarged on the unfortunate position of Royalty in this difficult period: 'We have talked it over, and we think we can meet some of the women afterwards, but the men, No – Never.' Kipling pointed out sourly that she need not worry about meeting the men if the Allies won, as they would all be tried for their offences. Then she wailed over the German Emperor, whom she had known since he was a boy – 'Who would ever have expected he would have done this?' 'All exactly like a woman in any other walk of life explaining how her family had members who were no credit to it.' Then she told him that

'Daisy', the Crown Princess of Sweden, acted as a check on the older generation. 'The Queen is one thing. *I* am very much the other. The Court you can believe is strictly neutral.'

'Poor little anxious, time-serving Court of Sweden,' said Kipling, 'skirmishing up and down those long passages.'[5] With a bad taste in his mouth from this conversation, Kipling went on deck and caught a cleansing whiff of the sea. They were entering harbour and the lean destroyers fell back. 'As we came into the shallow water our escort spread out, and drew aside, right and left of Boulogne Harbour, just like two black retrievers forbidden to come into the house.' And then to Paris in the twilight, to a flaming red sky and the silhouette of black buildings, the station dimly lighted. But the Place Vendôme was empty and silent; and a military car waited outside the Ritz. At dinner there were only fifteen people in the vast echoing halls, and the wartime waiters, anaemic youths dragged in from the streets. 'You can imagine the state to which the Ritz is fallen,' he wrote, 'when I tell you that I saw one waiter kick another man's behind, right in the middle of the dining-room.'[6]

Next day Kipling was received by Clemenceau. There was the great old man in his skull cap and white gloves, at last a politician whom he could admire without reserve. Their views on politics bore many striking resemblances. Clemenceau had for long observed that great military machine over the frontier growing into terrible maturity. He, like Kipling, detested political compromise and cowardice and was to stamp them out in France with brutal severity. Both men were ardent patriots, and were further united by a common contempt for the doctrinaire obstinacy of President Wilson. Kipling returned from his interview in a state of high excitement:

And so back from that amazing human explosive, Clemenceau, who, on the instant of my coming, held forth without break and so continued for forty coruscating minutes. All truth too, backed with very real power and the widest knowledge. I should say from what he said that *their* Government is the twin of ours, mentally and spiritually – same incompetence, same lawyers' explanations, same complete inability for anyone to admit that they were wrong in any particular, and the same furious intrigues. . . . It seems that the Ministry made absolutely and servilely every mistake that ours did – thought that the war would be short; thought that, if anything, France had more cannon than she needed, and in that belief countermanded orders for guns. Then he branched off into our (the allies) diplomacy, and the immense hash we had made, specially on the part of Russia, in our dealings with the Balkan States . . . he told me repeatedly that the German people, *qua* people, were fed up with the war of continuous victories 'always in the same place' . . . he was full of little touches, describing the Germans and what they think. He assured me that they have a growing horror at the thought of another winter campaign – a horror that it would need a lot of victories to counteract. He had no earthly doubt of the issue but – munitions, munitions, was his cry throughout.

From Clemenceau Kipling passed to Briand, and here he registered a very different impression. Back in redoubled force came all the old hatred for the politician, and he wrote home: 'Clemenceau's view of Briand is absolutely unprintable. He would endure, he says, a thousand Millerands sooner than one B.' Kipling found Briand in the midst of a difficulty. 'Oh no, not a crisis by any means; not even a crisislet or a crisisling – merely a readjustment.' The cause of the trouble was the fear of 'certain documents', the recurrent nightmare of French politicians, and Briand had spent the morning with his colleagues 'readjusting their little differences'. 'Altogether,' said Kipling, 'a politician's interview with the same L.G.-like* shrug and lean forward of the shoulders at critical points – a sort of political bedside manner. A wind-bag, yes, but of the most unscrupulous.'

Then came a memorable journey – first to Soissons via Compiègne – vivid impressions eagerly absorbed – a pale white street of pale white stone, and the houses smashed and burned – the car speeding on and on over the *pavé* – an entry into a tranquil, wooded valley, and a General called Nivelle, who told Kipling that his mother was English. Kipling climbed to a crow's nest in a sixty-foot acacia tree, and looking through the leaves and branches saw the whole countryside falling away in a long yellow slope, the grass perished, poisoned by German gas. He regarded with interest from his dizzy perch a surrealist landscape – trees like 'chewed tooth-picks', and the strangely impersonal smoke-puffs of the artillery salvos and the flung earth.

There were introductions to French sentries, who admired the *Jungle Books* with such unanimity that Kipling thought it was a put-up job by the General. And then with the strange incongruity of static warfare came a retreat from the realities of the front line, and a lunch of fifteen covers starting with crayfish and fillet of beef. Afterwards they entered the town, and to Kipling's alert senses it seemed a *dead* town. Grass was growing in the streets, and the gaunt skeleton of the Cathedral towered above the desolation. The silence was uncanny. Suddenly one heard a footfall far away, and sometimes saw a woman's

* Lloyd George.

face in a window. The shelling of Soissons was slow, methodical and maddening, 'like Devils ringing gongs'. When they approached the shattered Cathedral, Kipling thought that he could hear singing. 'Nonsense,' said the officer with him: 'But he forgot Sunday, and he forgot France. In a little, only partially-wrecked side-chapel some 100 people, mainly women, were gathered at service – kneeling before the altar and singing, not knowing whether or when the next shell might lift them out of the world. "*C'est stupéfiant,*" said our officer, but I saw his eyes fill with tears.' Kipling's own eyes were dim as he regarded those lines of pale faces in the strange light that filtered through the window, the little triumphant trickle of voices and the priest's deep bass against the silence broken by the thud of artillery.

His impressions on this tour became mixed, but certain things stood out in his mind – drinking orangeade in a peaceful dreaming chateau and sleeping in an echoing villa. 'Brekker at 9 tomorrow,' he wrote heartily to his family – 'a glorious day, but I don't like this incessant talking of French, and this everlasting R.K. jaw, who is ever and ever, Your own boy.'

Then to Rheims, where only 2000 people were left out of the original population of 100,000, and there he noted the sudden rattling of the few wheels still moving in the streets. As he contemplated the Cathedral his hatred for the Germans boiled up: 'Half the front is literally roasted to a horrible flesh colour.' The towers were smashed, the windows twisted and forlorn, the gargoyles maimed and defaced, the whole thing looking like 'some wretched mutilated human being'. Birds flew in and out of the windows, the floor tiles were broken, and the ancient oak doors opening from the Sacristy to the Cathedral were bent like pieces of paper. 'Put on your hats, Messieurs,' said the Sacristan, 'this is not consecrated. The Archbishop has declared it desecrated.' 'I can't tell you,' Kipling wrote, 'how I felt at the savagery and brutality of it all.'[7] They went away, 'sick and heavy at heart, and left that poor blinded burned horror alone in the great stillness'.

After Rheims he was taken to Epernay, and from there to a little hill-village built against a mountain crowned by a church. The winding road expired in pink ruins, blocks of shivered masonry against the sky, and a landscape as lovely as a picture in an illuminated mediaeval book. Then to Verdun, looking like a tiny Florence inside a fort, where he fell asleep to the clamour of the big guns among the hills and the roar of the river foaming through the weir. None could foretell the terrible destiny of Verdun, and it seemed then to Kipling that 'the Bosch leave Verdun alone because Verdun spanks Metz with big fat cannon if they drop shells there'. The view from the front of the club was of 'fat barges in a canal and adorable houses all alongside'. Then there was a ceremony – Kitchener reviewing with Joffre a French Army Corps in a rolling landscape of reaped fields and naked down-land, the Corps lying by the side of the road 'in a sort of pale blue drift like myosotis' – Kitchener walking down the dull blue line while the band played 'God Save the King' and the 'Marseillaise' and the aeroplanes pirouetted gaily overhead: 'It took about an hour and a quarter and moved one almost to tears. Puaux,* my nice Captain, frankly wiped his eyes. He hadn't seen an Army before, except in trenches.'

Again the impressions became confused – a villa in Alsace, and a brindled wolf-hound, a smell of the woods, and the wet ferns and rocks: then of a sector where, for the second time in his life, he experienced the sensation of being close to the enemy. There was a fatherly Colonel, 'who took us into the first line trenches, which are 7, or to be exact $7\frac{1}{2}$ metres – say the length of a cricket pitch – from the Germans ... and I had peeps at 'em through loop-holes blocked with plugs. I saw green sand-bags in a wilderness of tree trunks and stores and no Bavarians saw me.'

Kipling could not conceal his pride and exultation at being for a moment in the front line, even in this quiet sector and at an obviously safe moment. There is something a trifle distasteful and insensitive in the letter in which he described his adventures to John, who was soon to know the horrors of real war, and to be obliterated in the hell of Loos:

Dear old man,
   I hope you'll never get nearer to the Boche than I did. The quaintest thing was to watch the NCO gesticulating to his Colonel and me to keep quiet – and to hear a hopefully expectant machine gun putting in five or six shots on the chance, and then, as it were, stopping to listen. I don't mind trenches half as much as going in a motor along ten or twelve miles of road which the Boche may or may not shell.... It's a grand life though and does not give you a dull minute.

Back at Thom, five miles away, Kipling's old friend Perceval Landon, said: 'Now this is really dangerous,' for the Germans were in the habit of shelling Thom in their leisure moments. 'It's a beautiful Alsatian town, and well worth defiling,' said Kipling, but the Germans were not shelling that day and there was deep peace and silence.

* Kipling's escorting officer.

His attitude to Caroline at this time shows strong affection. He addressed her as 'Most dear and True'; 'Hurry up and let me know your Royal Mind, my Queen', and adds with spurious triumph: 'When I return be prepared for a new Domestic Tyrant. I'm somebody, and I've pulled the whiskers of death and don't you forget it.' He was astonished to discover that he was a household name in France: 'My dears – it is absolutely terrifying to me to find what I am in France. I haven't told you a tenth of the unbelievable things that have happened. The ex-avocat soldier in Alsace asked me, *under fire*, to explain how the idea of the *Jungle Book* came to me! and a man unseen in the darkness of a dug-out reached out his hands and shook mine, murmuring "*Le grand Rutyar*".'

On 15 August 1915 John Kipling went to France. There is a rather pathetic entry in Caroline's diary: 'John leaves at noon for Warley. He looks very straight and smart and young, as he turned at the top of the stairs to say: "Send my love to Dad-o".' The 'man-child' had gone to the wars, and from that moment began for the Kiplings a period of agony, covered by a frigid exterior restraint. It is perhaps doubtful whether Kipling's realistic mind nourished any genuine hope of his son's survival, but it never occurred to father, son, or mother that there was any alternative to immediate service.

The bad news was not long in coming. On 2 October came a message from the War Office that John was missing in the Battle of Loos on 27 September. John's Company Commander, in a letter of sober regret, described how the boy came to be missing. He was commanding No. 5 Platoon in the 2nd Battalion of the Irish Guards when they were ordered to attack a small wood:

No. 2 and 3 Coys. were ordered to attack, No. 1 and 4 being in support with picks and shovels. We advanced with one platoon from each of No. 2 and 3 in extended order, and the other 3 platoons of each Coy. behind in artillery formation. Your son led the Platoon in extended order from No. 2 Coy. We were shelled most of the way but remained in this formation till we reached the Wood, which was about 500 yds. long and 70 yards deep. The 2 leading platoons charged through the Wood, and when I got through with the platoons of my Coy. they were already digging themselves in about 30 yards the other side, and parallel with the Wood; at this time we were under machine-guns and casualties were getting numerous.

The Grenadiers and the Scots then came up on the right, and the Irish Guards on the right flank advanced with them right up to the Puits and Red Brick House, which were about 300 yards from where we were digging ourselves in. There were machine-guns in these buildings, and although they had been heavily shelled they opened from them a considerable fire and also from another Wood just beyond. Two of my men say they saw your son limping, just by the Red House, and one said he saw him fall, and somebody run to his assistance, probably his orderly who is also missing. The Platoon Sergeant of No. 5, however, tells me your son did not go to the Red House, but remained with the remainder of the 2nd Btn. digging themselves in just outside the Wood, but I think the former story the more correct one, and I am very hopeful that he is a prisoner.

Your son behaved with great gallantry and coolness and handled his men splendidly. I trust that your great anxiety may be allayed by definite news of his safety soon. Please accept my most heartfelt sympathy. I had a great affection for him.

Yours sincerely,
JOHN B. BIRD.

This was the second major blow of Kipling's life, and it intensified his horror and hatred of the Germans. He had envisaged this position with absolute clarity. His countrymen had disregarded his warnings – even flinched in boredom from their hero's writings – and now Kipling had to pay this terrible price. The lingering, pitiful spark of hope took some time to be extinguished. They made desperate efforts to ascertain John's fate. They went to the hospitals where the men of his Battalion lay wounded, to try to discover some survivors, some news one way or another, of that last assault. They were maddened by the uncertainty: 'What you say of our John is all quite true,' wrote Caroline to her mother, 'and if one could but know he was dead, one would accept it, but we do not know, and we do know stories too dreadful to write you of prisoners – it's this dreadful uncertainty, with all the horror of the fears it brings, that takes all one's life and spirit, *and*', she adds with strong meaning, 'until you in the US have had some experience, you cannot expect to know or understand the German and his devices, or to realize his various tortures.'[8]

As the hopeless weeks passed, the Kiplings' expectations ebbed, and Caroline wrote to Mme Cattani, in whose hotel they had stayed at Engelberg:

We must always keep a window open to hope, since so many officers have turned up after even a year of silence – but as the weeks go by our anxiety – always with us, becomes very heavy. If he met his death fighting for all the things we hold to be of value, we are honoured through him, and though our sorrow is no less, yet we realize he only did what many Englishmen have done and are prepared to do, and his loss, though so great a thing to us, is a little thing set against the greater.

Kipling smothered his agony in a terrible coldness: 'I don't suppose there is much hope for my boy,' he wrote to Dunsterville in November, 'and the little that is left doesn't bear thinking of. However, I hear that he finished well . . . it was a short life. I'm sorry that all the years' work ended in that one afternoon, but – lots of people are in our position, and it's something to have bred a man.' Yet another well-loved place was to be barred to him by torturing associations – Switzerland, where he and John had been happy in the keen Alpine air blundering about on skis, and he wrote years later to Mme Cattani: 'We have not the heart to come out there again. We generally go to the South of France for the Spring – to Cannes where we can climb up by car into the hills behind Grasse and smell the pines as the Spring snow melts from beneath them, and the anemones begin to come out.'[9]

And when Aunt Georgie saw Kipling for the first time since the death of his son, she said: 'I had not seen him since the death of his boy – and was greatly touched by his look. Quite well, he seemed, and younger and stronger than before, as if he had died and been buried and risen again, and had the keys of hell and of death.'

Kipling was numbed by his son's death and his grief is apparent in the bitter couplet:

> My son died laughing at some jest, I would I knew
> What it were, and it might serve me at a time when jests are few.

It is apparent, too, in the poem, 'My Boy Jack' (1916), put into the mouth of the mourning mother of a young seaman:

> 'Have you news of my boy Jack?'
>   *Not this tide.*
> 'When d'you think that he'll come back?'
>   *Not with this wind blowing, and this tide.*
>
> 'Has anyone else had word of him?'
>   *Not this tide.*
> *For what is sunk will hardly swim,*
>   *Not with this wind blowing and this tide.*
>
> 'Oh, dear, what comfort can I find?'
>   *None this tide,*
>   *Nor any tide,*
> *Except he did not shame his kind –*
>   *Not even with that wind blowing, and that tide.*

> *Then hold your head up all the more,*
> *   This tide,*
> *   And every tide;*
> *Because he was the son you bore,*
> *   And gave to that wind blowing and that tide!*

John had been a dark, short-sighted boy, whom his friends remembered with affection. He had not inherited Kipling's intellectual
powers, did not care for letters or books, and had sometimes caused
his father anxiety,[10] but he had in many ways a strong personality.
The formidable Caroline was clay in his hands, and when the Regiment was posing for its picture with Rudyard as Honorary Colonel,
John, standing above Kitchener who had a grease spot on his cap,
observed loudly: 'Kitchener will never make a Guardsman.' He was
obviously going to prove a smart soldier, but at seventeen his character
was still unformed.

Kipling never forgave the Germans for the death of his son. He
saw in the 1914 War a preparation for the next one, and was deeply
wounded that he only bored people, particularly the young, by his
habit of incessant reminder. Again, as in the case of Josephine, he
ruthlessly eliminated from his life anything that could remind him of
the dead child. Offered a bulldog bitch by Sir Roderick Jones, he
answered:

As to 'Mary'. It is a most generous and kindly offer that you make and
I'd love to accept it. *But*, – and here the children come in again, as *you* I
hope will never have reason to find out in your life. When all the world was
young and we were at the Woolsack, John, without shoes or stockings, owned
and was owned by one 'Jumbo', a brindle and white bulldog who chaperoned
him on his walks, played with him, and, being forbidden to sleep with him,
devoutly slept outside his door. John used to feed him currant buns and then
pick the currants out of his back teeth. All those good years you see, are
mixed up with the memories of a small boy and a large bulldog, and we didn't
realize how horribly alive they were till we talked over your letter. So – *not*
Mary, please, with her large, fool, devoted face and the same manners. She'd
bring too much with her into the house.[11]

'A bitter and sad business,' he said, 'even for such as know where
their boys are laid.'

As well as intensifying Kipling's hatred of the Germans, this loss
suddenly sharpened his growing resentment of the American attitude,
as will be seen in detail in the following chapter which contains little-

known correspondence between Kipling and Theodore Roosevelt. In May 1916, in response to a suggestion by Frank Doubleday that an 'important person should be sent out to the USA on a mission of friendship and goodwill', he replied curtly: 'That is the talk of the old world which died on Aug. 4. 1914. Men do not prove their friendship and goodwill now by their mouth but by their lives. You chose, after due thought, to commit moral suicide.'[12] Caroline, now almost entirely denationalized, fully shared these views, and their bitter anger was to grow in strength until, at the time of the *Lusitania* disaster, Caroline wrote to her mother: 'This morning we have the news that Germany has had her note accepted by America about the *Lusitania*, and all Americans of our generation and upbringing, undiluted by European dregs, must feel bitterly and lastingly ashamed.'[13]

In September 1916, when the situation seemed better, Kipling wrote gloatingly to Dunsterville:

It's a scientific-cum-sporting murder proposition with enough guns at last to account for the birds, and the Hun is having a very sickly time of it. He has the erroneous idea that he is being hurt, whereas he won't know what real pain means for a long time. I almost begin to hope that when we have done with him there will be very little Hun left. He plays our game splendidly. Every time there are new troops against him he proceeds to kill their wounded; consequently the new troops take rather less than two days to know how to deal with him. There is a legend that a man can get as much as eight days No. 2 field punishment if his officer sees him killing Huns. On the other hand the officer doesn't look too hard or too long.[14]

On 17 January 1917 he undertook a labour of love, the history of the Irish Guards.[15] Upon this work, which he intended partly as a memorial to his dead son, he lavished an immense amount of labour, recording the achievements of the Regiment down to Platoon level, but the massive two volumes which came with the sweat of his brow have not been found altogether satisfactory by Irish Guards officers.

When writing this book Kipling was forced, whether he realized it or not, to take refuge, in a delicate situation, in that compromise he so despised as a resort of politicians. And he was forced, moreover, to yield to it as much as any politician, and to sweeten the opinions he had expressed with such intemperance about Catholic Ireland – that 'pernicious little bitch of a country', 'that gang of criminals'. For he was now writing about Irish soldiers who had marched and died with his own son, and a somewhat different approach was required.

He seems to have made it without qualms of conscience, and a warm note is struck in the prologue to his history:

> Old Days! The wild geese are ranging,
>   Head to the storm as they faced it before!
> For where there are Irish their hearts are unchanging,
>   And when they are changed it is Ireland no more!

Apart from his visits to the front, he had come closest to the war visiting ships of the Dover Patrol and the Harwich Flotilla, and verses inspired by these naval occasions were his most vivid wartime achievement, particularly 'Minesweepers' with its haunting refrain: 'Send up *Unity, Claribel, Assyrian, Stormcock* and *Golden Gain*.' But Kipling's personal involvement in this terrible war had destroyed for ever the exhilaration he had once found in the portrayal of battle. He had become obsessed with the problem of pain and the nature of fear – the limits of human endurance before collapse. The agony of the individual in the face of this terror, and his acceptance of it, is poignantly caught in one of his greatest and most searing poems, 'Gethsemane':

> The Garden called Gethsemane
>   In Picardy it was,
> And there the people came to see
>   The English soldiers pass.
> We used to pass – we used to pass
>   Or halt, as it might be,
> And ship our masks in case of gas
>   Beyond Gethsemane.

> The garden called Gethsemane,
>   It held a pretty lass,
> But all the time she talked to me
>   I prayed my cup might pass.
> The officer sat on the chair,
>   The men lay on the grass,
> And all the time we halted there
>   I prayed my cup might pass.

> It didn't pass – it didn't pass –
>   It didn't pass from me.
> I drank it when we met the gas
>   Beyond Gethsemane.

And he felt not only grief and agony, but fury at such bungling of the authorities as had led to unnecessary slaughter in Mesopotamia:

> They shall not return to us, the resolute, the young,
>   The eager and whole-hearted whom we gave,
> But the men who left them thriftily to die in their own dung,
>   Shall they come with years and honour to the grave?
>
> Their lives cannot repay us – their death could not undo –
>   The shame that they laid upon our race,
> But the slothfulness that wasted and the arrogance that slew,
>   Shall we leave it unabated in its place?

In April a collection of stories entitled *A Diversity of Creatures* was published, and the same month found Kipling writing to C. R. L. Fletcher, the historian, on the subject of the corpse-factory in which the Germans were supposed to process their war-dead for pig-food:

And talking of Armies – the latest about cannon-fodder being turned into pig-food is very interesting and wholly logical. This is the last verse of an otherwise unprintable set of verses dealing with the subject:

> Charlotte, when she saw what Herman
>   Yielded after he was dead,
> Like a well-conducted German,
>   Spread him lightly on her bread.*[16]

Kipling visited the Italian front in May 1917, and we see him first at Modane, the turf of the valley studded with narcissi not yet in flower, cowslip and cranesbill and pruned orchards. He went to Rome, passing through the Mt Cenis with the spring upon it – pears and almonds together in bloom, the young wheat a foot high, a warm, fine rain falling, and the Campagna in the morning grey and green, with the white bullocks gravely regarding him; and at the Embassy in Rome, roses and wistarias out on the hot walls.

Here he attended the Beatification of a Carmelite Nun, and watched the splendid ceremony to the end 'when the golden litter had left through a far door and the whole crowd liquified, and flooded the Cathedral'. He lunched with a cardinal in his palace, a visit which

---

* The 'corpse-factory' in the First World War was a figment of Allied propaganda, but it was prophetic. In the Second World War concentration camp victims were processed to make soap, and the skin of tattooed prisoners tanned and made into lampshades for the wife of the Commandant of Buchenwald.

brought back memories of drives on cold spring days over the Tiber, and found a 'quiet, brooding, inner court facing a square of hot sunshine; a covered cloister, a climb up four flights of foot-worn stone stairs, and at last a long, long suite of rooms ... the final one all upholstered in yellow silk'.

After Rome he came to Udine, sprawling among green crops, and avenues of chestnuts with the pink and white petals already strewing the ground; the arcades, loggias and *campaniles* splashed in sunlight. Here he slept in a house 'bordered by a rushing stream of milky water in which the women washed their clothes while the wounded lay about in the healing soft sunshine'. There was an interview with General Cadorna and a breathtaking glimpse of Udine by moonlight – 'the moon full on the great square, dotted with blue lights. The town was silent, the moonlight slashed the fronts of the old buildings and the arcades and loggias showed like pits of blackness.' And when they came up to the front line they found a vivid light spring day; the roads were as white as bone and dry after days of wet. Every road was flanked by a little flushing water-channel, and lined with piles of limestone pebbles.

They came next to St Michael, the Italian Ypres, and Hill 60. 'The dead Italians had been carried down to the side of the river Isonzo below us, where they lay in 2 mile long cemeteries. You didn't need to be told it was a Golgotha. You felt it out there in the clean sunshine under the blue sky – felt it as though it were midnight. It was a land apart from anything else – it was the Carso, the Italians pronounce it with loathing.'

In July Kipling received news from a friend of an unfortunate episode at Westward Ho! and his answer throws an interesting light on his views on public-school morals:

This is perfectly sickening – specially when one knows, as you and I do, what the conditions must have been – and *above all* the sort of atmosphere that, mainly through the Masters' carelessness and neglect, must have been allowed to grow up. It makes me furious when I am told of cases of this sort by men without, as far as one can see, any memory of their own youth and boyhood. You can imagine for yourself what the old Coll would have been with a system of cubicles instead of the open dormitories and the Masters moving about at all hours through 'em – which is what saved us. But I don't think that as the world is today – and people are getting more reasonable than they were – that the thing will count against him in the future. And yet – how many men do we know who have risen to all sorts of positions, who when they were kids were – not found out!

I always go in deadly fear of the cubicle system at any public school. They have it at Wellington, and Eton, as we know, is . . .[17]

He was still ever prepared to castigate what he considered the treason of the politicians. A characteristic letter on 1 December 1917 explains this to his cousin 'Stan' Baldwin:

As to Lansdowne's letter to the D.T.* I fancy it appears there because the proprietor is a Hebrew, and was suffering from cold feet. It *is* a Semitic complaint. But the origin of his letter must be much more interesting. I am, as you know, a low-minded Soul and I expect the poor old bird (who is ga-ga) was worked upon as a 'patriot and a statesman' by someone – female for choice – in the Liberal interest. The Liberals have an idea – one gets at it now and again in queer places – that the war ought to be 'drawn' because that, in some insane way, justifies their contention that the war might have been 'avoided'. It is all mixed up with Asquith and a lot of loose talk about 'larger views', and 'detachment'. Brassey, who is also vehemently ga-ga, holds Lansdowne's opinions in advanced form. Of course, *au fond*, the whole fault rests with DORA, who should have known that the old imbecile meditated these performances. But it will pass over like the rest after a few juicy questions in the House, and it will add to the bewilderment of our enemies who never understand why we do all our mental toilet in public.

An eminent American reviewed Kipling's wartime activities with interest. Alexander Woollcott, who had observed with amusement Beatty Balestier's activities with the wolf-hounds in the Savoy, now wrote:

During the heyday of the AEF [American Expeditionary Force] Kipling, momentarily placated by our having sent two million soldiers to France, gave the *Stars and Stripes* the privilege of being the first to publish one of his poems. In acknowledgment, we sent a courier, accompanied by a blushing young orderly, to deliver the first copy off the press. Kipling received them, and it, at Brown's Hotel. The courier acquitted himself as instructed, and the incident was about to close, when the private, whose name I've forgotten and who was breathing heavily and obviously bursting with excitement, suddenly stepped forward, shook the gifted hand and said:
'My, Mr Kipling, it will be a great day when my folks in Georgia hear that I actually met the man who wrote the *Rubaiyat of Omar Khayyam*.'[19]

In 1917 Kipling was furious at learning that he had, without his knowledge, been appointed a Companion of Honour, writing to Bonar Law: 'How would you like it if you woke up and found they had made you Archbishop of Canterbury?' He still had not the

* This letter in the *Daily Telegraph* contained the suggestion that the time had come to make peace with Germany.

slightest interest in honours, however exalted, and four years later refused the Order of Merit almost without thought. Though he sternly disdained to accept any decorations, his friend Mrs W. M. Cazalet has provided an interesting account of his one exception:

'We were alone, and discussing many things and people. For some unknown reason, when talking to Edward Carson (a mutual friend) I said I had been dining with him the other day, and he had told me that he was one of the few people who had no *trinkets* ... and then I said that I did not think that he (Rudyard) had anything of that sort. He replied: "You are wrong for once. I *have* a decoration, and what is more you shall see it." He jumped up and ran across the lawn to the house and in a few minutes returned with a red box made of asbestos and shaped like a book. He sat down beside me, and took out of this sort of box-book, a copy of *Kim*. Bound in yellow paper and translated into French, it had a bullet mark right through it except for the last twenty pages, and thro' this hole tied by a piece of string was, hanging outside the book, a *Croix de Guerre*. He told me that a parcel containing this had arrived during the War addressed to Rudyard Kipling with a letter (which I read) from a French soldier saying that if *Kim* had not been in his pocket when he went into battle he would have been killed. With the consent of his parents he asked Kipling to accept his *Croix* as a token of his eternal gratitude. Kipling's simple appreciation was delightful to see, and very characteristic. When the war was over he went himself to France, and after great difficulty made the soldier take back his *Croix*, as he knew what it meant to him. As far as I know I am the only person to whom he showed his precious decoration, and I remember that when I told Mrs Kipling she was very surprised that I had seen it.'[20]

The soldier wrote that Kipling was indeed his saviour in that it was to his deep love of his 'sublime works' that he owed his life. He could certainly not do less than to send to Kipling the copy of *Kim* 'found' by the German bullet, but to the book he wished to add his most precious possession, his *Croix de Guerre* won on both French Colonial and European battlefields. He hoped that Kipling would accept it because it represented ten years of Colonial service during which he gained extra courage from the reading of Kipling's military stories of his English brothers. The letter ended, 'Your eternally thankful Maurice Hammoneau'.

Kipling accepted both the book and the Cross temporarily, but on the birth of Hammoneau's son in 1929, who was called Jean at Kipling's suggestion ('My boy's name was John, so yours must be Jean') and to whom he became godfather, he insisted that both book and decoration belonged to the child. In spite of protestations on Hammoneau's part Kipling sent them to France.

In 1917 Kipling undertook two tasks which did something to distract his mind from personal grief. When Lord Derby, Chairman of the Imperial War Graves Commission, had seen the original list of Commissioners he had said: 'You must have R.K., the soldiers' poet.' It was somehow appropriate that he who had lost a son should become one of the Commissioners, and that he should have been responsible for choosing the inscription set up in every war cemetery: 'Their name liveth for evermore.' It was, perhaps, a conventional tribute, and in strident contrast to it was the tragic disillusionment of Siegfried Sassoon, who could see only a vast and poignant oblivion in the slaughter and to whom the names cut on the Menin Gate Memorial were 'those intolerably nameless names'.

Kipling proved an immense success on the Commission. He remained a member for eighteen years, and was responsible for every inscription used by it. Its task was enormous – the exhumation, identification and reburial of a million British dead in permanent cemeteries set in gardens with tombstones and crosses, tenderly maintained in many cases by nationals of former enemy countries. But there was no headstone in this vast mausoleum for 'my son Jack', for John Kipling's fate was never determined and his body never found.

At the time of this appointment Kipling was invited by Dr Jameson to become one of the Rhodes Trustees responsible for the administration of the Rhodes Scholarships at Oxford for picked men from the Dominions, the United States and other countries. Rudyard knew little of Oxford's *mystique*, but he had been with Rhodes in South Africa when the scheme was launched, and Carrie had suggested practical improvements which had been adopted. He could throw himself without reserve into this enlightened project which would not only help to keep Rhodes's memory green, but would bring the flower of the Dominions' and American youth to the greatest University in England.

CHAPTER XVIII

KIPLING AND ROOSEVELT

KIPLING'S views on the 1914–18 War are revealed in greater depth in a remarkable exchange of correspondence between him and Theodore Roosevelt. Kipling had a tendency to hero-worship, with Rhodes for long an inviolate idol, and we have the feeling that after Rhodes's death he transferred some of this veneration to Roosevelt, a man of the same imperious stamp. The frankness of the two writers makes their correspondence of particular interest.

Bateman's,
BURWASH, Sussex.
Sept. 15. 1914.

Dear Roosevelt,

Your letters from England will have given you an insight into things as they are here. But I wish you could spend half a day with the Belgian refugees as they come into Folkestone. The look on their faces is enough, without having to hear their stories which are like tales from Hell. When people congratulate each other that So and So's womenfolk were shot outright one realizes a bit about German culture. As far as one makes out the rapings etc. were (and are) put through as part of a set plan to 'strike terror into the world'. Of course we in England may have these things happen to us: but frankly we are aghast at there being no protest from the USA against the Belgian dealings. It seems almost incredible that America, which has always stood so emphatically against these horrors, should be silent now. Neutrality is of course understood, but surely neutrality cannot bar her from putting herself on record as officially opposed to Louvainism etc.

It is in this direction that your help and leading will be of priceless value to us all. You say it is no use to be always in the vocative – that you are tired of talking. So is everyone except the Pacifists whose trade it is. That is the very reason that one must go on and on, even though the sound of one's own voice and the sight of one's own words makes one sick. The forces of ineffectualness *never* let up precisely because one can be ineffective at the minimum expenditure of energy and mind. I beseech you, therefore, to continue to testify. I know exactly what your reward is. I heard it the other day from a US journalist whose mission in life seemed to be to get the Bolsheviks 'recognized' by the powers. It ran on the familiar lines. 'Of course no one – W.* least of all – objects to fair criticism, but R.† is impossible. He's a crank, you know – etc. etc. . . . .' The more I look over the past years the more I see how right you were – even tho' you used the anti-English lever to get the beginning of the US Navy started in '96.

You *must* go on in the position of a gadfly – for the hide that you have to deal with is thick, and complacent beyond belief. In season and out of season keep your folk up to the *facts* of the case. But the really important thing is, 'what is going to happen to the US if Europe fails in this War?' Germany's victory would mean Germany dominating the Eastern Hemisphere by land and sea. In which case where does the US with its present fleet and no army come in?

For once I agree with the advanced Germans (they have left the Pan-German school behind), who say that with England out of it, Germany holds the US in the hollow of her hand. I needn't point out to you that the Monroe doctrine would become a scrap of paper not worth tearing up. I can only lament that you are not at the head of affairs to explain this to your people and to get them to arm steadily, but at once, by land and by sea. Otherwise, if Europe fails, there will be no place left for freedom and the decency of things in any part of the earth.

Another reason that I wish you were in office is that I don't think you would sit and bite your nails at the White House while your accredited representative at St James's admits that he can't get any answer to his telegrams to the US Ambassador in Berlin. You might regard that as discourteous – if not as an insult. England is rather set and determined to see the thing through though it says nothing of its losses individually and collectively – and we are all hit in our degree. And now I'll bring my infliction to a close. We've got to the state now where Death and loss somehow don't bite any more – a sort of anaesthesia which is very curious – as far as one's own soul is concerned.[1]

Theodore Roosevelt had written articles on the subject of the war, and Kipling felt that he had not gone far enough.

My only criticism of your articles would be that they are a little too remote in tone for the actual facts of the case: but of course – much water, or shall we say much blood, has flowed under the bridges since they were written. The necessity for immediate military preparation is not insisted upon strongly enough. As I see it, the US, for existing Teutonic purposes, *is* practically English. That is to say she has much the same assets as Belgium had – a vociferous public opinion and large financial means. Neither of these assets

* President Wilson.
† Theodore Roosevelt.

much concerns the Teuton since he disregards the one and annexes the other. It all seems to boil down to one point – the Allies are shedding their blood (and the butcher's bill is a long one) for every ideal that the United States stands for by the mere fact of her Constitution, not to mention her literature, press, and daily life.

If the Allies fail, all those things (which one has been taught to believe are eternal verities) will be challenged, and challenged very soon by the Conqueror. If the US cannot bring sufficient force to repel the challenge she will have to conform to the Conqueror's ideals. Meantime, and this is my point, the US is *not* arming in order that she may possess that sufficient force. For that reason very little that she says now matters much, and whatever she may say later will matter less. The fact set out in the *Outlook* that her prestige never stood higher and that she has made $100,000,000 by profits on War – wheat alone, has no bearing on the situation. If she has not armies and fleets she will go under. I am sorry that there is a schoolmaster,* instead of a man at the head of the US today, because I know something of the limitations of the Schoolmaster's mind. As to what you say about atrocities we are in rather close touch with that arena. Also the country is full of Belgian refugees; women who have been raped, to my large content don't talk about it, but those who have lost children and relatives are very eloquent.

A stiffening note in subsequent articles by Theodore Roosevelt caused Kipling to write again on 4 December 1914:

Dear Roosevelt,

I'm afraid I've been a long time answering yours of the 4th November, but I have had to be away from home a good deal, among the camps of the new armies.

Your articles, to my mind, cannot be bettered. With your usual courage, you have stated aloud, in regard to the position of the United States, what everyone in Europe has been thinking since the War began. Obviously, it is not a thing that any foreigner could utter. I see from the cabled summary of your later articles that you outline the possibilities of the situation after the War is ended. So far as the United States are concerned, I think your forecast will come true.

The more life and treasure spent in winning this War, the less will the victors be disposed to listen to any neutral's suggestions when the time comes to deal with the loser. That is only natural, but in addition to this, the United States is on record as having made no protest against any action that Germany took – from the invasion of Belgium to the violation of the Hague Convention. By what logic, then, will the United States protest against any action taken by the Allies? That – to put it shortly – is the impasse into which Mr Wilson (bless you for your illuminating flash-light on his family history) has prayerfully led his people. I imagine that later they may demand explana-

* President Wilson.

tions of the 'great and good'. At present they do not quite understand what they are at. You, who know world politics, do. As Lowell says: 'Once to every man and nation comes the moment to decide.'

But you yourself have said it all. There's no gratitude in a democracy, or they might realize you have put them under the greatest debt of your career. Instead of which you will get simply cussed.

Things are not going so badly here. I am, as you know, a black and unbending pessimist, but even I am beginning to feel, after much consultation with the men at the front, that we are turning the corner. Equipment is drawing abreast of men. (As you know we have had to equip our Allies, rather as it was in the old Napoleonic days.)

The Artillery question is being settled, and much transport and troops have been shifted. Our garrisons are rearranged – from Hong Kong to Gib. – and the Colonial contingents are in place. At present we haven't more than a million men under training. (I've been going round looking at them for the last six weeks in their camps and huts. They are rather interesting, both in physique and intellect and zeal to learn.) I don't say all England is yet an armed camp because there are gaps where you can go for ten miles without seeing troops, but so far as my wanderings have led me there is no road where you can go twenty miles without running into them in blocks. The second million will be coming on as soon as we can get the accommodation for them, and they ought to be able to fill the wastage in the first million. But we prefer to have our men thoroughly equipped and trained before using them.

The game is not going badly at the front either. Joffre seems happy and our people are not kicking. The French and we are carrying the weight of about two million Germans. They have been sending up their younger men and boys lately on our front. This is valuable because these are prospective fathers, and they come up to the trenches with superb bravery. Then they are removed, and new corps are sent in who have not seen too many of their dead.

There are not many tactics or finesse on either side – the aviators block that – and so the game reduces itself to plain killing. Our losses are not light, but by the circumstances and training of the German armies the German losses are not less than three times ours – which is a reasonable proportion. But don't believe that the Germans will slack off. They are good for at least a million more losses on our front alone – besides what they can stand from the Russians. They ought not to begin to weaken till they have lost a flat million of dead – not counting sick and wounded. We have got our bigger artillery into shape on the Western front, and I believe are reaching them farther back than before.   ·

I don't know for sure what the Russians are costing them, but my information is that in the cold on that Eastern frontier a wounded man who has to lie out even one night before being picked up is quite dead.

I fancy it is going to be a much longer game than people in the United States think, and, of course, Germany will do everything in her power to make friction between us. I can trace the effects of her agents, just like the smooth smear of water above a torpedo, in the letters that I get from the other side. The latest dodge is the 'unparalleled efficiency' boom and the stupidity of backing the wrong horse in a war 'that can have only one end'. I expect later that trade questions and 'conditional contraband' will be played for all they are worth. And we must put up with that too. We are expected to do the world's fighting and to keep the world comfortable while we are doing it.

But has it ever struck you that if the game goes our way, the largest block of existing Germans may perhaps be the eight million within your Borders? And precisely because, to please this Contingent and to justify his hereditary temperament, Wilson did not protest against the invasion and absorption of Belgium, Wilson will not be able to save for them the sentimental satisfaction of having a Fatherland to look back upon from behind the safety of the United States frontier. It seems a high price to pay for 'domestic politics'.

Thank you for what you say about my boy. He was not seventeen till the 17th August, but he managed to get in by Sept. 6. He is in the Irish Guards. Suppose my only son dies, I for one, should not 'view with equanimity' Mr Wilson (however unswayed by martial prejudice) advising or recommending my country how to behave at the end of this War; and I am but one of an increasing number of fathers. As I have quoted: 'Once to every man and nation', and Lowell was no small prophet.

Believe me as always
Most sincerely,
Rudyard Kipling.

The correspondence takes us next to 5 August 1917, when Kipling began by referring to Theodore Roosevelt's son Kermit: 'The two of them look well though naturally Kermit's spirited attempt to boil his son and heir on board ship had given them rather a shock. As is always the case in such matters it was the child who took the accident to heart least.' He continued:

I was specially interested in what you told me about yourself: and for once in my life I was thoroughly in accord with Wilson's attitude. What his intentions and motives were don't matter, but in keeping you back he is, as I see it, doing the best thing in the interests of the USA. The present game of war is no show for a middle-aged man. It means collapse at the end of a few days (we've had bitter and expensive experience in this line). If you were held at the base you'd fret yourself to bits to get forward. If you went up you would go out, but with no corresponding advantage to your country. But as long as you are in the USA there is still the element of strength and drive for the world to rely upon in the days when (as will surely happen) your pacifists, doubters, and General Sliemers begin to bleat. Then your power and strength can save and steady and rally and keep your faint hearts up to the mark. This is a service inestimably beyond any other that you could render to mankind. So, as I said, I applaud the Great and Good Wilson – though I don't know what was in his mind.

In November 1917 he wrote: 'Looking back the three years I find I have lost nearly everyone that I ever knew, which gives one a kind of superfluous age and impotence. I hope you'll not have to go through that furnace.'

On 21 October 1918, Kipling wrote an extremely frank letter about the activities of President Wilson, and proceeds to an onslaught on the Papacy:

What you wrote me about Wilson was in my own mind – and to tell you the truth – had been there from the first. But naturally that wasn't a sentiment one would avow even in a whisper. None the less, a great many people share it. And now that the past month has gone over and our position is what it is, very many people see what his initial delay – and worse still his neglect to make any preparations in the two years and seven months before he moved – actually mean. This War is *damned* hard on liars. One sometimes wonders how much blood that man might have saved while he was so busy saving everybody's soul: And God and the Government alone know how much he is hampering us in regard to Japanese action in Siberia, and our own in Ireland!

As you are perfectly aware, Civilization's great enemy is the Papacy. Not the RC religion of course, but the secular political head, unaltered in essence once since the beginning. In Canada, in Australia, and above all in Ireland, every place there is allegiance paid to the Papacy, there is steady, unflinching, and unscrupulous opposition to all that may help to win the War. Obviously there must be, because the defeat of the Central Powers means ruin to the Papacy materially and morally. Austria and Spain are St Peter's last hopes. If one breaks, the other goes, and – a consideration that has been in Rome's mind for many years past – the Modernists among RCs will get a free hand.

The revolt against the Papacy – as distinguished from the tenets of the RC Church – is of course spreading, and inclining by reason of the Pope's attitude towards the moral issues of the War. These things are elementary – you knew them before I did. I only repeat them for my own satisfaction. And now, at the eleventh hour, we in England are constrained – in order to please an immensely ignorant intellectual – to consolidate and confirm the power of a hostile Papacy in Ireland.

For that is what Home Rule means. That is one aspect and only one of our present position. But whatever the price, we must pay it for the help of the USA. My grief is that the head of the country is a man unconnected by knowledge or experience with the facts of the world in which we live. All of which must be paid for in the lives of good men.

Kipling showed great perspicacity in the matter of Wilson's Fourteen Points, and wrote about them to Roosevelt in a manner that would have been fully endorsed by his friend Clemenceau.

On 7 November 1918:

The guts of Europe are sliding into our laps day by day but at the one moment when we Allies ought to have our hands free to deal with a hemisphere *in extremis* we are tied up by his idiotic Fourteen Points. The only word of truth the Huns have spoken since the War was when they called them 'Theses'. They open the door to every form of evasion and quibble from the Huns and their friends all over the world.

It's trying the Nations who have lost a million dead apiece rather high when at the eleventh hour they have to explain to the Hun, who has brought mankind within sight of starvation, that they – reserve to themselves the interpretation of the 'Freedom of the Seas' phrase. To put it bluntly the USA which has grown up and thriven for 142 years under the lee of the British Fleet would have gone with the rest of us into oblivion two years ago.

An ape looking down under the palm tree on which he sits is reasonable compared to – but I needn't tell you. Simultaneous as to indemnities. The 14 P.s. have no word about those. All earth, it seems, must bear the cost of the War that was forced upon it, or if begun would have ended in a few weeks if the US had entered with the rest after the *Lusitania* was sunk.

Roosevelt replied with vigour:

I am stronger than ever for a working agreement between the British Empire and the United States; indeed I am now content to call it an Alliance. But there are only two Englishmen with whom I have continued in the slightest personal sympathy on these matters, or whom I could ever care to see again – Arthur Lee and yourself. In France, on the other hand, there is at least one public servant, Clemenceau, to whom I am much more closely knit than before the War; and with whom I can work in the heartiest accord. As regards the English leaders, I doubt if I can overstate the amused indignation I have felt when I, and such men as those I mentioned above, have been fighting tooth and nail to prevent Wilson from giving aid and comfort to Germany, and then have heard the English politicians and writers come out with enthusiastic praise and support of what Wilson was doing *against them*, and thereby so completely take away our weapons that it was only with the utmost caution that I have ventured to appeal for us to stand by England at all.

The English leaders of opinion have, with inconceivable folly, built up the utterly baseless myth that Wilson by much patience got a reluctant people to go to war. That is a simple lie; he did all he could to keep down the rising popular demand for war, and finally was swept off his legs by it, and hurried backwards into the conflict. For example, whenever we started a strong movement to denounce the neutrality doctrine, Bryce or Edward Grey, or Asquith, would come out with an impassioned support of Wilson's altruism, which would be quoted against us as showing that we were unkind and indeed wicked in saying that Wilson's neutrality was merely a bid for the pro-German vote.

Of course Wilson has not a vein of the idealist or the altruist in his whole make-up; he is simply a doctrinaire, which is something entirely different.

At the beginning of October he started a private negotiation with Germany on the basis of his fourteen points of peace, all of which Germany eagerly accepted; his theory was that he could still fool our people with fine phrases, and get them to accept a negotiated peace – a peace without victory – with the United States sitting at the peace table, not as one of the Allies, but as an umpire between the Allies and the Central Powers. However, by this time our people had thoroughly waked to the general undesirability of the Hun on this planet, and to the fact that we intended to put through the War beside our Allies, whether or not Wilson called them merely 'Associates'. I never saw a stronger protest than followed, and Wilson promptly turned a somersault and double-crossed the Huns instead of the Allies.

For once Kipling's strongly held dogmas were challenged by one holding his own views, and speaking with an equal authority. Kipling had written of America living for 142 years under the protection of the British Fleet. Roosevelt replied:

November 30th, 1918.
But now, friend, do not overstate your case. It is strong, and it needs no overstatement. You say that 'the United States existed for 142 years under the protection of the British Navy'. As a matter of fact for the first ninety years the British Navy, when, as was ordinarily the case, the British Government was more or less hostile to us, was our greatest danger. I am not condemning Great Britain. In those good old days the policies of the United States and Great Britain toward one another, and toward much of the outside world, were sufficiently alike to give a touch of humour to the virtuous horror expressed by each at the kind of conduct of the other which most closely resembled its own.

Roosevelt considered that Kipling's attitude towards America during the war had been exactly correct. He had never attacked her, which would have been foolish, but he had never been fulsome. He was incensed that Asquith, Grey, Bryce and Lansdowne, even Lloyd George and Balfour, should praise Wilson for one of the very attitudes which he summarized in his Fourteen Points, thus striking the weapons from Roosevelt's hands when he was attacking these attitudes:

The result of this ocean of praise for Wilson was that during the first nine months of the War he felt absolutely secure that he could do anything, and accordingly, as regards the War itself, he did almost nothing. Instead he indulged in rhetorical fireworks, and your leaders went into hysterics of applause over all of them, and praised him as a great idealist – a term to which he is about as entitled as Machiavelli was.

Let us quote one more letter to show how clear-minded Kipling was in the general confusion of opinion that followed the war about the manner of enemy we had faced and might face again. It was written in February 1919:

As you say, the fighting seems to be over, but the War is in full blast between a rather wearied Humanity and a Devil whose only hope now is to persuade people he is not so black as he was painted. I wish, later on, it might be possible for the League to send over some women-authors to look at the devastated districts of France and Belgium, and see what a thorough and conscientious Power for Evil we are up against. It would be of service.

Reading this correspondence in the light of later knowledge it is clear that Kipling was right. The record and character of President Wilson, and his tortuous negotiations through Colonel House, which afterwards came to light, fully justify the contemporary opinions that Kipling formed of him. Wilson was proceeding according to the disastrous perfectionist theory that a fundamental change had come over human nature, that he 'could reach the people over the heads of their rulers'. This theory was accepted by many eminent and able men, including J. M. Keynes.[2] Kipling knew that it was false. He knew that Wilson was merely sowing the dragon's teeth, and preferred to believe in the Old Adam. His views were fully shared by Clemenceau, as the aged Tiger sat impotently observing bastion after bastion being removed from twice-violated France.

CHAPTER XIX

THE POST-WAR YEARS

KIPLING emerged from the war with four preoccupations in mind – the continuance of his work, Ireland, India and Germany. The death of his son had drained him of personal emotion, and he turned to his political bugbears with corresponding alacrity. 'Rud and I feel as never before what it means now the War is over to face a world to be remade without a son.'[1] But he was not the same man as before, and his secretary, Dorothy Ponton, noticed certain ominous signs of deterioration – his step had lost its buoyancy, and he had now abandoned any pretence or conducting the practical side of his life, which was surrendered entirely to Carrie. But Kipling's segregation from the world at this time has been exaggerated, and although he preferred a small circle of neighbours at 'Bateman's', there were many visitors from outside.

On the Irish question Kipling associated himself completely with the policy of the *Morning Post*, continuing to send its editor, his old friend Gwynne, peremptory directives. As he turned more and more to the extreme Right in politics, Gwynne was indeed his staunch ally, supported by Lady Bathurst, proprietor of the *Morning Post* – two sad Rosinantes on this quixotic battlefield. But Kipling was in no doubt whatever as to his attitude. Murder must be taken by the throat, and the later apparent *volte-face* of the Irish Treaty, which he regarded as a cowardly and treacherous instrument, increased his contempt for politicians. This was further envenomed by his hatred of Ireland, and it is perhaps notable that the only Irish characters in his work whom he admired, such as Mulvaney, are those who were content to accept British control and contribute loyally to the consolidation of the British position. For the Irish who wished to break the British chain he had a far more critical appraisal: 'Ireland's attitude has been another eye-opener to the Catholics in the USA who at last are seeing that poor, tortured persecuted land at close quarters and are realizing what a dam' pernicious little bitch of a country she is and always has been.'[2]

In the meantime he sought relief from private sorrow and public anxiety in his work for the Imperial War Graves Commission. On 19 November 1918 he met the Prince of Wales, found him 'keen about it all', and successfully proposed the text for all altars in the cemeteries. When he declined the Order of Merit in 1921, he asked instead if the King would visit the graves. This invitation was to lead to the King's pilgrimage, and Kipling wrote the King's speech, devoting hours of anxious thought to it. His relations with his colleagues were excellent throughout, and he showed himself to be admirable on the side of the work he hated most – that of compromise. His developing adoration of the French was strongly reciprocated, and he would patiently continue to sign autographs all day in France, with no trace of the angry impatience he showed in England or America. At the Neuve Chapelle Memorial, Foch, who had taken little notice of anyone else, threw open his arms and cried: 'Oh! Keepling!' His poem 'France' had an electric effect upon that country, and even influenced the course of international relations:

> Furious in luxury, merciless in toil,
> Terrible with strength that draws from her tireless soil;
> Strictest judge of her own worth, gentlest of man's mind,
> First to follow Truth and last to leave old Truths behind –
> France, beloved of every soul that loves its fellow kind!

Sir Fabian Ware, the chief officer, related that, above all, Kipling loved the Imperial side of his work on the Commission on which the whole Empire was represented: 'He was a man of the strongest political prejudice, and would never meet my more radical friends such as Shaw, who always wanted to meet Kipling. His only excuse was that he was always preoccupied with foreign dangers, loathed those who ignored them, and happened to be right. He loved people who shared his opinions absolutely, such as Gwynne and Lady Bathurst. Everything was either black or white. There were no other colours.'[3]

The conclusion of the Armistice had not distracted Kipling's vigilant attention from the German problem. He was never one of those who were mesmerized by the brilliant 'organization of sympathy'. He realized with perfect clarity that the 1914 War, appalling in casualties as it had been, was only a stepping-stone on the road to Teutonic advancement. The Armistice negotiations and Germany's policy after it were to his realistic mind merely tactical preparations: '*Dec. 21. 1918.* The Huns are fighting tooth and nail now to drive in as many small points of friction and irritation as they can. So as to get a good run on before we begin to settle the peace terms. Go for the Huns' work in the past. Our Government has always carefully hidden what their efforts have been in England.'[4]

Kipling's work in 1918 was similar to that of 1917 in quantity, covering a fairly wide field. He spent much time on his Irish Guards history, produced a shilling volume of selected verse, and wrote a number of assorted verses including 'The Lathes', which dealt with the munition workers. He attended the necessary meetings of the Rhodes Trust, but refused office in connection with Service propaganda, although he agreed to help. His Irish Guards song was set to music by Edward German, and a verse over his forged signature appeared in *The Times*, which failed to discover the originator. Armistice Day brought unhappy memories of John, and Caroline concluded what appears to have been another, though minor, war by giving notice to her secretary on the last day of the year.

The health of both Kipling and Caroline remained bad, and they made a somewhat depressing visit to Bath in February 1919, where they were visited by a Mr Brooking from Warrington, with proposals to start a Kipling Society on a large scale, a project which filled Rudyard with apprehension and annoyance. On 10 April *The Years Between* was published and on the twenty-second Kipling wrote to Doubleday:

There is no sense in making a League of Nations if you don't put down an adequate force of police to watch the chief offender, and up to the present the USA don't seem inclined to help police the Hun border, and the Hun is the last tiger in the world with whom paper safeguards are effective. Every Hun and Bolshevik agency all over the world are now doing their damndest to divide civilization against itself, and, since not more than 10% of 'civilized' mankind trouble to do their own thinking, they are meeting with a certain measure of success.

I see the reviews of *The Years Between* in the English papers take this line sometimes, or lament (in the face of a cannibalistic Russia and India aflame), that there is no 'enlargement' or development of my 'gospel'. Naturally there ain't. If a man sticks to the second line of the first chapter of the Multiplication Table – 'Twice two are four' – he isn't likely to develop the proposition that they make five or three. If you care to look up some of my old Indian work in the old tales – *The Head of the District*, *One View of the Question*, and so forth, you'll see that what I wrote then covers what is happening in India today, just the same as the 'Walking Delegate' covers what is happening with your (and our) Labour movement.[5]

In June Kipling was distressed by trouble with his eyes, caused by the strain of reading galley proofs, and his letters again become angry and intolerant. Of Sir Alfred Mond, he wrote on 19 June to his Aunt Louisa:

Allah, for his own purpose, has created a pig called Mond Head of the Public Works, an 'Ebrew whose mere voice and presence is enough to put up the back of any and every committee that he presides over. Consequently, when Mond is trying to get anything done, or passed on a parliamentary committee he – just doesn't. That's all ... well the story as I got it, was of a particularly dead deadlock between Mond and one of his committee over some breach of Treasury accounts. 'And then,' said my informant, 'we send for Baldwin if we can get him.' It appears that Stan turns up in response to an SOS signal, smiles upon the assembly, explains the situation in that wonderful voice of his, and smooths the whole show out, on his personal popularity.[6]

Kipling's spirits were low and he carried out his work listlessly with automatically acquired skill: 'I'm busy as the Devil in a gale of wind at all sorts of jobs that don't seem to matter much. Nothing matters much really when one has lost one's only son. It wipes the meaning out of things. However the war is officially over which means that it has only gone underground where it is waged more ferociously than before.'[7]

In September Kipling decided to drop his work for a while, and went to Scotland to a beautiful place half-way down 'lone Glenart-ney's hazel shade', under the massif of the deer-forest. The water was low and clear, so that his fishing did not prosper, but he was content to look at the grouse, blackgame, pheasants and partridges without shooting them. Glenartney Forest was the name of this haven, with naked slopes running up 2500 feet, glens, corries, and rifts in the mountain side, burns with waterfalls and caves, and sweeps of heather – a queer country full of remnants and shielings and old dead roads and bracken. The air, he found, 'wiped the years off my back', but it failed to soften the asperity of his correspondence, and back at 'Bate-man's' in October we find him writing to Gwynne: 'The ideas and outlook are absolutely in line with the work which the "International Jew" at his worst has accomplished, and is accomplishing. The headlines about "Masonry" have been put in probably by an RC through whose hands the copy has gone; but the inspiration of it all must be looked for, I think, in Hunland, twenty to twenty-five years ago.'

In February 1920 Kipling was driven by some obscure impulse to take Caroline on a sentimental journey to the 'House of Desolation' at Southsea. It was all exactly as he had left it – the little passage crook-ing an elbow to the left, the greenhouse where the primulas had grown, and the steep stairs descending to the damp playroom below ground level. On the pillars in front were still engraved the ominous words 'Lorne Lodge'. Neither the passage of years nor world fame sufficed to efface the revulsion with which this detested place had inspired him: 'He talks of it all with horror,'[8] said Caroline. Indeed it seems that while the details of his mishandling had grown dim and blurred, the general recollection of his sufferings had been nourished and sustained by years of resentful meditation.

It was in this year in May that he went to London to see John's Memorial cast in bronze, dismissed it as a failure, and ordered it to be undertaken again: it was finished in June, and passed as 'most satisfactory'. His son's death preyed more and more upon his mind, and he began to link it up with industrial disturbance. To C. R. L. Fletcher the historian he wrote: 'I don't think you said enough about the systematic profiteering on organized Labour's part both in flesh and in money. Remember the big Union's first contribution to our distress was the pronouncement that conscription would mean revolution. For this cause my boy died at eighteen instead of at between nineteen and twenty, as he ought. I am glad to see you call Caillaux a traitor.'[9]

In the autumn of 1920 he and Caroline left on a journey to France to visit the ground over which the Irish Guards had fought. They arrived at the Chalk Pit Wood at the hour of day John fell, and passed by it at the hour he left the wood for the Red House. Then to Popperinghe and Arras – the greatest desolation of all, which they left 'after Rud had taken a photo for the old woman of Durham we met last night, going miles out of our way to do so'. This kindly incident, where Kipling photographed a son's grave for the benefit of a bereaved mother, showed that he took more than a formal interest in his work for the Graves Commission. And after this distressing pilgrimage, which had deeply moved them both, Caroline entered prosaically in her diary: 'The gardener gives notice – no reason assigned.'

Kipling felt nothing but depression as he surveyed the political scene. Deeply distrusting the future of India, he disposed of all his Indian securities. We have an interesting glimpse of how Kipling appeared at this time from a brilliant young intellectual of liberal bent, who as Sir Maurice Bowra was to become one of the most renowned of Oxford figures. Bowra was introduced to him by Victor Cazalet in the summer of 1921:

I was well acquainted with his books and full of curiosity about him. He had the famous face, so often and so truthfully depicted by Max Beerbohm, with the bushy eyebrows, the cleft chin, the receding forehead, the bristling, provocative moustache. But behind the thick spectacles was a pair of bright blue eyes, and his manner was unexpectedly friendly. He did not look at all well, and ate and drank very little. . . .

When I met him, Kipling's mind was still fixed on the war. He had lost his only son in it, and he may have had bitter regrets at using his influence with Lord Roberts to send a boy of seventeen, whose eyesight was as bad as his own, into the Irish Guards to be killed in the insane massacre at Loos. Most of the young people present had been in the war, and had no desire to talk about it, and Victor had lost a much loved brother in it. But Kipling brought up the subject and we had to respond. In retrospect I can see that at this time he had begun to shape in his mind some of the later, remarkable stories about the war and its effect on those who took part in it.

Kipling did not express any general views about the war and would probably have thought it wrong to criticize the generals, though he let off a few nasty cracks at Lloyd George. But he knew about the topography of the battlefields and was, as one might expect, full of curiosity about weapons. He had at his finger-tips a number of technical words, which he seemed to enjoy just because they were technical. . . . When the subject was exhausted, he turned to politics, in which he seemed to dislike everyone and to think all British policies wrong, and his language became coarser and cruder. He still hankered for some severe punishment for the Germans, though he did not specify what it should be or how it should be exacted. But what particularly exasperated him was Zionism. He called the Jews 'Yids', and had nothing too bad to say about Arthur Balfour, who had been the successful advocate of a national home for the Jews in Palestine. Kipling had the traditional English taste for Arabs, about whom he knew very little, but whom he may have liked on principle, because they were Muslims like some of the best troops in the Indian Army. He gave the impression that his views were formed less on reason than on rather hysterical emotions. Despite his courtesy, there was a note of violence in what he said, and I felt that fundamentally he was less sure of his opinions than he liked us to believe, and that his over-emphasis on certain matters was necessary to counter his chameleonic adaptability.[10]

On his next visit to France, in November 1921, Kipling received doctorates from the Universities of Paris and Strasbourg, and was greeted with rapture by the French as a national hero. They went to Hyères too, where his contentment was complete. At peace with the world, Kipling sat in a garden on a hot day, languidly watching a Camberwell Beauty fluttering round rock-cistus bushes bursting into white and rose, and a brimstone butterfly with an orange splash on its wings. His senses responded to the plant life round him, and he drew deep breaths of the scent of borage, myrtle, wild mignonette and asphodel. He drove through woods of cork oak, and collected delicate pink shells on the beach. His hotel was a mid-Victorian survival, with plain nourishing food – 'same as one gets in England y'know – and earnest committees to run everything. But the air, the flowers, the scent of hot pinewoods, the butterflies, the blue sea, and the island cannot be spoiled by the English.'

He ended his holiday at Cannes, where the weather broke tumultuously. There were thunderstorms in the mountains and then the hot angry wind blew from Corsica, threshing and bending double the date-palms on the Croisette, and a dull pewter sea foamed along the shore. He wrote exultantly, 'When the sun comes again all nature will take another leap forward into summer, and there will be a vast hatch-out of butterflies.'[11]

He met Bonar Law, who had come to rest on the Riviera under doctor's orders. Kipling observed with fascination how few resources in himself the stranded politician possessed. 'Twenty years of political life leaves a man with fewer resources . . . than I should have conceived possible . . . he plays one set of tennis per diem, and bridge when and where he can. Outside of that nothing except browsing over papers.' Bonar Law was frank about the matter. He told Kipling that a lifetime in politics killed a man for external interests. Kipling and Bonar Law had several political conversations, and although Kipling respected him he felt impelled to remark: 'It's curious to note how even a straight and good politician like B.L. inevitably gets to concern himself more in the means than in the ends of things. His talk is always of the *personalities* concerned in his game and not in his convictions.'[12]

Back in England Kipling turned again to work and politics. He was disappointed at a cinema version by Pathé of *Without Benefit of Clergy* which he felt missed all the essential points of his story. He continued to regard Germany's activities with the utmost suspicion:

I am rather interested in German reparations and the views of McKenna on the subject. The point that occurs to me is that the Hun was above all things methodical and far seeing; that he provided for every conceivable trouble ahead, as far as his mentality went. We know now that it went very far, and some of us begin to know that it is an open question whether we won the War. Now it is impossible that among his archives there should not exist his own *plans for what was to be done to the rest of the world in the way of making them pay up after he had won the War*. I am sure it would have been a well thought-out scheme, devised so as in no way to injure his own commercial development, while at the same time, holding the rest of the world in decent and industrious subordination. Where is that scheme that we may learn from it? Incidentally it may be that the actual means of keeping annexed or enslaved populations quiet while they worked for the Hun will be found to have been based on the use of poison-gas. I have no warranty for the last statement except what the past has taught one about the workings of the Hun mind.* [13]

He brooded angrily over Ireland: 'Did our land ever make so flagrant a deal with so flagrant a type of assassin?'[14] The word 'die-hard' had become current to describe those who held the views of Kipling, the *Morning Post*, and the Duke of Northumberland. It riled Kipling, and he suggested to Gwynne: 'Isn't "Kill-soft" the antithesis of "Die-hard"? Or would you prefer "Betrayhard" or "Betrayard"? There ought to be a name to throw back at 'em.' The 'outrage' of the Irish Treaty had now become an obsession. Remote as he was from the arena of battle, in the dust of which much prejudice might have been shed and many practical lessons learned, the 'Surrender' festered in his mind with morose persistence. It was now paramount in his wide repertoire of political grievances, the supreme Judas kiss. On 7 December 1921 Caroline wrote in her diary: 'Rud more depressed over the terms of South Ireland than he ever was during the War.'

December 1921 found him writing to Lady Bathurst, congratulating her on the *Morning Post*'s policy of strong criticism of the Government in a letter which clearly shows his political views at this time:

Bateman's.
13 December, 1921.

Dear Lady Bathurst,

I've been meaning to write to you for some time, and yesterday's splendidly dignified leader on 'Lost Causes' in the *Morning Post* makes me do it now.

I wonder if you realize what your paper has meant this year to the great multitude of bewildered and sickened people who have been unable to find any acknowledgment whatever of the plain laws of right and wrong in the Government-kept or controlled Press, and who have watched the whole ghastly business of organized betrayal (what an incompetent amateur Judas was, when you come to think of it!) going forward without one word of protest except from the *Morning Post*?

And of course it isn't only the Loyalist cause that is betrayed – it is every notion of right and fit and possible Government throughout the Empire. One can see that already in India where Allahabad, encouraged by the profitable example of 'The Free State of Ireland', is setting the note for Calcutta and Benares, so that the whole of India is set for organized crime and assassination which can now claim to be dealt with by Treaty, as a 'Nation'. In cold truth the Government have created a 'Free State of Evil' wherever Evil exists,

* Hitler referred to this possibility in *Mein Kampf*.

or tries to exist, in the world. And the *Morning Post* is the only paper that has said so and fought it and pointed out the consequences which everyone knows in his heart must inevitably follow.

There are an infinitely greater number of people than our self-centred Thieves' Kitchen can realize, who are thanking you from the bottom of their hearts for all that you and your influence have done and saved for the elementary decencies of life and truth. That is a debt which I feel sure will be admitted even in your life-time, and by the very people who are now bleating about 'the new era' etc.

I don't know what the next move of the Government may be but I expect it will be putting all sorts of pressure on every one to make them, if not commit themselves to blessing the present crime,* at least keep quiet about it. Then they can say later (as Haldane did about our unpreparedness in the War) that their action was taken at the behest of the Democracy.[15]

To Kipling's mind the problems of India and Ireland were perfectly simple, and exactly similar. Both countries were subject races who required firm government for the benefit of the governed, and he regarded any extension of self-government to either of them with horror. He seemed incapable of understanding that the two problems were in fact somewhat different – on the one side a vast heterogeneous sub-continent of warring creeds held together by British administration; on the other, a small country with a dark record of tragic misunderstanding with England, mature and passionately nationalistic, ready for self-government, and led by resolute men who were prepared to die and murder for their beliefs.

On 19 December 1921 he wrote again to Lady Bathurst:

I've been seeing Admiral Hall,† and he told me how MPs sidled up to him at the Division on the 'Surrender' and said: 'You know on which side our sympathies really lie. If we were free ... etc. etc.' It made me rather sick. Now, the point that occurs to me is whether there is any way of helping the Loyalists who want to get away from the wrath to come. I don't expect the murder-gang will let them leave Ireland if they can help it: but don't you think the public ought to be told, somehow, of the situation? In some ways it is almost as bad as the Russians and morally, of course, the shame to us is much the greater. Would the situation justify the starting of an Irish Refugee Fund? or would any English attempt to help lead to more outrages on the Loyalists? They are utterly unprotected: and after the frank admissions of almost everyone of the Ministry that England is bankrupt and can no longer protect life and property, there is no earthly reason why the Dail‡

* The Irish Treaty.
† Director of Naval Intelligence, and later a Member of Parliament.
‡ The Dail was the Parliament in the newly-created Irish Free State.

should not chuck 'the Treaty' and start in as what it is, a hostile power on our flank, amenable to no form of agreement or compromise.[16]

Kipling was not the only person whose temper was becoming exacerbated. On a visit to Spain in March 1922 Caroline wrote petulantly in her diary: 'Embark on ss *Ormuz*, Orient Line, for Gibraltar, 22. Arrive Algeciras, 23. To bed where I am likely to stop for some time. I am worn out and can't do these continual journeys doing all the work, their arranging, plus the usual work, but can't get Rud to realize it.' But her life continued to be restless and she accompanied Kipling to France in May 1922 on the King's pilgrimage to the War Graves. Kipling felt himself useful as a link between France, England and the Empire, and he was gratified by the praise given to the King's speech, and satisfied with his verses 'The King's Pilgrimage'. Rudyard and Carrie were already on a tour of the battlefields when they were asked to meet the King at Vlamertingue near Ypres. Kipling changed into official clothes in a peasant's cottage, and waited in bitter cold in the shelter of a wall for the King's arrival with Field-Marshal Haig, whose strategy, some thought, had done much to populate the graveyards. The King delivered the words Rudyard had composed for him in resonant tones and with splendid dignity – words noble but destined to be ignored: 'In the course of my pilgrimage I have many times asked myself whether there can be any more potent advocates of peace upon earth than this massed multitude of witnesses to the desolation of war.'

On 11 September 1922 occurred an incident which again roused Kipling's hatred for reporters and interviews. Mrs Clare Sheridan visited the Kiplings, whom she had known as a child. She was the daughter of their neighbours, the Frewens, and a cousin of Winston Churchill, and she had already made a name for herself as a sculptress. She presumably did not mention that she was on a commissioned tour for the *New York Evening World*, a paper holding intensely anti-British views. Ignorant of this fact, it is almost certain that Kipling spoke more freely on the subject of the USA than he would have done outside the family circle, and Mrs Sheridan composed her 'interview' from what she could remember of this general conversation, in which Kipling had probably spoken bitterly of American isolationism and the lamentable withdrawal by President Harding from Europe. It began, according to Clare Sheridan, on the lawn of 'Bateman's' where she asked Kipling what he had meant by the last verse of 'The King's Pilgrimage':

... There can no knowledge reach their grave
To make them grudge their death,
Save only if they understood
That after all was done,
We they redeemed denied their blood
And mocked the gains it won.

Without wholly accepting Thurston Hopkins's version of this unfortunate matter,[17] it is factually true that an 'interview' appeared in the *World* giving Kipling's views that the USA had entered the war so many years, days and hours too late – that they had cornered all the British gold – but that the British had saved their souls. The 'interview' produced a violent impact on both sides of the Atlantic, and Kipling denied that he had given an interview to Mrs Sheridan or said any of the things that were attributed to him. Caroline's version of the matter reads: 'Rud concerned to save the position as much as possible, for after all, they, the Frewens, are old friends and she came to Bateman's first as a child herself – and to see as little capital as possible is made out of it for anti-British propaganda for the papers. Never was hospitality so basely returned.'[18]

Kipling had been in poor health during the latter part of 1922, suffering from abdominal pains for which the doctors could find no cause. In the autumn, soon after his cousin Stanley Baldwin became Prime Minister, the pains became more severe and in November he underwent an operation. He was able to return to 'Bateman's' for Christmas but remained 'very low and depressed' until a sea-voyage with Carrie to the Riviera in the spring. With sunshine and change of scene his health improved and he began to write again.

The most important event for him in 1923 was the publication of his *History of the Irish Guards in the Great War*. He also delivered a speech at the Royal College of Surgeons, prepared the King's speech on Italy, and finished *The Janeites*, begun in 1922. He wrote *The Prophet and the Country*, *A Friend of the Family*, *London Stone*, and began that strange and macabre story *A Madonna of the Trenches*, which he had had 'long in his mind'. He began work on a brilliant, even stranger, fantasy, *The Wish House*, at the beginning of 1924, with its recurrent themes of cancer, agony and death. In October 1923 he was elected Lord Rector of St Andrew's University, and seized the opportunity of expounding his philosophy of life to the students in the spirit of 'If', a message which was ill received by the large section of the public which was now blind to his warnings and sick of his nagging. We shall examine in a later chapter the relation of Kipling's health to the dark side of his creative work. Here we may quote a significant passage from Caroline's diary: 'Rud at his new story. Rud quite hopeless with depression. Nerves and Nerves (story – *The Wish House*). Rud wretched. He worked on his *Wish House* corrections.'

On 23 May Elsie announced that she wished to marry Captain George Bambridge, a brother officer of John Kipling in the Irish Guards. Neither Rudyard nor Caroline was enthusiastic. 'We don't like the idea of losing her, and I am appalled at the change it will make,' wrote Caroline, and Kipling was seized with a strange jealousy of the man who was taking his only remaining child from him. The marriage took place on 22 October 1924, but Caroline was never able to reconcile herself to it, and could not refrain from making constant, dangerous and uncalled-for interferences in her daughter's married life, which were strongly resented, while Elsie's departure threw the Kiplings entirely upon each other.

1925 was a flat and uneventful year. During the week the house was empty and the clatter of youth had gone – two of his children dead, the other departed. The absence of children had darkened his life, and he wrote to Lady Bathurst after a visit to her house: 'It has been for us both one of the *very nicest* of our so many visits to you. I think that was because of the children being together and the feeling of "home" over them all. (I wonder if people with grandchildren realize how lucky they are!) It did Mrs Kipling all the good in the world for that reason.'[19]

Kipling remained restless and unsatisfied. He and Caroline made a Continental tour till 20 April, and in June he was down at Eton reading his work aloud to twenty-eight 'Lower School Imps' at the request of the Master, A. B. Ramsay.[20] He refused Lady Milner's request to write the Life of Lord Milner, and on 15 June resigned from the Rhodes Trust. The appointment as Secretary had been given to Philip Kerr (later Lord Lothian) and Kipling alone had brought objections against him, greatly mistrusting the appointment,[21] which, he felt, since Kerr was one of the detested 'Liberals' and an internationalist as well, opened the Trust to grave misrepresentations. Kipling's distaste for compromise or evasion made it impossible for him to pretend that he had resigned from ill-health or from pressure of work, when neither was true, and on 9 July his resignation was announced, and its reason became obvious.

He continued his triumphant career as a 'great man', receiving the freedom of the City of London on 3 July. Shortly afterwards Caroline noted: 'Brander Matthews tells us that Villars Stanford told him he was talking to Lord Tennyson before his death, and Lord T. speculating on his successor in the Laureateship, said that "young Kipling has more of it in him than any of the others". Interesting when one considers the then age of Rud.'[22]

The Kiplings were now living in a too close and unrelieved proximity in a house suddenly depressing without the noise of children. A heavy and joyless routine had settled upon it, and visitors were sometimes struck by the dead atmosphere of gloom surrounding the house in the hollow. A hint of this creeping depression is discernible in Caroline's last entry in her diary for 1925: '*December 31*. George and Elsie leave about noon. Her last visit before she goes to Madrid.* Rud cheered up by her visit and not too depressed by her departure. Rud sits these last few days a little in a chair. So ends the year. A very sad year for me with nothing ahead for the other years, but the job of living.'

---

* Captain Bambridge was taking up the post of Honorary Attaché at the British Embassy, Madrid. He had been there before their marriage, when he had transferred for a year in the same capacity to Brussels. Later they went to Paris.

CHAPTER XX

1926-1930

EVERY spare moment from Kipling's literary routine and frequent bouts of pain and illness was now devoted to politics. He kindled quickly to patronizing transatlantic comment – sat listening in silent fury to the smooth flow of exposition from the wife of Colonel Edward House, who opened the conversation at a luncheon party with the tactful inquiry whether he did not think that the present state of Ireland was a great improvement on the past. 'It takes summat to surprise me these days, but I own I was a little jerked ... she was more completely full of self and national esteem than anyone I had met in a long time.'[1] On 10 April 1926 he wrote in mock anger to Gwynne about the attempted assassination of Mussolini, in a passage which is the first of those in which he records his approval of the forceful methods of the Italian dictator, coupled with further contemptuous references to Ireland.

Dear Old Man,
   I was simply furious when I saw you allude to Lavinia Gibson* as a 'British subject'. It never struck me that Free Staters came under any other head than that of outbreaks of foot and mouth. These things depress me, but it is, all the same, a tremendous lift (in foreign parts) for Mussolini. I am only afraid that the woman might have injured his eyesight, as the shot was so near. I have never left England any year that I can recall since the War without being held up by some sort of Bolshevism. And yet Mussolini rides the storm quite serenely.[2]

   On 1 May 1926 he wrote to Lionel Curtis: 'You'll find Italy *very* interesting: and I wish you could come across Mussolini. What he has saved in strikes alone, in his land, is worth all the money. Do try to get at him.'
   Kipling combined at this time an incongruous zeal for the emergent Fascist Italy, under 'a strong man ruling alone', with a vigilant mis-

* An Irishwoman who had made an attempt on Mussolini's life.

trust of a soon-to-emerge Fascist Germany. He observed with sympathy the consuming interest and anxiety with which France was in 1926 watching the General Strike. He felt a private doubt as to whether the Government realized how vitally important it was that the Strike's collapse should be recognized as an accepted victory for civilization. 'I see our accursed priests (who can no more keep out of the spotlight than actors) are loose already; and there will be the old dope about "leaving no bitter memories" etc.' He believed that the 'hardest job would come over the settlement, when our tendency would be to forget our friends in our zeal to forgive our enemies, and our fear of depriving the Unions of any of their hard won privileges'.

And yet, the abolition of picketing, and the secret ballot before striking, are our first and most elemental needs, if the country is to be kept going. There will be the usual assertion: 'Oh, they have had their lesson and they won't do it again', and the intellectuals and the Godly will do their utmost to Versailles the Settlement. The ruin done to the country will be lightly brushed aside as a thing for the majority to bear and pay for uncomplainingly, while the face of the minority is saved. It is our one interest to use this opportunity so that our big industries can be started up again on a basis of security and confidence, working with the genuine Trade Unions on business lines. That way, we can build on the backs of these Revolutionaries double measure of the confidence they were out to destroy.[3]

Kipling now regarded his cousin Stanley Baldwin as a despicable Prime Minister. He had been disgusted by the readiness with which Baldwin had speeded the emancipation of India and Ireland, which had caused him to move, if possible, further to the right in politics, and to mutter bitterly: 'Stanley is a Socialist at heart.' But with warm memories of boyhood together he did not suddenly abandon this friendship as he did others on the grounds of political or moral delinquency. He and Carrie stayed often with the Baldwins at their house 'Astley' in Worcestershire and were equally welcome at the Prime Minister's official country residence 'Chequers'. His amicable relationship with Beaverbrook, however, was abruptly ended. Naively bemused by the true nature of Lord Beaverbrook's ambitions, Kipling had inquired directly what they were. 'Power without responsibility,' Beaverbrook had incautiously replied, and Kipling's devastating answer: 'I see, the prerogative of the harlot throughout the ages,' had been the death knell of their long friendship.*

---

* This phrase was later borrowed by Stanley Baldwin to use against Rothermere and Beaverbrook in the Westminster Election of 1931.

Kipling continued to take a keen interest in the technical side of journalism, which he linked in a nostalgic manner with his early days on the *Civil and Military*, writing to Gwynne on the subject of the 'lay-out' of a newspaper:

Dear Old Man,

Yes. Bates* is about as white as they make 'em, and – what a head! Thanks for the pulls. I've looked 'em over carefully. Thinking it all out, it occurs to me that the likes of you and me, who were bred among the presses, attach too much importance to, and credit our public with too much knowledge of, typography and the 'looks' of a page. I believe the secret of attraction lies more in the headlines than the body of the stuff.

He still regarded Westward Ho! with affection, and when acknowledging the receipt of Dunsterville's book on the subject, returned yet again to the question of the school's freedom from immorality:

No we were not like other schools. But don't you think you might bring out the amazing 'cleanness' of the Coll. as compared to other seats of learning, which for ages have been full of accepted beastliness. I can't recall anything in my time that in any way approached the scandals that other schools take as a matter of course. Can you? Bullying there was, as you and I know well, but nothing worse.[4]

In 1927 he fulfilled a lifelong ambition by making a journey to Brazil, arriving in Rio on 13 February, under the impression that he would do no work on the trip, encountering instead unremitting labour for five weeks in a tropical climate, and finding some difficulty in avoiding the hospitality of the Brazilian Government. On 5 October he went to France, where the Secretary of State for India, Lord Birkenhead, unveiled the War Memorial at Neuve Chapelle to the Indian dead, delivering a speech which Kipling described to Lord Lloyd as the finest funeral oration since Gettysburg.[5] Afterwards, at a luncheon attended by many French and English officers, including Foch, Kipling made a short and moving speech about the Indian soldiers fighting for England, and crossing a sea to do so which many of them believed to be peopled by malignant gods.

In the same year the Kipling Society was founded. Two years prior to foundation the first Secretary-to-be had written to Rudyard: 'While I hope that your shadow may not grow less for many, many years I have thought it advisable to be prepared for such an event by drafting some notes on a matter that I put before you last year. Yours sincerely, J. H. C. Brooking.'

* Sir Percy Bates, Chairman of the Cunard White Star Line.

Kipling's reactions to this proposal were immediate, and characteristic: 'As to the proposed Society it's a thing which, of course, I can't stop, but as far as my own feelings are concerned I certainly don't want it. I didn't wish to offend Brooking, who is a very sound man, by saying so when he first broached the idea: but if it has got to be done let it *be as private and quiet as possible.'*

Later, he wrote to Lionel Curtis: 'As to the Kipling Society, that is in the hands of Allah. Maybe the Committee will decide to chuck it. I don't think, myself, that there will be abounding enthusiasm on the subject. The generation that I tried to write for conked out between '14 and '18.'[6]

Kipling at this time came into contact with a man whom, by every convention of his life, he should have admired – Lawrence of Arabia – yet strongly resented him. Lawrence was present at a dinner at Brown's Hotel, and was by then a protégé of 'Effendi'. Kipling formed a strong distaste for him. The importance of Lawrence's audience may have excited him, but he appeared at his worst. According to Lawrence, the governing classes were all blood-suckers, living on the starving poor; no man should have more than £200 a year – otherwise he should be ashamed to look his fellows in the face. 'I remember,' said an observer, 'that when Rud called him half-baked, someone aptly added: "Not that, but he has been too long in the potter's oven, and is cracked." '[7] Although irritated by Lawrence, Kipling moderated his opinion when informed of his illegitimacy, writing to Doubleday on 4 November 1927: 'What you – or rather, what Lawrence, tells in his letter to you, is perfectly amazing, and when one has taken it in, it explains the whole uneasy soul of the man. One wonders why that explanation had not occurred to one before. Likewise it confirms one of my pet theories that to be the wrong side of the blanket doesn't breed the worst sort.'[8]

He continued to relax from illness on Continental motor tours on which he squandered the same richness of descriptive prose as in his most remunerative stories. Unlike many authors away from the desk, Kipling with a pen in his hand was incapable of writing a dull or woolly sentence. Every experience in travel was etched indelibly on the mind. Sometimes silent at the time, he registered every impression on these tours:

I had no thought or foreknowledge of what was coming, when the road began to twist among low hills, and we saw solemn olive trees powdered with the white dust of stone quarries – a strip of railway line and a loading dock alongside for the blocks of cheesy white stone that might have been cut out of Bermuda coral. Without any particular warning we ran slap into the Matoppos, but instead of the grave of Cecil Rhodes (on whom be Peace), we looked up among the bald and split rocks and saw a dead city. I have seen Amber in Rajputana – a city of stone abandoned at a King's command, and Chitore, a fortress of stone among jungle like a ship stranded on the rocks, which simply ceased to live after centuries of siege and wars – but this grey, toothless, eyeless thing, growing out of and into the living stone was more awful than either Chitore or Amber. I think the beauty of the day added to the horror and yet with the horror was the beauty and the pathos.[9]

As the years passed, the English winter crept more and more into Rudyard's bones, and he went each year in quest of sunshine. The pursuit took the Kiplings, among other places, to Algiers and Egypt. His ship left Marseilles port for Algiers in hard pale sunshine on an oily sea which immediately suggested flying fish to him. There were escorting dolphins leaping happily alongside, and a couple of turtle, which added to the delightful sense of escape, change, and movement. There was the arrival in the dark at Algiers, and the smells were exciting and new, a mixture of warm dust, petrol, jasmine and Arab. 'I have not smelt Arab before. He is milder than nigger, but not so nice as decent Asiatic.' He awoke to look out on a garden on the slope of a cypress-covered ridge, and beneath his window were orange trees heavy with 'bridal bloom'.

The whitewashed walls blazed with splashes of bougainvillea; jasmine grew like weed, and there were roses, sweet peas, violets with stalks a foot long, pansies, anemones and arum lilies. Flowering cacti and red-hot pokers were in full bloom, and behind all this mixed scent there was a tart background of camphor-like eucalyptus.

He walked down streets lined with ilexes and gums, and here and there a tamarisk with dust on its needles would remind him of India. In the native city there was beauty of colour, mystery and darkness, white Minars blinding in the sunshine and gaily tiled Mosque fronts. Kipling was extremely sensitive to sudden changes in atmosphere, and his mood of depression fell away from him in joyful surrender. He visited a three-hundred-year-old Moorish house with the original harem gardens – alleys of orange trees and at the end a marble fountain down whose channels the concubines had floated rose-leaves against each other for wagers of jewellery. There were montbretia flowers, iris, salvia and roses, magnolia trees thirty feet high thick with solid pink and white bloom, tree geraniums, Japanese dwarf trees, and great tile-lined pools under the shade of thousand-year-old olive trees.

The whole wonder lay out on a hill-side held up by hanging walls, terraces and Moorish tiled stairs swathed in rampant creeper. And the cobalt sea, pearl-white town and ranges of bluish-red hills, seen through or under waving fronds of date palms, plantain, bamboo or stiff-spired cypress, were beyond even exclaiming at. But, I confide to you that not once have we felt *securely* warm. Light blue sky and high fierce sun – yes! But under it all, like a knife half-sheathed, a wind or a breeze or a breath that says: 'Beware!'[10]

Kipling's strong residue of affection was now devoted to his small band of men friends, not least to F. N. Doubleday: '... and this, my dear old man, brings to you my old and unchanging love after close upon forty years of business too! And that's a record that very few couples can boast of.'[11] In extraordinary contrast to this mood of gentle affection is a violent outburst to Gwynne, in November 1929, against the Socialist, George Lansbury:

Look up the dossier of that living Christian Lansbury in the Potted Biographies and you will find that on Feb. 9. 1918, he wrote: Comrades of the Allied Countries. Comrades of the countries who are at war with ours. Comrades of the International. Our Comrades. Our tribulations are your tribulations. Our purpose is your purpose. Our hour is your hour. *And our hour comes.* The Russians' revolution has raised a sun in heaven which can never go out. We too hold our hands to it. We warm our hopes at it. *It is the token that our hour comes.* We are your friends, you workers of Germany and Austria – you workers of the whole world.'

'It is about time,' Kipling added savagely and with full justification, to Gwynne, 'that you fed 'em with their own vomit.'[12]

Rudyard found much consolation, at this somewhat depressing period of his life, in his London clubs, the 'Athenaeum' and the 'Beefsteak', and in two distinguished dining clubs, 'Grillions' and 'The Club'. He was sometimes a guest of his uncle, Edward Poynter, at Royal Academy Banquets, and was fond of an evening at the theatre.

Although he had accepted a number of University distinctions, he was a difficult bird to snare for their public functions. He was particularly reluctant to give public addresses, and is believed to be unique in academic history in having refused to deliver the Romanes Lecture at Oxford, the Leslie Stephen Lecture at Cambridge, the Gifford Lecture at Edinburgh, and the Reith Lectures of the BBC. But he unbent sufficiently in learned circles to accept an occasional tribute, one of the most notable being the gold medal of the Royal Society of Literature, which had been awarded only three times before – to Walter Scott, George Meredith and Thomas Hardy.

CHAPTER XXI

THE PROFESSIONAL MAN

THERE have already been many criticisms and evaluations of Kipling's work, and it is certain that a host of others will follow, for the quarry is deep, tempting, and inexhaustible. Some have sought, with deep psychological insight, to fathom his real springs of thought and action, and to penetrate the fiercely guarded innermost bastion of his thought. Others, like the Swedish philosopher Leeb Lunberg, have made erudite inquiries into the philology of Kipling's work and the sources from which it was derived; others again, like the Danish writer C. A. Bodelsen, have analysed with remarkable acuteness the 'obscure' stories which sorely puzzled some of Kipling's honest, if simpler, admirers in his later creative phase.

A biographer, attempting to describe his life, cannot be lured too far down these byways, and can only note the general trend of his writings and make some reference to the most significant. And here one is immediately struck by the violent fluctuations in his popularity and the esteem in which he was held. For Kipling, as for others, the idolatry was often greater abroad than in his own land. But in England, too, his triumph was at first almost complete – he had burst upon the country with the force of an electric shock, but had lived to see his reputation sadly eroded, and during the years of disillusionment he seemed, particularly to the young, an elderly blimp who symbolized the odious themes of duty, patriotism and military preparedness.

Yet there can be little doubt of Kipling's survival in the long term; as Maurice Baring observed, he is 'safe in the Temple of Fame, which once you have entered you cannot leave. For this Temple is like a wheel. It goes round and round, and sometimes some of its inmates are in the glare of the sun, and sometimes they are in the shade, but they are there; and they never fall out.'[1]

We have already noted the variations in Kipling's early work. They continued in the books published in his interim period. So far his greatest success had been achieved as a writer of short stories and of verse, and it is clear that he was anxious to show that he was not confined to these forms, but could also master the full-length novel. That he was wrong in this belief is clearly suggested by the appearance of *The Light that Failed* (1891), and *The Naulahka* (1892), which he wrote in collaboration with Wolcott Balestier. The first is a bad book, hardly to be classified indeed as a novel, and the second perhaps the worst that Kipling ever had a hand in. *The Light that Failed* was coldly received, and it was soon accurately described by hostile critics as 'The Book that Failed'.

Nor is it difficult to put one's finger on the weakness which prevented Kipling to the end from becoming a novelist. It was not that he was incapable of planning a full-length novel, but rather that his impatience, and weakness in the creation of character, made it difficult for him to sustain the reader's interest beyond the bounds of the short story, which was a perfect vehicle for his art. *Kim*, by far the most successful of his longer works, is not by any normal standards a novel at all, but a series of linked episodes in the progress of the Lama and Kim, most of which could be prised from their neighbours without disturbing the symmetry of the whole.

In the words of a contemporary critic: 'Kipling cannot escape from his own subjectivity. His *dramatis personae* melt away rapidly out of the memory, leaving us nothing but an admirably piquant and clever delineation,' while to another contemporary, Richard Le Gallienne, 'the characters are little more than pegs on which to hang an anecdote'. This shortcoming was not necessarily an impediment to the short story as practised by Kipling, but it was fatal in the novel.

'Kipling was rarely capable of creating a character,' wrote another critic. 'He could combine a collection of observed traits into a composite which would pass in ordinary daylight for a likeness; but there are few if any of his stories in which any single character gathers flesh upon his bones, inspires that flesh with nerves and a brain, and carries his progenitor away.'

We may test this undoubted truth by comparing Kipling's characterization with that of W. Somerset Maugham. They were the two most widely-read writers of the short story of their day, but unlike Kipling, Maugham was also, at his best, a most capable novelist. And the reason for this difference lies in the fact that Maugham was profoundly interested in the quirks of human nature and fascinated by the good and evil at war in every human breast. He fashioned his characters out of close observation, allowing them time to stretch and grow and become authentic, so that the reader could believe that he actually knew them, and could form for them a positive love or detestation. He did not hero-worship 'Great Men'. He was not interested in political issues or technical miracles. But the study of human frailty absorbed him, and that, no doubt, although he was a far less naturally gifted writer than Kipling, is why his characters remain printed on the mind – the odious Townsend in *The Painted Veil*, the contemptible Alroy Kear in *Cakes and Ale*, the cynical Dr Saunders in *The Narrow Corner* – while Kipling's Stricklands, Helders and Pycrofts dissolve without leaving a trace.

This weakness of Kipling's, however, did not impede him in the short story, which he continued to fashion with gem-cutting perfection, and we should remember Maugham's own tribute to him:

Rudyard Kipling alone among the English writers of the Short Story, can bear comparison with the masters of France and Russia. Though he captured the favour of the great public when first he began to write, and has retained a hold on it ever since, cultivated opinion has always been somewhat scornful of him. He has identified with an Imperialism which was obnoxious to many sensitive persons, and certain characteristics of his style have always been irksome to readers of fastidious taste. But he was a wonderful, varied, and original teller of tales. He had a fertile invention, a merit in any writer, and to a supreme degree the gift of narrating incident in a surprising and dramatic fashion. His influence for a while was great on his fellow-writers, but perhaps greater on his fellow-men who led, in one way or another, the sort of life he dealt with. When one travelled in the East it was astonishing how often one came across men who had modelled themselves on the creatures of his invention.

They say that Balzac's characters were more true of the generation that followed him than of that which he purported to describe; I know from my own experience that twenty-three years after Kipling wrote his first important stories, there were men scattered about the outlying parts of the world who would never have been just what they were, except for him. He not only created character, he created men. Rudyard Kipling is generally supposed to have rendered the British people conscious of their Empire, but that is a political achievement with which I have not here to deal; what is important to my present purpose is that in his discovery of the exotic story, he opened a new, and fruitful field to writers.

This is the story, the scene of which is set in some country little known to the majority of readers. It deals with the reactions upon the white man, of his sojourn in an alien land, and the effect which contact with peoples of another race has upon him. Subsequent writers have treated this subject in their different ways, but Rudyard Kipling was the first to blaze the trail through this new-found country, and no one has invested it with a more romantic glamour; no one has made it more exciting, and no one has presented it so vividly, and with such a wealth of colour. He had, like every writer that ever lived, his shortcomings, but remains notwithstanding the best short story writer that our country can boast of.[2]

Kipling wrote with greater ease and freedom from care in the American period than at any other in his life. In India, his stories and verse, remarkable as they were, had been the by-products of an overworked reporter. He had not been particularly happy in Villiers Street, but in Vermont he was far from interference, and in his house 'Naulakha' could rely on hours of peace and silence, with a Cerberus of a wife stationed at the entrance to his study to guard that privacy.

The collection *Many Inventions* was published in 1893, and again we are struck by the variation in subject and quality of the work it contained. There is a vivid story of a lighthouse, *The Disturber of Traffic*, with an opportunity for a display of technical knowledge brilliantly seized. In contrast, *A Conference of the Powers*, based on the conquest of Burma, is a return to the early subaltern-worship, and represents one of those moments when Kipling became ridiculously ashamed of his sedentary life. The literary man in the story sits back listening entranced to the gruff reminiscences of three young officers fresh from the Burma War. He discovers to his horror that they understand aspects of life that are a closed book to him, and ends by 'blaspheming' his own art. The 'Powers' of the title are the Pen and the Sword, and Kipling makes an abject surrender to the latter.

In the same collection, and more important, was *In the Rukh*, in which we are first introduced to Mowgli, who had been taking shape in his creator's mind, and which was the prelude to the next real exhibition of Kipling's genius – *The Jungle Book* in 1894 and *The Second Jungle Book* in the following year, which have been discussed in an earlier chapter. *Many Inventions* also contained the story *Brugglesmith*, perhaps the most perfect example of what happened when Kipling embarked on slapstick. We cannot lay down standards of humour, and Kipling's has brought delight to thousands. But to the fastidious reader the note is jarring, vulgar and percussive, and was to be repeated in such stories as *My Sunday at Home* (1895), *The Puzzler* (1906), *The Vortex* (1914) and *The Village that Voted the Earth was Flat* (1917). We know that Kipling loved these blatant effects, which often revealed a revenge-motif in which people are humiliated by being subjected to derision and laughter, so that besides being vulgar the stories are also cruel. But there was something in his nature that demanded occasional, orgiastic outbursts of low comedy. Tears

of mirth had poured down his cheeks as he composed *Stalky & Co.*,
and he laughed for three days over *My Sunday at Home*, finding that
such indulgence gave wonderful relief to his own pent-up feelings. The
popularity of such stories shows at least that there was a wide public
for them, but those who already found something a trifle repellent
in Kipling's work were further affronted.

But his touch was never surer than when, in 1893, his honeymoon
year, he wrote the memorable *Love O' Women*, in which the lecherous
gentleman ranker is conducted to a shameful end with a skill not often
surpassed by the author. Kipling's stories are often opened by a descriptive passage which sets the scene for the action, and never more
effectively than in *Love O' Women*:

> The horror, the confusion, and the separation of the murderer from his
> comrades were all over before I came. There remained only on the barrack-
> square the blood of man calling from the ground. The hot sun had dried
> it to a dusky goldbeater-skinfilm, cracked lozenge-wise by the heat; and as
> the wind rose, each lozenge, rising a little, curled up at the edges as if it were
> a dumb tongue. Then a heavier gust blew all away down wind in grains of
> dark coloured dust. It was too hot to stand in the sunshine before breakfast.
> The men were in barracks talking the matter over. A knot of soldiers' wives
> stood by one of the entrances to the married quarters, while inside a woman
> shrieked and raved with wicked filthy words.

No beginning could be more auspicious, but Kipling's handling of
the rest of the story sharply divided two of his greatest admirers. To
Edward Shanks, the end of *Love O' Women* – the climax when the
broken hero, riddled with syphilis, lurches from his litter to enter the
brothel where the woman he has ruined is employed – was sentimental,
unreal and repulsive, as were his words as repeated by the narrator,
Mulvaney: 'I'm dying Aigypt – dying.' But Maurice Baring did not
share Shanks's opinion, and his letter to him is an illuminating commentary, not only on this story, but on Kipling's work as a whole
as it appeared to a sophisticated and enlightened man of letters:

> My angle towards Kipling is very different from yours. It is a difference
> in time, being not of a contemporary, but still of a person who read all the
> early books when they first came out. I remember the little grey paper books
> appearing when I was at school, and I read *Life's Handicap* and *The Light
> that Failed* as they came hot from the press. I enjoyed his work from the
> point of view of one contemporary with its appearance, just as Max and
> [Hilaire] Belloc hated it from the same point of view. Do what one will, one
> is of one's epoch; one cannot escape it; and I think it is better to face the

fact and accept it and not try and jump out of one's epoch as Arnold Bennett used to do, haunted and spurred by a terror of not being up-to-date.

I feel sure you are right in thinking Kipling's 'third manner' his best. It is quite obvious that by then he had discarded all those superficial faults, vulgarities and the cheap cleverness which marred his early work, and had reached a higher plane of maturity and serenity and wisdom instead of the cheap would-be-wisdom of the precocious boy, so unripe in its over-maturity. But – but – but, there is something gone which never came back, something *else*, not only a glory and a freshness as of the dawn but a promise of marvellous things to happen in the future – things far too marvellous ever to happen. I feel like Fitzgerald did about Tennyson's *Maud* which no longer had 'the old champagne flavour'.

One example will show you the difference between us. *Love O' Women*, which you quote as an instance of Kipling at his worst, and contrast it with *The Wish House*, as an example of Kipling at his best, ranks, to my mind, among his twelve best stories, whereas I can hardly read *The Wish House*. I don't think *Love O' Women* in the least sentimental. I think it is alive and raw and quivering with authentic passion. It is not fair to quote the death scene and let it stand by itself, but when one knows the whole story the Shakespeare quotation from *Anthony and Cleopatra* is supremely appropriate and comes with a terrific force when reported by Mulvaney's lips. I assure you this opinion is neither a paradox nor an eccentricity nor peculiar to me, but is shared by a great many other people, and not only by my contemporaries. I once heard the story read out by Hugh Cecil to a mixed company of people older and younger than himself in his clear, high dry unsentimental voice, and it reduced everybody to pulp.

When Kipling wrote *Captains Courageous* he had great faith in the book, which he afterwards abandoned, admitting to Conland that it was not a novel at all. The book failed in this respect for exactly the same reasons as *The Light that Failed*. The author was using his newly acquired knowledge of the technicalities of cod fishing off the Banks to present a series of episodes in the lives of the fishermen. Again, the characters are mere cyphers who might, with little loss to the reader, be called X, Y and Z. Nor is the central figure, Hervey Cheyne, the pampered son of a millionaire, in any way credible. He remarks to his fellow-travellers in the liner in which he is a passenger: '... You can hear the fish boats squawking all around us. Say, wouldn't it be great if we run down one?' He is washed overboard and rescued by one of the fish boats, and then his period of discipline and rehabilitation begins. Kipling's account of this is so unconvincing as to be almost laughable, and we are left with the impression that Hervey Cheyne is yet another puppet of his creator's imagination, not a creature of flesh and blood; used merely to exhibit the virtue of the disciplined life upon a spoiled immature mind – a familiar theme in Kipling's work.

Yet the story of Hervey Cheyne's redemption might have been convincingly told if Kipling had troubled to develop Hervey's character at leisure, and provide a realistic description of the means, which must have been brutal, by which he was brought to subordination. He shows us instead the process completed in five pages, after about half an hour's conversation between Hervey and Disko's son Dan. After that the odious *enfant gâté* is a reformed character, humble and anxious to learn, with all the nonsense knocked out of him. As Shanks said: 'No novel can survive unhurt so light-hearted a slap in the face of obvious truth.'[3]

The Day's Work, containing the short stories written in Vermont, was published in 1898, and the high quality of these was the fruit of that sense of sudden accession of power which had come to him at a certain moment in America. Here we find two great stories of craftsmanship and machinery, *The Bridge Builders* and *The Ship that Found Herself*, which appeal even to those who are bored by this aspect of Kipling's art. In the first story he lavishes his descriptive powers upon the bridge-building, and upon the builders, Finlayson and his young assistant, 'recently an unlicked cub', who in fair weather and foul are spanning the River Ganges. It is a story of human skill and persistence in the face of inept administrators, again 'the strong man working alone', but we can also see in it traces of that symbolism so marked in his later work. The bridge is the emblem of the stabilizing effect of European civilization on India, and the story ends with Finlayson, delirious on a river island, imagining that the animals round him are a *punchayet* or meeting of the Indian gods.

There is symbolism, too, in *The Ship that Found Herself*. As the skipper of the *Dimbula* explained to the owner's daughter, the vessel had yet 'to find herself'. All the parts of the ship must learn to work together until they become a true whole, as in any human society man must learn to work, sometimes to yield and compromise, to resolve conflicting strains, so that the whole society may survive and become strong. And so, in this superbly wrought story, all the component parts of the vessel talk and sing in their struggle with the elements, and at last achieve harmony as they are riveted together by the sea in perfect unison.

Mistrust of democracy, particularly the American variety, is never long absent either from his stories or from his private correspondence.

It reappears here in a horse story, *A Walking Delegate*, where the Socialist horse, unhinged by abstract thought, wants political decisions to be made by the counting of noses; while, as if to counterbalance this nonsense, Kipling's reverence for administrators in difficulties, fighting famine, is the subject of *William the Conqueror*.

But students of Kipling, whether the blind idolators or the more perceptive admirers, are united in praise of another story in this collection – *The Maltese Cat*. In this story of polo Kipling wrote what is probably the finest description of a game in the English language. It is an animal story of which the polo pony, the Maltese Cat, is the hero, and is told so brilliantly that even readers ignorant of the game are held spellbound by the Cat's tactics, and the terse instructions he gives to the other ponies, for the Maltese Cat is the real captain of the side rather than the ostensible one, Lutyens.

It is wrong to assume, like some, that Kipling despised games. We have seen that he played several to the limits of his physical capacity, and polo was among those he had attempted ten years before. This story was written with particular pleasure since the 'Maltese Cat' was inspired by his own grey pony 'Dolly Bols'.[4] The Skidars team in the story, in which the 'Cat' played, were poor men who could not afford expensive ponies, whereas their opponents, the Archangels, could buy theirs from high-class stock. There is a moral here, that wealth and birth are not values in themselves, and there is another in the conclusion of the story. The Maltese Cat is injured in the game, saving Lutyens, his rider, from crashing into a goal post, and can never play again, appearing afterwards only as an umpire's mount: 'A flea-bitten grey with a neat polo-tail, lame all round, but desperately quick on his feet, and, as everybody knew, Past Pluperfect Prestissimo Player of the Game.'

'Player of the Game,' writes Bonamy Dobrée, 'that is the moral of the fable; but that the Game is worth more than the Player of the Game was a truth the Archangels had not learned; each player was too keen on his own prowess to forego any exhibition of personal skill for the sake of the side.'[5] It is significant that in this superb story Lutyens and the other humans are, as usual, figures without substance, while the character of the Maltese Cat is drawn with loving and tender care.

Perhaps we can get some idea of the variety, indeed unevenness, of Kipling's work by noting that the volume containing such masterpieces as *The Bridge Builders*, *The Ship that Found Herself* and *The Maltese Cat* also included *My Sunday at Home*, which, like Kipling's other stories of orgiastic mirth, has been the subject of erudite comment, but must surely convince most sensitive readers that humour was not his forte; and, at the end of the volume, *The Brushwood Boy*, which contains some of Kipling's most glaring lapses in taste and self-criticism.

The Brushwood Boy is one of Kipling's fabular stories, and deals with the fusion of dreams and reality. The dreams of the child, which always begin near a heap of brushwood near the shore, are poetical yet frightening; there is danger and terror in them, but they are also in a sense exciting and desirable, so that although the boy is puzzled and disturbed by these dream journeys, and by the girl who is his companion in them, he is also stimulated by an experience so different from the workaday world. There is a beauty and mystery about these occult wanderings which is completely dissipated when Kipling shows us the bewitched child developing into one of his idealized subalterns in India, and the picture of this clean-living military prig shatters in an instant the *mystique* of the Brushwood Boy:

Cottar was cantering across to polo, and he looked a very satisfactory figure of a man as he gave easily to the first excited bucks of his pony, and slipped over a low mud wall to the practice ground. There were more than Mrs Corporal Morrison who felt as she did. But Cottar was busy for eleven hours of the day. He did not care to have his tennis spoiled by petticoats on the court; and after one long garden-party, he explained to his major that this sort of thing was 'futile piffle' and the major laughed ...

'Comin' to the Fusiliers' dance tonight, Galahad?' asked the Adjutant.

'No, thanks. I've got a fight on with the major.' The virtuous apprentice sat up till midnight in the major's quarters with a stop-watch and a pair of compasses, shifting little pointed lead blocks about a four inch map.

The description of this smug paragon's return on leave, after winning glory in the field, to the stately country home and the adoring 'pater and mater' resembles some early Hollywood attempt to portray the English aristocracy, and is among the most embarrassing passages in all Kipling's work; and by now we can neither believe, nor rejoice in, the Brushwood Boy's hastily contrived union with his 'Dream Girl'.

Kipling's tender, personal side, so fiercely guarded, so much his own secret property, was revealed cautiously in the allegory *They*, and more fully in 'Merrow Down'. The agony of the past, the yearning for Josephine, the grief for all dead children are to be found in *They*. 'His sense or hope,' wrote Bonamy Dobrée, 'that dead children want to come back is poignantly phrased in the prefatory poem "The Return of the Children", which ends with Christ asking: "Shall I that have suffered the children to come to me hold them against their will?" '

There is a passage in *They*, when the narrator goes for the third time to the house where the ghost children are, knowing now that his own daughter is among them, a description of the Sussex countryside written with such care and virtuosity that one feels that in love of Josephine he made an almost self-conscious effort to create beauty, like the sudden spreading of a peacock's tail:

There came at last a brilliant day swept clear from the South-west, that brought the hills within hand's reach – a day of unstable airs and high filmy clouds. Through no merit of my own, I was free, and set the car for the third time on that known road. As I reached the crest of the Downs I felt the soft air change, saw it glaze under the sun; and looking down at the sea, in that instant beheld the blue of the Channel turn through polished silver and dulled steel to dingy pewter. A laden collier hugging the coast steered outward for deeper water, and across copper-coloured haze, I saw sails rise one by one on the anchored fishing-fleet. In a deep dene behind me an eddy of sudden wind drummed through the sheltered oaks, and spun aloft the first dry sample of autumn leaves. When I reached the beach road the sea-fog fumed over the brickfield and the tide was telling all the grasses of the gale beyond Ushant. In less than an hour Summer England vanished in chill grey. We were again the shut island of the North, all the ships of the world bellowing at our perilous gates; and between their outcries ran the piping of bewildered gulls.

Reality and 'the outer world' are closely intertwined in *They*, and the factual and fabular so mingled as to make definition difficult. But too close an analysis, in any case, destroys the fragile edifice of his imagination. It is an allegory of a limbo of lost children tended by a blind woman, children who are not yet ready for Heaven and come back for a space to inhabit earth. When the narrator of the story comes to the garden where the dead children play, 'his car is brought up against a yew tree clipped to represent a horseman, whose spear points to the visitor's breast; the yew is a traditional symbol of death, and the lance signifies that he is come to a territory which is forbidden the living to explore.'[6] The story is written with that quivering tenderness which possesses Kipling whenever he writes of children, and we should not probe too closely into its mechanics and symbolism:

All that we need is for the sense of the strange and the uncanny, of the achieving of the relief of sorrow by forbidden means that are at last realized as forbidden and put away, to grow on us as they grew on the narrator (who

on this one occasion at least we cannot but accept as Kipling himself) until
the heart-breaking moment of climax: the acceptance of grief that leads to
peace.[7]

He has realized at last that the children are only ghosts and can
bring no lasting comfort. Kipling's imagination never flagged in these
years, and the unceasing process of creation continued through *Puck
of Pook's Hill* and *Rewards and Fairies* to *Actions and Reactions* (1908).
His newly discovered love of England was revealed again in the story
An Habitation Enforced, in which his usual hostile attitude to Americans is reversed. An American couple, the Chapins, take a house in
Sussex and fall in love, as he had done, with the English countryside,
the people who live in it, and the ancient structure that holds it
together. Kipling was expressing his own conviction when he made
Chapin correct his wife: 'It's *not* our land. We've only paid for it.'
In the same collection we find *The Mother Hive*, a fable in which Kipling's hatred of Socialism, and of a society in which he thought men
were paid to do nothing and exonerated from their sins, is driven
home, and is yet another example of the preoccupation with England's
defence which he had expressed at the same period in 'The Dykes'.
Owing to the negligence of the Guard of the hive a wax moth enters
it (representing Socialist erosion), disobeys the law of the Queen Bee,
and disintegrates the life of the hive, which is eventually burned by
its human owner. Only a group of disciplined bees survives, creates
a Queen and swarms, preserved from anarchy by order and obser-
vance of the law. It is hardly necessary to labour the moral.

We have already seen how in *A Diversity of Creatures* (1917) Kipling
launched successfully into science-fiction, and as usual there is a wide
variety in this collection – a new note with the beautiful drug addict
of *In the Same Boat*, violent and revengeful mirth in *The Village that
Voted the Earth was Flat*, and at the end the story that brought brick-
bats showering on Kipling for sadism, cruelty and vindictive hatred
of the Germans – *Mary Postgate*.

Something more must be said of this story, which was called by Stanley Baldwin's son, Oliver, 'the wickedest story ever written'. It can
not be questioned that in writing *Mary Postgate* Kipling not only invited trouble, but positively entreated it. Nor can we doubt that he
had by this time a murderous hatred of the Germans for the havoc
they had brought into the world, for their love of war, their hideous
massacres of French women and children, and their barbarous sack
of Louvain.

But it can be strongly argued that *Mary Postgate* did not embody that hatred. It is the story of a repressed middle-aged spinster, companion to another woman, Mrs Fowler, in whose custody is a nephew, Wynn, who is killed in an accident in the Royal Flying Corps before the story begins. He is represented as an unattractive boy who treated Mary with indifference and even contempt. But all the frustrated love and tenderness in her nature has been lavished on Wynn, and the time comes when she and Mrs Fowler have to go through his pathetic personal leavings – boys' books, toys, broken gramophone records – putting all but a few in the garden incinerator. Mary goes down to the village for paraffin to make them burn thoroughly, and while she is there a German aeroplane drops a bomb which kills and mutilates a little girl.

Returning to the garden, she finds the German pilot, who has been forced down and terribly injured. In agony he asks for her help. By the light of the bonfire,

she saw, half hidden behind a laurel, not five paces away, a bareheaded man sitting very stiffly at the foot of one of the oaks. A broken branch lay across his lap – one booted leg protruding from beneath it. His head moved ceaselessly from side to side, but his body was as still as the tree's trunk. He was dressed – she moved sideways to look more closely – in a uniform something like Wynn's, with a flap buttoned across the chest. For an instant, she had some idea that it might be one of the young flying men she had met at the funeral. But their heads were dark and glossy. This man's was as pale as a baby's and so closely cropped that she could see the disgusting pinky skin beneath. His lips moved.

'What do you say' – Mary moved towards him and stooped.

'Laty! Laty! Laty!' he muttered while his hands picked at the dead wet leaves.

The climax of this story is determined with brilliant and revengeful certainty:

When she came through the rain the eyes in the head were alive with expectation. The mouth even tried to smile. But at sight of the revolver its corners went down just like Edna Gerritt's. A tear trickled from one eye, and the head rolled from shoulder to shoulder as though trying to point out something.

'Cassé. Tout cassé,' it whimpered.

'What do you say?' said Mary disgustedly, keeping well to one side, though only the head moved.

'Cassé,' it repeated. 'Che me rends. Le Medecin! Toctor!'

'Nein!' she said, bringing all her small German to bear with the big pistol. 'Ich haben der todt Kinder gesehn.' (I have seen the dead child.)

The head was still. Mary's hand dropped. She had been careful to keep her finger off the trigger for fear of accidents. After a few moments waiting, she returned to the destructor, where the flames were falling, and churned up Wynn's charring books with the poker. Again the head groaned for the doctor.

'Stop that!' said Mary, and stamped her foot. 'Stop that, you bloody pagan! ... Stop it,' she cried later across the shadows – '*Nein*, I tell you! *Ich haben der todt Kinder gesehn.*'. . .

She thumped like a pavior through the settling ashes at the thrill of it. The rain was damping the fire, but she could feel – it was too dark to see – that her work was done.

Another touch of realism, sinister in the extreme, is given at the end of the story. When Mary came in: 'She scandalized the whole routine by taking a luxurious bath before tea, and came down looking, as Mrs Fowler said when she saw her lying all relaxed on the sofa, "quite handsome".'

It was, as Oliver Baldwin said, a terrible story, but, in the opinion of some critics, essentially an example of Kipling's literary savagery. To Professor Bonamy Dobrée:

Kipling, of course, is not suggesting, as he has been accused of doing, that this is how people should behave; he is merely telling us 'This is what happens'. He is the realist. ... Terrible as Kipling's story is, one may wonder whether, if people would look into themselves, realize Mary's feelings about the dead Wynn, especially just then, when she is, so to speak, burying him; and imagine the shock she felt when she saw the mangled child, and then finding the man who had dropped the bomb, they could with certainty say they would have acted otherwise. Especially a woman.[8]

For a man, at such a crisis, would be what Wynn called a sportsman, and leave everything to fetch help, whereas in the case of a woman:

... Every fibre of her frame
Proves her launched for one sole issue, armed and engined for the same:
And to serve that single issue, lest the generations fail,
The female of the species must be deadlier than the male.

Professor Bodelsen agrees that in this story there is no justification for identifying the writer's attitude with that of Mary Postgate, but suggests other possible implications:

The most shocking thing about this tale is the suggestion of a sexual element in Mary Postgate's enjoyment of the German airman's agony. This is Sadism in the original sense of the word, and it is difficult to believe that he [Kipling] could have approved of that. ... It may well be that the story is meant as an example of the spiritual harm that Germany has done to the English: this is what it has come to, that a kindly and respectable English spinster finds herself turned into a torturer.[9]

'The English had begun to hate.' But even if Kipling need not be identified with the central figure, it cannot be denied that his understandable hatred of the Germans, increased a hundred-fold by the death of his own son in battle, grimaces at us from every line of the story.

It was said by Edmund Wilson that at this period Kipling 'codified his snobberies', that he fled for refuge to the solid amenities of conservative English rural life. But in fact he was far from anxious for too close a relation with the local gentry, preferring the 'Hobdens' of the rural scene, whom he saw as the bones of English history, but who accepted him with a certain reserve. His snobbery, if it could be called that, remained a liking for men at the head of enterprises in which he was deeply interested – at this time such men as Sir Percy Bates, who planned and built new Cunarders, or Lord Stanhope, who as First Lord of the Admiralty presided over the British Navy.

But we should remember that although he had long been angrily involved, from a distance, in politics, this interest was always secondary to his work as a writer and his love of the countryside. The fires of his political interest were blown upon and kept glowing redly by what he thought the criminal mishandling of issues on which he held passionate views. But his writing remained the central interest of his life.

CHAPTER XXII

A DARK VALLEY

═══════

KIPLING's violent contortions in public affairs, and some aspects of his later writings can be readily explained by an examination of his medical history. He suffered from duodenal ulcers. He endured constant and often acute pain, vomiting, haemorrhages, and ultimately perforation, leading to death. The following records of an illness so bravely and patiently borne that many of his friends were unaware of it is taken chiefly from the pages of his wife's diary. Some quotations from letters to his daughter and son-in-law are added. During the latter years of the illness Caroline herself was often sick and weary with bodily strain and anxiety.

Travelling about as he did, Kipling consulted many doctors about his pain, and the following are on record as having seen him: Dr Ironside Bruce; Dr Melsome; Dr W. Christie; Dr Lang; Dr Alcock; Sir Humphrey Rolleston; Dr Curtis; Lord Dawson of Penn; Dr Graham Hodgson; Dr Evans; Dr Jarvis; Dr Roux; Dr Bres; Sir Maurice Cassidy. His surgeons included Sir John Bland-Sutton, Mr Miles, Sir Alfred Webb-Johnson and Mr Peter Stanley. The following list is interesting as an indication of the cause of his pain according to different opinions:

1915	Gastritis	'The Doctor'
1917	Internal Chill	?
1918	Irritability of the stomach	Dr Ironside Bruce
1919	Adhesion of the liver and colon	Dr Melsome
1921	Septic foci in the teeth	Sir J. Bland-Sutton
1922	Old ulcer with inflamed colon and lower bowel	Dr Christie with Dr Miles
1931	Adhesion to operation scar. Umbilical hernia	Sir John Bland-Sutton. Lord Dawson in consultation
1932	Colic from overdoses with aperients	Dr Evans
1933	Ulcer at mouth of duodenum	Dr Roux and Dr Jarvis

Every year from 1915 onwards Caroline Kipling's diaries and other family papers contain ominous references to the constant discomfort, and often agony, in which Kipling gallantly produced his vast output. In 1915 a doctor diagnosed gastritis and put Kipling on a strict diet, and for the next two years he was continually ill and miserable. In 1918 we find such entries as: *Apr. 23*. Wretchedly ill all night and during the day. *Apr. 29*. Not at all well. *May 7*. He has a severe go of pain in the evening. *May 8*. Goes to see Bland-Sutton and it is decided to photo his inside. *May 10*. Miserable all day. *Aug. 30*. Rud sick and miserable. In February 1919 he 'had his old pain back', and on 5 February: 'Bad night – great pain and till the 7th wretched with a lot of pain.' In 1920: *Mar. 3*. His old pain back again. *Mar. 4*. Overwhelmed with depression and return of his pain. *May 6*. A return of his pain. *July 17*. Rud has his pain. *Aug. 1*. Rud has a return of pain. *Aug. 16*. Is more than usually wretched with a more than usually severe go of pain.

This deplorable catalogue continued without break or alleviation to the end of his life. In 1921 the doctors fell back upon a panacea much favoured at the time, the removal of all his teeth, but this failed to touch the radical cause of his malady and in the same month – February – the wretched entries begin again: *Feb. 12*. Rud has a lot of pain. *Feb. 13*. Rud has a pretty miserable day. *Feb. 15*. Rud more wretched than ever in the afternoon. *Feb. 18*. Rud in pain.

By July 1922 Caroline found him 'very ill, yellow and shrunken, like an old man. Very worried, and difficult not to let him realize I am.' These anxieties continued. The first X-ray examination showed that another must be made under an anaesthetic. Kipling was haunted by the dread of cancer. He had convinced himself in his drawn-out illness that there could be no other explanation of an assault so agonizing and sustained.

The examination of 14 February 1922 did something to remove this particular dread. 'The doctors,' said Caroline, 'discover no trace of any sign of the much to be dreaded cancer. *An old ulcer* is found; a large area of inflammation in colon and lower bowel from which there has been a haemorrhage, which has caused his anaemia.' They brought him to Brown's Hotel and started treatment, a heavy dose of Epsom salts every morning; bowels washed out twice a day, and no solid food.

'Rud's nights are dreadful with pain. He does not often sleep more than an hour and a half. On the 10th and 11th Nov. 1922, he had two nights of agony, more than any before.' The doctors decided to operate and Kipling was taken to a nursing home, where he saw his lawyer, making a fresh will, signed papers and attended to his business affairs before being drugged into torpor. December found him back at 'Bateman's' – 'gloom and depression only from Rud; unliftable as far as one can see'.[1]

In spite of these moods of abysmal depression inseparable from such an illness, he bore his afflictions with superb courage. 'He suffered,' said his daughter, 'frightful and incessant pain over a very long period with the patience of an angel. He never complained, and never snapped. The most he ever said, when doubled up in agony, was: "Just leave me alone; I'll be all right soon."'[2]

Indeed it is an astonishing tribute to the creative vitality and courage of this man that he could, in the midst of this prolonged misery and constant dread of cancer, continue to keep up his output. And it was not only in fiction that he was pouring out his inventive genius. We stand astonished at the vast bulk of letters to his friends, most of it in his own handwriting, that went forth during these years – those letters so buoyant and gay, full of unforgettable descriptive passages and flashes of youthful fire.

An account of Kipling's physical condition should do much to explain his occasional asperities. He was constantly deluded by brief cheating periods of improvement and hope, but in 1926 a new enemy stepped into the breach and he was attacked by severe pneumonia; and when this long bout had spent itself Lord Dawson next detected 'a flutter in his heart'.

This melancholy medical catalogue continues year by year, month by month, and often week by week and day by day, until June 1928 when Caroline Kipling's health, never robust, and harassed by emotional strain, broke down. She joined Kipling under Lord Dawson's care for prolonged tests and examinations, and was put on a rigid diet. The diary entries are broken from now on, and we may assume that Kipling concealed his pain from her whenever he could. Caroline's now persistent illness increased Kipling's profound depression, although he attempted to make light of it all in his letters, writing on 8 December 1930: 'Of course I've added to the joy of nations by a riotous inside, but that I can manage.' And on 26 December: 'I've abandoned my eternal "digestive" pills, which were playing the deuce with my innards, in favour of agarol, and for three weeks now have been free from pain. You don't know what that means after years of discomfort. I couldn't have stuck the last strain, I think, if I'd been doubled up as usual.'

Kipling's depression from now on was increased by a steadily deteriorating conjugal relationship. As his health declined, Caroline exercised upon him a more rigorous control. This control was partly due to a genuine anxiety about his physical condition, and partly to an incorrigible possessiveness of character. Ever since the old, evil Beatty Balestier days, Caroline had been a possessive woman, and this failing grew upon her with the years. She was jealous of the influence her daughter Elsie had upon her husband, and she had spoiled her son John, who was not intimidated by her. She had, as we have seen, become almost denationalized now – so English that she would talk of 'we' as opposed to the Americans. After John's death she was bitter about America's tardy entry into the war, and this grief further assisted her divorcement from her own people. Her domination over her husband was by now to some extent justified by the need for devoting her own ailing but stubborn system to the sustenance of his. But this devotion was not all the story. Kipling, she thought, was hers, and that closed the issue. She resented with extraordinary jealousy any intrusion upon this monopoly. Perceval Landon was one of the few encouraged to visit him, and was allowed to take a cottage in the grounds of 'Bateman's'.

Nor was she any longer willing to be regarded as a mere accessory to Kipling's distinction, and from now on fretted him by an excessive protection. She strengthened her control over all the minor details of his life. When he went out for an evening walk she was there to see that he came back. When there were guests her eyes followed his every movement. The only telephone in the house was situated in her bedroom. Caroline even resented Rudyard reading *Stalky & Co.* to Margaret Mackail, with whom he had been brought up.

Ill health overshadowed his entire later life. He was driven in upon himself, and was now too often denied access to the outside world. He had become a guarded flame. Caroline herself was threatened with diabetes, and an atmosphere of illness brooded over the house. It was almost as if the *Feng Shui* had returned again, yet such was the magnetism of Kipling that many of his friends still ventured to enter the house. Here they would find the ailing couple – Kipling delighted with fresh companionship – good wine, poor food, and ill-warmed rooms, and Kipling suddenly in the middle of a fascinating story breaking off and saying, 'You finish it Carrie,' which she would do, according to Mrs Cazalet, with 'funny little sniffs'. One intimate friend said that she never saw Caroline read a book, but only newspapers, and that her conversation when the women had left the dining-room was about her servant problems, but this ignores the fact that Kipling constantly called upon her for the *mot juste* in a story or verse, which she readily and ably supplied.

Various unnecessary conjectures have clouded this true picture. It has been wrongly said that Caroline kept Kipling short of money. When he wanted money at the Beefsteak Club or the Athenaeum, he cashed a cheque like anyone else. He often found himself without money, however, because it used to fall through a hole made by the wearing of a heavy knife in his pocket.

Kipling was emotionally incapable of making any protest against this increasing control of his life. Contrary to the impression he presented to the world, he was in fact a timid and sensitive man immersed in the realms of creation. On the world outside this kingdom he had many theories, but of practical knowledge in his later years, little. He was further removed from the means of gaining it. Either in the hollow at 'Bateman's', or in the excursions to Brown's Hotel, or in the foreign travel, they were always together. Their mutual gloom and sickness increased, and we have already noted as early as July 1901 the strange neurotic depths to which Caroline could sink. Yet all might have been well if she could have relaxed her possessiveness to the extent of realizing that the only hope was to send him abroad for several months, to the new climates and scenes that so excited and rejuvenated him – not to accompany him herself but to let him go with Gwynne, with Landon, or some other friend, when he could have returned with redoubled affection – but this she could not do.

Rather was her vigilance increased as his health declined. Kipling, as we have observed in his dealings with Beatty Balestier, was timid, and he feared Caroline's scenes. This fear showed itself in ridiculous little ways. Kipling had two book-ends at 'Bateman's'. He gave one of them to his surgeon Sir John Bland-Sutton and kept the other himself as a token of their friendship. He accompanied the gift with earnest injunctions 'not to tell Carrie'. Characteristically she noticed this absence, and when Kipling died she sent the other one to Bland-Sutton, saying that as he had one he had better have both.

Matters between them finally came to such a pass that one night Kipling opened his heart to an intimate friend after Carrie had gone to bed. He said that he could not stand it any longer, that he was never allowed to escape from the atmosphere of 'Bateman's'. He complained that although Caroline would invite people to 'Bateman's' she could never realize that it was necessary for him to get away and see his friends alone. The suggestions that have been made that Caroline exercised the same control in London are not borne out by the entries in her diaries. Far more often than not, Kipling lunched or dined out at his Clubs. When they drove up to London by car from 'Bateman's' Caroline would drop Kipling at 'the usual place', which was at the foot of some steps. Sometimes she might not see him again before he returned for the night.

Caroline's threats of self-violence terrified Kipling, and the terror made him even more submissive. All this, coupled with the constant physical pain, reduced him to a terrible condition. He wrote beseechingly to one of his friends, 'Come down as many week-ends as you can. I am so bored.' He was forced sometimes to take these letters up to the post office and post them himself, as Caroline would look at his letters and cross-question him as to whom they were for. Sometimes when Gwynne went for a week-end to 'Bateman's' Kipling would take him out for a walk, exclaiming with the glee of a schoolboy, 'Idle day today', and pitching his hat into the air; and in the evening he would lie beside the fire like a cat.[3] He so treasured these moments with his friends that he used to shave, with the *Morning Post* propped up before him, in the same room in which Gwynne was having his bath – making comments on the letter-press.

Kipling was devoted to Caroline, and he was intensely grateful for all she had done for him. He could never forget, too, that she had given him Josephine. He could look back on their long, fruitful married life, and to its beginning – the memory of the world's adventure faced together in youth. But her behaviour had perilously strained his nerves. Her care for him had become an obsession, and he could not summon up the courage to make even a temporary escape.

Deprived now of any form of exercise, he concerned himself more and more with military matters. No detail was too small for him. He would come to Lord Stanhope with carefully worked-out schemes for the decentralization of drill-halls in London. He was keenly interested in the training of youths to ride motor-cycles so that they could act as scouts in wartime – cycles with solid tyres for rough country, and carrying sub-machine guns. He spoke always about the coming war, the advent of which he clearly predicted. He had no patience with those who failed to understand the threat or to do their duty, and was infuriated when Ramsay MacDonald recommended the King to confer a peerage on a man who had been a conscientious objector in the last war. Enraged that such a person should be occupying a

bench in the same House as such idols as Milner and Allenby, Kipling
wrote savagely:

> Oh belted sons of Treason,
> Pass onwards to the Lords,
> Where six safe months in prison
> Can win such great rewards!
> From Jutland to Judaea
> Bob up ye dead and sing!
> He'll sit with wicked Beatty
> And Allenby and Byng.

> Through toil and tribulation
> And tumult of our war,
> He sought the consummation
> Of peace for evermore,
> A million fell beside him,
> By land and air and sea,
> In order to provide him
> With breakfast lunch and tea!

Kipling's insatiable curiosity continued throughout his later life.
Friends, and even vague acquaintances, were grilled on technical subjects. This, of course, was an old habit, a way of gathering material,
and no better description of it has been given than that by Sir Roderick
Jones, who watched Kipling in action in South Africa:

'One morning Kipling looked in at my office in Cape Town and
said he had a rather important consulting engineer from the Rand
coming to see him that afternoon at tea-time – would I come too?
I did.

'We three sat in comfortable chairs in Kipling's study, each with
our tea beside us. At first our talk was general. But very soon the
engineer became witness in the box, Kipling a cross-examining barrister, and I the dumb audience. The gold mines on the Witwatersrand
were even then, as now, the greatest in the world, and machinery and
methods employed were the best that science and industry could produce and money could buy.

'Our witness in the box was an expert and an authority on all the
ramifications of gold mining, and Kipling's purpose was to extract
from him the cream of his knowledge – which he did by encouraging
the man to talk and himself being a patient listener, but one ready

to pounce down upon the man, the moment he faltered, with searching questions of a highly technical character. All the time Kipling kept his eyes, those piercing eyes sheltered by great shaggy eyebrows, fixed upon his victim, not to mesmerize him, as one might think, but because he was intensely interested and burning with a desire to hear more and yet more from the man who was talking. Only occasionally would he jump up from his chair, and almost spring to the desk behind him and scribble just two or three words as a reminder. Then he would sit down quickly again and galvanize the man to further effort and exposition by some stimulating comment or interrogation.

'This process went on without a halt for over two hours and when, at nearly seven o'clock, the engineer and I walked down the hill together from "The Woolsack", the engineer declared that he had never had such a grilling in his life, and he felt like an orange squeezed dry of its juice. A few days later when I was dining with Kipling he recalled every one of the salient points made by the engineer, and I was astonished at the way in which, relying simply upon his memory, that I soon learned to be prodigious, and upon his two or three scrappy notes, he had sifted and retained all the grain and separated it most skilfully from the chaff.'[4]

This tedious habit was also noted by Sir Ronald Storrs, who described Kipling's meeting with King Feisal:

Feisal was in London, faithfully attended by Haddad ... and I was doing my best, by introducing him to publicists and politicians, to further his cause. On such occasions I persuaded him to wear his Arab robes, with no little difficulty, for so remote was he from the London atmosphere that he really believed he would create a better impression in faultless evening dress. Not all these great men seemed to realize that it was the politics and not the literature and archaeology of the Arab world that he had come to discuss. After enduring a ten minute questionnaire from Rudyard Kipling as to the size, number, origin, and significance of camel brands in the Hejaz, he asked me in Arabic over the poet's shoulder: 'Does this man take me for a camel dealer?'[5]

Throughout illness and depression this remarkable mind maintained its steady focus upon foreign and military affairs. He was refreshed by visits to General (later Field-Marshal) Sir Archibald Montgomery-Massingberd, and after one of these Carrie wrote to the General's wife: 'We did so delight in our visit to you. Rud had not been so cheerful for months – and last night when the PM talked such rot, he said: "There is still Salisbury Plain."' Kipling proposed to the General an ambitious scheme for using horses in an elaborate cere-monial in the Tattoo, and when the General had indicated the intrinsic difficulties of the scheme, replied ruefully:

Dear General Sahib,
I'm afraid the Cavalry are right. Obviously if the Horse had been capable of doing anything on his own, something like that item would have been produced long ago. Horses *are* fools. But what about 'Mechanized Lancers' – horses and Tanks doing musical rides together? Has that ever been tried? Seems to me that there might be some rather pretty figures in it.

And later he wrote to the General with a suddenly startled enthusiasm:

Telepathy again! All three of us were talking about you two only a couple of days ago as we were going along the Hog's Back North, and wondering when we should see you again. And now you've got the First Division at Aldershot! When you are settled in perhaps you'll come over for a quiet Sun-day with us. The welcome will be the warmest, tempered by the knowledge that so far as human cunning can do it India is lost to the Empire.

The passion for detail continued. Kipling wrote to Lord Stanhope asking him whether a seaman of fifty could have been in the 'Black Fleet'. Stanhope did not know what this meant, but discovered that it was a term applied to the period of the change-over from sail to steam. Months later Stanhope came upon the use Kipling had made of this information in a story in the magazine *Idler*, about parrots in Trinidad.[6]

Constant among Kipling's anxieties remained his love of France, but he failed completely to realize the havoc which had been caused in her national character by the losses in the 1914 War, the venality of her politicians, and the weariness and cynicism of her people. His mind began to go back now to that first visit to France in boyhood – how long ago – when his adoration for her had been formed. He had first arrived in Paris – 'my city', as he called it, in 1878. He was then twelve years old, and in his delightful book *Memories of France* he described his arrival in Paris and the life of that era. He spoke of 'my Exposition', and felt that he owned the whole country.

At the Exposition had been the head of the immense Statue of Liberty, the work of Bartholdi. The Statue was offered to the United States of America by France, and was placed and unveiled in 1886 on Bedloe's Island in New York Harbour. Young Kipling would run up the wooden staircase inside the head, and gaze through the empty eye-sockets, from which he could see the world at his feet. And one

day an old man had said to him: 'Young man, I see that you are
English; you can now say that for once in your life you have seen
through the eyes of Liberty': but to Kipling, 'It was through the eyes
of France that I really commenced to see.'

CHAPTER XXIII

SWAN SONG

RUDYARD'S deterioration of health was accompanied by a change in his manner of writing. The collections *Debits and Credits*, published in 1926, and *Limits and Renewals*, in 1932, contained stories which puzzled many of his readers, for they were dark, involuted, and sometimes agonizing – stories which if, in the words of a critic, they had been 'the work of a young and unknown writer the average editor might have condemned as ridiculously obscure, or dismissed as perversely morbid'.

The regular appearance of a certain type of subject at once struck his readers. In *Dayspring Mishandled* he threaded a gloomy labyrinth of treachery, disease and death. *The Woman in His Life*, a sentimental dog story, begins with a harrowing description of a nervous breakdown. *Unprofessional* is based on cancer and suicide: the theme of cancer is again to be found in *The Eye of Allah* and *The Wish House*, while *A Madonna of the Trenches* is a story of cancer and suicide in a setting of shell-shocked hysteria and ghostly visitation.

The causes of this preoccupation with sickness should now be obvious, but Kipling's 'late' manner was not an entirely new manifestation of his art. He had deviated from the 'straight' method of story-telling, as used in *Plain Tales from the Hills*, as long ago as 1904 in *Mrs Bathurst* and in *They*. He now gave a further twist to this technique and used it more often, thinking that the old method was played out.

It has been pointed out that these experiments tended to become 'a kind of greatly concentrated novel, usually dealing with a fairly long period in the lives of one or more characters, and this involves a high degree of concentration if the story is to be of his usual length – 15 to 20 pages'. And it is clear that Kipling saw this intense compression as a desirable end in itself, although it was by no means a new characteristic in his writing.

For years he had been in the habit of dipping a pen in Indian ink, and re-writing each manuscript, considering every paragraph, sentence and word, and ruthlessly cutting out dead wood. After a time he would re-read the story, and usually found that it required 'a second shortening'. And then would come a third reading where further deletions might be made. There were obvious dangers in this method, for as C. S. Lewis wrote: 'Even an athlete can be overstrained. Superfluous flesh should be sweated off, but a cruel trainer may be too severe in judging what is superfluous. I think Kipling used the Indian ink too much. Sometimes the story has been so compressed that in the completed version it is not quite told – at least I still do not know exactly what happened in *Mrs Bathurst*.'[1]

The late stories are indeed pared to the bone to such an extent that some of them demand the most concentrated attention, but more importantly they are distinguished by another trait. Kipling seems to be setting elaborate puzzles in the manner of certain Victorian painters in their 'problem' pictures, giving a limited help in their solution. It is as though he said to the reader: 'There, I have given you enough clues. Work it out for yourselves.' But he is conceding less and less, and although the stories are full of grace notes, the clues are deeply hidden.

A close study of these stories shows that they are composed with layer upon layer of meaning, close packed like the skin of an onion. In *The Eye of Allah*, *A Madonna of the Trenches*, and *The Gardener* four or five different interpretations can be placed upon the stories, which means that four or five different tales are contained in each story, although the average reader will only notice the obvious one. As an example of this Bodelsen points out:

The Eye of Allah is on one level a story about what happens to a group of people in a mediaeval monastery; on another level it is a story about a premature discovery (the microscope); on a third it is about the impact of the Renaissance on the mediaeval world picture; on a fourth about the attitude of the artist, the physician, and the philosopher to science, and on the fifth about four aspects of civilization personified as the artist, the scientist, the philosopher, and the Church dignitary and statesman, and illustrated by confronting them with an emblem of the new science: the microscope.[2]

Kipling had also used this method to a lesser extent in *Rewards and Fairies*, knew exactly what he was doing, and was certain it was right:

I worked the material into three or four overlaid tints and textures, which might, or might not, reveal themselves according to the shifting light of sex, youth and experience. It was like working lacquer and mother o' pearl, a natural combination, into the same scheme as niello and grisaille, and trying not to let the joints show. So I loaded the book up with allegories and allusions. ... It was glorious fun; and I knew it must be very good or very bad, because the series turned itself off [i.e. like a tap] just as *Kim* had done.

But the public did not regard Kipling's 'late' manner as glorious fun. They wanted him to continue writing the sort of stories long familiar to them, like those in *Plain Tales from the Hills* or *Life's Handicap*. They were baffled by the ambiguity of the new ones, and dispirited by their macabre emphasis upon cancer, fear and death. And the critics, understanding his purpose little more than the public, reviewed the stories coldly. But Kipling refused to turn from his new method, although he realized that his readers could no longer understand him. He was to write in his autobiography: 'As soon as you find you can do anything, do something you can't,' and he persevered in spite of the bewilderment of the public and the hostility of the reviewers.

The most characteristic and famous stories in the new manner were *The Bull that Thought, A Madonna of the Trenches, The Eye of Allah, The Gardener* and *The Wish House*. Kipling could not complain if his purpose was misunderstood by the average 'Kipling fan', for it has required much modern scholarship to unravel the skein; and even now we must beware of being carried away by speculation, and reading into these stories meanings that were never in Kipling's mind. But in some of them his intentions now seem clear. *The Bull that Thought* is a perfect example of the subtle concealed fable in which he was now interested – in this case about art, the artist and the public, with particular reference to himself.

Like *The Eye of Allah* this story has layer upon layer of meaning, although at a first reading it seems to be a simple tale related to Kipling by the French wine-grower, Voiron, of a magnificent bull, Apis, from the Camargue, who triumphs in a bull-fight because he can think, and is able to create havoc because he departs from the recognized habits of bulls. But in fact the story is an allegory on art and the artist, and the art theme is soon apparent if we know how to look at it. The bull resents being asked to give an encore of a performance in the bull-ring at Arles, 'because no artist will tolerate being asked to repeat himself', a reference to the new and unpopular manner Kipling was now attempting. He had developed 'a breadth of technique that comes of reasoned art, and above all the passion that arrives after experience'.

Of the matadors of the bull-fight described in the story, Villamarti is famous, but a show-off, and is quickly humiliated by Apis. The other matador, Chisto, is 'a laborious middle-aged professional who had never risen beyond a certain dull competence'. When his turn comes, Voiron, watching, saw him 'as the least inspired of all; mediocrity itself, but at heart, and it is the heart that conquers always, my friend – at heart an artist'. Apis, who has spurned the flashy Villamarti, responds wonderfully to Chisto, and together they put on a superb display. Villamarti, seeing his rival's success, tries to join in but is chased off by Apis, and the pantomime ends with Chisto leading the bull to the gate through which few return alive, his arm round Apis's neck, and saying: 'Gentlemen, open to me and my honourable little donkey.'

The bull-fight scenes with Chisto in the ring are described in terms that suggest a work of art: a drama, a comedy, sometimes a ballet. They are a parable about the mysterious ways of poetic inspiration, exemplified by the way in which the hitherto mediocre artist Chisto is 'inspired' ... by the bull to attain heights of art hitherto denied him; and it is also a symbol of the way in which the poet responds to the challenge of his subject; that private experience from which he must distil, in the words of Kipling, ... 'the passion that arrives after experience'.[3]

But another theme can be found in the story beside that of artistic inspiration. The grisly details of the bull-fight, the disembowelments, the crashing of animal bodies against wooden barriers, are a return to Kipling's 'brutal realism'. He had not written in this vein for a long time, and he did so now with a definite purpose. For these horrors are to be taken to represent the terrible battles France had fought in the Great War: Voiron calls Apis 'this Foch among bulls', so that another layer of the story is a fable of the greatness of France and of her art, and at the end of it Voiron and Apis's owner drink a toast to 'her'.

Of all the stories of Kipling's 'late' manner *A Madonna of the Trenches* is the most brilliantly written. Like several others, it was set in the Masonic Lodge of Instruction, and like *The Wish House* is a story of sublime love. Strangwick, the central character, has a nervous collapse at the Lodge. He has been a 'runner' at the front, and in a superbly written passage he babbles of trenches strutted by human skeletons to keep their walls together, and floored by corpses stuffed under the duckboards, which make a horrible creaking sound when trodden on in frosty weather.

But Keele, the Lodge Warden, who was in Strangwick's unit in France, does not believe that these things were the real cause of his collapse, but that he was using them to conceal some greater horror.

Under pressure from Keele it transpires that Sergeant Godsoe, whom Strangwick has known at home from childhood and called 'Uncle', has for long been in love with Strangwick's aunt, Bella Armine, their tragedy being that each is already married. They can be united only by death, and both yearn for its arrival. Bella is dying of cancer, and tells Godsoe the moment she expects to die. At that moment she manifests herself to Godsoe in the trench, and he kills himself to be with her. The victory of love over death, which is the theme of the story, is accomplished. But Strangwick saw Bella and Godsoe in that trench, and this was the real cause of his collapse: 'He was lookin' at 'er an' she was lookin' at him. I saw it, an' me soul turned over inside me because – because it knocked out everything I'd believed in. I 'ad nothin' to lay 'old of, d'ye see? ... There wasn't a single gordam thing left abidin' for me to take hold of, here or hereafter, if the dead do rise – and I saw 'em – why – why *any*thing can 'appen.'

The Wish House is another story, pitiful and harrowing, in which Kipling enshrines that belief in a sublime love and readiness for sacrifice which he believed to be the ultimate compassion, the supreme emotion of which a human being is capable, in a setting of witchcraft and occultism. It is written in his most spare and sinewy prose, the horror accentuated by the matter-of-factness, the fabular and the actual cunningly blended, and the whole pierced by shafts of horrible realism. It is the story of a woman who, for love, has taken upon herself, by a pact in witchcraft, the agony of another person – the worthless man who has deserted her. The clues are provided more generously than usual in the poem preceding the story, 'Late came the God', in which the agony of cancer

> Daily renewed and nightly pursued through her soul to her flesh –
> Mornings of memory, noontides of agony, midnights unslaked for her,
> Till the stones of the streets of her Hells and her Paradise ached for
> her. ...
>
> And she built an Altar and served by the light of her Vision –
>   Alone, without hope of regard or reward, but uncowed,
> Resolute, selfless, divine.
>   These things she did in Love's honour...
> What is a God beside Woman? Dust and Derision!

Mrs Ashcroft, an elderly retired servant, tells her friend Mrs Fetley how she has taken the illness upon herself by asking the mysterious Token of the Wish House to be allowed to do so. There is no glamour

or excitement in the Wish House. It is simply an empty house in a
suburban row, with a shuffling, wheezing elemental inside it – well
in keeping with the dead sick-room atmosphere of the story. The man
has recovered without ever knowing the reason, and Mrs Ashcroft
has never before told anyone of her pact and her cancer. There is something that makes one shudder in the way Kipling describes her doing
so:

'Liz,' she tells Mrs Fetley, 'There's no mistakin' when the edges are
all heaped up, like – same as a collar. You'll see it. An' I laid out
Dora Wickwood, too. *She* 'ad it under the armpit, like.'

But Mrs Ashcroft is pathetically anxious to be assured that her
squalid agony – 'God's croolty' – will succeed in keeping her man:

'But the pain *do* count, don't ye think, Liz? The pain *do* count to keep
'Arry – where I want 'im. Say it can't be wasted, like.'
'I'm sure of it – sure of it, dearie. You'll 'ave your reward.'   .
'I don't want no more'n this – *if* de pain is taken into de reckoning.'
'T'will be, t'will be, Gra.'

Equally memorable, and with a theme that uplifts rather than har-
rows, is *The Gardener*, which Kipling placed at the end of *Debits and
Credits* with the object of drawing particular attention to it. Like *The
Wish House* it is a story of compassion, and like *The Bull that Thought*
appears at first glance a clear and straightforward one: of an un-
married mother who loses her son in the war and visits his grave in
a war cemetery, being shown its position by one of the gardeners.

The mother, Helen Turrell – how impersonal these Kipling names
are – has for years passed off the boy as her nephew, and he was
publicly known as such, but she has found the strain of this deception
almost unbearable. Reaching the cemetery, she does not know where
to find the grave:

A man knelt down behind a line of headstones – evidently a gardener,
for he was firming a young plant in the soft earth. She went towards him,
her paper in her hand. He rose at her approach and without prelude or saluta-
tion asked: 'Who are you looking for?'
'Lieutenant Michael Turrell – my nephew,' said Helen slowly and word
for word, as she had many thousand times in her life.
The man lifted his eyes and looked at her with infinite compassion before
he turned from the fresh-sown grass toward the naked black crosses.
'Come with me,' he said, 'and I will show you where your son lies.'
When Helen left the cemetery she turned for a last look. In the distance
she saw the man bending over his young plants; and she went away, supposing him to be the gardener.

The reference here is to the Fourth Gospel, *John* 20:15, when Mary Magdalene goes to the tomb for the body of Jesus, finds him standing there, and speaks to him without realizing who he is, 'supposing him to be the gardener'.

On one layer of *The Gardener* we find a story of an upper-class Englishwoman, suffering agonies through her code of respectability; on another a story of the mercy of God to sinners. The gardener in the war cemetery relieves Helen of her terrible burden of deception by revealing his knowledge that the dead soldier whose grave she is seeking is her son. The revelation is equivalent to rolling away the stone of the Sepulchre, as did the angel in the New Testament account, and that this was Kipling's meaning is made clear in the accompanying poem:

> One day of all my years –
> One hour of that one day –
> His Angel saw my tears
> And rolled the Stone away.

The same technique is to be found in *Dayspring Mishandled*, a 'revenge' story of a savage feud between a genuine and a spurious bibliophile in which literary forgery takes place (Kipling typically going so far as to forge a mediaeval manuscript himself before writing the story); and in such tales as *Unprofessional*, *The Prophet and the Country*, *The Manner of Men*, and *The Janeites*.

But although the invention never flags, there are signs of exhaustion in *Limits and Renewals*. We have seen the reason for Kipling's obsession at this period with fear, pain and cancer; with the moment when the moral fibre disintegrates under intolerable pressure. He is absorbed in a man's private hell of fear, in the breaking-point which proclaims psychological collapse. But there is always tender sympathy with the 'misused clay', and in 'The Coward', one of the 'Epitaphs on the War' based on the Greek Anthology, he wrote of a man shot for cowardice:

> I could not look on Death, which being known,
> Men led me to him, blindfold and alone.

One has the impression, in these last stories, that Kipling, although perhaps unaware of it, is farther and farther from his audience, concocting his mysterious brews in solitude. And in many of them he had abandoned action completely, allowing conversation to take its place, as in *The Janeites* and *The Wish House*, which for some made these stories impossible to read. But he did something to placate his public by returning to dog stories with *Thy Servant A Dog* which, unlike *The Dog Hervey*, which had been the story of a dog as seen by a man, tries to fathom the mysterious, opaque mind of the animal. His public turned with a sob of relief from cancerous to canine themes, and leaped upon *Thy Servant A Dog*, which sold 100,000 copies in six months.

The swing of some modern critics towards Kipling has been largely based on these 'late' stories. 'What narrative there is,' said Lord Radcliffe in a lecture to the Kipling Society, '– often there is little – runs like a root below the surface of the story, and all that shows above ground are the shoots that tell by implication what lies underneath. Kipling had forged one more of his remarkable tools.'[4]

Yet it would be as mistaken to overpraise these stories as to revile them. Like Lord Radcliffe, we would be

sorry if attention came to be concentrated too closely on his late manner. It often fails to make effect, even to convey its point, by the sheer complexity of the structure, the dedication to jargon, the withdrawal. After all, prose must remain an art of communication. Words are to speak to the ordinary willing reader, rather than to the devotee or the researcher. The artist has no right to retire so far that only through prayer and fasting can his voice be heard.[5]

CHAPTER XXIV

A DARKENING SCENE

By February 1930 Carrie's health had become almost as miserable as that of her husband. Crippled by rheumatism and now a confirmed diabetic, she was ordered abroad by her doctors. They sailed for the first time to the West Indies, taking with them Lady Milner's daughter, Helen Hardinge. After a somewhat churlish refusal, in the Kipling manner, of an invitation by the Governor of Jamaica to visit him, they began to tour the islands. Their progress was curtailed when Carrie succumbed to appendicitis and was placed in hospital in Bermuda; Rudyard was left alone in lodgings for four months, his longest separation from Carrie during forty years of married life.

He began to wonder how to extricate himself and his sick wife from the island, which had been rendered repulsive to them by throngs of Americans who had left their 'dry' country in order to get drunk there. Kipling's distaste for America was now such that he told the long-suffering F. N. Doubleday that even if an operation proved necessary, Carrie would refuse to have it in New York. The United States, he added, was 'not a civilized country for the sick'. He would not dream of returning home through America, and decided to do so through Canada.

The Dunhams came to meet them in Montreal, and at once called at the Ritz-Carlton Hotel where the Kiplings were staying, finding 'Uncle Rud' in a somewhat dictatorial mood.

We children [said Miss Josephine Dunham] stayed behind to give Father and Mother the first chance, and then we went in and saw Uncle Rud. We shook hands with him, and 'Don't touch me,' he said. He had a cold. In the sitting-room was Aunt Carrie, standing near the door. We were so glad to see her again; and she looked sick, and very thin. Her hair, at least in front, is now pure white. They began talking about Italian steamers. Carrie had complained that the delicate manipulations of the temperature were undertaken solely on behalf of the bananas. She thought that the Italians had the finest Mercantile Marine in the world, but Rudyard observed:

'They're not a good crew to drown with. I'm very particular about the people I drown with.'

Someone came to the door with an offer to Carrie to appear on the cinema. Kipling dismissed the man, and coming back into the room said: 'It's you they want, darling – I can just see you in the Movies.'

Father told Uncle Rud the story of the American surgeon, way back, who before starting to operate would always spit on his knife for good luck. Mother was quite horrified; she had been married to Father for over thirty years and had never heard the story.[1]

Kipling spoke of what he regarded as the horrible situation in Bermuda of heavy drinking among Americans, and the demoralizing conditions prevailing there. The Dunham daughters attempted to persuade the Kiplings that these people were only the scum of America. The telephone rang shortly after their arrival, and Kipling answered it: 'Publicity picture – what's that? . . . Oh, a talking movie. Nothing doing.'

The Kiplings [continued Miss Dunham] are appalled at our way of handling people entering the country. I spoke of how interested we were to see Canada and how we had never been in it before except to pass through it for a short distance at night years ago. We also spoke of how interesting it was to see so many signs in both French and English, and how tolerant the Government seemed.

'We always do that,' said Uncle Rud. The French and English in Canada apparently lead a separate existence side by side. We found from Uncle Rud that Canada's tie with England is practically nothing at all. England has no control over her Government, and the only link is the Governor-General who has no power whatever. They only have him 'to please the ladies'; there is absolutely nothing to prevent Canada breaking away any day.

'Only,' he said, 'we've been together so long – for 300 years.' He says that the modern way is to allow the dominions great latitude, great freedom of Government, and a right to get out whenever they wanted to. B.* said yes, that she supposed it was better to make them fond of England, than to hold them together by oppression; and I said I supposed it was the best way to keep the Empire together. Just then the telephone rang and Uncle Rud went. When he came back he said, 'It's the *only* way to keep an Empire together. . . . When you have grown up children, you have to give them a latch-key – India, however, is not a dominion. The Hindus are in many ways a somewhat degenerate race.' They married pathetically young, and Uncle Rud says they are 'the children of children'. The young Hindus are brilliant to a degree around the age of 21. They can pass the most difficult examinations that would baffle and stump a white boy. But soon they begin to peter out, and

* Miss Beatrice Dunham.

die around 40. The women get worn out and die about the same age too. The English, Uncle Rud says, are in control of India because the Indians want them. The Indians long ago saw how beautifully the small parts were run that the English had jurisdiction over, and wanted them to come in and settle their disputes for them and keep some kind of jurisdiction over them. Gandhi was spoken of, and I asked Uncle Rud whether he thought that he was sincere.

'Not the least little bit,' he said. 'Gandhi is just a paste-board front.'[2]

Back home, Kipling wrote to his friend Sir Percy Bates. It is a letter which shows his regard for Caroline's waning health, and his own passion for amateur technical detail:

You have my sympathy about reading at meals. I've been doing it for more than three weeks, as the wife has been ill with something too like inflammatory rheumatism to please me. It wasn't the genuine article, but it fled about from joint to joint in an ugly way. I take my meals alone, and have rediscovered the ancient fact that reading at grub is dam bad for the innards. But I read the *Rambler* and the *Tatler* (the old lot), and of course, all the papers which make me savage.

As to *my* new ship, with the proper stern, her name will be the *Magnalia*, which being translated literally, means 'Mighty Works' – as see Cotton's *Magnalia Christi. You* would like to call her the *Imperia*, but as the Empire is out of commission, that will not be any good. She will not, as your Board will suggest, be called *Magnolia* by the foolish public, because every Englishman knows something about *Magna* meaning great, (and it comes before Charta); and it is a fine full and sonorous title without any of the arrogance that caused the Gods to open up the *Titanic*. Also it can't be twisted into Yiddish, like the *Levi Nathan*.* I will *not* travel on her because nothing this side Gehenna would make me go to New York, but I will give her my blessing and, if I live so long, I will try to come down to her launch.[3]

* *Leviathan.*

CHAPTER XXV

TWILIGHT AND EVENGLOW

THE Kiplings left Burwash on 20 February 1931 for Egypt, where they remained until April, dallying for a fortnight on the way home. Another visit to Paris in June, and one to Oxford in September, seem to have been the only excursions from home other than the normal ones to London. Kipling did little work during the year – less than in any previous year. A few verses, the Bermuda parrot story, a skit, and the preparation for his French speech, appear to have made the total of his work, although he collected some old material for his book of humorous stories, published in March.

His health throughout the year was, on the whole, poor, with considerable pain, accounting almost certainly for the lack of work. His literary inactivity was increased by anxiety on account of Caroline, who was attacked by gout and eye trouble. The Budget in September worried them considerably, and perhaps accounted for their decision to get rid of their cars and the chauffeur, Taylor, who had been with them for twelve and a half years. There is, however, a super-tax entry of £9426.

Kipling's intense resentment of the course pursued by the Baldwin Government in 1931 caused him to write to Gwynne about his cousin and childhood companion: 'I am glad you've got on to the fact that S.B. is a Socialist at heart. It came out of the early years, when he was in that sort of milieu among some of the academic Socialist crowd – unconsciously but none the less effectively.'

In November he commented:

Dickens is out of date for the public, or you might make Ian* write a leader about Mrs Gummidge 'thinking of the old 'un'. That is all that S.B.'s speed is come to. Since Balfour's 'darkness and composure' talks I can't recall anything like it. S.B. and Mac are of one kidney – almost like the old Nigger 'brudder Bones' gags. But Mac excelled himself with his speech about dying

* Ian Colvin.

a dreamer. He didn't think of the poor devils that died while he was more than dreaming how to spoke the War.

He felt acutely the American Debt débâcle. He believed that behind the rigidity of the American attitude lay the knowledge that England was spending enormous sums upon giving her 'working classes' a higher standard of living – 'and it is a bit hard to answer 'em when they say: "You pay out three or four hundred million on your social reform stunts, and you can't cough up twenty million for your just debts!" '[4]

To Bates he wrote violently on the subject of education: 'The reason we don't cut "education", is because it is a Trades Union of 250,000, mostly females of sensitive years. It's a "vested interest" and the child doesn't matter a dam. You'll hear that bitch-pack throw tongue before long.' He mistrusted extensive popular education, and was fond of saying that it did not help a milkmaid to milk or a ploughman to plough.[5] One of his friends, Lieut. Colonel Thwaites, observed of him at this period that he was surprised by the violence of Kipling's conservatism. The bestowal of the 'flapper vote' and Baldwin's 'Safety First' slogan infuriated him, and his growing intolerance became noticeable to others:

'He had a poor opinion of many classes of the community. He instanced to me the case of one of his gardeners. This young fellow, working at Burwash, enjoying good wages, with a rent-free house, thought to "better himself" by going to Australia. Kipling acquiesced, and facilitated a passage. Six months or more later the young fellow turned up again and begged Mr Kipling to reinstate him. He complained that he had been asked in Australia to "ride the boundaries" or whatever the phrase is; he had been called upon at any hour of the day or night to round up cattle, or sheep; had been expected to off-saddle and sleep in the open, and, in other words to live "an uncivilized life". Kipling relished telling me that he had pleasure in turning away from his door so poor a specimen of an Englishman.'[6]

Kipling's last collection of stories, *Limits and Renewals*, was published on 8 April 1932, but although he continued to write, his mind was becoming increasingly engrossed in politics. His political antagonism to his cousin now appears complete. He refused an invitation from Bates to visit Ottawa – 'One can't tell the truth about things. You want someone who will watch that triple ass Thomas – and Baldwin.'[1] The advent of Hitler placed beyond doubt his long-held and brilliantly perceptive convictions of Germany's aggressive intentions: 'The Were-Wolf has got tired. He's been a man for twelve years, and has got all out of mankind that he needs. At least he can't get any more – so it is time for him to change shape. In less than a year he will be clamouring for the return of his Colonies, as "necessary for his self-respect". You wait and see!'[2]

Kipling had a peculiar dislike for biography, which he often referred to as the 'Higher Cannibalism', a fear which probably sprang from his deep reserve about his own private life, and which was increased by the stirring of dead memories. There was so much in his own past which he could not bear to think about – Josephine radiant in the garden at Naulakha, the Vermont feud, John blown to pieces at Loos, and now the same horror beginning all over again, while the English, whom he had so frequently warned, went their old fatuous way to cinema and football field, unlistening, uncaring. He even refused a request from Sydney Cockerell to write a book on Lady Burne-Jones, 'the beloved aunt', who had died in 1920, so fearful was he of stirring the sleeping ghosts. His feminine and perhaps distorted sensitivity emerges from the letter of refusal he wrote to Cockerell:

I quite see your point because, as you say, some of her letters might bring back things to me: but my objection stands, tho' it be a selfish one. I'm too fond of her, and loved her too much in my childhood and youth, to share my feelings with *any* public. This here biography and 'reminiscer' business that is going on nowadays is a bit too near the Higher Cannibalism to please me. Ancestor-worship is all right, but serving them up filleted, or spiced or 'high' (which last is very popular) has put me off.[3]

Although he winced from many episodes in the past, he became occasionally nostalgic about the happier memories of childhood. When he had written to his Aunt Georgie before her death the memories would sometimes come back of the felicity with which he had knocked on the front door of 'The Grange', a little boy with bursting carpet bag, and the 'running wild' at Epping. He spoke of

the earliest days in the old long store room at Wilden, when you used to chase me out of it, and herd up Stan after brekker for his cod-liver. Not to mention the Loughton summer when you objected to the smell of barnyard manure on our boots at meals and you were *not* sympathetic over the details of pig-killing. D'you remember the stranger who broke in from the Dalleys' kitchen when you were singing: 'Oh those blue eyes, those eyes of blue', and we sniggered (we *were* little beasts) – when his compliments turned you turkey-coloured and there was much – much more afterwards.[4]

It was a period of recurring pain and disability. James, Kipling's original Aberdeen terrier, died, to his infinite distress, but a younger, Mike, remained to console him in his loss. There was a certain amount of work in 1932 – *Proofs of Holy Writ*, in which Ben Jonson and Shakespeare discuss the Authorized Version of the Bible; a speech for the Prince of Wales; the verses 'The Flag Ship' and 'A Fox Meditates'; an appreciation of Mary Kingsley, *Meditations in Flight*; and some French notes. He prepared for the American market a selection of verse and prose with the title *A Pageant of Kipling*, and attended to the production of the vast Sussex Edition of his work in thirty-five volumes. Figures at the end of the year show a gross income of £32,831, from which normal income tax of £7989 plus approximately £9000 super-tax were deducted. It was also a year which offered to the Imperialist the immense satisfaction of hearing the King use Kipling's own words in his address to the Empire on Christmas Day.[5]

Kipling's infirm body kept his mind preoccupied with illness and operations, and rendered him particularly sympathetic with those in similar trouble. He had again left England and from Monte Carlo wrote to Lady Bathurst in February 1933:

Your news is disturbing *except* that you say the trouble has been dealt with. The knife is so much better than the disease. I am rejoiced that the special horror of the thing – the return through darkness and bewilderment, and the fear that goes before getting on the table seem to have been spared you. All of which does not in the least spare the wretched carcase that goes under the knife, and that takes it out of the Soul. Isn't it curious how personality splits beneath anaesthetics, and how one comes to consider what one has always called 'oneself'.[6]

He was not happy at Monte Carlo: 'All the old MC have rallied to the flag and the King of Sweden leads them, assisted by the King of Denmark, and Miss Evelyn Laye, who calls everyone within hail of her table "darling".'[7]

As though realizing that his creative life was now over, Kipling turned to the revision of old work. On 5 October 1933 he published his *Collected Verse, 1885–1932*. His practical literary competence is shown by the fact that he undertook single-handed the forbidding task of correcting the proofs of this vast mass of print, classifying the verses, indexing them, and arranging them in chronological order. In spite of the fact that this was a year of incessant pain, he did not flinch from his dreary and difficult task, refused to delegate it, and performed it with outstanding skill. His spirits during the soulless routine work were remarkably high. He wrote to Trix, who was well again:

Oh, very dear daughter of my mother!
... For the moment I am in a small and pernickety Hell. 'Tis thus. They (Hodder & Stoughton) are bringing out another issue of my inclusive edition of collected verse. The last was in '26. Since then a mass of verses have accumulated and 'tis I must read the proofs of the whole thing and wheel them into some sort of order. (Now I am *not* orderly) and that has meant a set of proofs the size of a small hayrick – some of them old and long ago set up in stereo, so that any alteration must be gouged out of, and plugged into the stereo metal. Technically this is called 'Mends'. They are marked by little pink pieces of paper gummed over what was the original. I make as few 'mends' as I can. The rest is fair white paper on which, as they are first proofs, I can make all the alterations I want. ... Well they arrive in duplicate – some in triplicate – in wudges of from two hundred to a hundred pages all neatly tied up with paper-tummy bands (and I am *not* neat!). I cleared my writing table to the bone, and spread 'em out yesterday and they all got mixed as the wanton eels. They are all back again in their belly bands and harnessed with additional ones of red elastic so that they can't get off and 'commit poetry' with other wudges. And the whole blessed thing is about eight hundred pages.[8]

He concluded this great volume with an appeal to possible biographers, as futile as it was unreasonable, to leave his private memories in peace:

> And for the little, little, span
> 　　The dead are borne in mind,
> Seek not to question other than
> 　　The books I leave behind.

1933, the year of ill-omen, passed, and while the slave-pens were being hammered together at Dachau and Sachsenhausen, the English remained suspended in their delicious trance. At this lamentable period, when 11,500,000 people signed the Peace Ballot, when Canon Sheppard's pacifist sermons were filling St Martin-in-the-Fields, and a subversive vote was passed with acclamation at the Oxford Union, Kipling was now coldly assessing the number of years left before the deluge. In January 1934:

Here's the Hun getting into position for – '36? or a year later? I don't suppose anything will teach our people anything. Personally I shall be grateful if we are allowed three years, but given our present administration and our disturbing internal influences, I can't see why the General Staff should not strike before that time. We aren't merely asking for it; we're imploring it: and that damn League of Nations Union is rotting out all the Schools ... we have lost years in slush.[9]

He railed in despair at the contrast between the pacifism prevailing in English schools and universities, and the flaming racial doctrines and brutal fanaticism that were being pumped into the eager and bright-eyed Teutonic youth.

He went back to France sick with forebodings, and in a retreat soothingly called 'L'Enchantement Mongiers' the healing spirit of the country he loved did something to alleviate his misery. Yet it was never absent. The villa was wild and deserted but sometimes he would see *camions* loaded with coal and wood and pine-cones, and feed the five starving cats until they grew sleek and purring. There were 'almonds almost crazy with bloom, and the bees who have come in to plunder, quite so. They are banded, rather savage ladies who have been losing their tempers over the ragged and frost-bitten rosemary.' One day he found himself on a terrace set with orange trees, a loquat, and a peach in full bloom. And beneath this there were brilliant-hued cocks and hens and a nun pigeon on the vivid grass, where the low wild irises were flowering. Kipling was stupefied with the beauty: 'Under the sunlight and the slashing shadows of the loquat leaves, it all composed like a marvellous piece of Jap cloisonné lacquer-work.' And when they climbed out of this enclave into a biting wind on the naked side of the hill it was, he thought, like coming out of the Garden of Armicha to the landscape round the Dark Town.

On his return to England in March 1934, he began busying his restless mind with abuse of Professor Laski, and in urging, five years before the steps were taken by those whose business it was, the immediate commencement of air raid precautions. In that month he wrote to Gwynne: 'Get someone to work out the amount of cellar-room and the rest of it; and *keep on pegging away with figures.* Absurd? Yes. But the only way of putting the wind up the people is by going on just those lines. The Govt. will pretty soon say that you are "panic-mongering". Your answer is: "No. We only want a chance to live. Your present system don't give it."' He continued his old nagging about politicians, and again Baldwin does not escape the lash: 'You are quite right about the sensitiveness of S.B. and R.M. as to what they call "personal attacks" – which means any rude criticism not couched in official phrases. But did you ever know any politician who was otherwise in England?'[10]

In pleasant contrast to these depressing events was Kipling's interest in the construction of the great Cunarder '534', afterwards to become the *Queen Mary*. He wrote long letters packed with intricate amateur marine detail and suggestions to Sir Percy Bates, letters which often astonished Bates with their insight and common sense.[11] He measured out the vast proportions of the liner in his fields at 'Bateman's', and stood amazed at the acreage filled on his land by this plotting of the hull of the leviathan, stem to stern, and across the beam. She looked even more gigantic on land, he thought, than she would at sea, marked out with two white diamonds – stretching over a meadow and a half.

Kipling's own personal '534' had been sent in for winter painting, and refit. The numbers had to be scratched through and *Queen Mary* painted below, the house flag renewed, and three coats of varnish applied. She was the little wooden boat on the pond at 'Bateman's', used by the visiting children, her proportion six feet overall, and in heavy service that summer on the pond, carrying babies. He kept in close touch with Bates, who was obviously flattered by the interest of this eminent man. Bates sent Kipling, through his secretary, the proposed life-boats stations' list of the new liner, and Kipling replied exuberantly:

I haven't been specially fit, but I'm a heap better than I was. And here's as far as I have got with my latest ribaldry – based on the boat-stations list that your Secretary sent me.

Namely:

> Such as in ships of awful size
>   Into the seas descend,
> Are given Tyrian broideries
>   And bathrooms without end.
> But me no chromium plumbing thrills,
>   Nor Tudor Banquet Hall;
> It is her watch and station-bills
>   I study first of all.
>
> So, when that first down-Channel night
>   Breaks, in full gale, today;
> And Ushant's seven mile of white
>   Foretells a rabid Bay; –
> Above my earliest cup of tea
>   Contentedly I think
> Of those who have to sail with me
>   And (peradventure) sink.[12]

Four pages of the medical extract from Caroline's diaries support her opinion of 1934 – that it was a 'year that was not easy for either of us'. Kipling's work was greatly reduced again, and nothing of importance emerged. Over three months were passed in Cannes, a fortnight in Jersey, a week-end at Deal and another at Cirencester with the Bathursts. The excursions to London, so welcome to Kipling, when he could visit the Beefsteak Club and escape from the clammy atmosphere of 'Bateman's', were few – the ten days spent there in December were the first since July. He assisted a little with ideas for the Pageant of Parliament in the Albert Hall earlier in the year, wrote an ode for the Australian Government at their request, started one dog story, and helped with the scenario of *Soldiers Three*. There is mention of *A Pageant of Kipling* and his *Collected Dog Stories* appeared in September.

Kipling was unfortunate not to have survived into the days when really great prices were paid for the scenarios of motion pictures. As it was, on 3 February 1935 Alexander Korda offered him £5000 for *Toomai of the Elephants*, an offer which was accepted. This contract was clinched by Caroline, whose business sense never deserted her in spite of the fact that she was so 'wretchedly ill that I can neither read, write or talk, and all these days and many more besides I have existed, not lived. There had to be a smash some day.'[13]

Kipling had meditated now, for some time, how he could finally express his sombre views about the wrath to come. He selected a meeting of the Royal Society of St George on 6 May 1935 as a suitable forum. Into this restrained speech, the obvious sobriety of which indicates the control he had placed upon his emotions, he sought to put, in a reasonable, academic form, all the despair of thirty years' unacknowledged foresight. He was not a good public speaker. Nor did he enjoy the practice of oratory. Rather was he a dutiful reader-out of inspired devotional exercises. It seemed to him that the moment had now come for a final effort to rally his compatriots. He had found that violent dialectics, however brilliantly pursued, either in prose or verse, were fruitless. With a conscious subordination of the passions that were boiling within him, with an icy dismissal of his own personal sacrifices in the war, and with – perhaps, most difficult of all – a forgiveness to the indifference, to the boredom excited by his warnings, Kipling breasted his audience.

His son was dead; his health was appalling; his warnings had been despised. He was never the most patient of men. Shafts of hatred and anger had pierced his correspondence, fed by illness, but created by no simply analysable cause. He faced his distinguished audience and spoke in a quiet, passionless voice:

Great Britain's quota of dead in the War was over eight hundred thousand when the books were closed in '21 or '22. It would be within the mark to say that three-quarters of a million of these were English. Furthermore, a large but unknown number died in the next few years from wounds or disease directly due to the War. There is a third category of men incapacitated from effort by the effects of shock, gassing, tubercle and the like. These carry a high death-rate because many of them burned out half a life's vitality in three or four years. They too, have ceased to count.

All these were men of average physique, and, but that they died without issue, would have continued our race. The selective elimination of so many men of one type, and their children, led to an extensive revision of all standards of English thought and action.

Now, there were a number of persons who, for various motives, had dissociated themselves from the War at the outset. These, however, were all able to answer to their names at the close of hostilities, and to rejoin the national life with a clear field before them.

Still they were not happy. There is a necessity laid upon man to justify himself to himself in order that he may continue to live comfortably with himself. Our initial errors, as we all know, are trivial. It is what we say and do to prove to ourselves that our errors were really laborious virtues which build up the whole-time hells of this life.

So it was in exact accord with human nature that, very shortly after the War, a theory should have sprung up that the War had been due to a sort of cosmic hallucination which had affected the nations concerned with a sort of cosmic hysteria. This theory absolved those who had not interested themselves in the War and, by inference, condemned those who had; thus supplying comfort and moral support where needed. Naturally the notion bore fruit. For this reason.

Most children and all nations, when they have hurt themselves, instinctively run indoors and ask to be told a pretty tale. So it is with us, and so to us, too, a tale was told. (You may remember we were all a little fatigued at the time.) The special virtues of our tale was that its moral bases were as inexpugnable as the most upright preceptress could desire. Here they are:

All pain – whether it comes from hitting one's head against a table or from improvising a four years' war at four days notice – is evil. All evil is wicked. And, since of all evils, war gives the most pain to the most people, wickedest of all things is war.* Wherefore, unless people wish to be thought wicked, they must so order the national life that never again shall war in any form be possible.

* An unconscious reversal of Bentham's famous principle.

Granted the first premises, the rest of the reasoning is unanswerable – on paper. But why the entire Commination Service should have been addressed by ourselves to ourselves is a little obscure. For if there was a converted nation since the days of St Augustine, it was us.

A little later – in '22 or '23 – on the heels, you might say, of Rachel mourning for her children – our electorate was enlarged by the enfranchisement of all Englishwomen over twenty-one.

This gave renewed impetus to our national ideal of an ever-rising standard of living and the removal of want, discomfort, and the accidents of life from the lives of all our people. To this end we built up, and are now building, gigantic organizations to control and handle every detail of those lives. But for reasons which I shall try to show, we chose – we chose – not to provide that reasonable margin of external safety without which even the lowest standard of life cannot be maintained in this dangerously congested island.

The world outside England had other preoccupations. Like ourselves it had dealt – had been compelled to deal – with an opponent whose national life and ideals were based on a cult – a religion as it now appears – of War, which exacted that all his nationals should be trained at any cost to endure as well as to inflict punishment.

In this our opponent was excusable. He had won his place in civilization by means of three well-planned Wars, waged within two generations. He had been checked somewhat in his fourth War, but soon after the close of it – in '24 or '25 – seemed to be preparing for a fifth campaign.

In this also our opponent was excusable. His path was made easy for him. Stride for stride with his progress towards his avowed goal, we toiled, as men toil after virtue, to cast away a half, and more than a half of our defences in all three elements and to limit the sources of their supply and renewal. This we did explicitly that we might set the rest of the world a good example.

That the rest of the world – down to the little uneasy neutrals who had seen what can happen to a neutral at a pinch – was openly or furtively trying to arm itself against whispered eventualities, had nothing to do with our case. It was laid upon us to set the world an example, no matter at what risks. And we did.

For several years – more than ten, I believe – our responsible administrators dwelt, almost with complacency, on the magnitude of the risks we were running, and on our righteousness in running them, and through all those years our people were made to appear as if they loved to have it so.

But through all these irrecoverable years a large part of the world outside England had not been idle.

Today, State-controlled murder and torture, open and secret, within and outside the borders of a State, State-engineered famine, starvation and slavery are requisite; State-imposed Godlessness, or State-prescribed paganism, are commonplaces of domestic administration throughout States whose aggregate area is between one-fifth and one-fourth of the total land surface of the Eastern hemisphere. These modern developments have been accepted in England without noticeable protest even from quarters usually quick to protest.

Nevertheless the past year has given birth to the idea that our example of State-defended defencelessness has not borne much fruit, and that we have walked far enough along the road paved with good intentions. It is now arranged that, in due time, we will take steps to remedy our more obvious deficiencies. So far, so good; but if that time be *not* given to us – if the attack of the future is to be on the same swift 'all-in' lines as our opponents' domestic administrations – it is possible that before we are aware, our country may have joined those submerged races of history who passed their children through fire to Moloch in order to win credit with their Gods.

And yet, the genius of our race fights for us in the teeth of doctrine! The abiding springs of the English spirit are not of yesterday or the day before. They draw from an immemorial continuity of the Nation's life under its own Sovereigns. They are fed by a human relationship more intimate and more far-reaching than the world has ever known. They make part of a mystery as unpurchasable as it is incommunicable.

Kipling was fortunate in that his inspiration never flagged. His mind teemed with plots, and unlike many writers he was extremely generous in putting his ideas at the disposal of others. The talented Lord Dunsany had already endeared himself to Kipling by making the only human speech at a deplorable public dinner they had attended together, a dinner at which Kipling had writhed in fury as a member of the Cecil family descanted on the virtues of the League of Nations. Kipling was strongly drawn to Dunsany, and in May wrote him an interesting letter:

Private.

Bateman's
30th May, 1935.

Dear Dunsany,

Here is a thing which has come up in my head which I can't handle because I don't know present-day Irish (Mick) language and backgrounds. So I send it on to you to consider. Substantially I have made it boil down to three or four IRA – rebels – Mountain Men, or cattle of that kidney, who, for their own purposes, politics, row about a girl or what you please – have fired into – set alight, bombed or otherwise terrorized a neighbour's house. Or, alternatively they have waylaid and hammered a man in the dark, or cut off a girl's hair (you have a large choice in the matter, I believe). Anyway, they find themselves landed with a dead or dying person who must be disposed of before the dawn breaks.

They discuss the situation among themselves and finally pick up the corpse and bear it off with intent to dispose of it in a kindly bog. En route, they find that there has attached himself to their little procession an odd-looking person in some sort of clerical garb that they can't identify. He seems to have taken on himself charge of the whole situation – even to the extent of turning round and furiously (sic) bidding them, in dumb show, to (sic) to go on when they (Irish fashion) begin to waver in their precise objective.

It is his amazing eyes that they notice first of all. Then it dawns on them that he is not of this earth, and, further, that he is mad – a mad ghost.

In great fear they follow his signals to the lip of the bog, where he takes charge of the committal and delivers a sermon on the dead and on Ireland at large. It is rather a notable sermon – as you will find when you try to write it; he being, or, rather, having once been, Dean of St Patrick's in whose crypt his body, he tells them, lies. Cut it off at that point, or if you like add frills and grace-notes at discretion – such as one of the lads telling the tale at Confession, or something of that kind.

You are the only one who can do it with comprehension and venom. So I put it to you.

Always sincerely,
RUDYARD KIPLING.

Valentine Williams,* too, speaks of Kipling's generosity to young authors. In spite of the difference in their age and literary attainments, he always treated Williams on equal terms as a fellow-author, and although Williams was not deceived, he was much encouraged by this attitude. One day Kipling began to question him about his experiences in Macedonia, in the Balkan War; and out of their talk proceeded to evolve a short story centring about the figure of a Macedonian Komitaji, which Kipling insisted Williams should write. 'In his enormous kindness to young writers he subsequently sent me several letters on the subject, elaborating "our" story, as he called it, in great detail.'[14]

During the summer of 1935 Kipling wrote a 'Just So Story', *Ham and the Porcupine*, for Princess Elizabeth's Gift Book, and a poem, 'The King and the Sea', which was widely circulated in the press. It was now again Caroline's turn to be ill, and for her sake they went to Marienbad for a cure, although to travel through Germany was a painful ordeal for both of them. But once there Rudyard found deep happiness, and he told Frank Doubleday that he had not seen such woods and hills since leaving Vermont,[15] although the cure did nothing to improve Caroline's health. The Kiplings had spent from February to early May in Cannes, and returned for another month there in August. These were the main departures from Burwash during

* Author of the spy story *The Man with the Club Foot.*

1935, but they spent a few days on the *Berengaria* watching the Jubilee Fleet Review in the Solent in July. On 1 August Kipling began work on his autobiography, which was posthumously entitled *Something of Myself* at the suggestion of Sir Alfred Webb-Johnson, President of the Royal College of Surgeons, who edited it. We have already observed Kipling's reticence, and it is nowhere better exhibited than in this cautious, tantalizing work. Vividly written, eminently readable, it yet masks every intimate detail of his past. We have already seen that he felt adverse events so strongly that he could not bear to think about them, preferring to suppress them. He was thus denied the release from grief which many authors obtain through their writings. The reader will search this baffling work in vain for any reference to the Vermont tragedy, to the deaths of Josephine or John, to Flo Garrard or Mrs Hill. These memories were excised from his mind by a surgical cut.

His political bitterness continued as the situation further deteriorated, and in September we find him writing: 'The present situation is beyond all my knowledge and experience – except so far as it confirms my conviction that the tender mercies of the *righteous* are worse than the rages of the heathen. If you've got to crusade, you ought to have something better than a surplice for the job. It only needs de Valera for the next League President to round out the whole cycle of collective delirium.'[16]

In spite of these asperities, he remained a charming host at 'Bateman's' to those he liked. Sydney Cockerell returned from a visit deeply impressed. He had been met by Kipling at the door, and they talked for two hours in the famous study with the utmost gusto, like old friends. They talked of the old Burne-Jones, Morris, Crom Price days, of 'my dear Sara Anderson (the best secretary I ever had)', of Cambridge and Aunt Georgie, Abyssinia, of the deplorable military and naval weakness of England, and the folly of her politicians.

He told Cockerell how, when at Cannes in the previous spring, he had written a new dog story, about the dog that noses for truffles. He had found that all the best truffles came from Cahors, and with the aid of the Mayor of Cahors and one or two French agricultural officials had learned everything about their growth at the roots of a tiny species of oak tree. He recited a long poem, which he told Cockerell he could not print, about the strife between Jew and Arab under the British Mandate which he had observed on his visit to the Middle East, a poem which took the form of a history of the Jewish race.[17]

This poem has never been printed in full, and only three copies exist.

One was held by the late President of the United States, Franklin D. Roosevelt, one by Sir Winston Churchill's trustees and one by the Royal College of Surgeons:

But Abram said unto Sarai, 'Behold the maid is in thy hand. Do to her as it pleaseth thee.' And when Sarai dealt hardly with her she fled from her face.

Genesis 16:6.

In ancient days and deserts wild
There rose a feud – still unsubdued –
Twixt Sarah's son and Hagar's child
That centred round Jerusalem.

(While underneath the timeless boughs
Of Mamre's oak 'mid stranger-folk
The Patriarch slumbered and his spouse
Nor dreamed about Jerusalem.)

But Ishmael lived where he was born,
And pastured there in tents of hair
Among the Camel and the Thorn –
Beersheba, South Jerusalem.

But Israel sought employ and food
At Pharaoh's knees, till Rameses
Dismissed his plaguey multitude,
With curses, toward Jerusalem.

Across the wilderness they came
And launched their horde o'er Jordan's ford,
And blazed the road by sack and flame
To Jebusite Jerusalem.

Then Kings and Judges ruled the land,
And did not well by Israel,
Till Babylonia took a hand
And drove them from Jerusalem.

And Cyrus sent them back anew,
To carry on as they had done,
Till angry Titus overthrew
The fabric of Jerusalem.

Then they were scattered North and West,
While each Crusade more certain made
That Hagar's vengeful son possessed
Mohammedan Jerusalem.

Where Ishmael held his desert state
And framed a creed to serve his need –
'Allah-hu-Akbar! God is Great!'
He preached it in Jerusalem.

And every realm they wandered through
Rose, far or near, in hate and fear,
And robbed and tortured, chased and slew,
The outcasts of Jerusalem.

So ran their doom – half seer, half slave –
And ages passed, and at the last
They stood beside each tyrant's grave,
And whispered of Jerusalem.

We do not know what God attends
The Unloved Race in every place
Where they amass their dividends
From Riga to Jerusalem.

But all the course of Time makes clear
To everyone (except the Hun)
It does not pay to interfere
With Cohen from Jerusalem.

For 'neath the Rabbi's curls and fur
(Or scents and rings of movie-kings)
The aloof, unleavened blood of Ur,
Broods steadfast on Jerusalem.

Where Ishmael bides in his own place –
A robber hold, as was foretold,
To stand before his brother's face –
The wolf without Jerusalem.

And burdened Gentile o'er the main,
Must bear the weight of Israel's hate
Because he is not brought again
In triumph to Jerusalem.

Yet he who bred the unending strife,
And was not brave enough to save
The Bondsmaid from the furious wife,
He wrought thy woe, Jerusalem.[18]

Rudyard and Carrie voted at the General Election of 1935 which placed Baldwin in office with a large majority. Kipling could not now conceal his contempt for his cousin. He was disgusted by Baldwin's attitude towards India, and regarded the policy of sanctions against Italy in the Abyssinian War as midsummer madness. Nor did he welcome his seventieth birthday, which fell in December, remarking to a friend: 'You have my acutest sympathy over what you delicately call the "nuisance of growing old". A train has to stop at some station or other. I only wish it wasn't such an ugly and lonesome place, don't you?'[19]

It was perhaps because he saw the writing on the wall that Kipling tackled his autobiography with greater zeal and interest than he had shown for years, and this book was presumably finished by the end of the year. His mind and writings began to turn to the eternal verities. He assured his Aunt Edie that he had no fear of death: 'Bless you for your note which has just come in. He who puts us into this life does not abandon His work for *any* reason or default at the end of it. That is all I have come to learn out of my life. So there is *no* fear!'[20]

On 22 December 1935 Kipling wrote to his friend, Theodore Roosevelt, his mind soaring above the normal literary routine and the bitter political hatreds:

Yes – Man's an interesting critter and we don't know much about him. The fun will begin (and the theories will be altered) when it dawns on someone that the ultimate call of the beast is next door to – or intimately affected by – the Cosmic Ray, or some variation of that Ray. You'll find it all set out in the verses that follow my yarn 'Unprofessional' in *Limits and Renewals* but – seriously it is curious to watch how, just now: the advance-guard of Research is skirmishing along the borders of Matter and Spirit and finding out that that frontier like the Abyssinian one is 'debateable'.

On 8 January 1936 he wrote again, now for the last time, and his thoughts were again appropriately tranquil and elevated. Roosevelt had sent him a book called *Man the Unknown*, and Kipling had mused deeply over it. After some reflection he wrote:

Now I've read *Man the Unknown* – and more than once. It is enormously interesting but – don't you think that in the end he re-establishes that fact that Man *is* Unknown – as unknown as the internal combustion engine, every detail of which is explicable *except* the nature of the Spark that causes the mixture to explode? So it may be with us.

We seem to be set in a revolving universe from which we draw some sort of power – for 25,000 days or so. Then either we are removed from the cycle of the Power, or Power removes itself from us, by a series of processes which men of science and research give names to. And that was all the Astrologers of old arrived at. Man, they said, was composed of 'Hormones', which Hormones were due to, or affected by the 'influence of the stars' – i.e. powers inconceivably beyond our imagination but the Source of all Creation and all Modifications of the Created ... in one point Carrel* is as consistent as, say Hammurabi. He thinks of a 'goal', and an ultimate elevation of man to wonderful new heights and power and intelligence – always the 'something round the corner'. It seems to me that his appliance and mechanisms apart – man has been pretty much what he always has been; – 'an imperfectly denatured Animal intermittently subject to the unpredictable reactions of an unlocated spiritual area'. He, like the Universe, will continue to go round and round, not necessarily upward, if there be any direction in infinite space and time.[21]

Suddenly, on 9 January 1936, Kipling fell violently ill in the night, and was taken to the Middlesex Hospital. His surgeon was Sir Alfred Webb-Johnson, who had first met Kipling through Bland-Sutton and was now an intimate. He approached the bedside at 3 a.m. Webb-Johnson found that Kipling was suffering from a perforated duodenum, and in illustration both of Kipling's tranquil courage at the supreme moment, and also of his terse descriptive powers, the surgeon explained that all medical textbooks contain long descriptions of the painful symptoms of this condition in a variety of forms, but that when he approached the bed and said quietly: 'What's the matter, Rud?' Kipling replied: 'Something has come adrift inside.' 'This,' said Webb-Johnson, 'brilliantly summarized the matter.'[22]

Three poignant entries close Caroline Kipling's diaries. These documents, amounting to nearly fourteen thousand pages, span the entire married lifetime of the couple. United in youth by the compelling bond of Wolcott Balestier, they had faced the world together. She had sustained him through the years while his genius ripened, and there were many memories shared in common. They had winced together from the brutal demeanour of Beatty Balestier; they had triumphed over a financial crisis; they had sailed the Seven Seas; they had solaced each other in their personal sorrows. She had nourished and preserved his astonishing success. Her possessiveness had indeed chilled their relations in the latter years, and his absorption in a world of the mind

* Author of *Man the Unknown*.

had led to a disciplinary control of the mechanics of life. But when he went, it was the end of a chapter for Caroline. The patient curator was suddenly deprived of her charge; the years of success and rugged commercial struggle had come to a sudden end. Quietly, finally and briefly her diary entries for 1936 read: *Jan. 9* London. Rud signs his Will. *Jan. 12* Rud taken ill and to hospital in the early morning for an operation. Webb-Johnson sees him at 3 a.m. and later operates. *Jan. 18* Rud died at 12.10 a.m. Our Wedding Day.

Kipling died on 18 January 1936, and was cremated in secret at Golders Green Crematorium on the evening of Monday, 20 January. His ashes were buried in Westminster Abbey on Thursday, 23 January – the day when George v's body was brought to London to lie in state in Westminster Hall.

'The King has gone,' they said, 'and taken his trumpeter with him', and Kipling's death was, of course, submerged in the greater tragedy. It required the departure of a much-loved King to deprive him of the full measure of public grief that would otherwise have been revealed. But the *Daily Telegraph* wrote: 'In the midst of her greater sorrow, England was not unmindful yesterday of the poet who above all others has honoured her achievement in undying verse.'

After the committal of the urn to a grave beside those of Charles Dickens and Thomas Hardy, the great congregation which filled the North and South transepts joined in singing 'Recessional'. He was interred in Poets' Corner. The Service was moving and impressive: 'I am the Resurrection', 'I know that my Redeemer liveth', and 'We brought nothing into this world'.

The bier was brought from St Faith's Chapel on the shoulders of the bearers. It was covered with the Union Jack, on which rested four wreaths. Beneath the flag was the marble casket containing the dead poet's ashes. The Prime Minister was among the pall-bearers, and the bier rested between lighted candles at the altar steps. Psalm 121, 'I will lift up mine eyes', was sung. The Lesson, from 1 *Corinthians* 15, was in perfect sympathy with Kipling's character, and St Paul's robust plea for immortality rang through the transept. It was followed by 'Abide with me', and the lovely hymn was rendered with haunting beauty.

The Dean spoke the words of the committal, and the white marble urn was removed from the bier and lowered into the grave, which was covered by a purple slab, later replaced by a stone bearing the inscription: 'R.K. 1865–1936'.

CHAPTER XXVI

A BACKWARD GLANCE

WE have now traced this busy, toilsome, successful life to its close. We are left in no doubt that Rudyard Kipling was a great artist, a major writer of genius, and although his reputation passed through many vicissitudes, his immortality seems assured. But although Kipling's impact was so enormous as to influence the lives of men in distant lands who had not even seen him, we cannot escape the fact that there was something in him which made him repellent to many intelligent people, even to some who otherwise admired his supreme gifts as an artist. For it must be clearly recognized that Kipling was hated as intensely as he was loved. 'Hardly any reader,' wrote a critic who did not take either extreme view, 'likes him a little. Those who admire him will defend him tooth and nail, and resent unfavourable criticism of him as if he were a mistress or a country rather than a writer. The other side reject him with something like personal hatred.'[1]

How far such hatred can cloud an otherwise objective mind may be seen in George Orwell's essay on Kipling published in 1942. Here we are told, with fatuous generalization, that during five literary generations every enlightened man has despised him; that his view of life cannot be accepted or forgiven by any enlightened person; that revelling in sadism and brutality, and descending into 'abysses of folly and snobbery', he is 'aesthetically disgusting'; and that most of his verse 'is so horribly vulgar that it gives one the same sensation as one gets from watching a third-rate music hall performer recite "The Pigtail of Wu Fang Fu" with the purple limelight on his face ...'[2]

Here is a critic so deeply repelled by certain aspects of Kipling's mind that his ability to comment becomes entirely vitiated, and his attack meaningless and ludicrous. But even here it is possible to detect a love–hate attitude, for Orwell goes on to say, although in a grudging and surly manner, that there is much in Kipling's verse

that is capable of giving pleasure to people who know what poetry
means:

At his worst, and also his most vital, in poems like 'Gunga Din' or 'Danny
Deever', Kipling is almost a shameful pleasure, like the taste for cheap sweets
that some people secretly carry into middle life. But even with his best passages one has the same sense of being seduced by something spurious, and
yet unquestionably seduced. Unless one is merely a snob and a liar it is impossible to say that no one who cares for poetry could get any pleasure out
of such lines as:

For the wind is in the palm trees, and the temple bells they say:
'Come you back, you British soldier; come you back to Mandalay!'

But although we may safely attribute a love–hate attitude to Orwell
himself, the hatred is naked, and he is only the most extreme of many
who were conscious of it. There were other, less biased men of intellect
who found something repulsive in Kipling, and their opinions should
not be ignored, although he has already proved more durable than
most of his detractors.

We are not likely to reach a balanced estimate of Kipling by listening
either to those who detested him root and branch, and were disgusted
by the whole Kipling ethos, or to the blind idolaters, 'the Service
people who read *Blackwood's'*. Perhaps the right mental attitude from
which to regard him is that which recognizes his genius as an artist
with reservations about the uses to which he put it. Long ago, in his
glorious emergent youth, his most vicious tormenter, Max Beerbohm,
clearly recognized this genius, and his hatred was due to the fact that
he believed that the gold had been insensitively transmuted into baser
metal, and a rare gift brutally squandered.

There were many others who continued to hold this opinion
throughout Kipling's literary career, and nowhere shall we find the
irritants in Kipling set forth more temperately or with greater understanding than in C. S. Lewis's essay, 'Kipling's World'.[3] Here we have
a critic convinced of Kipling's genius, who yet becomes saturated after
prolonged reading of his works:

I have never at any time been able to understand how a man of taste could
doubt that Kipling is a very great artist. On the other hand, I have never
quite taken him to my heart. He is not one of my indispensables; life would
go on much the same if the last copy of his works disappeared. I can go
even further than this. Not only is my allegiance imperfect, it is also incon-
stant. After I have been reading Kipling for some days together there comes

a sudden check. One moment I am filled with delight at the variety and solidity of his imagination; and then, the very next moment, I am sick, sick to death, of the whole Kipling world. Of course one can reach temporary saturation point with any author; there comes an evening when even Boswell or Virgil will do no longer. But one parts from them as a friend: one knows one will want them another day; and in the interval one thinks of them with pleasure. But I mean something quite different from that; I mean a real disenchantment, a recoil which makes the Kipling world for the moment, not dull (it is never that) but unendurable – a heavy, glaring, suffocating monstrosity.[4]

It is a not uncommon reaction, and we should try to grasp its causes. To a modern generation his supposed imperialism was displeasing, and even exposed him to accusations of having a Fascist inclination. As we have seen, Orwell admits the absurdity of this charge. To repeat his comment on 'Recessional':

'Lesser breeds without the law.' This line is always good for a snigger in pansy-left circles. It is assumed as a matter of course that the 'lesser breeds' are 'natives', and a mental picture is called up of some *pukka sahib* in a pith helmet kicking a coolie. In its context the sense of the line is almost the exact opposite of this. The phrase 'lesser breeds' refers almost certainly to the Germans, and especially the pan-German writers, who are 'without the law', in the sense of being lawless, not in the sense of being powerless. The whole poem, conventionally thought of as an orgy of boasting, is a denunciation of power politics.[5]

And no one is more unsparing than Kipling in his denunciation of corruption and incompetence in Government, undermining the labour of the worker in the field – Finlayson with his bridge, the heroine of *William the Conqueror* in her famine district, and many another thwarted hero. Dislike of Kipling stemming from this cause was therefore based on a misunderstanding, but there were other, and more potent reasons for intellectual disdain.

He was, above all else, the poet of work, discipline and responsibility. A man's working life had been before a strangely neglected field:

Mr Osborne may be a merchant, but *Vanity Fair* has no interest in his mercantile life. Darcy was a good landlord, and Wentworth a good officer, but their activities in these capacities are all 'off stage'.... Business comes into Dickens only in so far as it is criminal or comic. With few exceptions imaginative literature in the eighteenth and nineteenth centuries had quietly omitted, or at least thrust into the background, the sort of thing which in fact occupies most of the waking hours of most men.[6]

And not only does he exploit this almost virgin field; he allows it to dominate his writing as no author had done before. He is far more absorbed in the task he is describing than the men who are performing it – the Roman centurion on the Wall, the marine engineer, the galley slave: 'the rhythms of work – boots slogging along a road, the Harrild and the Hoe devouring their "league-long paper-bale", the chuckle of a water wheel – echo through Kipling's verse and prose as through no other man's.' And what chiefly emerges is a passionate belief in the indissoluble bond created between men by shared experience, by dangers or hardships endured together in the past, in war or elsewhere. Nothing, for Kipling, can eradicate such experience:

> Oh, was there ever sailor free to choose,
>   That didn't settle somewhere near the sea?
> We've only one virginity to lose,
>   And where we lost it, there our hearts will be!

And behind the concentration on work, angering and disgusting many of liberal and independent minds, is the insistence on an iron discipline. To such minds there was something horrible in the gusto with which Kipling, again and again in his writing, describes the process, essential in his opinion, of 'licking a raw cub into shape'. This theme is the backbone of *Captains Courageous*; it runs through innumerable stories and poems, and is developed with particular relish in the Mulvaney stories. For the sufferer to claim any personal rights is to Kipling a subversive and heinous offence. '"My rights," said Ortheris with deep scorn, "my rights! I ain't a recruity to go whinin' about my right to this an' my right to that, just as if I couldn't look after myself. My rights! 'Strewth A'mighty. I'm a man."' And as one reads, it seems almost that a man does not exist for Kipling until this process has taken place – that he is only raw material.

The philosophy of the process is summed up at the end of *A Walking Delegate*, one of Kipling's less tolerable animal fantasies, where the yellow horse (an agitator) has asked the old working horse: 'Have you no respec' whatever fer the dignity o' our common horsehood?' He gets the reply: 'Horse, sonny, is what you start from. We know all about horse here, an' he ain't any high-toned pure-souled child o' nature. Horse, plain horse, same ez you, is chock-full o' tricks an' meannesses an' cussednesses and monkey-shines. . . . Thet's horse, an' thet's about his dignity an' the size of his soul 'fore he's been broke an' raw-hided a piece': 'Reading "man" for "horse", we have here Kipling's doctrine of Man.'[7]

This insistence on the need for subjection, often by barbarous means, aroused more hatred against Kipling among progressives even than his alleged imperialism, for it amounted to something like a doctrine of original sin, repugnant to many modern trends of thought. Readers, seeing themselves in the role of tormented rookie, were horrified by the vision and outraged by the cure, taking refuge in accusations of Kipling's Fascism and public-school brutality. But, as Lewis wrote, there is no solution along those lines:

It is a brutal truth about the world that the whole everlasting business of keeping the human race protected and clothed and fed could not go on for twenty-four hours without the vast legion of hard-bitten, technically efficient, not-over-sympathetic men, and without the harsh processes of discipline by which this legion is made. It is a brutal truth that unless a great many people practised the Kipling *ethos* there would be neither security nor leisure for any people to practise a finer *ethos*.[8]

And even Orwell is forced to concede that 'he sees clearly that men can only be highly civilized while other men, inevitably less civilized, are there to guard and feed them. It would be difficult to hit off the one-eyed pacifism of the English in fewer words than in the phrase: "Making mock of uniforms that guard you while you sleep".'[9] In other words:

Unless the Kipling virtues – if you will, the Kipling vices – had long and widely been practised in the world, we should be in no case to sit here and discuss Kipling. If all men stood talking of their rights before they went up a mast or down a sewer or stoked a furnace or joined an army, we should all perish; nor while they talked of their rights would they learn to do these things.

But if we accept this harsh logic we can still deplore the avid approval with which Kipling describes the process of 'raw-hiding', and his complete failure to observe its effect upon those who carry out the chastisement. In his eagerness to emphasize the cleansing virtues of discipline he seems entirely indifferent to the motives and emotions of those who administer it. It is clear that, to Kipling, the old soldiers who reduce young recruits to blubbering wrecks do so from the highest motives – they are making soldiers of them. He seems not to understand, or else not to care, that Mulvaney and Ortheris may derive a sadistic pleasure in inflicting punishment on men entirely at their mercy and denied the freedom to protect their 'rights'. How are we to reconcile this bleak insistence on discipline with the contempt for authority and the anarchy described with such blatant glee in *Stalky*

& *Co.*, in the boys' endless battles against the masters? How to explain it in the light of the discipline of the 'House of Desolation', which left such lasting scars on Kipling's shuddering flesh?

There are moments when we feel that he forgets whether 'the game that is more than the player of the game' is a good game or a bad one – whether in fact the end is sufficient to justify the suffering. Sometimes it seems that the despised characters in some of his stories might well have been the heroes, had he merely shifted the angle; that the masters of *Stalky & Co.* might have been presented as admirable disciplinarians instead of inept clowns. And at such moments we begin to wonder whether, behind the doctrine of work and discipline, there was an uncertainty of mind and an obscurity of vision.

Three other elements in his work jarringly affected many of Kipling's readers. The first was his passion for the closed circle of intimates, the inner ring with an exclusive knowledge. It is not surprising that he became an ardent Mason. This strong instinct for being 'inside', for 'belonging', pervades his work from beginning to end, from the knowing hints of privileged social information at Simla which his position as a journalist by no means justified, to the stories of his last years, so many of them set in the Lodge of Instruction. Hence the slapstick farces which are almost always concerned with crude hoaxes perpetrated on outsiders by a group of intimates. From this obsession with the closed circle came the 'knowingness', the casual assumptions, which produced such contemptuous irritation: 'If you open him at random, the chances are that you will find him enslaved to some Inner Ring.... His jungle is not free from it. His very railway engines are recruits, or Mulvaneys dressed up in boilers. His polo ponies are public school ponies. Even his saints and angels are in a celestial civil service.'[10] And even the enjoyment of the gentle irony of Jane Austen's novels is turned into the pretext for yet another secret society in *The Janeites*.

Another irritant was the fact that, for whatever reason, Kipling had early formed a preference for the man of action to the man of ideas. This, to many writers, seemed a lamentable and abject choice. To some it seemed that by this servile option he had almost betrayed his own calling. To Edmund Wilson, his attitude was due to a failure of nerve:

He lacked faith in the artist's vocation. We have heard a good deal in modern literature about the artist in conflict with the *bourgeois* world. Flaubert made war on the *bourgeois*. Rimbaud abandoned poetry as piffling in order to realize the adventure of commerce; Thomas Mann took as his theme the emotions of weakness and defeat of the artist overshadowed by the busi-

nessman. But Kipling neither faced the fight like Flaubert, nor faced the problem in his life like Rimbaud, nor faced the problem in his art like Mann.
Something vulgar in his middle-class British way, something perhaps connected with the Methodist Ministers who were his grandfathers on both sides,
a tradition ... which had a good deal of respect for the powers that governed
the material world and never thought of putting the artist on a par with them
– something of this sort prevented Kipling from playing through his part,
and betrayed him into dedicating his talents to the praise of the practical
man. Instead of *becoming* a man of action like Rimbaud ... he fell into the
ignominious role of the artist who prostrates his art before the achievements
of soldiers and merchants, and who is always declaring the supremacy of
the 'doer' over the man of ideas.[11]

If these were the most common reasons for distaste among Kipling's
more critical readers, there seemed to many to exist a final blemish
which cannot be ignored. This account of his life has shown that there
was much in his mind and writing to jar on a sensitive ear, a common-
ness that at times seems wilfully assumed, and lapses of taste like unresolved discords. His letters, always contrived, as we have seen, to
deny the slightest glimpse of intimacy, even to lifelong friends, are
often couched in a breezy, lower-middle-class, synthetic style, like a
hearty extrovert in the locker-room of a provincial golf course, referring to 'the missis' and 'the kids', and with 'them' always rendered
as 'em. To many it seemed that in a man with so superb a command
over the language, such an affectation was difficult to forgive, or if it
was not an affectation, but a natural impulse, that it revealed a streak
of vulgarity in his nature, some craving to descend for comfort and
reassurance to the level of lesser men.

Bound up with this coarse strand was the abuse of dialect, the mutilated words which also alienated many readers of taste, and it is
a curious fact that when Kipling wrote dialect his ear was far from
perfect. He often uses it when it would be more effective not to do
so: it is carried to ridiculous lengths in the Mulvaney stories, and the
effect of the stylized cockney and preposterous Irishisms is, in the end,
one of fundamental falseness which falls upon the ear like an untuned
piano, like a cuckoo in June.

Nor did Kipling appear to realize that many of his lines, thus
mangled, would not only have been improved but even rendered
beautiful by being translated from cockney into standard English.

As, if we omit the cockney:

> So it's knock out your pipes and follow me!
> And it's finish up your swipes and follow me!

> Oh, hark to the big drum calling,
> Follow me – follow me home!

Or:

> Cheer for the sergeant's wedding –
> Give them one cheer more!
> Grey gun horses in the landau,
> And a rogue is married to a whore.

Most of the dislike of Kipling was centred on these main grounds of criticism. Some of them were the fruit of political bias, others the natural reaction of fastidious critics, and they should be remembered when we look back on his long and triumphant career and his massive influence on the minds of men.

It has been said that no writer since Dickens has made an equal impact upon his age. Streets and frontier towns were named after him; branches of the Kipling Society thrived in five countries. All over the world were admirers of Kipling in their thousands, and the popularity of his books ensured that he was a best-seller throughout his lifetime, and for years after his death. He was, pre-eminently, the author for ordinary men and women and they remained his unquestioning devotees – sailors, soldiers, engineers and administrators, those, in fact, who kept the wheels turning. An artist to his fingertips, he yet wrote deliberately in a manner that offended many intellectuals of his own craft, and he was stonily indifferent to their sneers. It is some measure of his popularity that of all twentieth-century writers he is probably the most frequently quoted, and that phrases of his have become almost part of the language and are familiar to many unaware of either their context or their significance. To quote but a few: 'East is East, and West is West'; 'The white man's burden'; 'What do they know of England who only England know?'; 'The female of the species is more deadly than the male'; 'Somewhere East of Suez'; 'Paying the Dane-geld'.

Early in life he had found himself in a strange and exotic land, living a life of adventure and responsibility at a time when most boys of his age were still in the classroom. He had edited a newspaper, been given servants and horses, lived with soldiers, and consorted with princes; and a sudden and intoxicating success had leaped upon him almost unawares. He is our only social historian of the contemporary Indian and Anglo-Indian theatre: 'What was caught and reflected by that young man's eye, fascinated, enraptured and appalled, was the essential brittleness and violence of the scene, the violence of nature, with the burning heat, with flood and famine, with sudden pestilence and death, and the violence implicit in a social tension that could neither be permanently justified nor immediately released.'[12]

As a young boy he had been congratulated on his poems by the Viceroy of India, but he made the bold decision to leave all his Indian triumphs behind him, almost as though he had felt a call. He had gone alone, with a handful of books, to challenge London, and it had fallen like the walls of Jericho. He had experienced a strong elation and belief in his own powers, a furious creative vitality in his 'daemon'.

But as he grew older, and in spite of the love of his parents, we are always aware of his loneliness, of a profound and unnatural reticence, a fierce instinct of self-protection, which may have been his sour legacy from the 'House of Desolation', whose rigours he never forgot, and his reason for seeking refuge in the closed circle. Perhaps this morbid sensitiveness was why the Vermont feud, which now seems to us trivial and ridiculous, wounded him so cruelly. It was deepened by the most agonizing personal blow of his life, the death of Josephine, and this shattering bereavement was why, among so much that was harsh and masculine, his writing about children was always of such quivering tenderness.

His pessimistic realism increased as one ardent belief after another was exposed and turned cold by disillusionment. The South African War was the watershed between the two moods. Here, where the might of the Empire was used in overwhelming superiority, he saw only bungling and criminal incompetence. But once he had realized that his former idols – the 'General Sahibs' at the higher elevation and the 'Brushwood Boys' at the lower – had failed his expectations, his confidence was sapped. His fundamental convictions were not changed, but something – the first flaming belief – had gone.

It was a sharp rebuff to views so long held, though his continuing anxieties soon replenished the springs of thought. But it was now a less confident and arrogant chauvinism that he began to urge, a need for constant vigilance. The early over-confidence in the English grew into something like despair, and his certainty of approaching doom distorted his opinions on other topics. In 1914 it all came about as he had long predicted to an indifferent world. At last the 'greasy altars' were forcibly deprived of their devotees; the cricket and football fields were gaunt and deserted, and became barrack squares or balloon sites. The 'flannelled fools' and 'muddied oafs' were pressed into the new armies, and John Kipling was obliterated at Loos.

After the First World War Kipling began almost immediately to

issue warnings against the next, and to make the same pleas against
dismantling the armed forces. But he was now preaching to an
exhausted world, sickened of war and fighting; his message was by
now completely inert, and he reached his lowest ebb, both in popularity and influence, in the 1920s and early 1930s. To a new generation
of youth, smugly contemptuous of the mess their elders had made of
the world, the Kipling virtues of courage and discipline had become
not merely tedious but actively repulsive. We are told by the American
critic Lionel Trilling:

> We must make no mistake about it – Kipling was an honest man and he
> loved the national virtues. But I suppose no man ever did more harm to the
> national virtues than Kipling did. He mixed them up with swagger and
> swank, with bullying, ruthlessness, and self-righteousness, and he set them
> up as necessarily antagonistic to intellect. He made them stink in the nostrils
> of youth.... Up to the [Second World] War I had a yearly struggle with
> undergraduates over Wordsworth's poem, *The Character of the Happy War-*
> *rior*, which is, I suppose, the respectable father of the profligate *If*. It seemed
> too moral and 'manly', the students said, and once when I remarked that
> John Wordsworth had apparently been just such a man as his brother had
> described, and told them about his dutiful and courageous death at sea, they
> said flatly that they were not impressed. This was not what most of them
> really thought, but the idea of courage and duty had been steeped for them
> in the Kipling vat and they rejected the idea with the colour.[13]

Kipling was denied the melancholy satisfaction of seeing his forebodings come to pass once more in even more terrible guise. Instead,
he lingered on through the dreadful twilight years, dying three years
after Hitler's advent to power, his belief in the cowardice and venality
of politicians amply confirmed. It is a fitting place to leave him. There
has been no attempt in this account of his life to ignore his faults and
quirks, but when history arrives at her calm verdict she will surely
regard Kipling as a prophet of penetrating, if narrow, vision, a man
of stainless honour, and a descriptive and inventive writer of God-
sent genius.

We can only conjecture what thoughts passed through his mind in
the last hours. We should like to believe that he remembered the happy
days of challenge and adventure, that there were memories of the
tamarisks and eucalyptus groves in India, and those breathless evenings
when the 'night got into his head' and he wandered entranced through
the native city under the brilliant stars; that he remembered, too, the
foggy days in Villiers Street, and the dingy chambers where he worked
so late, with the trains whistling and clanking at Charing Cross, when

the books were written which would proclaim the emergence of a new master. But it is improbable that the mind of the disillusioned old man dwelt for long on the past. It is more probable that it was occupied with the destiny of the people in whom he had once passionately believed; who had set him up and worshipped him, failed him and forgotten him, but who, when the supreme moment came and he was dead, recovered before an astonished world the ancient virtues he had so long urged upon them in the years of trance.

APPENDIX A
KIPLING'S DELIRIUM

———

*Dictated by him, after passing the crisis of his illness,
in New York, March 1899 (see page 197).*

I BEGAN by going upstairs to large, empty, marble rooms on top floor of Hotel Grenoble and there finding illustrated paper and newspaper clippings containing letters and correspondence from a New York girl, called – to the best of my recollection – Bailey or Brady – accusing me in great detail of having larked around with a great many girls both before and after marriage; letters couched in vilest personal style. I was much moved by these. They were calculated to make harm between wife and myself. I came down again. Hiatus.

I went up once more to top of hotel, finding large roof gardens filled with members of New York society, who spoke to me of Miss Bailey's correspondence. I characterized the girl as an unclean-minded person, using a sharp word. I took something to drink and some fruit, where-upon the entire roof garden began to revolve. At this point Theodore [Roosevelt] appeared on the scene, who was in the pay of Miss Bailey (or Brady) and New York society to be revenged on me for calling her opprobrious names. He informs me, with great concern, that Miss Bailey is really a well-wisher of mine and has a wonderful sub-marine boat which could take me and family in course of night or two to see Robert Louis Stevenson. I am pleased at this but am still very ill owing to mixed drinks and melon on roof garden. I suddenly come across wife with children and both servants, much upset, saying she judges it best in the interests of our own happiness to go to Samoa in said boat. I do not remember at this point whether we were kidnapped or voluntarily embarked on a year's cruise.

We enter the submarine boat which sinks through warm water and an indescribable journey commences, where we touch submarine ports and hear most extraordinary noises. We rise to the surface one grey morning dawn and behold a wonderful landscape. At this point I am first conscious of nurses in the shape of stewardesses. Miss Ryerson's face is impressed on me first. The arrangements of the boat are perfectly indescribable, but this point is the first at which constraint is more or less used upon me.

Just as we were settling down to a year's cruise the boat suddenly rises under New York town hall. I am arrested by policemen. I am lying on a black iron bed. Have family and servants go over to Grenoble. Theodore confesses he was in this joke and the nurses reveal themselves as lady reporters for the *New York Journal*. A big police-man comes up with the information that I am to be tried for being found drunk and incapable in New York town hall, but this is New York's revenge against me personally.

At this point I am first conscious of a good many sick-room appliances which are used while I am waiting. I wait from six in the morning until midday, hearing the crowd of the population of New York assembled overhead, watching magic lantern flashes coming through the roof and swearing at the lady reporters. One of them (Miss Warner) attempts to justify herself. The other (Miss Ryerson) prepares a ruffle for the foot of my bed and informs me that I will be brought into court in that condition.

The room moves slowly until I am finally brought out into the sun-shine in the presence of some 80,000 people and then taken away and told that bail is refused. I spend all that night in a moving room that forces itself away through sand. At this point Dr Conland takes me for a thirty-five-mile drive in a big railway which he says was built by the city money for the benefit of the town council. We travel within a few miles of the north side of Conn. Conland tells me this, the ground opening up in front of us and closing behind. I pass my sister, seeing her face for a moment. I pass gigantic earth-cutting field of Irishmen hastening to England. I return to rooms in town, here to find that bail is again refused and that I am to stay with a strange woman, who was Miss Ryerson, in room number 8.

All this is underground. I have great difficulty in finding room 8 but woman's husband and children show me the place. At this point I begin to wonder why I am always lying down. Find myself in subter-ranean landscape, trees, glades, fields of brown satin all in deep twi-light underground. Here I meet the élite of New York dining at little tables, and for many hours I am subjected to most brutal remarks and insults.

At this point I hear Dr Conland's voice, telling me to lie down and not to mind. Am aware that some crack volunteer cavalry troops are in the neighbourhood. Men and women at the dining tables discuss wisdom of lynching me on account of my remarks about Miss Bailey.

I wander away from number eight and hide with a negro family. I hide with Dr Conland and at last escape into a trackless desert where I try to sleep.

A detachment of officers overtakes me, is not sure whether I am Kipling but puts revolver to my head and says if I stop snoring for an instant I will be shot. *I snore!* (This must have been the oxygen.) I come back to find country altered. More troops come in from Wisconsin, Idaho and the South, all with the intent to lynch me, but a very old woman from Oklahoma informs me that a detachment of Oklahoma volunteers are perfectly willing to fight for me. She lived in a den and they were the rummiest lot I ever saw. The locality throughout, I was informed, was on or near 126th Street and was a mountainous country underground, little tables spread about in the valleys and men and women in evening dress dining. They were people who wished the lynching. There was an interval here and five young men of the New York troops, whom I knew recognized me but would not lynch me, examined me copiously and minutely on questions of Indian Army detail, a very large proportion of the New York troops being drilled and organized on the lines of native cavalry, and to my excessive disgust using the same slang.

Some of the young men would have it that I had been a lieutenant of Indian cavalry the greater part of my life, and I distinctly remember, after one of these examinations when I had invented boldly, seeing their ignorance, statements concerning Baluch and Pathan regiments, that I said to myself: 'If ever I get out of this mess alive I will write an article on American superficiality and carelessness that shall hurt.' I also remember composing fragments of some article.

One of the young men with his troops deliberately protected me when I was hiding in the cottage at the time the trains loaded with Wisconsin lynchers were coming through, by saying that his orders were to occupy this building in military strength. Three times that young man saved me. Fires and fighting broke out all along the mountain. I hide in mountain village and here watch trains, filled with drunken lynchers, roaring down the mountain passes.

Here Miss Warner takes the lead and I am conscious of her voice for a long time telling me to lie down. As this is part of the hiding from the lynchers I readily consent. I lose Carrie and the children. Am threatened and at last I find Carrie in the mountains and make a break for the sea, descending on a wet, howling, rainy night to seaside village opposite the shores of Ireland. Here we all take refuge (wife, Conland, myself and both nurses) in an anchored ship, which belongs as far as I can remember to the Rothschilds or some firm of equal standing, a sailing ship which lacks her bows. The skipper is there and two agents representing the Rothschilds. We state our case and meet a person of most extraordinary appearance.

At this time I am dressed in the clothes of an abbé without any undergarments. (This must have been the first introduction of night-gowns instead of pajamas.) I attempt to pass myself off as a book agent, aforesaid abbé, aforesaid Irishman, and many other people according to the company I meet on ship. Ship's agents say they cannot sail on account of water. We wish to go because that is the night in the year when the Irish descend on this village from Ireland and carry off all the women.

Dr Conland takes command and gets hold of agents and insists on sailing. I am let down under Miss Warner's charge in amid-ships of ship. We find to our horror that the hold is full of Irishmen, some two hundred of them, who wish to capture ship for their own orgies. We spend four hours in fitting bow of ship, trying to warp ship out of harbour. Foul weather and the Irish in the hold by some means can keep her back. At last lady and daughter arrive with steam barge made of iron in which they wish to cross. We explain we cannot get ship away on account of Irish in hold. They then say: 'Why don't you come ashore?'

The night is very cold and frosty. We walk out of ship and find a road at top of 200 foot cliff, descend other side and go straight aboard a pitch black German ship subdivided into cabins. Then I begin to wonder why I am not master of my own action. I am put on a table or bed and suffer many indignities. We sail away and reach, as I believe, England. Am kidnapped and taken to horrible house in a garden of weeping willows, rocks and running water, inhabited by eight married couples, all men like Theodore and young Janeway.

Here my mental distress is very great, because whenever I attempt to get up I am pushed down by the neck, and all food has an indescribable taste (peptonoid). I try to get some communication from my wife and find it impossible. I cannot tell for sure whether I am in England or America. Once I escape as far as a sleepy English town but a bearded young man brings me back again. The restraint and taste of the food sets me to thinking and for a long time I debate whether I am or am not insane because it occurs to me that all insane people have an idea that all their food is drugged and that they are under restraint and that people are after their money.

At odd times I hear the eight young married couples talking in low

voices over some plan or other, and, so far as I can gather, I am to
be the last to die in some big tontine scheme. (That was very beautiful
when the woman said I was to be the last to die.) At this point things
become more hazy. So far as my memory serves me, the delirium beginning with the black German ship then duplicated itself from the
step where I left the Rothschild wooden ship off the American coast,
and this time I am landed in America, but this time, as before, I am
conscious of Dr Conland's voice.

I discover a theory that I am mad and am perfectly convinced that
I am under wrongful restraint. I escape again once more and get into
the wings of a theatre in New York or the lower part of an elevator
shaft of a newspaper office in New York. Here, in a voice which even
now I can remember as thick and guttural, I proceed to address the
janitor and a few other people on my wrongs, demanding that at least
the English Government shall take care of me whatever my condition
may be. I pity myself and weep at intervals, and at the same time I
am distinctly conscious of thinking of Charles Reade's novels of
wrongful incarcerations in an asylum, and just when I think I have
made an impression I hear Dr Conland's voice. He came down the
elevator shaft, together with Miss Ryerson, whom I hated; she turned
up always. They sat down, one each side of me quite patiently without
any sign of anger, and let me talk. Then I felt a hand on my neck.
(That was a thing that made me mad.) It troubled me that all my
remarks were delivered in a lying-down posture. How I moved from
place to place I did not know, but I used to find myself lying down.

Here again the delirium became indistinct, but shortly after this I
am conscious for the first time of a great heat in my own body, and
I ride five times around the world with the second Army division of
the American Army all mounted on red ponies with natural leather
fixings, by the light of a green comet, halting beside Behring Straits
with a sense of having accomplished magnificent deeds, not one of
which I can remember. We swept all through Russia, we allowed the
second Army division to sweep their army.

After this the landscape changed, the heat increased and I began
to descend into the bowels of the earth and down a shaft over green
settees and sofas. At this point I was conscious that a gigantic joke
had taken place just before I began the descent, that it was my duty
to know all about because Conland did. Conland and Miss Ryerson
were with me. I was very ill from thirst and faint and pretended to
be exhausted with laughter over this excellent joke. From time to time
Conland would pick me up and turn me over.

The heat increased. We came out once more on a lot of Russian steppes and plateaus, two of which had the names I had translated from Russian newspapers fifteen years ago in the old *Civil and Military Gazette*. There my memory fails me altogether. The last I remember is Conland turning me again on a green settee and our coming out into a black volcanic country where I understand there is no water for hundreds of miles.

N.B. The submarine voyage to Stevenson was duplicated. The first time I went by myself. The second the wife arranged to go on the grounds that it would be better for us all. This I understood had some-thing to do with Miss Bailey and the allegations made against me and I was deeply distressed. In the same way the experiences in the sailing ship off the Irish coast were duplicated. I was distinctly con-scious of wondering when I was with my wife whether the experience would turn out the same as when I had taken that ride before by myself.

One very curious feature of the wandering on 126th Street was that I found that not only had the New York newspapers worked up this sensation, namely my being victimized at the City Hall and held up to the derision of the city, but that the enterprising newspaper had published a red book detailing the whole of my experiences as I went through them. This book I would find from time to time and read. The experiences continued unbroken from my first in-carceration under the City Hall down to my flight from the Island of Cream where the Irish came over and we had a row with the Irish in the hold.

Conland's voice was the one thing that I recognized throughout my trouble. I knew that something was very badly wrong, but I under-stood from him that whatever it was it was none of my business to find out but to lie low and let it blow over. Sometimes it was a sand-storm; sometimes it was an attack of a train load of lynchers, but my business as I understood it was to lie on the ground and, so long as Conland was by, never to raise my head. I hated Theodore more intensely than I ever hated anyone. When it was found out that he had been in league with Miss Bailey and the rest of New York society to play this town hall trick on me, he would come to me and say: 'I am afraid you must not mind this. I could not help doing it', and he would stick things into me. I am very polite to him, meaning later to kill him when I got well. I also hated Miss Ryerson and Miss Warner. Miss Ryerson was dressed throughout in soubrette style, with short skirts, clock stockings and high heels. Among other things I sent a cable to the English Government about this affair. I said there was *casus belli*. That was after this tremendous joke was being played on me, being found with nothing on but a nightgown in New York town hall.'[1]

HONOURS AND AWARDS

14 December 1899 *Caroline Kipling's diaries*: Lord Salisbury's Secretary comes down to offer Rud a KCB which he declines feeling he can do better without it. We are much pleased to be offered it however.

6 November 1903 *Letter from A.J. Balfour to R.K.*: I have reason to believe that if you were disposed to accept that honour, the King would be pleased to confer on you the KCMG. It could not in my opinion, and in that of the Secretary for the Colonies, be better bestowed; and I am certain that the English speaking world are, in this matter, of our mind. Your admirable literary gifts have not merely resulted in pleasure to innumerable readers; they have made the citizens of this widely scattered Empire known to each other as they have never known before. It is no small thing to have infused into so many dwellers in the narrow routine of everyday work some flash of that sympathetic insight into the ways of other men of other climes which you have done in so abundant a measure; it is – if not from a literary yet from a national point of view – an even greater thing that you have always held up before your countrymen the Imperial ideal in its noblest shape. May I be allowed to add that as one of your oldest admirers – an admirer before a single one of your books was published in this country – it would give me very peculiar pleasure to be the channel through which this public recognition of your services reaches you. Earnestly trusting that you will look favourably on the proposal. PS. It is I hope unnecessary to add that the acceptance of the offer would impose not the smallest limitation on your absolute freedom of utterance on all subjects at all times.

7 November 1903 *Footnote to above letter written by R.K.*: Lord Salisbury sent R. Macdonald to me in the month of December 1899

to offer me a KCB. It is cheering to note how I have advanced during
the last few years in the opinion of our generous Government. Rudyard Kipling 'KCMG.'

7 November 1903   *Caroline Kipling's diaries:* Mr Balfour writes to
ask if he may propose R.'s name for KCMG. A letter of appreciation.
He will call it backed by the approval of one Mr Lyttelton, recently
made Colonial Secretary. Rud declines. Evidently title conferring
is as slack as other Government business and they know nothing
about the KCB of 1899.

Undated draft (7 November 1903)   *From R.K. to A. J. Balfour:* I have
to thank you for your letter of yesterday and to assure you of my
entire appreciation of the honour you propose as well as of the more
than flattering terms in which you propose it. But I find my position
has not changed since 1899 when Lord Salisbury was kind enough
to offer me a somewhat similar distinction and that such honours
must continue outside my scheme of things.

28 May 1917   *Caroline Kipling's diaries:* Stan Baldwin comes from
Bonar Law informally to say the Prime Minister will give Rud pretty
much any honour he will accept. Rud says he will not accept any.

6 June 1917   *Caroline Kipling's diaries:* Rud to the House of Commons to see Stan Baldwin. He hears a rumour at his Clubs that
his name is on the list of Knights of the new Order of the Empire
and sees Bonar Law's Secretary as B-L is away ill. Secretary assures
him his name will not be sent in without consulting him and Rud
warns him it must not be.

30 June 1917   *Letter from Acting Secretary, Order of Companions of
Honour to R.K.:* Your name appears in the list of those who have
been recommended to the King for the Order of the Companions
of Honour and I should therefore be obliged if you would fill up
the enclosed form and return it to me at your earliest convenience.

1 July 1917   *Caroline Kipling's diaries:* Our day starts with a letter
from the Secretary of the new Order Companions of Honour, saying
Rud's name is down. They have not consulted Rud and he wires
to say so, and adds he does not intend to accept. He also wires Bonar
Law to that effect.

1 July 1917   *Telegram from A. Bonar Law to R.K.:* The notice sent to you is intended to ascertain whether you wish it or not. If not, so reply, and that is the end of it. I did not know that list had been completed to the extent of sending out these notices or I should have stopped yours at least till I had communicated with you as I know your views.

2 July 1917   *Letter from R.K. to Bonar Law:* Many thanks for your wire of Sunday about the Companions of Honour. I am sorry to have added to your work but there is absolutely nothing in the Acting Secretary's letter to indicate that the matter was not irretrievably settled. On the face of it it looks as though the Prime Minister's prerogative included recommending his fellow-subjects to the King's notice without consulting them beforehand. This opens the way to a new form of frightfulness which I don't think people should be called upon to endure – even in wartime. How would *you* like to be waked up on a Sunday morning by a letter from the Acting Secretary of the Clerical Aid Society informing you that your name was among the list of Bishops that had been recommended to the King? Wouldn't you assume that the Archbishop of Canterbury had landed you at last into his fold and wouldn't you at once collaborate with me in a bill against the imposition of arbitrary honours on the King's loyal subjects? So you see how earnest was my appeal to you for help.

3 July 1917   *Letter from A. Bonar Law to R.K.:* I am sorry you have been troubled about this question of an Honour and I would have written you sooner but I have been excessively busy the last two days. I quite understand your position but as it happens a quite different course has been adopted with regard to these Honours from that previously adopted, inasmuch as the preliminary notice in the form of a circular has gone direct from the Palace instead of through the Prime Minister. I do not think that this is a good plan and it will not probably be adopted again, but in any case there will be no more publicity about the matter than if it had happened in the ordinary way.

15 December 1921   *Letter from Lord Stamfordham, Private Secretary to the King, to R.K.:* I am commanded by the King to inform you that it will give His Majesty much pleasure to confer upon you the Order of Merit – in recognition of the eminent services you have

rendered to the Science of Literature and of the almost unique estimation with which your works are regarded throughout the British Empire. Will you kindly let me hear at your earliest convenience whether the fulfilment of this wish of His Majesty's would be agreeable to you?

Abstract of correspondence in Royal Archives. Confidential.

1. *30 January 1916. Robert Bridges to Stamfordham initiating the name of R.K. for the* OM: It is plain that he is the greatest living genius that we have in Literature and it is generally thought that he has been passed over on account of his politics. The only other reason I could think of would be that he has written so much in slang and low dialect. But much of his later work is altogether above any such reproach and some of it is extremely beautiful on any standard. ... I do not know Mr Kipling personally and am clear of any prepossession one way or the other.

2. *3 February 1916. Stamfordham replies:* H.M. realizes that R.K. has undoubted claims for recognition of his great genius and will bear in mind your strong support.

3. *28 May 1921. Sir Herbert Warren putting R.K. forward for* OM: ... has done invaluable and untold service in keeping the Empire together and of course many of the poems and phrases are household words for the English speaking race.

4. King discusses the names of Kipling and J. M. Barrie with the PM on 3 November 1921.

16 December 1921   *Caroline Kipling's diaries:* Rud looks over the letters and with characteristic lack of interest passes over one from the Lord Privy Seal's Office which is a proposal sent by the King through Lord Stamfordham ... an OM ... a quaint letter.

17 December 1921   *Caroline Kipling's diaries:* Rud decides he cannot accept the OM offered by the King and writes his letter.

17 December 1921   *Letter from R.K. to Lord Stamfordham:* In reply to your letter of the 15th the fact that the King has been pleased to signify his approval of my services to Literature will be to me the great honour of my life. But as regards the conferment upon me of the special honour suggested I would ask you, while presenting my humble and loyal duty to H.M., to pray that H.M. may be graciously pleased to hold me excused.

13 January 1922   *Telegram from editor, Daily News, to R.K.:* Wayfarer in Nation announces your refusal of OM. Will you kindly confirm or deny this. Have you any comment to make.

14 January 1922   *Telegram from London Agency, New York World, to R.K.:* Would be glad to publish any statement you care to make explaining why you decline Order of Merit.

14 January 1922   *Telegram from Herbert Bayard Swope, Executive Editor, New York, to R.K.:* Unprecedented act in declining order merit subject deep interest to your many American admirers. New York World would be glad to have your cable its expense statement as to reason you took this action.

14 January 1922   *Caroline Kipling's diaries:* Rud is greatly upset by wires from newspapers about his refusal of the OM. No word have we said to anyone, so our disgust at its being let out is great.

16 January 1922   *Letter from Lord Stamfordham to R.K.:* Many thanks for your kind letter; but I must take the responsibility for the newspaper announcement with regard to your having been offered the OM. The fact is that since the publication of the New Year's Honours Gazette several suggestions have reached here, directly or indirectly, that the Order of Merit should have been conferred on you. It was felt due to the King, in whose gift alone is the Order of Merit, that the public should be made aware that these suggestions had already been anticipated by His Majesty.

17 January 1922   *Caroline Kipling's diaries:* A letter from Lord Stamfordham to say he is responsible for the newspapers announcing that the OM was offered Rud by the King. An amazing thing.

18 January, 1924   *Letter from Lord Stamfordham to R.K.:* Although I have before me your charming letter of 17th December 1921, I write on behalf of my Sovereign to say that His Majesty has heard indirectly that there is an idea that perhaps you might now be disposed to view differently the communication I then made – that it would give the King much pleasure to confer upon you the Order of Merit for the reasons which I mentioned in my letter of 15th December 1921. If this rumour be correct I am to assure you that His Majesty will be delighted to do now what he so much wished to do at that time.

18 January 1924   *Letter from Stanley Baldwin to R.K.:* Would you care for an OM? I gathered from what you once told me that you wouldn't but I don't want to leave office without putting it to you. Of course it is the King's gift alone and I could only suggest it unofficially. Let me know by return.

19 January 1924   *Telegram from Stanley Baldwin to R.K.:* I know for certain that 'Yes' would give enormous pleasure in many quarters.

19 January 1924   *Caroline Kipling's diaries:* A letter from Stamfordham offering Rud the OM is a difficulty.

21 January 1924   *Letter from R.K. to Lord Stamfordham:* I deeply regret that any such report as you allude to should have reached the King. When you were good enough to see me at the Palace, two years ago, I explained more fully than one could in writing the reasons that prompted my action at the time. My work makes it unnecessary I hope that I should protest my loyalty to the King and the Empire but as I ventured to tell you in our talk I am convinced that whatever I may be able to do towards these ends in the troublous future ahead will be best and most serviceably carried through without acknowledgement in the public eye. My rewards for what I may have done in the past are great indeed since my Sovereign has thought once and again to honour me so markedly for it. Will you then present my most humble duty and gratitude to H.M. and of your kindness lay before him the motive which has governed me throughout.

23 January 1924   *Letter from Lord Stamfordham to R.K.:* The King has read your letter of the 21st inst., and desired me to say how much he appreciated the disinterested spirit that has led you to adhere to your previous decision, the reasons for which His Majesty quite understands.

Abstract of correspondence in Royal Archives. Confidential.
    1. *7 January 1922. Memo from Wigram to Stamfordham:* I spoke about R.K. to the King who did not favour the idea of our informing the press about the OM. H.M. said he thought you had better write to Massingham and tell him privately. I then suggested that you might write to R.K. himself, and explain matters as he might not wish it to be known that the King has offered him the OM and H.M. had no objection.

2. *Stamfordham to Massingham:* With reference to the comments in last week's *Nation* upon the New Year's Honours I think it is well that you should know that some time before the publication of the Gazette the King proposed to confer the OM upon Mr R.K. who however asked to be allowed to decline the proffered honour.

3. *Massingham's reply:* Many thanks for your kind letter. I can't understand K.'s refusal unless it was personal modesty. The OM is a very great honour and the standard of admittance has been kept very high.

4. *13 January 1922. R.K. to Stamfordham:* I confess I have been horrified to see this week newspaper statements in regard to my having been offered an OM as I have not, of course, communicated the contents of your letter by word or hint to anyone. The letter itself came direct to my hand – not through my secretary – and lay in the box until answered. I am more disgusted than I can say over this latest example of newspaper enterprise.

5. *21 January 1922. An open letter in John Bull* congratulates R.K. on declining it.

6. *20 November 1923. Lord Derby to Stamfordham:* Points out how much the War Graves Commission has owed to R.K.'s imagination. Would it be acceptable to H.M. if he (Derby) were to suggest to Baldwin that R.K. should get the OM. It might be delicate for Baldwin to suggest it himself.

7. *21 November 1923. Stamfordham replies:* No use. R.K. declined it.

8. *January 1924. Note by Sir Francis Bryant (Stamfordham's Confidential Secretary):* At the request of Mr Baldwin Sir Ronald Waterhouse informed Lord Stamfordham that Mr Kipling had changed his mind and would now be prepared to accept the OM. Sir R. Waterhouse said Mr Baldwin proposed therefore with the King's approval to write and offer the Order to Mr Kipling. H.M. did not approve of Mr B. making the offer and directed Lrd. S. to do so on H.M.'s behalf. As Mr B. and Mr K. are cousins it is difficult to understand how Mr B. could have been so misled as Mr K. shows in his reply.

Postscript: Kipling had been suggested for the OM long before the incidents recorded above, namely as successor to George Meredith. Lord Esher had been consulted by Lord Knollys and had replied (2 June 1909) that Meredith's death did not mean that a direct successor in the OM must necessarily be found. Thomas Hardy was not in his opinion up to the standard despite *The Dynasts*. 'Kipling has done more for the Empire than any living writer. He has done a mass of work of unequal value – some *very* bad. On the other hand he has written some things of the highest national importance. Personally I think he has earned the Order of Merit for having – with his pen – accomplished for the Empire quite as much as Cromer or Kitchener.' All the same his own choice at that particular juncture would unhesitatingly be James Bryce.

Evidently Knollys passed this letter to John Morley for his comments for he wrote on 6 June: 'Cordially agreed that novelist should not necessarily succeed novelist. I have not a word to say against Hardy, whom I like very much as a man, and much admire as a writer. I have deep doubts about Kipling in spite of his genius and imaginative vigour. I think there would be some criticisms.' Advocates Sir George Trevelyan.

POET LAUREATESHIP

Note from Mrs Bambridge: In 1892 the Laureateship fell vacant at the death of Lord Tennyson, and it was not until 1896 that Alfred Austen was appointed. Lord Salisbury had 'thought of R.K. for the job' and Arthur Balfour was most insistent that R.K. be sounded on the subject. The answer was (as it was to all such offers) that he thought he could be of more use to the country and do better work if he were free to write as he chose.

Extract from original letter to Lord Baldwin from Ian Malcolm: That ass Alfred Austin was made PL [Poet Laureate] in 1896 – after much hesitation and reflection. I was bottle washer at Hatfield then. Lord S. certainly thought R.K. for the job though he blows his trumpet rather loud sometimes and A.J.B. more than 'thought of him' and wanted him to take it. So he was sounded and the answer was just as you [Lord Baldwin] said and as one might have expected.

Extract from a letter to Lord Baldwin from Lady Violet Bonham-Carter: I don't think my Father ever offered R.K. the Laureateship, in fact I'm practically *sure* he didn't (tho' he did *think* of doing so). The vacancy occurred when we were on the Admiralty Yacht and I remember very well my Father discussing the problem with me. The *obvious* choice was Kipling. Bridges was the alternative in my Father's mind. What weighed with him was the very reason you

[Lord Baldwin] gave – that Kipling was inspired and could not write to order. Bridges with his chiselled gift would be more likely to be able to do so. He wrote offering it to Bridges. ... As you know, Bridges proved a barren Laureate.

In 1913 Bridges was appointed by Asquith as being 'more likely to write to order' and fall into line than R.K. who, it was thought, would probably refuse again. In 1930 Ramsay MacDonald would not have thought R.K. possible nor would he have been allowed by his party to make the appointment.

SOURCE NOTES

The Kipling Papers are now the property of the National Trust. Caroline Kipling's diaries, previously part of the Kipling Papers, were not given to the National Trust and have been destroyed.

The Dunham Collection consists of unpublished Balestier family papers which were in the possession of Dr Dunham, Kipling's brother-in-law, in New York.

Mrs A. M. Fleming (Trix Kipling) wrote at considerable length to Lord Birkenhead in answer to written questions and this material has never before been published.

Rudyard Kipling's works are given by title only.

CHAPTER I   A PEACEFUL CHILDHOOD

1 *A Kipling Primer*, p. 13, Chatto & Windus, 1900.
2 Frederick W. Macdonald, *As a Tale that is Told*, p. 115, Cassell, 1919.
3 Lockwood Kipling's diary, the Kipling Papers.
4 Lecture by Dr Vaughan Bateson on 'Kipling Links in Yorkshire', *Yorkshire Post*, 14 January 1937.
5 C. Hilton Brown, *Rudyard Kipling*, p. 21, Hamish Hamilton, 1945.
6 Macdonald, *As a Tale that is Told*, p. 2.
7 The Kipling Papers.
8 Extracts from Miss Plowden's *Fond Memories*, unpublished.
9 ibid.
10 Mrs Margaret Mackail (*née* Burne-Jones) to author.
11 Mrs A. M. Fleming (Alice [Trix] Kipling), 'Some childhood memories of Rudyard Kipling', *Chambers Journal*, March 1939.
12 *Something of Myself*, p. 4.

CHAPTER II   THE HOUSE OF DESOLATION

1 *Something of Myself*, p. 6.
2 ibid., p. 6.
3 Mrs A. M. Fleming to author.
4 ibid.
5 Mrs A. M. Fleming, 'Some childhood memories'.
6 Mrs A. M. Fleming to author.
7 ibid.
8 *Something of Myself*, p. 8.
9 ibid.
10 Mrs A. M. Fleming to author.
11 Extracts from the diary of

Kipling's grandmother, Mrs Macdonald, 1872, the Kipling Papers.

12 Georgiana Burne-Jones, *Memorials of Edward Burne-Jones*, vol. II, p. 3, Macmillan, 1904.

13 ibid., pp. 45–6.

14 Mrs Margaret Mackail to author.

15 ibid.

16 Stanley Baldwin to author.

17 Herbert Baker, 'Architecture and Personalities', p. 193, *Country Life*, 1944.

18 Stanley Baldwin to author.

19 Mrs A. M. Fleming to author.

20 Lockwood Kipling's diary, the Kipling Papers.

21 Mrs A. M. Fleming to author.

22 Caroline Kipling's diaries.

23 Mrs Bambridge (Elsie Kipling) to author.

24 ibid.

CHAPTER III   EPPING INTERLUDE

1 Letter from Mrs Constance Frost to author.

2 Mrs A. M. Fleming, 'Some childhood memories'.

3 *Something of Myself*, p. 20.

CHAPTER IV   WESTWARD HO!

1 R. M. A. Owen to Murray Brooks.

2 General L. C. Dunsterville to author.

3 ibid.

4 H. A. Tapp, *The United Services College, 1874–1911*, Gale & Polden, Aldershot, 1934.

5 L. C. Dunsterville, *Stalky's Reminiscences*, p. 31, Cape, 1928.

6 G. C. Beresford, *Schooldays with Kipling*, p. 20, Gollancz, 1926.

7 General L. C. Dunsterville to author.

8 Letter from Mrs Constance Frost to author.

9 Beresford, *Schooldays with Kipling*, p. 20.

10 General L. C. Dunsterville to author.

11 W. G. B. Maitland to author.

12 *Something of Myself*, p. 34.

13 General L. C. Dunsterville to author.

14 Letter in possession of Lieut.-Colonel Pettigrew.

15 *Something of Myself*, p. 22.

16 *Souvenirs of France*.

17 General L. C. Dunsterville to author.

18 ibid.

19 The Kipling Papers.

20 *Something of Myself*, p. 25.

21 Beresford, *Schooldays with Kipling*, pp 65, 112–13.

22 H. C. Bailey in the *Daily Telegraph*, 18 January 1936.

23 *Stalky and Co.*, p. 217.

24 *Something of Myself*, p. 36.

25 Tapp, *The United Services College*, p. 13.

26 Mrs A. M. Fleming to author.

27 ibid.

28 Edward B. Shanks, *Rudyard Kipling*, p. 32, Macmillan, 1940.

29 Mrs A. M. Fleming to author.
30 *Something of Myself*, p. 38.
31 H. M. Swanwick to Murray
    Brooks, 1937.

32 Beresford, *Schooldays with
    Kipling*, pp 116–17.

CHAPTER V   THE YOUNG JOURNALIST

1 *Something of Myself*, p. 40.
2 The Kipling Papers.
3 Sir Henry MacMahon to author.

4 The Kipling Papers.
5 Sir Louis Dane to author.
6 The Kipling Papers.

CHAPTER VI   MILITARY INCLINATION

1 *Something of Myself*, p. 55.
2 George Orwell, 'Rudyard
   Kipling', *Horizon*, February
   1942.
3 John Fraser, Yeoman Gaoler,
   Tower of London, to the author.
4 H. R. Goulding, *'Old Lahore'*,
   printed at the *Civil and Military
   Gazette* Press, Lahore, 1924.
5 The Kipling Papers.
6 ibid.
7 ibid.
8 ibid.

9   ibid.
10 ibid.
11 Mrs A. M. Fleming to author.
12 The Kipling Papers.
13 E. G. Haward to author.
14 *Something of Myself*, p. 52.
15 ibid., p. 64.
16 The Kipling Papers.
17 Charles E. Carrington, *Rudyard
    Kipling* pp 64–5, Macmillan,
    1955.
18 The Kipling Papers.
19 Mrs A. M. Fleming to author.

CHAPTER VII   THE EARLY WORK

1 Edmund Gosse, *Questions at
   Issue*, p. 258, Heinemann, 1893.
2 William Archer, *Poets of the
   Younger Generation*, p. 225, John
   Lane, 1901.
3 George Moore, *Avowals*, ch. 8,
   privately printed, 1919.
4 Henry James in his introduction
   to *Mine Own People* by Rudyard
   Kipling, United States Book
   Co., 1891.
5 Max Beerbohm, 'Kipling Entire'
   in *Around the Theatres*, vol. I,
   Heinemann, 1903.
6 Archer, *Poets of the Younger
   Generation*, p. 228.

7 W. Dixon Scott, 'The Meekness
   of Mr Rudyard Kipling' in *Men
   of Letters*, p. 48, Hodder &
   Stoughton, 1916.
8 *On Greenhow Hill*.
9 Andrew Lang, *Essays in Little*,
   pp 204–5, Longmans Green,
   1912.
10 A. G. Gardiner, *Prophets,
    Priests and Kings*, p. 327, Dent,
    1917.
11 Lang, *Essays in Little*, p. 199.
12 ibid., p. 200.
13 Letter from Maurice Baring to
    Edward Shanks.

CHAPTER VIII   LONDON OVERTURE

1 William Gaunt, *The Aesthetic Adventure*, p. 139, Cape, 1945.
2 ibid., p. 180.
3 Mrs A. M. Fleming to author.
4 Letter of Sir Desmond MacCarthy to author.
5 The Kipling Papers.
6 *Something of Myself*, p. 87.
7 *Pall Mall Gazette*.
8 *Something of Myself*, p. 80.
9 Mrs A. M. Fleming to author.
10 The Kipling Papers.
11 Frank Harris, *Contemporary Portraits*, p. 85, the author, New York, 1915.
12 *The World*, 2 April 1890.
13 Mary R. Cabot's account of Kipling in Vermont, papers of F. Cabot Holbrook, Brattleboro, Vermont.
14 Arthur Waugh, *One Man's Road*, p. 176, Chapman & Hall, 1931.
15 Dunham Collection, New York.
16 ibid.
17 ibid.
18 Waugh, *One Man's Road*, p. 186.
19 Sir Desmond MacCarthy to author.
20 Mrs A. M. Fleming to author.
21 Ethel, Lady Dilke to author.
22 M. A. Belloc Lowndes, *The Merry Wives of Westminster*, p. 65, Macmillan, 1946.

CHAPTER IX   LONDON CONQUERED

1 The Kipling Papers.
2 Mrs A. M. Fleming to author.
3 The Kipling Papers.
4 Dunham Collection, New York.
5 Charles Morgan, *The House of Macmillan 1843–1943*, pp 147–52, Macmillan, 1943.
6 The Kipling Papers.
7 Caroline Kipling's diaries.
8 The Kipling Papers.
9 Caroline Kipling's diaries.

CHAPTER X   TRAVEL AND AMERICA

1 Caroline Kipling's diaries.
2 The Kipling Papers.
3 Mary Cabot's account of Kipling in Vermont.
4 ibid.
5 ibid.
6 Statement of John Bliss, Kipling's neighbour in Brattleboro.
7 Testimony of August Rhode, cabinet-maker in Brattleboro.
8 Caroline Kipling's diaries.
9 Edith Catlin Phelps, *Personal Recollections of Mr and Mrs Rudyard Kipling*.
10 C. O. Day, *Rudyard Kipling: As seen in his Vermont home*.
11 Mary Cabot's account of Kipling in Vermont.
12 Lady Milner in the *Empire Review*.
13 Mary Cabot's account of Kipling in Vermont.
14 Mrs Sheppey to author.
15 Statement of Tucker Reid, farmer of Brattleboro.
16 Howard C. Rice, *Rudyard Kipling in New England*, Revised edition, Book Cellar, Brattleboro, USA, 1951.

17 *Letters and Friendships of Sir Cecil Spring Rice*, edited by Stephen Gwynn, vol. I, p. 173, Constable, 1929.
18 Chalmers Roberts to author.
19 The Kipling Papers.
20 General A. S. Little to author.
21 The Kipling Papers.
22 Caroline Kipling's diaries.
23 *Something of Myself*, p. 123.

CHAPTER XI   THE END IN VERMONT

1 F. F. van de Water, *Rudyard Kipling's Vermont Feud: on the relations of Rudyard Kipling and Beatty Balestier*, John Day, New York, 1937.
2 ibid.
3 Miss Josephine Dunham to author.
4 ibid.
5 Dunham Collection, New York.
6 Beatrice Kaufman and Joseph Hennessey, eds, *The Letters of Alexander Woollcott*, p. 222, Cassell, 1946.
7 Dunham Collection, New York.
8 Testimony of August Rhode.
9 Mrs Sheppey to author.
10 Mary Cabot's account of Kipling in Vermont.
11 van de Water, *Rudyard Kipling's Vermont Feud*.
12 Mrs Sheppey to author.
13 Julian S. Mason, *A Yale Footnote to Kipling*, printed for the Yale Library Associates by the Yale University Press, 1937.
14 The Kipling Papers.
15 Mary R. Cabot's account of Kipling in Vermont.
16 *Brattleboro Reformer*, 15 May 1896.
17 ibid.
18 Mary Cabot's account of Kipling in Vermont.
19 Mrs Gale (Beatty Balestier's second wife) to author.
20 Testimony of Dr Hogle to author.

CHAPTER XII   ENGLAND

1 The Kipling Papers.
2 ibid.
3 ibid.
4 General L. C. Dunsterville to author
5 Mrs Margaret Mackail to author.
6 The Kipling Papers.
7 ibid.
8 Dunham Collection, New York.
9 *Something of Myself*, p. 134.
10 Dunham Collection, New York.
11 Will M. Clemens, *A Ken of Kipling*, p. 82, New Amsterdam Book Co., New York, 1899.
12 Carpenter Collection, Library of Congress, Washington.
13 *Something of Myself*, p. 137; Burne-Jones, *Memorials of Edward Burne-Jones*, vol. II, pp 45–6.
14 The Kipling Papers.
15 William Roberton, *The Kipling Guide Book*, p. 28, Holland Co., Birmingham, 1899.
16 The Kipling Papers.
17 *Something of Myself*, p. 149.
18 Dr H. Bell, *The Times*, 20 December 1937.
19 Caroline Kipling's diaries.
20 George Orwell, 'Rudyard

Kipling', *Horizon*, February 1942.
21 The Kipling Papers.
22 Statements of Mary Cabot and Sir Roderick Jones.
23 Caroline Kipling's diaries.
24 *Something of Myself*, p. 148.

25 ibid.
26 From the collection of Sir Shane Leslie.
27 Roberton, *Kipling Guide Book*, p. 15.
28 Clemens, *A Ken of Kipling*, p. 82.

CHAPTER XIII AMERICAN TRAGEDY

1 The Kipling Papers.
2 Clemens, *A Ken of Kipling*, pp 31–8.
3 The Kipling Papers.
4 Dr Dunham to author.
5 *Something of Myself*, p. 49.
6 Caroline Kipling's diaries.
7 Arnold Bennett, *Books and Persons*, p. 161, Chatto & Windus, 1917.

8 The Kipling Papers.
9 ibid.
10 Angela Thirkell, *Three Houses: Reminiscences*, p. 86, O.U.P., 1931.
11 The Kipling Papers.
12 Statement of Mrs Greenwood to author.
13 Caroline Kipling's diaries.
14 The Kipling Papers.

CHAPTER XIV THE BOER WAR

1 The Kipling Papers.
2 Caroline Kipling's diaries.
3 The Kipling Papers.
4 Lord Newton, *Retrospection*, p. 203, John Murray, 1941.
5 Caroline Kipling's diaries.
6 ibid.
7 George J. Younghusband, *Forty Years a Soldier*, pp 203–4, Herbert Jenkins, 1923.
8 Julian Ralph, *War's Brighter Side*, pp 203–4, C. Arthur

Pearson Ltd, 1901.
9 Nourah Waterhouse, *Private and Official*, p. 76, Cape, 1942.
10 Extract from article published in *Birmingham Post*, 22 January 1936.
11 H. A. Gwynne to author.
12 *Something of Myself*, pp 158–61.
13 The Kipling Papers.
14 Was in the possession of Countess Roberts.
15 A local inhabitant to author.

CHAPTER XV A WANING CONFIDENCE

1 *Something of Myself*, pp 165–6.
2 Cyril B. Falls, *Rudyard Kipling*, pp 189–90, Secker, 1917.
3 *From Sea to Sea*.
4 Mark Kinkead-Weekes, *Kipling's Mind and Art*, p. 230, 1971.
5 ibid., p. 231.
6 ibid., pp 233–4.
7 The Kipling Papers.

8 Gardiner, *Prophets, Priests and Kings*, p. 235.
9 Francis W. L. Adams, *Essays in Modernity*, John Lane, 1899.
10 W. H. Auden, 'The Poetry of Encirclement', *Tribune*, 24 December 1943.
11 Arthur Bryant, *English Saga*, p. 272, Eyre & Spottiswoode, 1940.
12 Shanks, *Rudyard Kipling*, p. 193.

CHAPTER XVI   FROM WAR TO WAR

1 Mrs Bambridge to author.
2 The Kipling Papers.
3 Mrs Bambridge to author; H. A. Gwynne to author.
4 Herbert Baker, *Architecture and Personalities*, p. 27.
5 ibid.
6 Mrs Bambridge to author.
7 Mr Cook to author.
8 Letter in possession of Sergeant Johnstone.
9 Miss Wynne to author.
10 ibid.
11 The Kipling Papers.
12 A. B. Filson Young, *The Complete Motorist*, p. 285, Methuen, 1904.
13 ibid.
14 The Kipling Papers.
15 ibid.
16 Caroline Kipling's diaries.
17 The Kipling Papers.
18 ibid.
19 William Rothenstein, *Men and Memories: Recollections*, vol. III *Since Fifty*, p. 101, Faber, 1939.
20 Carrington, *Rudyard Kipling*, p. 373.
21 *Something of Myself*, p. 186.
22 Marcus Crouch, *Puck Country*.
23 Carrington, *Rudyard Kipling*, p. 381.
24 J. I. M. Stewart, 'The unfading genius of Rudyard Kipling', address to the Kipling Society, 1965.
25 The Kipling Papers.
26 ibid.
27 Dunham Collection, New York.
28 ibid.
29 Gardiner, *Prophets, Priests and Kings*, p. 293.
30 The Kipling Papers.
31 Kipling to H. A. Gwynne, the Kipling Papers.
32 ibid.
33 ibid.
34 Mrs A. M. Fleming to author.
35 Kipling to Stanley Baldwin, the Kipling Papers.
36 Letter from Field-Marshal Lord Chetwode to author.
37 The Kipling Papers.
38 ibid.
39 ibid.
40 ibid.
41 ibid.

CHAPTER XVII   1914–1918

1 The Kipling Papers.
2 Caroline Kipling's diaries.
3 Nelson Doubleday Collection, Princeton Univ. Lib.
4 Caroline Kipling's diaries.
5 The Kipling Papers.
6 ibid.
7 ibid.
8 Dunham Collection, New York.
9 Mme Cattani to author.
10 Kipling to H. A. Gwynne, the Kipling Papers.
11 Letter in possession of Sir Roderick Jones.
12 Nelson Doubleday Collection, Princeton Univ. Lib.
13 Dunham Collection, New York.
14 The Kipling Papers.
15 Caroline Kipling's diaries.
16 The Kipling Papers.
17 ibid.
18 ibid.

19 Kaufman and Hennessey, eds, *Letters of Alexander Woollcott*, p. 224.

20 Mrs W. M. Cazalet to author.

CHAPTER XVIII   KIPLING AND ROOSEVELT

1 All the letters in this chapter are preserved in the Library of Congress, Washington.

2 John Maynard Keynes, *The Economic Consequences of the Peace*, Macmillan, 1919.

CHAPTER XIX   THE POST-WAR YEARS

1 Caroline Kipling's diaries.
2 Letter to F. N. Doubleday, Nelson Doubleday Collection, Princeton Univ. Lib.
3 General Sir Fabian Ware to author.
4 Letter to F. N. Doubleday, Nelson Doubleday Collection, Princeton Univ. Lib.
5 ibid.
6 The Kipling Papers.
7 ibid.
8 Caroline Kipling's diaries.
9 The Kipling Papers.
10 C. M. Bowra, *Memories: 1898–1939*, pp 187–9, Weidenfeld, 1966.
11 The Kipling Papers.
12 ibid.
13 ibid.
14 ibid.
15 Letter from Kipling to Enid, Lady Bathurst.
16 ibid.
17 R. Thurston Hopkins, *Rudyard Kipling's World*, R. Holden, London, 1925.
18 Caroline Kipling's diaries.
19 Letter from Kipling to Enid, Lady Bathurst.
20 Caroline Kipling's diaries.
21 ibid.
22 ibid.

CHAPTER XX   1926–1930

1 The Kipling Papers.
2 ibid.
3 ibid.
4 ibid.
5 Lord Lloyd to author.
6 The Kipling Papers.
7 Chalmers Roberts to author.
8 Nelson Doubleday Collection, Princeton Univ. Lib.
9 Kipling to Claude Johnson, quoted by Lady Troubridge and A. Marshall, *John, Lord Montagu of Beaulieu*, pp 109–10, Macmillan, 1930.
10 The Kipling Papers.
11 Nelson Doubleday Collection, Princeton Univ. Lib.
12 The Kipling Papers.

CHAPTER XXI   THE PROFESSIONAL MAN

1 Shanks, *Rudyard Kipling*.
2 W. Somerset Maugham, 'The Short Story', vol. 25 of *Essays*, Royal Society of Literature, 1950.
3 Shanks, *Rudyard Kipling*, p. 133.
4 Carrington, *Rudyard Kipling*, p. 219.
5 Bonamy Dobrée, *The Lamp and*

The Lute, p. 152, Clarendon
Press, 1951.
6 Roger Lancelyn Green, *Kipling
and The Children*, p. 175, Elek,
1965.
7 C. A. Bodelsen, *Aspects of*

Kipling's Art, p. 97, Manchester
University Press, 1964.
8 Dobrée, *The Lamp and The Lute*,
p. 132.
9 Bodelsen, *Aspects of Kipling's
Art*, p. 102.

CHAPTER XXII A DARK VALLEY
1 Caroline Kipling's diaries.
2 Mrs Bambridge to author.
3 H. A. Gwynne to author.
4 Sir Roderick Jones to author.

5 Sir Ronald Storrs, *Orientations*,
p. 506, Nicholson & Watson,
1937.
6 Lord Stanhope to author.

CHAPTER XXIII SWAN SONG
1 C. S. Lewis, 'Kipling's World',
Literature and Life: Addresses to
the English Association.
2 Bodelsen, *Aspects of Kipling's
Art*, pp 91–2.

3 ibid., pp 60–1.
4 Lord Radcliffe, address to the
Kipling Society, 26 October
1966.
5 ibid.

CHAPTER XXIV A DARKENING SCENE
1 Dunham Collection, New York.
2 ibid.
3 The Kipling Papers.
4 ibid.

5 Enid Bagnold (Lady Jones) to
author.
6 Lieut.-Colonel Thwaites to
author.

CHAPTER XXV TWILIGHT AND EVENGLOW
1 The Kipling Papers.
2 ibid.
3 Letter in possession of Sir
Sydney Cockerell, dated 6
October 1932.
4 The Kipling Papers.
5 Caroline Kipling's diaries.
6 Letter from Kipling to Enid,
Lady Bathurst.
7 ibid.
8 The Kipling Papers.
9 ibid.
10 ibid.
11 Sir Percy Bates to author.
12 The Kipling Papers.
13 Caroline Kipling's diaries.

14 Valentine Williams, *The World
of Action*, p. 375, Hamish
Hamilton, 1938.
15 Carrington, *Rudyard Kipling*,
p. 502.
16 The Kipling Papers.
17 Sir Sydney Cockerell's diary,
unpublished.
18 Poem in possession of the Royal
College of Surgeons.
19 Carrington, *Rudyard Kipling*,
p. 503.
20 The Kipling Papers.
21 Dunham Collection, New York.
22 Sir Alfred Webb-Johnson to
author.

CHAPTER XXVI   A BACKWARD GLANCE

1 C. S. Lewis, 'Kipling's World', *Literature and Life*: Addresses to the English Association.
2 George Orwell, 'Rudyard Kipling', *Horizon*, February 1942.
3 In *Literature and Life*: Addresses to the English Association.
4 Lewis, 'Kipling's World'.
5 Orwell, 'Rudyard Kipling'.
6 Lewis, 'Kipling's World'.
7 ibid.
8 ibid.
9 Orwell, 'Rudyard Kipling'.
10 Lewis, 'Kipling's World'.
11 Edmund Wilson, *The Arrow and The Bow*, pp 48–9, Cambridge, USA, 1941.
12 Lord Radcliffe, Address to the Kipling Society, 26 October 1966.
13 Lionel Trilling, 'Kipling' in *The Liberal Imagination*, p. 93, Secker, 1951.

APPENDIX A   KIPLING'S DELIRIUM

1 The Kipling Papers.

KIPLING'S MAJOR WORKS

⎯⎯⎯⎯

Schoolboy Lyrics
1881 Civil and Military Gazette
Press, Lahore

Echoes by Two Writers (RK
and his sister 'Trix')
1884 Civil and Military Gazette
Press, Lahore

Quartette by Four Anglo-
Indian Writers (Mr and Mrs
K, RK and 'Trix')
1885 Civil and Military Gazette
Press, Lahore

*Departmental Ditties and
Other Verses*
1886 Civil and Military Gazette
Press, Lahore
1890 Thacker, Spink, London and
Calcutta
1890 United States Book Co, New
York (as *Departmental
Ditties, Barrack-room Ballads
and Other Verses*)

Plain Tales from the Hills
1888 Thacker, Spink, Calcutta
1890 Frank F. Lovell, New York
1890 Macmillan, London

*Soldiers Three: A Collection of
Stories*
1888 'Pioneer' Press, Allahabad
(Indian Railway Library No1)

1890 Simpson Low, Marston,
Searle & Rivington, London

*The Story of the Gadsbys: A
Tale without a Plot*
1888 A. H. Wheeler, Allahabad
1890 Sampson Low, Marston,
Searle & Rivington, London
1890 John W. Lovell, New York

In Black and White
1888 A. H. Wheeler, Allahabad
1890 Sampson Low, Marston,
Searle & Rivington, London
1897 Outward Bound edition,
vol. 4, New York.

Under the Deodars
1888 A. H. Wheeler, Allahabad
(No 4 in Indian Railway
Library)
1890 Sampson Low, Marston,
Searle & Rivington, London
1898 John W. Lovell, New York

*The Phantom Rickshaw and
Other Tales*
1888 A. H. Wheeler, Allahabad
1890 Sampson Low, Marston,
Searle & Rivington, London
1890 John W. Lovell, New York
(with *Wee Willie Winkie* as
Indian Tales III)

Wee Willie Winkie and *Other
Child Stories*

1888 A. H. Wheeler, Allahabad
1890 Sampson Low, Marston, Searle & Rivington, London, as *Wee Willie Winkie and Other Stories*

The Courting of Dinah Shadd and Other Stories
1890 Harper & Brothers, New York

The Light that Failed
1890 J. B. Lippincott, New York
1891 Ward, Lock, Bowden, London (*Lippincott's Magazine* [English] edition)
1891 Macmillan, London (15-chapter version)

The City of Dreadful Night and Other Places
1891 A. H. Wheeler, Allahabad
1891 Sampson Low, Marston, Searle & Rivington, London

Letters of Marque
1891 A. H. Wheeler, Allahabad (1-vol. edition)
1891 Sampson Low, Marston, Searle & Rivington, London (Vol. 1 only; Vol. 2 suppressed by RK)
1895 Unauthorized edition published in America, including *The City of Dreadful Night and Other Places*

Letters of Marque, with revised text, included in *From Sea to Sea*, Vol. 1

American Notes, including 'The Bottle Imp' by R. L. Stevenson

1891 M. J. Ivers, New York – Ivers American Series No 230

Mine Own People
1891 United States Book Co, New York

Life's Handicap
1891 Macmillan, London
1891 Macmillan, New York

The Naulahka (with Wolcott Balestier)
1892 William Heinemann, London
1892 Macmillan, New York

Barrack-room Ballads and Other Verses
1892 Methuen, London
1892 Macmillan, New York, as *Ballads and Barrack-room Ballads*

Many Inventions
1893 Macmillan, London
1893 D. Appleton, New York

The Jungle Book
1894 Macmillan, London
1894 Century, New York

The Second Jungle Book
1895 Macmillan, London
1895 Century, New York

The Seven Seas
1896 D. Appleton, New York
1896 Methuen, London

Soldier Tales
1896 Macmillan, London
1896 Macmillan, New York (as *Soldier Stories*)

The Kipling Birthday Book (compiled by J. Finn)
1896 Macmillan, London
1899 Doubleday & McClure, New York

*Captains Courageous: A
Story of the Grand Banks*
1896 The S. S. McClure Co,
London and New York
(copyright edition)
1897 Macmillan, London
1897 Century, New York (first
trade edition)

An Almanac of Twelve Sports
(illustrated by Sir William
Nicholson)
1898 William Heinemann, London
1898 R. H. Russell, New York

The Day's Work
1898 Doubleday & McClure, New
York
1898 Macmillan, London

*A Fleet in Being: Notes of
Two Trips with the Channel
Squadron*
1898 Macmillan, London
1913 included in *From Sea to Sea*,
Vol. 2, American edition

Stalky & Co.
1899 Macmillan, London
1899 Doubleday & McClure, New
York

*From Sea to Sea: Letters of
Travel*
1899 Doubleday, McClure, New
York
1900 Macmillan, London (as *From
Sea to Sea and Other
Sketches*)

Kim
1901 Doubleday, Page, New York
1901 Macmillan, London

*Just So Stories for Little
Children*

1902 Macmillan, London
1902 Doubleday, Page, New York

The Five Nations
1903 Methuen, London
1903 Doubleday, Page, New York

Traffics and Discoveries
1904 Macmillan, London
1904 Doubleday, Page, New York

Puck of Pook's Hill
1906 Macmillan, London
1906 Doubleday, Page, New York

Collected Verse
1907 Doubleday, Page, New York
1912 Hodder & Stoughton,
London

Letters to the Family
1908 Macmillan, Canada

Actions and Reactions
1909 Macmillan, London
1909 Doubleday, Page, New York

Rewards and Fairies
1910 Macmillan, London
1910 Doubleday, Page, New York

A History of England (by
C. R. L. Fletcher and
Rudyard Kipling)
1911 Clarendon Press, Oxford/
Hodder & Stoughton,
London
1911 Doubleday, Page, New York

The Fringes of the Fleet
1915 Macmillan, London
1915 Doubleday, Page, New York

A Diversity of Creatures
1917 Macmillan, London
1917 Doubleday, Page, New York

Twenty Poems
1918 Methuen, London
1918 Macmillan, Canada

The Years Between
1919 Methuen, London
1919 Doubleday, Page, New York

Rudyard Kipling's Verse,
1885–1918 Inclusive edition
1919 Hodder & Stoughton,
London
1919 Doubleday, Page, New York

Letters of Travel 1892–1913
1920 Macmillan, London
1920 Doubleday, Page, New York

Land and Sea Tales for
Scouts and Guides
1923 Macmillan, London
1923 Doubleday, Page, New
York (as *Land and Sea Tales*
for Boys and Girls)

The Irish Guards in the Great
War (2 vols.)
1923 Macmillan, London

Kipling Calendar
1923 Hodder & Stoughton,
London
1923 Doubleday, Page, New York

Songs for Youth, from
Collected Verse
1924 Hodder & Stoughton,
London
1925 Doubleday, Page, New York

'They' and the Brushwood Boy
1925 Macmillan, London
1926 Doubleday, Page, New York

Debits and Credits
1926 Macmillan, London
1926 Doubleday, Page, New York

Sea and Sussex from Rudyard
Kipling's Verse
1926 Macmillan, London
1926 Doubleday, Page, New York

Songs of the Sea
1927 Macmillan, London
1927 Doubleday, Page, New York

Rudyard Kipling's Verse,
1885–1926 Inclusive edition
1927 Hodder & Stoughton,
London
1927 Doubleday, Page, New York

A Book of Words: Selections
from speeches and addresses
delivered between 1906 and
1927
1928 Macmillan, London
1928 Doubleday, Page, New York

Poems 1886–1929
1929 Macmillan, London
1930 Doubleday, Doran, New
York

Thy Servant a Dog
1930 Macmillan, London
1930 Doubleday, Doran, New
York

Selected Poems
1931 Methuen, London

East of Suez
1931 Macmillan, London

Humorous Tales
1931 Macmillan, London
1931 Doubleday, Doran, New
York

Animal Stories
1932 Macmillan, London
1938 Doubleday, Doran, New
York

Limits and Renewals
1932 Macmillan, London
1932 Doubleday, Doran, New York

Souvenirs of France
1933 Doubleday, Doran, New York
1933 Macmillan, London

Rudyard Kipling's Verse, 1885–1932 Inclusive edition
1933 Hodder & Stoughton, London
1934 Doubleday, Doran, New York

Collected Dog Stories
1934 Macmillan, London
1934 Doubleday, Doran, New York

A Kipling Pageant
1935 Doubleday, Doran, New York

Something of Myself for My Friends Known and Unknown
1937 Macmillan, London
1937 Doubleday, Doran, New York

Uncollected Prose, vol. I
1938 Macmillan, London (Sussex edition)
1941 Doubleday, Doran, New York (Burwash edition)

Uncollected Prose, vol. II
1938 Macmillan, London (Sussex edition)

1941 Doubleday, Doran, New York (Burwash edition)

Sixty Poems
1939 Hodder & Stoughton, London

More Selected Stories
1940 Macmillan, London

A Kipling Treasury: Stories and Poems
1940 Macmillan, London

Rudyard Kipling's Verse Definitive edition
1940 Hodder & Stoughton, London
1940 Doubleday, Doran, New York

A Choice of Kipling's Verse made by T. S. Eliot with an Essay on Rudyard Kipling
1941 Faber & Faber, London
1943 Charles Scribner's Sons, New York

Twenty-One Tales: Selected from the Works of Rudyard Kipling
1946 Reprint Society, London

A Choice of Kipling's Prose Selected and with an introductory Essay by W. Somerset Maugham
1952 Macmillan, London
1953 Doubleday, New York, as *Maugham's Choice of Kipling's Best*

BIBLIOGRAPHY OF PUBLISHED MATERIAL

ADAMS, FRANCIS, *Essays in Modernity*: Mr Rudyard Kipling's Verse (John Lane 1899)

ARCHER, WILLIAM, *Poets of the Younger Generation* (John Lane 1901)

AUDEN, W. H., 'The Poetry of Encirclement', article in *Tribune*, 24 December 1943

BAILEY, H. C., 'Kipling, Imperial Poet the World Acclaimed', obituary notice in *Daily Telegraph*, 18 January 1936

BAKER, SIR HERBERT, *Cecil Rhodes by his Architect* (Oxford University Press 1934)

Architecture and Personalities, Country Life, 1944

BALLARD, ELLIS AMES, *Introduction to a Summary of the Works of Rudyard Kipling* (privately printed, Philadelphia 1930)

BATESON, DR VAUGHAN, 'Kipling Links in Yorkshire', lecture, printed in *Yorkshire Post*, 14 January 1937

BEERBOHM, MAX, 'Kipling's Entire' in *Around the Theatres*, vol. I (Heinemann 1903)

BENNETT, ARNOLD, *Books and Persons* (Chatto & Windus 1917)

BERESFORD, G. C., *Schooldays with Kipling* (Gollancz 1936)

BIRDWOOD, FIELD-MARSHAL LORD, *Khaki and Gown* (Ward Lock 1941) *Birmingham Post*, 22 January 1936

BODELSON, C. A., *Aspects of Kipling's Art* (Manchester University Press 1964)

BOWRA, C. M., *Memories: 1898–1939* (Weidenfeld & Nicolson 1966)

BROWN, C. HILTON, *Rudyard Kipling* (Hamish Hamilton 1945)

BRYANT, ARTHUR, *English Saga* (Collins 1940)

BUCK, E. J., *Simla Past and Present* (Bombay 1925)

CARRINGTON, CHARLES E., *Rudyard Kipling, His Life and Work* (Macmillan 1955)

CHARLES, CECIL, *Rudyard Kipling, the Man and his Work* (J. Hewetson & Son 1899)

CHARTERIS, EVAN, *Life and Letters of Sir Edmund Gosse* (Heinemann 1931)

CHEVRILLON, A., *Studies in English Literature: Rudyard Kipling* (Librairie Plon, Paris 1936)

CLEMENS, WILL M., *A Ken of Kipling*: being a biographical sketch of Rudyard Kipling, with an appreciation and some anecdotes (New Amsterdam Book Co., New York 1899)

CRANE, CHARLES EDWARD, *Pen-drift* (Stephen Daye Press, Brattleboro)

DAY, REV. C. O., *Rudyard Kipling as seen in his Vermont Home*, newspaper article written by the Congregational Minister at Brattleboro 1899

DENNY, SIR HENRY, *A Kipling Shrine*

DOBRÉE, BONAMY, *The Lamp and the Lute* (Clarendon Press, Oxford 1929)

DUNSTERVILLE, L. C., *Stalky's Reminiscences* (Cape 1928)

DUTTON, CHARLES, 'He knew Kipling', article in *The Commonwealth*, 3 June 1938

ELIOT, T. S., *A Choice of Kipling's Verse: Introduction* (Faber 1942)

ERVINE, ST JOHN, 'Kipling', review of *Life* by Hilton Brown in the *Spectator*, 21 September 1945

FALLS, CYRIL, *Rudyard Kipling: A Critical Study* (Secker 1917)

FIRTH, J. B., 'Kipling: Poet and Prophet of Empire', obituary notice in *Daily Telegraph*, 18 January 1936

FLEMING, MRS A. M. (Alice 'Trix' Kipling), 'Some childhood memories of Rudyard Kipling', article in *Chambers Journal*, March 1939

GARDINER, A. G., *Prophets, Priests and Kings* (Dent 1917)

GAUNT, WILLIAM, *The Aesthetic Adventure* (Cape 1945)

GEROULD, KATHERINE FULLERTON, 'The Remarkable Rightness of Rudyard Kipling', article in *Atlantic Monthly*, January 1919

GOSSE, SIR EDMUND, Questions at Issue (Heinemann 1893)

GOULDING, COLONEL H. R., *Old Lahore* (*Civil and Military Gazette* Press 1924)

GREEN, ROGER LANCELYN, *Kipling and The Children* (Elek Books 1965)

GUEDALLA, PHILIP, *Collected Essays* (Hodder & Stoughton)

GWYNN, STEPHEN (ed.), *The Letters and Friendships of Sir Cecil Spring Rice*, vol. I (Constable 1929)

GWYNNE, H. A., 'A Personal Tribute by an old Friend', obituary notice in *Morning Post*, 18 January 1936. Unsigned but from internal evidence clearly written by Gwynne.

HAMILTON, GENERAL SIR IAN, *Listening for the Drums* (Faber, 1944)

HARRIS, FRANK, *Contemporary Portraits* (The author, New York 1915)

HENDRICK, B. J., *Life and Letters of Walter Page* (Heinemann 1924)

HOPKINS, THURSTON, *Rudyard Kipling's World* (R. Holden, London 1925)

IRELAND, GORDON, *The Balestiers of Beechwood* (privately printed Washington DC 1948)

JACKSON, HOLBROOK, *The Eighteen Nineties* (Grant Richards Ltd)

JAMES, HENRY, *Mine Own People: a critical introduction* (United States Book Company, New York 1891)

KAUFMAN, BEATRICE, and HENNESSEY, JOSEPH (eds), *The Letters of Alexander Woollcott* (Cassell 1946)

KEYNES, JOHN MAYNARD, *The Economic Consequences of the Peace* (Macmillan 1919)

KINKEAD-WEEKES, MARK, *Kipling's Mind and Art* (1971)

KIPLING, LOCKWOOD, obituary, *The Times*, 30 January 1911

KIPLING, RUDYARD, 'An Undefended Island', address delivered to the Royal Society of St George, 6 May 1935. Printed in *Nineteenth Century* No. DCC, June 1935

KNOWLES, F. L., *A Kipling Primer*, including biographical chapters, an Index to Kipling's principal writings and bibliographies (Chatto 1900)

LANG, ANDREW, *Essays in Little* (Longman's 1912)

LE GALLIENNE, RICHARD, *Rudyard Kipling*: A criticism (John Lane 1900) *Rudyard Kipling's Place in Literature* (1919)

LEWIS, C. S., 'Kipling's World' in *Literature and Life: Address to the English Association*

LIVINGSTON, FLORA V., *Bibliography of the Works of Rudyard Kipling*

LOWNDES, M. A. BELLOC, *The Merry Wives of Westminster* (Macmillan 1940)

MACCARTHY, SIR DESMOND, 'Rudyard Kipling, His Place among English Writers', obituary notice in *Sunday Times*, 19 January 1936

MCCARTHY, JUSTIN, *Reminiscences*, vol. II (Chatto 1899)

MACDONALD, FREDERICK W., *As a Tale that is Told*: recollections of many years (Cassell 1919)

MacMUNN, LT GENERAL SIR GEORGE, *Rudyard Kipling, craftsman* (Hale 1937)

Kipling's Women (Low 1933)

MARTINDELL, E. W., *Bibliography of the Works of Rudyard Kipling* (John Lane 1923)

MASON, JULIAN S., *A Yale Footnote to Kipling* (printed for the Yale Library Associates by the Yale University Press 1937)

MASTERMAN, LUCY, *C. F. G. Masterman* (Nicholson & Watson 1939)

MAUGHAM, W. SOMERSET, 'The Short Story', in *Essays*, vol. 25 (Royal Society of Literature 1950)

MEYNELL, VIOLA (ed.), *Friends of a Lifetime*, letters to Sydney Carlyle Cockerell (Cape 1940)

MOORE, GEORGE, *Avowals* (privately printed 1919)

MORGAN, CHARLES, *The House of Macmillan, 1843–1943* (Macmillan 1943)

MORTIMER, RAYMOND, *Channel Packet* (1942)

New York Tribune, 11 and 12 May 1896 (Report of Kipling–Balestier Case)

NEWTON, LORD, *Retrospection* (John Murray 1941)

NICOLSON, HAROLD, *Helen's Tower* (Constable 1937)

ORWELL, GEORGE, 'Rudyard Kipling', article in *Horizon*, February 1942

PALMER, JOHN, *Rudyard Kipling* (Nisbet 1915)

PHELPS, EDITH CATLIN, *Personal Recollections of Mr and Mrs Rudyard Kipling*

Phoenix, files of the Brattleboro newspaper

PONTON, DOROTHY, *Rudyard Kipling at Home and at Work* (privately printed)

QUENNELL, PETER, article in *New Statesman*, 13 October 1935

RADCLIFFE, LORD, Address to the Kipling Society, 26 October 1966

RALPH, JULIAN, *War's Brighter Side* (C. Arthur Pearson Ltd 1901)

The Reformer, files of Brattleboro newspaper, particularly 15 May 1896 for Kipling–Balestier case

RICE, HOWARD C., *Rudyard Kipling in New England* (The Book Cellar, Brattleboro, Vermont, 1951)

ROBERTON, WILLIAM, *The Kipling Guide Book* (Holland & Co., Birmingham 1899)

ROBINSON, E. KAY, 'Kipling in India', article in *McClure's Magazine*, New York, July 1896, by the former editor of the *Civil and Military Gazette*, Lahore

ROTHENSTEIN, WILLIAM, *Men and Memories: Recollections*, vol. III, *Since Fifty* (Faber 1939)

SCOTT, W. DIXON, *The Meekness of Mr Kipling* in 'Men and Letters' series (Hodder 1916)

SHANKS, EDWARD, *Rudyard Kipling: a study in literature and political ideas* (Macmillan 1940)

STEWART, J. I. M., *The Unfading Genius of Rudyard Kipling*, address to the Kipling Society

STODDARD, CHARLES WARREN, *Rudyard Kipling at Naulakha*

STORRS, SIR RONALD, *Orientations* (Nicholson & Watson 1937)

SYKES, SIR FREDERICK, *From Many Angles*, an autobiography (Harrap 1942)

TAPP, H. A., *The United Services College, 1874–1911* (Gale & Polden, Aldershot 1934)

THIRKELL, ANGELA, *Three Houses* (Oxford University Press 1931)

TRILLING, LIONEL, 'Kipling' in *The Liberal Imagination* (Secker 1951)

TROUBRIDGE, LADY, and MARSHALL, ARCHIBALD, *John, Lord Montagu of Beaulieu: a Memoir* (Macmillan 1930)

WARD, A. C., *Twentieth Century Literature* (Methuen 1928)

WATER, F. VAN DE, *Rudyard Kipling's Vermont Feud*

WATERHOUSE, NOURAH, *Private and Official* (Cape 1942)

WAUGH, ARTHUR, One Man's Road (Chapman & Hall 1931)

WILDE, OSCAR, *Intentions* (Methuen 1891)

WILLIAMS, VALENTINE, *The World of Action* (Hamish Hamilton 1938)

WILLIAMSON, KENNEDY, *W. E. Henley: a Memoir* (Harold Shayler 1930)

WILSON, EDMUND, *The Arrow and the Bow* (Cambridge, USA 1941)
The World (newspaper) 2 April 1890. Interview given by Rudyard Kipling
YOUNG, A. B. FILSON, *The Complete Motorist* (Methuen 1904)
YOUNGHUSBAND, MAJOR-GENERAL SIR GEORGE, *Forty Years a Soldier*
  (Herbert Jenkins 1923)

BIBLIOGRAPHY OF UNPUBLISHED MATERIAL

The Kipling Papers, including more than 1,000 letters between Kipling and his family, many other letters, press cuttings, etc.

Mrs Rudyard Kipling's diaries from 18 January 1892 (their wedding day) to 18 January 1936 (day of Rudyard Kipling's death).

The Dunham Collection. Balestier and Dunham family letters, the property of Dr Theo Dunham, all unpublished. New York.

Nelson Doubleday Collection, Princeton University Library. Large collection of letters between Kipling and his publisher and friend F. N. Doubleday.

Roosevelt Papers. Correspondence between Kipling and Theodore Roosevelt. Library of Congress, Washington DC.

C. E. Norton Papers, Houghton Library, Harvard.

Milner Papers, New College, Oxford.

Bathurst Letters. Letters from Kipling to Lady (Enid) Bathurst, proprietor of the *Morning Post*.

Dunsany Letters. Correspondence between Kipling and Lord Dunsany.

Cattani Letters. Correspondence between Mr and Mrs Rudyard Kipling and Madame Cattani, proprietress of hotel at Engelberg where they spent 5 winter holidays 1909–1914. Correspondence continued to 1935.

Sir Shane Leslie's Collection, including letters from Kipling to Moreton Frewen 1907–1918.

Sydney Cockerell's Collection, including 4 letters from Kipling to Cockerell 1932–1934; 3 letters from Sara Anderson (secretary in succession to Ruskin, Burne-Jones and Kipling) to Cockerell 1932–1939; extract from Cockerell's diary after visit to Batemans, 27 September 1935.

Recollections of Kipling by Chalmers Roberts, for 15 years F. N. Doubleday's representative in London. 12 pages of typescript recollections written for the author. Much information about Kipling's attitude towards America.

Extracts from Dorothy Ponton's diary while governess and secretary in Kipling's household. 60 pages of typescript.

Letters from Kipling to Sergeant Johnson of Rottingdean about the Rifle Club, 1901 and 1904.

Letter from Maurice Baring to Edward Shanks about Kipling and his work, dated 15 April 1940.

The Carpenter Collection, including Dr Conland's letters, and letters of Mrs S. A. Hill. Library of Congress, Washington DC.

New York Public Library. The Owen D. Young and Howe Collection of letters.

Columbia University. The Brander Matthews letters.

'Annals of Brattleboro' by Mary Cabot (partly published in Vermont Historical Papers), including an account of Kipling's life in Vermont by a close friend and extracts from her journal.

Sir Roderick Jones. 13 typed foolscap pages of notes on Kipling written for the author.

Miss E. Plowden, *Fond Memories*, unpublished memoirs.

Collection of Howard C. Rice, Jnr, Brattleboro, Vermont.

Holbrook Papers. Private papers of F. Cabot Holbrook, Brattleboro, Vermont.

GENERAL INDEX

References to Kipling's works are listed at the end of this index

REFERENCES TO KIPLING'S WORKS